THE

BAKER

IN ME

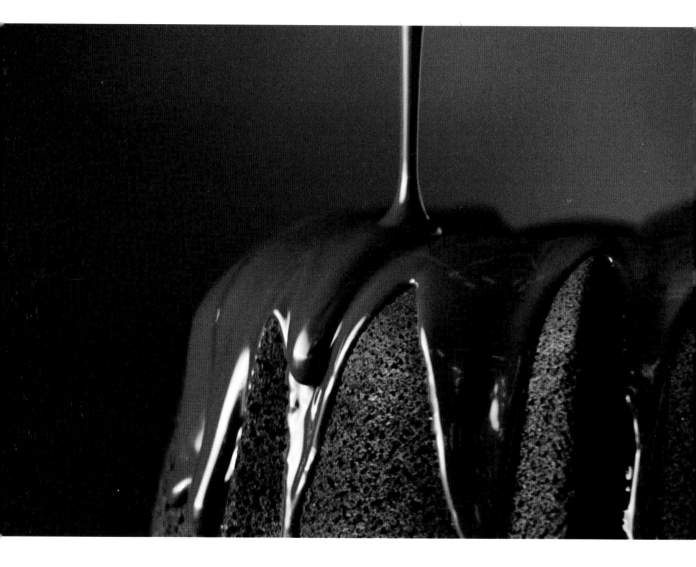

THE BAKER IN ME

DAPHNA RABINOVITCH

(A BORN BAKER)

whitecap

Whitecap Books is known for its expertise in the cookbook market, and has produced some of the most innovative and familiar titles found in kitchens across North America. Visit our website at www.whitecap.ca.

EDITOR: Jordie Yow
DESIGN: Andrew Bagatella
FOOD PHOTOGRAPHY: David Scott
FOOD STYLING: Olga Truchan
PROOFREADER: Patrick Geraghty

Printed in Canada

Library and Archives Canada Cataloguing in Publication

Rabinovitch, Daphna, author
The baker in me / Daphna Rabinovitch.

ISBN 978-1-77050-242-0 (bound)

1. Baking. 2. Cookbooks. I. Title.

TX763.R33 2015   641.81'5   C2015-903095-1

We acknowledge the financial support of the Government of Canada, the Province of British Columbia through the Book Publishing Tax Credit.

Canada

21 20 19 18 17 16 1 2 3 4 5 6 7

For Skip *and* Jacob, *whom I love even more than I love baking.*

CONTENTS

VIII FOREWORD

X INTRODUCTION

2 COOKIES

124 BARS AND SQUARES

172 ALL THINGS CHOCOLATE

218 MUFFINS, BISCUITS AND SCONES

270 QUICK AND YEAST BREADS

302 A CUPBOARD FULL OF CAKES

398 PIES, TARTS AND FRUIT DESSERTS

468 ACKNOWLEDGEMENTS

470 INDEX

FOREWORD

For a long time now, perhaps a couple of decades, friends, family, colleagues, publishers, even total strangers, have been asking me when I would write a cookbook. I always hemmed and hawed and muttered, "Well, perhaps someday." What I really thought was, "What could I offer?" It's true I love to bake. Make that I LOVE to bake. I NEED to bake. I almost CRAVE to bake. It is, aside from my family and friends, what I am most passionate about. Passion is a funny word—it has been flung about a lot and runs the risk of losing its meaning—but I can't think of another word that delivers the sheer joy, unconditional love, diehard commitment and innate satisfaction that I derive from baking. I've always LOVED to bake. It is as much a part of my identity as being a sister, daughter, wife and mother. In fact, I think I was born a baker—I have perennially cold hands. Part of me is convinced that is one of the reasons that I bake so well.

I can still remember the white cake my mom used to make most Friday nights for dinner. Now, over 35 years later, I remember the goose-down softness of the white cake crumb. The way it melted in your mouth. The, oh-so-slight golden tinge at its edges. The bordering-on-gritty dark chocolate icing that my mom made from scratch to top it. In fact, in all modesty, I think I can recall every sweet thing I have ever eaten. And believe me, there have been many, for I may have been born a baker but I was also born with a seriously sweet tooth. The chocolate éclairs from a favoured patisserie on Côte-des-Neiges in Montreal. My first homemade chocolate chip cookie. The dense gooey brownie that I relished on my first trip to New York.

Of course I love to cook as well. It's part of my life and how I express myself creatively. I develop recipes for a living and there are not a whole lot of things that are more satisfying than creating a chicken recipe or vegetable side dish that you know hits all the right notes, that has the perfect balance of flavours and, more importantly, that people will make and enjoy. Still, to paraphrase Robertson Davies, what's bred in the bone is forever lodged in the flesh and that's how I feel about baking.

It's not just the mixing together of lovely ingredients—unsalted gold-en-hued butter, melding with the sweetness of luxe brown sugar or the sultry melting of chocolate in a pot—I love to know why. And when. And how. Why does the size of the crystalline edges of the sugar matter so much in the creaming process? Why is the preferred ratio of good pastry three to one? Why are there three different kinds of cooked meringue and which one is better in which scenario?

I love everything about baking and want to try and impart that love and joy to you.

INTRODUCTION

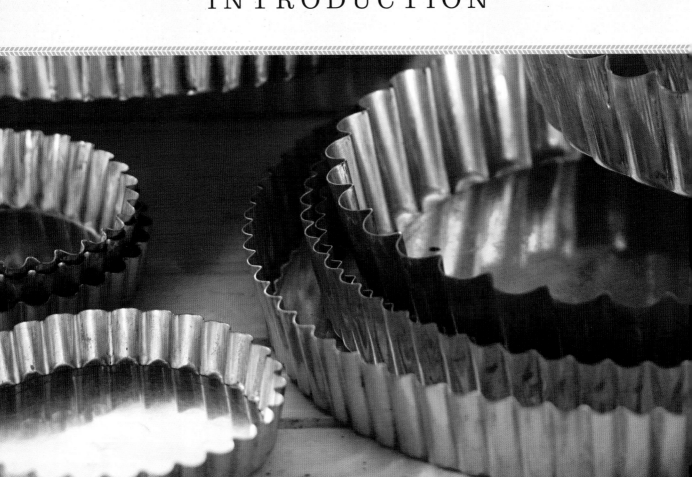

6 BAROMETERS OF SUCCESS

7 MEASURING

10 TESTING FOR DONENESS

11 THE GREATEST GIFT OF ALL

13 BASIC INGREDIENTS (AND ALL YOUR THE SCIENCY STUFF THAT GOES ON BEHIND THE SCENES)

43 A FEW TECHNIQUES TO TUCK INTO YOUR APRON

50 EQUIPMENT

R IGHT OFF the bat I have to start by saying that although I completed my *stage* at a hotel restaurant and then moved on to be a pastry chef (and then an executive pastry chef), I am, at heart, a home baker. I can whip up a towering *croquembouche*, its cream-filled puffs tethered together by golden strands of spun sugar, or a multi-layered Dobos torte or an orange scented Rigó Jansci, yet I derive the same, if not more profound, satisfaction by baking off cookies in my home kitchen on a Sunday afternoon. It must be something about a Sunday afternoon, because although I feel like I've been baking my whole life, my earliest memories are of baking with my mother on Sunday afternoons while my father took my two sisters to the local Y. It wasn't so much that I didn't want to go with them—all my friends congregated there on Sunday and there were plenty of activities. I much preferred, however, the warmth of my childhood kitchen, standing beside my mother, stirring together one of the recipes she had painstakingly inscribed on lined cue cards. It was in childhood that I discovered my spiritual and holistic home—the kitchen.

Like so many people of my generation, I didn't start off pursuing a culinary career. I didn't even know enough to consider it. Instead, I took delight in academia, pursuing a couple of degrees until one summer when, while working in Northern Ontario at an Outward Bound Canada wilderness school, it hit me that I should just do what I love to do. I should just bake.

So, off I went. First I spent a year in Toronto working at two bakeries, honing my gift for precision and earning a reputation as a stickler for quality. Then I made my way to San Francisco to attend a year-long course at Tante Marie's Cooking School, tucked between Little Italy and the colourful wharf.

At Tante Marie's, I had the immeasurable good fortune and privilege to study with some of the best, most creative, innovative and thoughtful cooks and bakers. Their influence shapes me to this day. I learned about chocolate and cakes from the expert chocolatier, baker and cookbook author Alice Medrich, who brought truffles to America long before anyone even knew that bittersweet chocolate existed. I learned bread baking from the redoubtable Beth Hensperger, author of more than half a dozen books on bread making. I spent Saturdays with Jim Dodge, one of the most formidable pastry chefs in the Bay area. It was magical. Joyce Goldstein came to the school to teach as did Brad Ogden, Perla Meyers and Joyce Jue. My fellow students and I would go out and eat at restaurants run by the likes of Thomas Keller, Wolfgang Puck and Jeremiah Tower.

Or we would head up Columbus Avenue during our lunch break to North Beach, which houses Little Italy. We would sweep into Molinari Delicatessan, an amazing Italian deli, and seduced by the rows of pink cold cuts and the allure of huge barrels of Parmigiano-Reggiano, throw our meagre student budgets to the wind and order hefty sandwiches of transparent prosciutto, robust cheese, fragrant basil and garlicky roasted red peppers. They were such heady days. We spent the day whipping up cioppino, beef Wellington or flaky aerated puff pastry. We rummaged through the town, scouring food stores for the best dried porcini mushrooms, bakeries for the deepest and most dense tortes and cookery shops for the sharpest chef's knives. One of the best things about the year that I spent in California was my roommate Cathy Byrd, who loved to eat, try new things and never seemed to gain any weight. We got along famously.

After my year and stage were up, through the kindness of Carole Field (whose home I used to house-sit while she travelled), I was lucky enough to audition for and get a job in Tuscany, Italy. It was the beginning of summer when I moved to the Badia a Coltibuono, located halfway between Florence and Sienna, and I immediately fell down to earth. The cooks at the Badia a Coltibuono (Abbey of the Good Harvest), of which I was now one, didn't cook chicken the way they did at cooking school, they roasted it high and quick. They had rigid rules about what type of pasta to serve with what type of sauce, and they forbade cheese from ever, under any circumstance, accompanying a seafood pasta. Their bread had little if any salt and no fat. So I started to learn all over again.

That's one of the greatest rewards about a culinary career. You never stop learning. There's always a new ingredient, a new technique or a new inspiration.

I learned so much during my stint in Italy. Of course I travelled a great deal, breathing in all of the famous sites and meeting warm and generous people who invited me to their homes to sample the local specialties. One of my most vivid memories is being on the train to Modena when a young student sitting beside me told me about a small, out of the way restaurant that I simply had to visit. We navigated our way there and I went in on my own, not without a little trepidation. The meal was memorable: squash ravioli with a fried sage butter sauce, the squash light, ephemeral and delicate, encased in a toothsome homemade pasta. But more than the food I ate, it was the way I cooked in Italy that changed my life. In the North American culinary capitals—New York, San Francisco and Toronto—the bud of local, seasonal, regional and authentic food had started to grow. In Italy, it was already centuries old.

Refrigerators in most Italian's homes, even grand homes like the Badia, were and are small. Through necessity and through their culinary heritage, people shop for groceries and bread almost every day. Perusing the fruit and vegetable stalls to see what is the freshest or has just come into season, and including the vendor in your menu preparation, is a way of life in Italy. So are heated debates about food, with seemingly everything up for grabs from which pancetta is the best, to whether the Milanese know risotto better than the Venetians, to which pasta best suits an artichoke sauce.

Lorenza de Medici, who oversaw the Badia, had a spectacular garden in the back. All I had to do every morning was make my way to the local butcher in Montevarchi and then step outside to decide what to serve both for lunch and for dinner. That imprint has never left me.

It was in Italy that the blush of first love that prompted my flight to San Francisco was stoked and blossomed into an intense lifelong infatuation. I learned that a cautious hand with sugar makes the best sweets and to appreciate the intense depth of flavour you enjoy when you don't fuss too much. It was in Italy that I learned to trust my hands. The flour in Italy is much lighter than in North America, meaning that all of the recipes I learnt in San Francisco didn't work at all. I had to feel my way, without any formula, while making pastries, bread and all variety of baked dessert. I learned how to truss, to whisk, to place lardons and to tell just by the thickness of a soup if it was right. I learned confidence, the hallmark of being comfortable in the kitchen.

And I just kept right on learning, adding experience and knowledge and making more than my fair share of mistakes. As a professional pastry chef, I learned how to batch up recipes so that they made 250 cookies instead of 24, the art of efficiency and the promise of presentation. I became even more of a purist, insisting on the very best and most authentic, and eschewing crazy fads (blueberries in bagels? Really??). At *Canadian Living Magazine,* under the expert and patient tutelage of Elizabeth Baird, I learned the discipline of developing and recipe writing. I learned never to make assumptions when writing recipes, as well as how Canadians cooked and baked. I read, ate, baked, ate, cooked, baked and read.

With time, my insatiable curiosity about how ingredients worked the way they did and why took a turn and became a desire to learn about the historical and sociological elements in food. Why do Jewish bakeries make such incredible bread? How did chocolate go from that slightly bitter drink introduced by the Aztecs to the sensuous form it takes today? Who made the first brownie? This book answers some of these questions.

While I'm in confession mode, I'll admit that I love words (talking, not so much). I love their power; how, when spun together, they create this map of wonder, leading you somewhere enchanted, thoughtful and cavernous. I am in particular awe of writers who, with deft economy, can stop you in your tracks, make you sit a bit straighter, think a bit deeper. I can still remember the time when I read what turned out to be one of my favourite books and I just stopped—a paragraph held me in thrall for at least 10 minutes. I reread it several times and then finally called a girlfriend to read it to her. I harbour no ambition to be a novelist nor do I believe that any of my paragraphs will be passed from friend to friend, but I do hope that my words will bring you the confidence and desire to bake. I hope that the instructions I give you lead you through the recipes and guide your hand through stirring, whisking and folding, and that the explanations demystify some of the science behind baking so you can march right into the kitchen and take charge. But most of all, I hope that you will learn to love baking as much as I do.

So, let's stop talking and start the adventure together.

BAROMETERS OF SUCCESS

YOUR OVEN AND TEMPERATURE CONSIDERATIONS

The most fundamental tool in your kitchen, more important than measuring ingredients properly or perhaps even the quality of your ingredients, is your oven. Without your oven, there is no baking, and the temperature your oven settles at is tantamount. Professional bakers have an expression that summarizes it succinctly. Actually, it's not even an expression, just two words: "time" and "temp." Without the right temperature, nothing good can come from your oven and without the right timing, much of your baking will get lost. Many people assume that their home ovens are accurate but ovens can fluctuate wildly and be off by 25–50°F (14–28°C). It's hard to imagine trying to bake a cake properly under these conditions.

It's well worth your time to visit a local cookery store and invest in a mercury-based oven thermometer. You'll find it indispensable. It will let you know your oven temperature is correct and where your oven's hot spots are located. Test your oven regularly with an oven thermometer and get it calibrated once or twice a year.

Give your oven plenty of time to preheat. This usually takes about 20 minutes, although it can be longer or shorter depending on the oven. If you slide a cake into an oven that is still preheating, the batter will simply

melt (as opposed to inflate and set) and you'll be left with a sad little puck instead of the jewel your family was waiting for. On the other hand, if your oven is too hot, your pastry will burn before the filling has time to set. In either event, your family will be crushed.

Temperature relates to more than the oven. For the great majority of baking (pastry products excluded), ingredients should be at room temperature. It's virtually impossible to cream cold butter and even harder to trap air bubbles in sloppy, too-soft butter. The same applies to eggs.

Take this scenario, for example: You've just spent five minutes creaming together some lovely room temperature butter with granulated sugar and you've reached the optimum fluffiness and lightness of colour. Then, you add cold eggs, straight from the refrigerator. All of a sudden, your mixture starts to separate and look curdled. This is what happens when you use cold eggs. The temperature of the eggs has re-solidified the butter, essentially ruining the suspension of air bubbles. Once you add the flour mixture, the curdled look will disappear, but your cake will not achieve the impressive heights it otherwise would.

All of the recipes in this book were developed and tested in a conventional radiant oven. The heat in a radiant oven comes from the bottom, where the heat coils are located, eventually filling the oven. Convection ovens, on the other hand, are equipped with little fans at the back that blow the heat around, intensifying the heat and shortening the baking time. I consider myself lucky since the stove I have is gas on top with an electric oven, called a "dual fuel" in the industry. If you prefer baking in a convection oven, reduce your oven temperature by 25°F (14°C). If your oven is equipped with a convection bake setting, as mine is, there is no need to reduce the temperature. Be mindful, though, as your baked goods may be ready a few minutes early. In general, breads are best baked in a convection oven, while cookies, squares, pies, muffins, quick breads and butter-enriched doughs (i.e. sticky buns or babkas) can be made in either a radiant or convection oven (although I personally prefer a radiant oven). Almost all cakes, cheesecakes, tarts, brownies and delicate cookies fare best in a radiant oven.

MEASURING

Successful baking relies on accurate measuring. During the writing of this book, I spent many sleepless nights trying to decide whether I should weigh my ingredients or use volume measurements. Of course, when I was a pastry chef, we weighed everything and it is, hands down, the most accurate way to bake. Volume measurements carry certain risks. Depending on how you measure your flour, you can have up to ¼ cup (60 mL) more flour than what is required. And although this is changing, it's been my experience that most home bakers do not have scales and tend not to weigh their ingredients. So, after countless conversations with peers and fellow bakers (thank you, Heather), I have decided to use cup measurements for the recipes in this book. The exceptions are chocolate and cream cheese, which are always called for by weight, and butter, which is called for by volume and by weight. I always eyeball the measurement when I cut my block of butter, so to ensure accuracy, I always weigh it as well.

Even without weighing, however, you can and will be a great baker. For accurate volume measuring, you need to understand that different ingredients must be measured in different ways and sometimes even with different utensils. Buy the right tools. Dry measuring cups are for measuring dry ingredients such as flour and sugar. They are available in graduated sets of 1 cup (250 mL), ½ cup (125 mL), ⅓ cup (80 mL) and ¼ cup (60 mL). Try to buy straight-sided stainless steel cups—the latter because they'll wear better, and the former because they are more accurate than cups with sloped or curved sides. I have about 3 sets of cups so that I am never searching for the cup size that happens to be in the dishwasher.

There are two different ways to measure flour using a dry measure. The first method involves spooning flour into a dry measuring cup until the flour mounds slightly, at which point you level it off using the blunt edge of a knife. The second method requires you to dip the entire dry measure into the bin of flour, lightly scooping out enough flour so that it too is mounded, then again using the blunt edge of a knife to level off the flour, allowing the excess to fall back into your bag or bin of flour. **The method used throughout this book is the second method, the scoop and sweep method.** It's really important to use the flour as it is once it's been levelled off. Tapping the dry cup on the counter top to see if it's level will compact the flour and make it look like you don't really have enough, when in fact you do. Before measuring the flour, aerate it slightly by fluffing it with a fork, in case it has compacted in your cupboard.

The exception to this rule is when I call for cake and pastry flour, where I spoon and sweep. The compact nature of cake and pastry flour means that the spoon and sweep method is more accurate.

Granulated sugar is measured the exact same way, by scooping and then levelling off.

Brown sugar, since it is so much denser, must be packed into a dry measuring cup. This is also true of other raw and moist sugars.

Always use the dry measure called for and not a measure that's larger than the amount you need.

When measuring, pay attention to the wording of a recipe. Does the recipe call for 1 cup (250 mL) of tightly packed raisins? Is the packing done loosely or firmly? This is especially true when it comes to cake and pastry flour. There is a world of difference between "1 cup (250 mL) of cake and pastry flour, sifted" and "1 cup (250 mL) of sifted cake and pastry flour." In the former, you are being asked to measure the flour and then sift it. In the latter, the requirement is to sift the flour first and then measure it. The difference can be up to 2 or 3 Tbsp (30–45 mL) difference of flour, which will definitely alter the outcome of your baking.

Use a set of graduated measuring spoons for very small measures. When measuring baking powder, baking soda, salt and the like, follow the dip and sweep method. Simply put your spoon into the required ingredient, say, baking powder, remove the spoon with the powder heaped and then level it off. It's always a good idea to do this somewhere other than over the bowl you'll be working with, in case you accidentally spill more than you need into the bowl. The same applies when you're measuring small amounts of liquid ingredients.

There's nothing worse than not finding your measuring spoons when you need them or having to stop and wash your tablespoon measure, so I always have two sets to simplify my baking. Again, I find stainless steel to be the most accurate and reliable.

For any type of liquid, use a Pyrex or glass measuring cup. Pour the liquid into the measuring cup and determine its accuracy by getting right down to the counter to see for yourself. Don't be tempted to hold it up to your eyes and gauge it that way. It's also important not to use an oversized Pyrex measuring cup if you're only measuring a small amount of liquid. For instance, do not use a 2-cup (500 mL) wet measure if you're only measuring ¼ cup (60 mL), it will be off. Stick to a 1-cup (250 mL) measure.

I remember how horrified I was when, one summer while I was at our cottage in the Laurentians, my mother used some wet measures to measure flour. Not only did she pack the flour right into the 1-cup (250 mL) glass measure but she then tapped it on the counter to make sure she had the right amount. Don't get me wrong, my mother happens to have been an excellent baker. But I'm a bit of a nut about this and here is the reason why.

To understand the science behind the use of different measuring cups, you have to go back to high school chemistry class. Do you recall your science teacher talking about the meniscus line? It's the curved surface line of water and is the primary reason why you can't accurately measure any liquid in a dry measuring cup. To fill the cup properly and completely, the meniscus line would have to rise above the rim of the cup, which is basically impossible—the liquid would spill over, leaving less than a full cup.

Similarly, you shouldn't use wet measures to measure dry ingredients. You cannot level flour or sugar off at the top edge, leaving you to guess that it's at the 1 cup (250 mL) mark. You might be tempted to shake the wet measure so that it levels off on its own, thereby compacting the ingredient and making it more than you need.

For ultimate success, use large, room temperature eggs, unless it's specified that they should be cold. Use unsalted butter. Find a national brand of flour that you like which produces consistent results and stick with it. Buy a small inexpensive scale and start to measure your butter. Before you know it, you'll be back at the same store, investing in one that is of better quality and you'll start to weigh more and more of your ingredients.

TESTING FOR DONENESS

Knowing how to tell when your baked good is ready can be tricky if you're not used to it. As with so many other things in your kitchen don't forget that you are the best judge. Use your nose, in other words. You will always be able to tell when a brownie, cookie or cake is nearing the completion of its baking cycle when you start to smell its sweet aroma.

I have tried to give the time as well as a visual clue to help determine when a recipe is done. Always check it at the first indicated time, just to be on the safe side. But don't be a slave to the timer (an essential tool if there ever was one). The visual clue is just as important.

If a recipe calls for inserting a cake tester, use a metal cake tester, a wooden skewer or even a paring knife. Insert this into the centre of the cake. It should come out with a few moist crumbs clinging to it. The edges of the cake should be just beginning to sneak away from the sides of the pan. This is the most common test for brownies, pound cakes and dense tortes, as well as some bars, muffins and flourless cakes.

The other way to tell if a cake is done is to press it lightly in the centre with your fingertips. It should feel springy and set. If you're baking a denser cake, such as the Devil's Food Cake (see p. 179), it will still feel springy with no indentation left after having been very lightly pressed.

For pies, the best way to tell if they're done is to ensure that the crust is golden and that the fruit's juices are bubbling and thickened.

Most cakes and other baked goods should be baked in the pan that the recipe specifies. If the pan you choose is slightly smaller or larger, the baking time may be off. This will also apply if you use a heavier-gauged pan than what is called for.

THE GREATEST GIFT OF ALL

And before we get to even more suggestions and the guts of this book, one parting send-away on how to bake for success: One of the greatest gifts you can give yourselves on your road to becoming an accomplished baker is the gift of organization. I learned this way back in cooking school and it has proved to be one of the best lessons I could have possibly absorbed. It is as true now when I have a larger kitchen as it was when I worked in amazingly cramped quarters. I have one whole cupboard dedicated just to my baking ingredients, organized in my own idiosyncratic way. The flours are bunched together, the sugars are too, everything in its place and easy to find. This way, I can review, at a glance, what I need to replace and what I have enough of. I like to keep my flours and sugars in canisters that have wide openings so I can dip my measuring cups in easily. I also make sure that they are airtight so that I don't get any little buggy surprises when

I'm about to bake. The chemical leaveners, vanilla, other flavouring agents and sprinkling sugars are on the next shelf, with the chocolates, chocolate chips and other chips on the shelf above that.

I keep all of my measuring tools organized in one place as well. The dry measures are stacked and handy and my measuring spoons have a place of honour right beside them. The wet measures in different volumes are stacked just above them. I have two large jars, one ceramic and one glass, right beside my oven, filled with spatulas and wooden spoons, as well as differently shaped whisks and stronger spatulas. I have umpteen stainless steel bowls, all neatly stacked in the cupboard underneath my baking supplies. I tend to lift the entire stack out at once and keep it on the counter so that I have the right-sized bowl for whatever I need, be it mixing or for my mise en place (see p. 43).

Brushes too are kept separate and woe to the person who uses one of my soft bristled ones—the ones that are just meant for brushing flour off of pastry—on the outdoor grill!

Call me neurotic but this type of organization means I don't have to search from here to kingdom come to find something.

There is definitely a mindset to being a professional or home baker. Back when I lived in San Francisco, Mary Risley, the founder of the cooking school I attended, informed the students that there were two basic personalities in the culinary world: those who become chefs or cooks, and those who become bakers or pastry chefs. She explained that the first type of personality was looser and perhaps a bit more intuitive. After all, you can throw in a pinch or two of cayenne and the dish won't fail. If your soup is too salty, all is not lost, you can add a potato to solve the problem. A baker, on the other hand, HAS to be more precise since an extra ½ tsp (2 mL) of baking powder or baking soda can inextricably alter or even spoil a cake. At first, I took affront at this statement. Are you saying I'm not as creative as the person making boeuf bourguignon? Since then, I've come to appreciate the veracity of her words. Baking is a science and I am constantly learning about how different ingredients interact with each other. But it's truly a creative endeavour as well, one where you can let your imagination and will run wild (once you are on intimate grounds with the science behind it all).

BASIC INGREDIENTS (AND ALL THE SCIENCY STUFF THAT GOES ON BEHIND THE SCENES)

One of the things that makes baking so extraordinary and so magical is the fact that from just a few simple ingredients—butter, sugar, flour, eggs, a few flavourings—gorgeous, flaky, airy, melt in your mouth, chewy, tart, gooey and crispy desserts and creations are made. Whether they succeed or falter will depend on the quality of the ingredients you bring to your baking counter. The ingredients should be of the best quality that you can afford. Why make an insipid cookie with margarine and flavoured chips when you can make a truly memorable one with fresh unsalted butter and real chocolate chips. Why spend the time on a lemon meringue pie if you're only going to use bottled lemon juice? Freshly squeezed lemon juice—boisterous and puckery—spells the difference between lifeless and stellar. What follows is not a comprehensive list but a list of the basics you will need to feel like an accomplished baker.

Butter .... pg. 13

Sugar .... pg. 16

Flour .... pg. 24

Chemical Leaveners .... pg. 28

Salt .... pg. 31

Eggs .... pg. 32

Chocolate .... pg. 33

Vanilla .... pg. 40

Spices .... pg. 41

Nuts .... pg. 42

Dairy Products .... pg. 42

BUTTER

Let's face it, baking is nothing without butter. You just have to resign yourself to it and get on with it. I can wax rhapsodic about butter but the scene in the movie *Julie and Julia* says it all. It's near the beginning, and Julia Child (played by Meryl Streep) and her husband have just arrived in Paris and have gone out to a bistro to eat. Julia Child orders some fish and after she takes the first bite she puts down her fork and sighs, reverentially, exclaiming, "Butter!"

And that's all there is to say really. Everything is better with butter. Ask any pastry chef what ingredient is indispensable to them and the answer will always be butter. I'm not advocating injudicious consumption of butter. There are clearly many places where the amount of butter can and should be reduced. By the same token, however, there are many dishes that simply cry out for butter and nothing whatsoever will stand in its place. Pastry without butter is simply not worth eating. Can you imagine a croissant made without butter? I shudder at the very thought; no flakiness, no flavour, no flair. You can always tell the difference between cookies and cakes made with butter and those lowly cousins who were made with margarine or oil. Many sauces are regal and flavourful on their own while some just reach altogether different spheres of deliciousness when finished with a pat of butter.

Butter is available in both salted and unsalted varieties. I urge everyone who wants to bake to use unsalted butter. It's fresher, has a slightly sweeter taste and allows you to be the author of how much salt you want in your recipe.

Be mindful though: not all butter is created equal. The texture and even the flavour of the butter can depend on the season and the manufacturer. Much like olive oil aficionados, I recommend that you do a taste test and then stick with the butter you prefer. Feel the butter before you buy it. Good quality butter will be quite firm. Softer butter, even when it's been refrigerated, has a higher percentage of water than is optimal. Butter should be about 16% moisture, but some brands will add more water to reduce the cost. If the butter has too much water in it, your pastry will come out tougher; you won't be able to capture as many air bubbles when you cream butter together with sugar for a cake and your

baking will suffer all around. Even if the firmer butter is more expensive, indulge. Your baking will thank you. Butter with less moisture in it will be firmer, will be able to hold more air and generally will make tender and flakier pastry.

Really good butter should be dense, showing no air bubbles or holes inside. When you cut into it, it should cut cleanly, without crumbling into many pieces. It should also smell very fresh with nary a whiff of rancidity. To keep butter as fresh as possible, store it in the middle of the refrigerator, not in the butter box on the side of the refrigerator door where it will be subject to frequent variations in temperature. Butter attracts stronger odours, so store it tightly wrapped, well away from strongly odoured foods.

Many professional bakers do not recommend freezing your butter. They prefer to keep the butter refrigerated for up to 3 months. Freezing butter, they contend, can play havoc with its moisture levels, producing grainy or dewy room temperature butter.

For baking, room temperature butter essentially means that the butter is about 65–68°F (18–20°C). Since not many people I know will stick an instant reading thermometer into their butter, an alternate way of telling whether your butter is the right temperature is to push a (clean) finger into the butter. The impression left should remain without any oozing or the butter falling in on itself. Room temperature butter is soft enough to expand and fill with air bubbles during the creaming process, yet stable enough to hold those very same air bubbles in suspension. Many cookbooks instruct the baker to cut the butter into largish pieces and to use the microwave to hasten the process of bringing butter to room temperature. If you're going to do this, do it in 10-second increments on the very lowest heat power. Check the butter often, it should be soft and pliable, not almost melted. Another technique that is also widely used is to cut the butter into pieces and then separate them on a plate to decrease the amount of time the butter needs to come to room temperature. Or, cut the butter into small pieces and start beating them on a low speed, until creamy. Make sure you use low speed or else you'll end up with small pieces of butter scattered around your kitchen. I prefer to bring my butter to room temperature either overnight or for a couple of hours sitting on my kitchen counter.

In some of the recipes in this book, especially for some of the Jewish holidays, I call for oil instead of unsalted butter. Be sure to use a flavourless oil, such as vegetable oil or canola oil. All of the recipes in this book that call for oil were tested with canola oil.

Sugar plays an essential role in the drama that happens during baking. It goes without saying that sugar of any kind will sweeten your baking. That is its primary function. Baked goods without sugar are, well, just not dessert. I tend to liken sugar to salt. Use just the right amount and it will enhance whatever dish or dessert you're making; use too much, and all you'll taste is sweetness (or saltiness, as the case may be). But there is so much more that sugar contributes to baking.

In baking, sugar is considered a liquid ingredient since it liquefies upon contact with any sort of liquid, be it eggs, melted butter, oil or even fruit juice. This is readily evident when you caramelize sugar. Upon contact with heat, aided by the addition of water or not, sugar will melt and start to caramelize or get darker. The same thing happens to sugar in the heat of an oven. As your item bakes, the sugar in the cake, pie or cookie starts to melt and imparts a golden colour to the sides of your golden white cake, the crust of your pecan pie or the undersides of your chocolate chip cookie.

Sugar, especially granulated sugar, also contributes significantly to the tenderness and texture of cakes. When you cream butter with sugar, air becomes trapped between the fat and the grains of sugar. The size of the sugar crystal is directly proportional to the amount of air that is incorporated. The smaller the crystal, the less air that is developed. The larger the crystal, the more air. If you look at a sugar crystal under a heavy duty microscope, you'll see that it has fine crystalline edges. It is these sharp edges that bite into the fat and open up the pores that grow to become air cells. Other ingredients, such as the leavening and flour you choose, then guarantee that the air remains suspended in the batter. The air cells expand during baking, ensuring that the baked good rises and becomes tender. Sugar also slows down the development of gluten in wheat flour, causing the cell walls to stretch slowly so that your cake can rise to the maximum before the structure is set by the oven's heat.

It's the same type of activity or friction that allows egg yolks and egg whites to expand and become thick and velvety beaten egg yolks or voluminous and billowy egg whites. When granulated sugar is whisked with whole eggs or egg yolks, air is trapped between the crystals of the sugar and suspended in the expanded egg yolks. When the item in question is baked, the trapped air inside the batter expands, leavening the baked good. Adding granulated sugar to egg whites breaks down the egg whites' tightly wound coils of protein, allowing air to be absorbed. Sugar delays

the coagulation of whole eggs, providing desserts sufficient time to incorporate more air before setting. In terms of egg whites, sugar provides stability and structure, allowing the beaten egg whites to hold their shape. The addition of sugar also means that the beaten egg whites are moist enough to withstand the withering power of the oven heat.

This is why the vast majority of cakes and other baked goods call for granulated sugar. Made from either sugar cane or beets, it has the rough shape and chemical make-up to provide the sweetness, tenderness and colour that characterizes dessert making. It's important to note that granulated sugar and superfine sugar are not the same. Superfine sugar, due to its much finer crystals, is appropriate for an angel food cake, where the air bubbles and structure come from the whipping of the egg whites and not from the creaming process. Superfine sugar will also dissolve much faster than the larger crystals of regular granulated sugar, and thus you will often see superfine sugar called for in meringue recipes, fruit sauces and the like. To make your own, simply buzz up some regular granulated sugar in a food processor for several minutes.

The finer crystals of superfine sugar also mean, however, that you will never be able to get a sufficient number of air bubbles for a regular cake. At the time of this book, sugar is milled a bit finer than say, five or ten years ago. What this means is that the edges are not quite as rough as they used to be and you are actually getting a bit more sugar per cup. This has a number of consequences, both for our waistline and for our baking.

I'm not going to indulge in a talk about weight (after all, this is a baking book!), but for the purposes of baking, the finer milled sugar means that you have to strictly follow the guidelines for creaming butter with sugar and make sure enough time is provided to get the right number of air bubbles. This is the only time these air bubbles will develop. Once you add the eggs, the opportunity is lost. No matter how long you beat the eggs for, you will never be able to develop more air and the extended beating may even tamper with your baked good.

In addition to tenderness, much of a baked good's texture depends on how much sugar you use. Cookies are a prime example. If your cookie recipe has a lot of sugar in it, it will be crispier than one with less sugar. Less sugar (or more brown sugar) will make your cookies soft and chewy. If your shortcrust pastry has sugar in it, as they tend to do, they become crispier and take on a more golden-hued colour than regular pastry.

Sugar is hygroscopic, meaning it attracts and helps retain moisture. The amount of sugar and the kind you use can significantly alter how moist your baked good is and how long it will stay moist. In this case, granulated sugar does not reign supreme. Honey and corn syrup are the masters here and baked goods that are sweetened with these liquids will stay moist the longest. Second in command is brown sugar or any soft sugar.

Sugar also freezes at a lower temperature than water, so sweetened custards, gelati or ice creams will not freeze as rock hard as ice cubes, making consumption that much more enjoyable.

Yeast too depends on sugar. It's sugar's job to kick-start yeast by feeding it, which enables fermentation and thus allows a bread to rise. If you've made bread before, you're familiar with the technique of adding a small amount of sugar to the water in which the dried yeast will proof. Yeast loves sugar, devouring it greedily and enabling the starch in the flour to convert to sugar. This conversion produces the carbon dioxide that ultimately leavens the bread.

Lastly, sugar can help prevent dry ingredients from clumping together. Take for example, the Chocolate Birthday Cake on page 317, in which the brown sugar is whisked together with the flour, leaveners and such. The sugar helps separate the dry ingredients from each other in the bowl, aided by a whisk. Consequently, you don't need to whisk as much once you pour in the wet ingredients, making for a tender final product.

All sugars should be stored in an airtight container in a cool, dry place. They should last up to 2 years.

GRANULATED SUGAR The most commonly used sugar in baked goods. It is made from either beet or cane sugar. See above for a description of its myriad functions.

CASTER OR SUPERFINE SUGAR Caster or superfine sugar acts much like granulated sugar, it simply has smaller grains. As mentioned above, caster sugar is ideal when the sugar in a recipe is required to dissolve quickly. It's also used in cakes such as angel food cake, where its finer grains can add volume but not weigh the batter down when added to the dry mixture.

ICING SUGAR Basically this is granulated sugar that has been ground or powdered. An anti-caking agent (between 3 and 5%) is almost always added to help prevent clumping. It is most definitely not a substitute for granulated or brown sugar. You will most often see it called for in icings or in some shortbread cookies, where it more easily dissolves than granulated sugar.

BROWN SUGAR Adorned with a moist, cakey texture, brown sugar is simply white granulated sugar with some molasses added back into it. Grains of brown sugar are smaller and softer than the grains of white granulated sugar, so it's often not used in the creaming method—although exceptions are many. The addition of brown sugar will mean your cookies are softer and moister because of the liquid in brown sugar. It also means your chocolate cakes will be more chocolatey tasting. Always pack your brown sugar when measuring it and store it in a really tight, airproof container. If it does clump and harden, simply add a piece of bread, an apple wedge or one of those terracotta discs that retail stores sell to get it soft again. Although not quite as sweet as white sugar (there's about a 4% difference), you can substitute brown sugar for white in most recipes in equal amounts. If your recipe calls for brown sugar and you find yourself out of it, simply add 1 Tbsp (15 mL) of fancy molasses to 1 cup (250 mL) of granulated sugar, which will yield 1 cup (250 mL) of brown sugar. Currently, brown sugar is available in dark and light varieties. I personally find the dark too aggressive for my liking, so all of my recipes have been tested with light brown sugar.

DEMERARA SUGAR Made from sugarcane, it has a dark brown colour and is moister than granulated sugar. Generally, demerara sugar can be substituted with dark brown sugar cup for cup.

MUSCOVADO SUGAR This is an unrefined brown sugar made from sugarcane. It tends to have more molasses than dark brown sugar, and thus a stronger flavour, but in a pinch it can be used to replace dark brown sugar.

PALM SUGAR This sugar is becoming more popular due to its low glycemic index. It is cup per cup as sweet as granulated sugar. Derived from the coconut or sago palm, it is most typically sold as a solid block. Consequently, it requires grating before incorporating into a recipe.

TURBINADO SUGAR Most often used for sprinkling on pies and cookies, this coarse, dry sugar is made from sugarcane.

CORN SYRUP Corn syrup is not a naturally occurring sugar. It must be manufactured by adding an enzyme to cornstarch that converts the starch to sugar. After a few other ingredients are added, you end up with corn syrup, which, as a result, is quite highly refined. Available in both dark and light or clear varieties, corn syrup is most often used to prevent crystallization or to provide moistness. Unless colour is an issue, the two varieties can be used interchangeably.

HONEY The world of honey is so varied, it's hard to know where to start. There are roughly 500 different varieties of honey produced globally, some single blossom honeys (the honey collected from a single type of blossom), some multi-blossom honeys and some specific to a particular region. Most commercially available honeys tend to be a blend of several honeys, to ensure uniformity. Whatever type you opt to use, there are a number of considerations to weigh. First, honey is not 100% purely sweet. It's made up of about 18% water, meaning it's not quite as sweet as granulated sugar and has fewer calories *by weight* than sugar. On the other hand, because it does contain water and is a liquid itself, it's highly hygroscopic, meaning anything baked with honey will be moister than if it were made with granulated sugar (it will also be a bit denser). Not only will it be moister, but it will stay moister longer. Honey, like corn syrup, will delay or prevent crystallization, making sorbets and ice creams velvety smooth. Generally, the darker the honey, the more pronounced its flavour. Refrigerating honey will encourage honey to crystallize, so always store in a dark place at room temperature. For every 1 cup (250 mL) of granulated sugar, substitute ¾ cup (180 mL) honey and reduce other liquids in the recipe by ¼ cup (60 mL). You will need to reduce the oven temperature (since honey encourages browning) and add ½ tsp (2 mL) baking soda for every 1 cup (250 mL) of honey.

MAPLE SYRUP As with other liquid sweeteners, baked goods sweetened with maple syrup will tend to be denser and moister than those made with granulated sugar. Maple syrup is slightly less sweet than granulated sugar. There seems to be some controversy about how much maple syrup to substitute for 1 cup (250 mL) of granulated sugar. I have read anything from ¾ cup (180 mL), to 1 cup (250 mL) to 1½ cups (375 mL). It will depend on your personal preferences. I prefer to err on the side of just sweet enough so I tend to substitute 1 cup (250 mL) of granulated sugar with ¾ cup (180 mL) of maple syrup. Completely eliminating granulated sugar from a recipe and substituting it wholly with maple syrup is not recommended. As with honey, if you do substitute some of the granulated sugar with maple syrup, it's necessary to decrease the amount of liquid called for in the recipe by ¼ cup (60 mL), or alternatively to increase the flour by ¼ cup (60 mL). As a general rule, the denser the syrup, the darker and more concentrated the flavour of the syrup.

MOLASSES This dark, syrupy liquid almost always comes from cane sugar and is removed from the raw sugarcane juice during the refining process. Generally used in addition to granulated sugar, molasses imparts a deep caramel flavour to baked goods and, because it is an acidic ingredient, can be used to activate baking soda. Molasses is also considered a hygroscopic ingredient so that baked goods containing molasses tend to be moister than those made with granulated sugar only. There are actually quite a few varieties of molasses, although some can be tricky to find. Fancy molasses, the kind called for in the recipes in this book, is the highest grade of molasses available and results from the pure juice of the sugarcane that hasn't yet had any of the sugar extracted from it. Fancy molasses is lighter in colour than the other molasses types and has a sweet, almost burnt sugar taste to it and can be somewhat tangy.

Light molasses is produced after the first boiling of the sugar cane. It tends to be quite light in colour and quite sweet because only a small amount of sugar has been extracted. It's also known as Barbados, table or first molasses. Dark molasses, frequently referred to as second or full molasses, is the result of the second boiling after more sugar is extracted. It is darker in colour, thicker and less sweet than refined or light molasses.

Cooking molasses is a blend of fancy molasses and blackstrap molasses (see below). Thicker and darker than fancy molasses, it has a more full-bodied flavour and texture.

Blackstrap molasses is the highly concentrated, very dark syrup produced after the third and final boiling. Quite bitter, it should never be used as the main sweetener in baking and should be used sparingly.

BROWN RICE SYRUP Although not called for in this book, brown rice syrup is becoming increasingly popular as an alternative to white sugar because it is mistakenly believed to be significantly healthier as it is less refined. Brown rice syrup is the result of fine meal brown rice that is cooked until the starch in the rice is broken down into sugar. The liquid that results is boiled down until it becomes a thick, brown syrup. It tends to be considerably less sweet than granulated sugar and cannot easily be substituted for regular granulated sugar. Baked goods made with brown rice syrup tend to be a bit crisper than those made with white sugar. You will have to experiment until you're happy with the results.

AGAVE Sometimes sold as "nectar" and sometimes sold as "syrup," agave can be used to replace granulated sugar, but with caution. Because agave is 1.4 to 1.6 times sweeter than sugar, you use less but you will also have to adjust the liquid in your recipe, as you would with honey. For example, you can substitute honey or maple syrup with an equal amount of agave, or 1 cup (250 mL) of white or brown sugar with about ⅔ cup (160 mL) of agave, but you will also need to reduce the amount of liquid respectively by ¼ cup (60 mL) or 2 Tbsp (30 mL). It's also best to mix the agave with the fat called for in the recipe or with some of the liquid ingredients. Reducing your oven temperature by 25°F (14°C) is usually helpful as well. Baked goods made with agave also tend to be darker in colour. Agave is generally available in light, amber, dark and raw varieties. Light agave is really the only one that should be used in baking. The darker as well as the raw variety are generally considered too strongly flavoured for all-purpose baking.

SUGAR SUBSTITUTES Although I kind of frown on using these products (why not just make a really amazing dessert and have a very small piece), I do recognize that many people use sugar substitutes in their baking. If you're using a product such as Splenda, simply replace each cup of granulated sugar with a cup of Splenda. If you're using a more specific product, such as Splenda Brown Sugar Blend, use ½ cup (125 mL) for every 1 cup (250 mL) of brown sugar and increase the vanilla by ½ tsp (2 mL).

There are a few caveats to keep in mind when using a sugar substitute. If you're creaming together butter and a sugar substitute for a cake or a cookie, the mixture will remain a bit grainy no matter how long you cream. Once you add the eggs, the mixture will most likely curdle, but will come back together when you add the dry ingredients. Most cakes and biscuits made with a sugar substitute, although sweet, will not yield the impressive height you might otherwise expect. (Look at the beginning of this section for an explanation of the creaming process.) Cookies and other baked goods made with a sugar substitute will also not brown quite as much and may take 3–5 minutes LESS time to bake, so watch your oven! In addition, desserts made with a sugar substitute will not store for as long as those made with conventional granulated sugar.

FLOUR

Flour is one of most fundamental ingredients in baking. Butter is just butter and sugar is just sugar, but add some flour and you can achieve anything from flaky, quick puff pastry, to ethereal biscuits or dense and chewy breads. The key is what kind of flour to use.

The first thing you really need to know about flour—even before what kind, because in fact it will determine what kind—is that all wheat flour contains protein, to varying degrees. When these proteins come into direct contact with a liquid, they form a new protein called gluten, a web of strong and flexible strands that provide structure for all baked goods. Gluten, once it's wet, binds the flour and liquid to achieve an elastic and flexible dough. The less gluten you develop, the softer and more tender your baked product will be. Conversely, the more gluten you develop, the chewier and springier the baked good. And so, depending on what you want to make, it's important to differentiate between wheat flours and how much protein each one contains.

I will be concentrating mostly on the flours called for in this book, mostly made from wheat flours.

ALL-PURPOSE FLOUR This flour, as its name surely suggests, is the master of versatility. It is usually a combination of what's called hard wheat and soft wheat. The protein content of all-purpose flour ranges from 9–12%. Most manufacturers have their own proprietary blend and trademark style. As I recommend with butter, try out several national brands and then stick with the one that you most prefer. I will never forget one incident that occurred when I was Test Kitchen Director at *Canadian Living Magazine*. It was the middle of summer and so of course we were testing all of the cookie recipes for our Christmas issue (magazines typically work about 6 months ahead). Much to our dismay, none (and I mean none) of the cookies worked. They fell apart, spread too much and were, quite frankly, a disaster. I racked my brains for what could be causing such failure. After some investigation, it came to light that someone had purchased an unknown flour, sold on deep discount. Problem solved. We returned to the flour we preferred and voila, all of the cookies baked up beautifully and deliciously.

All-purpose flour is sold as bleached or unbleached. Technically, all all-purpose flour is, to some extent, bleached. When wheat is freshly milled into flour, carotenoid pigments in the wheat give the flour a slight yellowish tint. Over time, about 12 weeks, these pigments oxidize naturally, changing the yellowish colour to a creamy white colour. Early in the 20th century, scientists developed a method to expedite this process by using chemicals. Bleached all-purpose flour is bleached with either benzoyl peroxide or chlorine gas. These chemicals bleach the flour a stark white and, in fact, alter the protein content, somewhat lowering it. This makes the flour less prone to form strong gluten, which is why some bakers, such as one of my personal pastry goddesses Rose Levy Beranbaum, are more inclined to use it (because it more closely resembles cake flour that has been chlorinated—more on that below). Bleaching does not affect the nutritional flavour of the flour and is not harmful whatsoever.

Many bakers can discern a difference in flavour between bleached and unbleached flour, so prefer the latter. However, an equal number will tell you that bleached all-purpose flour is preferable due to its lower protein content. Their contention is that baked goods made with bleached flour improves their baking, enabling them to produce more tender cakes, cakes that boast a softer texture and cakes with a more vivid colour. You most likely will not be able to notice a significant difference between cookies made with unbleached flour versus those made with bleached flour. However, you will notice a difference in an angel food cake, which will be lighter, softer and whiter when made with bleached all-purpose flour.

Today's flour is pre-sifted more than 100 times during the milling process, so it's no longer necessary to sift all-purpose flour before using it. However, flour does settle, so I recommend aerating it with a spoon or fork before measuring it. It's also helpful to transfer the flour from the bag in which you bought it to a container with a wide opening. It's much easier to dip a 1 cup (250 mL) dry measure into a large canister and then sweep it clean than it is to do so in a 5 lb (2.3 kg) bag of flour.

In this book, I have used mostly bleached flour for the biscuits, scones, muffins, cakes, pies, cookies and as a thickener for pies. For quick breads, heartier cakes and all of the yeast breads, I have used unbleached all-purpose flour. If you don't want to have two flours on hand, an unbleached all-purpose flour will work on all of the recipes.

CAKE AND PASTRY FLOUR This is actually a category that encapsulates three different kinds of flour: cake flour, pastry flour and "cake and pastry flour." Cake flour is made from very soft wheat and has about 8% protein. Pastry flour is quite similar to cake flour but has a protein level of about 9%. Both of these flours are not easily available in commercial form, being used mostly by professional bakers. What is available in Canada, however, is a blend called cake and pastry flour, with a protein content ranging from 8–10%. All cake and pastry flour is chlorinated, which basically means that it's been bleached to an ivory white colour. With a lower protein (hence gluten) level and a lower pH level, cake flour tends to produce not only a sweeter taste but also a finer, more velvety crumb. It's the higher acidity of cake flour that lowers the temperature at which the proteins coagulate, meaning that the network of gluten sets quickly in the oven. Accordingly, cakes made with cake flour can support more sugar and butter and better absorb liquid. Many cake experts say that fat adheres to the surface of chlorinated flours better than those flours that have not been chlorinated, which results in better aeration and lighter, airier cakes.

Because cake flour is so finely milled, it tends to clump upon sitting. You must sift cake and pastry flour before using. Be mindful though, whether you sift before measuring or after measuring is determined by the wording in the ingredient list. If a recipe calls for "2 cups (500 mL) cake and pastry flour, sifted," then you sift the flour after you measure it. Conversely, if the recipe calls for "2 cups (500 mL) sifted cake and pastry flour," you sift and then measure.

All the recipes in this book that call for cake and pastry flour have been spooned into a dry measure until the flour is overflowing and then levelled off with the blunt edge of a knife.

In a pinch, you can substitute all-purpose flour for cake and pastry flour. Use ¾ cup (180 mL) of all-purpose flour plus 2 Tbsp (30 mL) of cornstarch for 1 cup (250 mL) of cake and pastry flour.

BREAD FLOUR As the name suggests, this is a higher protein flour—between 12.5 and 14%—best for use in breads and other yeasted products. The high amount of protein in bread flour enables bread and other yeasted wonders to dramatically expand yet still hold their shape. Bread flour is almost never bleached since that would strip it of some of its protein. Bread flour comes in white or whole-wheat forms, organic or otherwise.

WHOLE-WHEAT FLOUR Whereas the bran and germ of the wheat shaft is removed from all-purpose flour, the two are left intact when whole-wheat flour is milled. This explains the somewhat coarse texture of whole-wheat flour and its colour. Since the entire grain is used, whole-wheat flour is more nutritious and contains more fibre than white all-purpose flour, although it has less protein. It imparts a nutty toasted flavour wherever it's used. Because the wheat germ contains fat, whole-wheat flour can become rancid very quickly. It's best to buy it in small quantities and store it in the freezer (you don't have to thaw whole-wheat flour before using it).

If you regularly bake with whole wheat, then you know to expect a baked good that is chewy, nutty and somewhat heavier than a comparable item made with all-purpose flour. Yeasted breads made with all whole-wheat flour tend to be quite heavy and dense. I have found it beneficial to substitute only about 60% of the white flour with whole-wheat flour for a lighter textured bread. In non-yeasted baked goods, it's best to replace only up to half of the white flour with whole-wheat flour, or, again, you may end up with a heavier result than anticipated. A good alternative to keep in mind if you want to go the whole-wheat route is to substitute all-purpose flour with whole-wheat cake and pastry flour, sometimes available at specialty or bulk stores.

Whole-wheat flour is available in both regular milled and stone-ground varieties. If you purchase the latter, be prepared for a slightly nuttier flavour and crunchier texture in your baked goods.

WHEAT GERM/WHEAT BRAN Back when I was a pastry chef, the rage du jour was wheat germ and wheat bran. Due to popular demand, I added it to almost all of my muffins and many of my quick breads. Nowadays, these two lovely ingredients are not quite so *de rigueur*, but deserve a place in your baking pantry nonetheless. Tiny but nutrient dense, wheat germ is the part of the wheat shaft that sprouts and grows into a new plant. Regularly left out when milling white all-purpose flour due to its propensity for rancidity, wheat germ (which comes from the word germinate), contains fibre, protein, vitamin B and is high in carbohydrates. You can add it to most muffins, quick breads or hearty cakes along with the dry ingredients to add nuttiness and increase the recipe's nutritional quota. In general, you can add up to 3 Tbsp (45 mL) of wheat germ or wheat bran without affecting the overall ratio of dry to wet ingredients in your baked good. Store bottles of wheat germ in the freezer or refrigerator (like whole-wheat flour, there's no need to thaw before using).

Wheat bran is the outer layer of the wheat kernel. Much like wheat germ, it's high in carbohydrates, calcium and fibre. Add it to muffins, cookies or quick breads as you would wheat germ and store much the same way.

CORNMEAL   Cornmeal is made from ground, dried corn kernels. It is available in yellow, white and blue, although for the purposes of baking in this book, only yellow cornmeal is considered. When you add cornmeal to a quick bread or a muffin, it imparts a coarse, crunchy texture and a nutty, toasted corn flavour. Store stone ground cornmeal in the refrigerator and regular cornmeal in a cool dry place.

CORNSTARCH   Most commonly used as a thickener or as an addition to flour to impart tenderness to shortbread cookies, cornstarch is the ground starch isolated from the whole corn kernel. It has twice the thickening power of regular white flour and results in a clear, not cloudy, mixture. If you've ever made a lemon meringue pie that has turned soupy, you'll know that there are a couple of things to keep in mind when using cornstarch. First and foremost, it's imperative to adhere to the timing when thickening a mixture with cornstarch. Cornstarch, when mixed with a liquid and then heated, will thicken as it reaches a full boil. If you continue to cook it much longer than that, and stir it too vigorously, the granules that absorbed the liquid and swelled to thicken it will break down and the mixture will thin out. At this point, the mixture is irrecoverable. You just have to start again. Store cornstarch in its original container in a cool dry place.

CHEMICAL LEAVENERS

In baking, there are three types of leavening, the process or agent that makes a cake or pastry or bread rise. First, there is mechanical or physical leavening. Physical leavening occurs when butter is creamed with sugar and pockets of air are formed in the mixture. This air will then expand in the heat of the oven, allowing the flour and eggs to set the risen structure.

It also happens when air is whipped and then trapped in egg whites. The same is true when you're making pie or puff pastry and butter is enmeshed between layers of dough. As the butter melts, the resulting steam pushes the layers apart, creating a delicate, flaky pastry.

Biological or natural leavening is at work when yeast is called for in a recipe. Yeast feeds on the sugars in the starch of the flour, which causes these microscopic, single-celled organisms to thrive and multiply. As the yeast feeds, carbon dioxide is created. Then, as the yeast expels carbon dioxide, the gas bubbles are caught in the bread's developing gluten web, causing the bread to expand and rise.

Chemical leavening comes into play when either baking soda or baking powder is used. These products are necessary when a natural leavener is not suitable or when physical leavening alone is simply insufficient to give the baked good the oomph it needs to rise. You will often see chemical leaveners coupled with physical leavening to ensure the lightest, most tender baked good.

CREAM OF TARTAR Cream of tartar, one of the key ingredients in baking powder, is used mostly when whipping egg whites. The acid in cream of tartar provides stability and strength to the egg whites, firming up their proteins, which, in turn, allows them to hold the volume and shape they've achieved.

BAKING POWDER Most of the baking powder you buy these days is double acting baking powder. Essentially this means that the baking powder starts to work upon contact with a liquid when it releases a small amount of carbon dioxide (a result of the reaction caused between the acid and the alkali). The second reaction occurs when the batter reaches a certain temperature in the heat of the oven. This is when the baking powder releases its full power, expanding the gas cells as the structure of the batter sets, giving a full rise to the cake.

Baking powder is made up of baking soda, an acid to use up all of the soda (usually tartaric acid) as well as cornstarch, which prevents the acid and the baking soda from absorbing too much moisture and drying out.

Too much baking powder can cause a batter to taste bitter or cause the batter to rise rapidly and then collapse (because the air bubbles in the batter grow too large and break, causing the batter to fall). Cakes will have a coarse, fragile crumb with a fallen centre. Too little baking powder results in a tough cake that has poor volume and a compact crumb.

Baking powder readily absorbs moisture from the air and can deteriorate quickly as a result. It has a shelf life of about 3 months. To test for efficacy, combine 1 tsp (5 mL) of baking powder with ½ cup (125 mL) of hot water. If it bubbles up vigorously, the baking powder is still good. If no reaction occurs, then it's time to buy a new can.

BAKING SODA   Baking soda, also known as sodium bicarbonate or bicarbonate of soda (alkali) is about four times as strong as baking powder. It is used and activated in recipes that contain a liquid and an acidic ingredient (often the two are the same) such as vinegar, citrus juice, sour cream, yogurt, buttermilk, chocolate, unsweetened cocoa powder (although not the Dutch-processed variety), honey, molasses, brown sugar, maple syrup and some fruits. Baking soda starts to react and release carbon dioxide gas as soon as the batter is moistened, so you have to work quickly and get your baked good directly into the oven.

Being heavy handed with baking soda can cause a soapy taste in your baking and encourage a coarse, open crumb.

Baking soda has a shelf life of 6–9 months if stored in a sealed container in a cool dry place. Remember to store the box in a plastic bag since exposure to any moisture in the air can rob it of its ability to leaven. Just be sure not to use the baking soda that you use to deodourize your refrigerator when you bake.

Chemical leaveners, such as baking powder and baking soda, do not actually create new bubbles in a batter or dough. Rather, they work their magic by releasing carbon dioxide that enlarges the bubbles already created during beating or creaming (physical leavening).

People often ask why some recipes call for both baking powder and baking soda. Shouldn't one be sufficient to leaven the baked good? The quick answer is that both are called for when baking soda is called for in sufficient amounts to neutralize acidity but in insufficient amounts to provide the requisite leavening. Baking soda, it should be noted, also tends to cause baked goods to brown more than baking powder. Cookies made with baking soda only will spread more than cookies made with a combination of baking soda and baking powder or baking powder alone. You'll see that throughout the book, when I make a cake, muffin or quick bread, the instructions call for whisking together the dry ingredients really well. This distributes the baking soda or powder as well as the salt or any spices called for throughout the batter, so that no one part of the batter is getting too much leavening.

SALT

In baking, salt is as important as sugar, in my opinion. Salt is meant to enhance and enliven all of the other ingredients in a recipe. Without salt, your cookies will taste flatter than usual, your cake will lack that special oomph and your custard will come out bland. When working with yeast, salt is especially salient. Salt can kill yeast, which is why it's almost always mixed in with the flour once the yeast has proofed. Salt also helps slow yeast, allowing the dough the time to properly develop its flavour and texture.

Although many coarse salts are available, they are not optimal for baking. Fine sea salt or free-running table salt are the best options since they disperse easily into the dry ingredients and dissolve readily. Many cookies, scone and biscuits bake quickly in the oven so a salt that melts easily and quickly is required. Kosher or coarse salt is harder to measure and will not disperse as evenly in your dry mixture. If kosher salt is all you have, use 1¾–2 tsp (9–10 mL) of kosher salt for every 1 tsp (5 mL) of regular salt.

EGGS

As much as butter, sugar and flour, eggs play an essential role in baking, performing an extraordinary myriad of functions. They form part of the liquid content of a cake, contribute to texture, colour and richness, help bind together different ingredients to provide structure and act as leaveners to boot.

Many baked goods, in addition to baking powder and baking soda, rely on eggs for leavening. Many cake recipes, for example, call for egg yolks to be beaten with sugar until thick and pale coloured (see the Lady-fingers on page 122, for example). When you whip together egg yolks with sugar, air is trapped between the crystals of the sugar and suspended in the expanded egg yolks. When the item in question is baked, the trapped air inside the batter expands, leavening the baked good.

Eggs also provide structure to baked goods. Eggs tend to coagulate at a relatively low temperature, which can be altered by the inclusion of sugar or salt in a batter. The important thing to remember is that this coagulation provides the structure of the cake until the flour has had enough baking time to set and firm up.

Eggs add tenderness to a cake because of the high fat content of the yolk. They also provide their own inimitable flavour, especially in recipes where they claim star status, such as mousses, sabayons and custards.

Whole eggs are natural emulsifiers as well, because the yolks contain lecithin. This property enables eggs to bind fats to a liquid, creating wonderfully satin custards and ice creams and tender and delicate crumbed cakes.

Eggs are also natural thickeners, since they can hold up to four times their own weight in moisture once they coagulate. See the section on tempering (see p. 46) to discover how to proceed with thickening a custard or the base of an ice cream.

Finally, eggs provide a golden colour to many baked goods, again mostly because of the yolk. Compare the downy whiteness of an angel food cake, made only with egg whites, to the sunny golden richness of a pound cake. Eggs also provide colour when used as a glaze. The darker you want the surface of your bread to be, the higher the percentage of fat should be included in the glaze. Egg yolks, on their own, will provide the richest looking colour (as will melted butter or whipping cream), due to their high fat content. If you want a shiny finish, such as is desired on a hot cross bun, use the whites only.

All of my recipes were developed and tested with large eggs. I have called for large eggs in each recipe as a reminder.

CHOCOLATE

Like everything else in your pantry, you should start with really good chocolate. And really good chocolate—no matter its nomenclature—tends to be expensive. To avoid paying for an inferior product, here are some clues to help you choose the best.

Always look for the words cocoa butter, cocoa solids, cocoa mass or cocoa liquor on the ingredient list. Together, cocoa butter and chocolate liquor (a combination of cocoa solids, which are bitter, and cocoa butter) make great chocolate. Optimally, the cocoa butter should be listed among the first two of the ingredients and the ingredient list should not include vegetable oil or shortening. Some manufacturers add vegetable oil or shortening in an effort to reduce the amount of cocoa butter, which is quite expensive. However, unlike cocoa butter, those two ingredients offer nothing in terms of flavour. The ingredient lists for both semisweet and bittersweet chocolate should include cocoa solids, cocoa butter, sugar, pure vanilla or vanillin and possibly lecithin, which is an emulsifier.

Really good chocolate should appear glossy, have a deep and rich colour and sport a smooth surface. The chocolate should show no evidence of bloom or discolouration, which indicate that it has been stored for too long and has been subject to temperature fluctuations (more on that later).

Chocolate should introduce itself even before you taste it. Premium chocolate has a strong, rich, deeply chocolatey aroma. Once you eat it, it

should melt in your mouth almost immediately. Part of the reason good chocolate is so divine is because cocoa butter has a melting point exactly that of our own internal body temperature. Vegetable shortenings have a much higher melting point so that chocolate made with them does not and cannot have the same mouth feel or richness. The chocolate should melt uniformly and have a good long finish. It should never be gritty (a sure indicator of too much sugar) nor feel waxy or greasy.

Really good chocolate should taste somewhat complex. You may find yourself tasting a slight overtone of coffee (after all, chocolate comes from a bean), perhaps cinnamon or tobacco, red wine or even berries. I remember the first time I tasted Valrhona chocolate in San Francisco, I was immediately and surprisingly reminded of berries, which I had never really experienced before. Avoid chocolates that are cloyingly sweet or leave an aftertaste.

Premium chocolate should not feel waxy or pasty and should break into clean shards when chopped with a knife or chocolate fork. If it's crumbly or pasty, that's a sign of too little cocoa butter.

The recipe you use and the type of dessert you're making will determine what kind of chocolate you should be using. For instance, if you're making the Passover Chocolate Cake on page 327, it's important to use the best quality chocolate you can since it's essentially the primary ingredient and flavour of the cake. Conversely, if you're baking a cake with many levels of flavouring, perhaps a square with nuts or a multi-layered cake, the best chocolate is a more casual semisweet chocolate, since this type of chocolate won't get lost or overpower any of the other elements in the baked good. In general, the darker the chocolate and the more bitter and intense its flavour, the better it will wed with other flavourings such as eggs, butter and sugar without sacrificing its inherent complexity. Conversely, unlike a sweet milk-chocolate bar, it may be too intense for eating out of hand. I, for one, simply cannot eat any chocolate that is higher than 75% cocoa on its own.

To understand the personality of the different kinds of chocolate, please see the list below.

UNSWEETENED CHOCOLATE Unsweetened chocolate is 50–58% cocoa butter with the rest made up of cocoa solids. Unsweetened chocolate contains no sugar and cannot be eaten out of hand. It is usually sold in 4-oz (125 g) blocks or bars and it is as bitter as cocoa powder.

BITTERSWEET CHOCOLATE Bittersweet chocolate is the result of some sugar and a little vanilla being added back to the chocolate liquor along with some more cocoa butter. Chocolate liquor is made up of 50–60% cocoa butter and the rest cocoa solids. The wonderful thing about baking with bittersweet chocolate is how dramatically the flavour of your desserts can change depending on the particular brand you use. Nowadays, you can find bittersweet chocolates with a cocoa content anywhere between 55% and 95%. However, some of the higher cocoa chocolates are not as suitable for baking. When testing the Fudge Truffle Tart on page 204, I tried it with Baker's semisweet chocolate, Callebaut's bittersweet chocolate and an 80% bittersweet chocolate. The first two worked out beautifully, whereas the tart made with the higher cocoa content (and consequently much less sugar) came out too bitter.

It's crucial to remember that as you increase the cocoa content, you not only remove sugar but you add cocoa butter as well. These two ingredients affect texture and mouth feel. High percentage chocolate can also wreak havoc when making ganache—often called for in the pages of this book. Classically, ganache is equal parts chocolate and whipping cream. For ganache to be successful, the chocolate has to have the correct proportion of chocolate solids to soak up the hot whipping cream. Since chocolate with higher percentages of cocoa tend to have more chocolate solids, the proportions are thrown off, and more cream is required. Otherwise, you're left with a grainy and oily mass. Until high-percentage chocolates become the norm, most recipes in baking books, as is true of mine, develop and test their recipes with a moderately bittersweet chocolate, hovering between the 50 and 68% mark. For best results, try to use a bittersweet chocolate with these percentages.

Bittersweet chocolate is the best type of chocolate when you're baking deeply chocolatey desserts. Its depth of flavour, complexity and sweetness make the chocolate dessert sing without being pushed to the side by other flavourings.

SEMISWEET CHOCOLATE Unlike Europe, where there are very strict standards about what constitutes bittersweet and semisweet chocolate, the lines are a little more blurry in North America. In general, semisweet chocolate is very similar to bittersweet chocolate but with more sugar. Consequently, it's a little less complex and a little sweeter. This is not to say it's inferior. Some semisweet chocolates can be better than bittersweet chocolate made by another manufacturer. By law, semisweet chocolate must contain a minimum of 35% cocoa, but most come in around the 50% mark. Because it's a bit sweeter than bittersweet chocolate, semi-sweet chocolate is easier to eat out of hand and is better suited to desserts where a pure, unrestricted but sweet flavour is demanded.

Both semisweet and bittersweet chocolate can be purchased as a varietal chocolate or as a single-origin chocolate. While most chocolates are a blend of varietals from around the world (giving their manufacturers the ability to consistently achieve their own proprietary taste and attributes), varietal chocolates come from the same variety of cocoa bean. Single-origin chocolate is also made from varietal beans, but those which hail from a single plantation, area or origin. Callebaut and Cacoa Barry make some really interesting single-origin chocolates as do other well-known manufacturers.

MILK CHOCOLATE Milk chocolate contains cocoa liquor, milk or dry milk solids, flavourings and additional fat (usually vegetable shortening) as well as sugar and vanilla. Since the cocoa content is only 10–15%, milk chocolate has a much less pronounced chocolate flavour. The addition of milk, either dry or condensed, imparts to milk chocolate the creaminess that we so often associate with it. As with bittersweet chocolate, there is a movement to introduce "dark" milk chocolate to the market, with some varieties showing up with as much as 40% cocoa content, which, in essence, melds a deeper chocolate flavour to the milky sweetness.

WHITE CHOCOLATE White chocolate has been dubbed the "Great Imposter" since it's not really a chocolate at all. It doesn't contain any chocolate liquor, only cocoa butter, and in reality not every brand even contains that. Always look for a high percentage of cocoa butter and refrain from buying any white chocolate that contains vegetable shortening. Good white chocolate should never be pure white, but should instead be a creamy ivory. White chocolate is very temperamental and not suited to melting. It also turns rancid quickly, so buy only what you need and don't store it for too long.

COCOA POWDER Remembering that chocolate liquor is made up of both cocoa solids and cocoa butter, it's easy to visualize how brittle and unpalatable those cocoa solids would be with the removal of the cocoa butter. This is what cocoa powder is made from. The cocoa solids, sans the cocoa butter, are formed into a pressed cake using hydraulic pressure. The cake is then ground into a powder.

There are two different types of coca powder: Dutch-processed and natural. Dutch-processed cocoa (also called alkalized cocoa) has been treated with an alkali during processing which neutralizes its innate acidity, mellows its flavour and transforms its colour to a beautifully dark, almost reddish brown. In essence, the less acid it contains, the smoother, more mellow the cocoa powder. Because it has already been alkalized, most recipes using Dutch-processed cocoa powder call for baking powder. Dutch-processed cocoa powder, invented by Conrad Van Houten in the early 1800s in Holland, is the form most preferred by Europeans.

Natural (or non-alkalized cocoa powder) has a darker, more intense or bitter flavour and is more common among American bakers and in American grocery stores. Because it has not been alkalized, natural cocoa powder requires baking soda as a leavener, which also helps to neutralize the acidity naturally present in the cocoa.

One of the most confusing things for novice bakers is when to use which type of cocoa powder, and multiple theories abound. Some baking experts say they can be used interchangeably, as long as when you substitute Dutch-processed cocoa for natural cocoa, you add some acid, such as cream of tartar. Similarly, it's okay to replace natural cocoa for Dutch-processed cocoa if you add some or increase the baking soda, usually by about ¼ tsp (1 mL) per ½ cup (125 mL). The food scientist Harold McGee, author of the renowned *On Food and Cooking: The Science and Lore of the Kitchen,* declares that eggs neutralize the pH in most batters, so if eggs are included in the recipe, either type of cocoa will do. It's really quite confusing and unless you want to do a lot of experimenting, not very helpful.

The general consensus is that the cocoa powders can be used interchangeably when there is no leavening required, such as in ice creams, most drop cookies, puddings and chocolate shortbread cookies. Similarly, when the amount of cocoa powder is small, say ½ cup (125 mL) or less, then either can be used. If a recipe only calls for baking soda, then use natural cocoa powder. If baking powder is called for, or more baking powder than soda, use Dutch-processed cocoa powder. Whichever type of cocoa powder you use, make it the best you can. Throughout this book, I have used a Dutch-processed cocoa unless otherwise specified.

MELTING CHOCOLATE All you need to do to melt chocolate brilliantly each and every time is understand the nature of chocolate and follow a few simple rules.

Always chop your chocolate before you melt it. Larger pieces take longer to melt, and because the chocolate pieces will melt unevenly, you risk scorching some of the chocolate. The finer you chop the chocolate, the less time it will be exposed to the heat and the more uniformly it will melt.

I prefer the old fashioned method of melting chocolate, melting it in a *bain-marie* or water bath. If I'm only melting a small amount, say an ounce or two, I will use the microwave. If I am melting chocolate together with butter, I melt them both in a saucepan directly over very low heat since the butter protects the chocolate from burning.

To make a bain-marie, fill a saucepan one-third full of hot water. Place the chopped chocolate in a heat-proof bowl large enough to sit above the rim of the saucepan. The water in the saucepan should be simmering and not boiling. Chocolate is incompatible with even SMALL amounts of moisture, so if the water bubbles too vigorously and a droplet accidentally plops itself into the bowl of melting chocolate, it's pretty much game over. The chocolate, regardless of what stage it's at, will seize or clump together. Seized chocolate is irrecoverable in most cases. Sometimes you can recover it by adding a droplet or two more of slightly warm water, stirring gently where the chocolate has nastily started to seize. Slowly widen the circumference of your stirring, adding another drop or two of water, until the chocolate has returned to its former glossy self. Adding a fat such as clarified butter or cocoa butter can also help. Sometimes, however, all you can do is throw the chocolate out and start over. This is also why you don't want to stir the melting chocolate with a wooden spoon that may contain minute traces of water lurking in the cracks of the wood.

So here you are, bowl over a pot full of barely simmering water. Try not to stir, even if you're tempted to, until at least 10% of the chocolate has melted. If you stir too soon, not enough of the chocolate will have melted and the liquid chocolate will stick to the unmelted chocolate, causing it to re-solidify. Once three-quarters of the chocolate has melted, remove the bowl from the top of the double boiler. The residual heat in the bowl will finish the melting.

Although small amounts of liquid sound the death knell for chocolate, you can safely add larger quantities of liquid to melted chocolate with much success, as long as you do it all at once and use the correct proportions. The general rule of thumb is that you can safely add 1 Tbsp (15 mL) of liquid for 2 oz (60 g) of chocolate. To clarify, if you are melting ¼ lb (125 g) of chocolate, you can safely whisk in 2 Tbsp (30 mL) of, say, whipping cream or butter without ruining your melted chocolate. Stirring in

1 Tbsp (15 mL) however would cause it to seize. Even if you quickly added the second tablespoon, the damage would have been done.

Higher percentage chocolate is somewhat more stable than, for example, bittersweet chocolate, and so requires a higher heat to melt it. Never substitute chocolate chips when melted chocolate is part of a recipe. Chocolate chips are designed and engineered to retain their shape even in the heat of the oven during baking and often do not melt smoothly. I also find their texture waxy and their flavour a little too sweet compared to high quality chocolate.

STORAGE All chocolate should be stored in a very cool, dark place, away from strongly odoured foods, and it should not be subject to fluctuations in temperature or moisture. Unsweetened, bittersweet and semisweet chocolates can be stored for up to 18 months, whereas milk and white chocolates can only be stored for up to 4 months.

BLOOM "Bloom" is the term used when chocolate develops unattractive whitish streaks or blotches on its surface. There are two different kinds of bloom, characterized by different conditions. The first type is called "fat" bloom and is caused by too much heat, either during its processing or storage, or perhaps even in the front seat of your hot car on the way home from the local chocolate shop. When the temperature of the chocolate rises too high (above 90°F/32°C), some of the cocoa butter separates and melts. The melted cocoa butter rises to the surface of the chocolate where, once the chocolate has cooled again, it re-crystallizes and solidifies, creating those whitish looking streaks. In the industry this is called "being out of temper." The second type of bloom, "sugar" bloom, occurs when the surface of the chocolate comes into contact with too much moisture, say from condensation or from storing your chocolate in the refrigerator. When moisture hits the surface of the chocolate, the sugar in the chocolate dissolves. Once the moisture or water evaporates, the sugar re-crystallizes and turns the top of the chocolate grey or white and sometimes even gritty.

Most bloomed chocolate can be melted easily and used in your baking. The only exception to this is bloom on a newly opened package of chocolate. My recommendation would be to discard the chocolate since the invisible water may have invited bacteria into the chocolate, causing it to spoil. If chocolate has bloomed in a new package you don't know how long ago it bloomed or where it was stored, unlike chocolate that may have recently bloomed on your shelf.

VANILLA

One of the most essential flavourings in baking, vanilla ranks as the second most costly spice in the world (after saffron). This is due to the fact that the flowers of the vanilla orchid open and die within a few hours and must be pollinated by hand to ensure that the fruit sets. The fruit (or beans) needs to mature for about 9 months before it can be picked. Once harvested, it undergoes a lengthy fermentation and aging process, in some cases for up to 2 years. As the beans age, they turn from green to a shrivelled dark brown or black.

Vanilla is unique among dessert flavourings: it can be used to support or enhance other flavours, especially chocolate, nuts and fruit, can mellow harsh elements and can even act as a flavour in its own right.

VANILLA BEANS Where vanilla beans are grown deeply impacts the flavour of the bean. Basically there are four different kinds of vanilla beans: Mexican, Bourbon (so named for the Bourbon Kings of France, with no connection to the spirit, and otherwise known as Madagascar vanilla), Indonesian (or Java) and Tahitian vanilla beans. The Mexican variety is strong and intense, whereas the Bourbon vanilla bean is smoother, richer and sweet. Madagascar vanilla is by far the most popular type, making up more than half of the vanilla consumed globally. Indonesian vanilla is the second most popular, while the Tahitian vanilla is very popular due to its delicate, fruity flavour. The latter is also very plump and aromatic.

To split open a vanilla bean, simply place the bean on a flat work surface. Using the tip of a small paring knife, cut the bean, almost all the way through, lengthwise. Then, using the dull side of the knife, scrape out the tiny seeds and add them to your recipe. Often whole vanilla beans are used to flavour a poaching liquid or custard. See the recipe for Vanilla Roasted Plums or Banana Cream Pie. If you keep your vanilla beans in an airtight container in a cool, dark, dry place, they may very well last up to a year or more. Make sure that they stay supple and soft. If they show any indication of drying out, use them as quickly as possible.

Alternatively, you can add half of a supple vanilla bean to 2 cups (500 mL) of granulated sugar to create vanilla sugar.

VANILLA EXTRACT Pure vanilla extract is made by macerating crushed or chopped vanilla beans with alcohol, which are then blended with sugar and water. Intensely flavoured, deep and almost mystically aromatic, there is no comparison between pure vanilla extract and imitation vanilla. Try to add vanilla near the end of blending or creaming so that it retains its potency and its rich flavour. And, please don't balk at the cost. When it comes to vanilla, a little goes a long way, so it's a savvy investment.

VANILLA PASTE This new product is increasingly becoming more popular. Vanilla paste is a combination of pure vanilla extract and the seeds of the vanilla bean, sugar, water and, generally, some kind of thickener. In general, although more viscous than vanilla extract, it can be substituted equally for vanilla extract. In truth, vanilla paste doesn't have more flavour than vanilla extract, although the visual appearance of thousands of small seeds speckling your baked good is lovely.

SPICES

I'm not going to go into the pros and cons of each individual spice. Suffice it to say that the fresher the better. Even dried herbs and spices will spoil if kept too long or stored improperly. Light, heat and moisture all contribute to the breakdown and spoilage of spices, so be sure to store your spices in a cool, dry, dark place. Buy only what you need at a supermarket with a high turnover rate. I personally am big on grinding my own spices whenever I can, most commonly with cardamom and nutmeg.

Individual varieties of nuts are discussed throughout the book. All nuts should be stored in the freezer and, in most cases, should be toasted before using, to enhance their flavour and smell.

DAIRY PRODUCTS

For all of the recipes in this book, 2% milk is used. There is no need to use whole or homogenized milk and 1% or skim milk lacks the necessary richness, moisture and storage qualities that 2% milk provides.

Buttermilk is one of the most useful dairy products you can keep in your refrigerator. Made by culturing skim (or non-fat) milk with bacteria, this wonderful liquid produces cakes with a moist, tender crumb, and biscuits or scones with a slight tang and flaky interior. Baking with buttermilk lends your baking an old fashioned goodness. Do not use buttermilk when regular milk is called for. All baking recipes that call for buttermilk will also call for some baking soda, since the acid found in buttermilk activates baking soda. To make your own buttermilk or soured milk, pour 1 Tbsp (15 mL) of lemon juice into a 1-cup (250 mL) wet measure. Fill the wet measure to the 1-cup (250 mL) mark with regular milk. Let the mixture stand for about 5 minutes to allow it to thicken.

I also frequently call for sour cream. It's essential to use full-fat sour cream in your baking since the lower fat variety often contains thickeners and gums that dissolve when placed in the oven, making your baked goods heavy and dense. Non-fat sour cream is even worse because, aside from the thickeners, it has an extraordinary amount of water destined to imperil all of your baking efforts. Stick with the 14% fat variety and you'll be fine. Like buttermilk, you'll often see that the recipes calling for sour cream also call for baking soda since, again, it's the acid in the sour cream that activates the baking soda. If you find yourself out of sour cream, you can use buttermilk or yogurt in its stead, although you may need to use slightly less.

Yogurt is also wonderful in baking. Here again, it's important to use a minimum of a 3% fat yogurt, and even a 6% fat yogurt should be considered. Lower fat or non-fat varieties will be too thin and may contain an array of extra sugar, gums, stabilizers and thickeners.

Whipping cream (35% cream), 10% cream and 18% cream are also called for in a few of my recipes. Be sure to store these creams in the coldest part of your refrigerator and to check the best before date. Whipping cream is the only cream that can whip up and retain its volume, so you should never substitute other creams for whipping cream. However, due to its richness and butterfat content, it is rarely used as the liquid of choice when making cakes, since it will weigh down the batter. The exception is recipes that contain an acidic ingredient such as lemon juice. These tend to call for whipping cream since dairy products with a lower fat content (the majority, since whipping cream registers 35% on the butterfat scale) would make the batter curdle. In one or two instances, I call for non-dairy whip topping in an effort to allow my kosher friends to partake of a dessert. In all of these cases, regular whipping cream can be substituted.

When I call for cream cheese in my recipes, I am specifically referring to a cream cheese that is thick and dense, most often sold in 8-oz (230 g) packages. When developing and testing these recipes, I used only Philadelphia cream cheese. If you prefer another brand, feel free to use it but please avoid the whipped varieties, which are not suitable for cheesecakes.

Mascarpone cheese comes in at a whopping 90% butterfat but between you and me, nothing else can really act as a substitute if you want a decadently rich, luxurious tiramisu or tart. Considered a double- or even triple-cream cheese, mascarpone cheese is quite perishable and should be used quickly after purchase. It also tends to break down if over beaten, so tread cautiously.

A FEW TECHNIQUES TO TUCK INTO YOUR APRON

MISE EN PLACE Even though I've said it a few times throughout this book, there is no substitute for being organized. The French call it *mise en place* or "everything in its place." Good and steady baking doesn't come from wingin' it. What mise en place really means is getting all of your ingredients ready and measured even before you start the recipe. You'll be happier and your baked goods will be happier too. Start by reading the recipe carefully from beginning to end and make sure that you understand it. Then check that you have all the requisite equipment and preheat the oven. The third step is to measure out all of your ingredients. There's nothing worse than making a cookie or cake or whatever and finding out, halfway through, that you don't have baking soda. Or that you should have melted the chocolate with the butter and didn't. Or that your whipped egg whites should have been whipped after the egg yolks and now they're going to stand around, sadly deflating while you whip up those darn egg yolks.

BLIND BAKING Tart shells and pie shells often need to be partially or fully prebaked before they are filled with a fruit- or custard-type filling. This is a technique referred to as blind baking. To blind bake a crust, line your baking shell with a large piece of parchment paper, making sure it fills the inner edge. Then fill the shell with pie weights, dried rice or dried beans. Again, press lightly on the weights to make sure that the shell is completely and evenly filled. The pie weights prevent the pastry shell from puffing up. A pastry shell is done when it's no longer shiny but matte and either lightly golden for partially baked shells or golden for fully baked shells.

CARAMELIZING SUGAR This technique probably raises the intimidation factor for most people because its finicky reputation precedes it. Cook sugar too little and you're left with insipid, flavourless caramel. Cook it too long and you're left with a foul smelling, burnt mixture. What to do?

There are two ways of caramelizing sugar, the dry method and the wet method. Since the wet method is more foolproof, I'll start with that one. Start off by combining sugar and water in a heavy-bottomed saucepan. You can stir the sugar or swirl the pan to ensure the sugar is evenly moistened. This is the only time you should stir the sugar. Once the pot is set on the stove, do not stir. Over a medium-high or high heat, bring the sugar to a boil. The important thing at this stage is not to stir it and to have a pastry brush dipped in water close by. Stirring the sugar at this point encourages some of the sugar to re-crystallize (firm up), leaving you with a hardened mass. Use a wet brush to brush down the inner sides of the saucepan to remove any sugar crystals that may sneak into the boiling sugar. This is an important step. It doesn't really matter if your brush is saturated with water and this water seeps into the sugar mixture. It will just take a little longer to caramelize. What does matter, however, is that the sides of the saucepan are free from any sugar crystals. Sugar crystals caught on the side of the saucepan and not incorporated into the sugar that is heating up can fall back into your sugar and encourage the whole mixture to crystallize or solidify. Then you have to start all over. I prefer to caramelize my sugar over medium-high heat to ensure an even caramelization and reduce the risk of crystallization. If my saucepan is a little uneven, or if my caramel is developing unevenly, I move the pot around the source of the heat to make sure all of the mixture is caramelizing at the same rate.

For some recipes in this book, you will need a candy thermometer to gauge the correct temperature. If you're just making caramel, however, you will be able to eyeball when the caramel is ready and even to smell it. As the sugar mixture boils, the water evaporates, the bubbles slow and the syrup becomes thicker and more viscous. Then the sugar will start to caramelize or turn a pale golden colour. At this point, you can swirl the pan gently to ensure that the caramel is cooking evenly. Invariably, many people think this is the finish line. More often than not, that's not the case. The caramel will still be too pale and not have a fully developed flavour. Holding the saucepan with a kitchen mitt, tilt the pan ever so gently so that you can see the thin layer of caramel that clings to the bottom of the pot. This layer is the best gauge of your caramel; it should be an amber or reddish brown, much the same colour as a copper penny. If you're using a very small saucepan, it may be more difficult to ascertain since the caramel may look much darker than it actually is. Again, try to tilt the pot to get a better look at the bottom shallow layer, or dip a small whisk into the mixture and hold the whisk up to the light to gauge what colour the sugar is. Then make haste. As soon as the correct colour is achieved, remove it from the heat and stir in the room-temperature butter or cream or whatever other ingredient is called for, since the caramel will continue to darken even after it is removed from the heat. Once you've made caramel a few times, pay attention to the smell. Once the sugar mixture is JUST past the point where it starts to smoke, take a few whiffs. This is what perfect, deep, rich caramel smells like. Never, ever leave your sugar unattended once it starts to colour because before you know it will become a black smoking mess.

Making the caramel by the dry method is much the same as above with the exception that you don't dissolve the sugar in water first. Rather, you place the sugar directly into a skillet so the sugar has more surface area in which to melt. Then you just let it melt over a medium heat, stirring it very occasionally, so that it all caramelizes at the same time and to the same colour. Some pastry chefs prefer this latter method while others swear that the wet method produces a less cloudy caramel.

CREAMING You'll see constant reminders (see the introduction to the cookie and cake chapters) of just how important this method is to good baking. When you cream room temperature butter together with granulated sugars, the crystalline edges of the sugar dig deep into the butter, burrowing in until hundreds of little air pockets are created. These air pockets grow into air cells.

Other ingredients, such as the leavening and flour you choose, then guarantee that the air remains suspended in the batter. The air cells expand during baking, ensuring that the baked good rises and becomes tender. The other thing to remember when you're using the creaming method is to make sure that your butter and sugar are creamed together for an appropriate amount of time. The butter-sugar mixture should turn from a yellow mass to an ivory coloured mixture.

FOLDING Overmixing is often the culprit behind a tough cake or a leaden mousse. The way to avoid these pitfalls is to use a method called folding. Folding allows you to mix together two seemingly disparate ingredients while retaining as much air, lightness and integrity as possible.

To fold properly, use a plastic spatula and cut straight through the centre of the bowl, going all the way to the bottom. Sweep the spatula along the bottom and then up the side of the bowl, folding the mixture onto the surface. Give the bowl a quarter turn and then repeat the motion. Keep repeating this process until all of the ingredients are combined. Every few turns, be sure to scrape and sweep the sides of the bowl, to fold in any unmixed ingredients.

Always fold in parts. If you have a large amount of egg whites to fold into a batter, for example, start off by folding in between one-quarter and one-third of the egg whites to "lighten" the batter and make it more willing and easier to fold in the remaining egg whites, which should be added in two or three remaining folds. The rule of thumb in folding is to ALWAYS fold the lighter mixture, in parts, into the heavier mixture, and not the other way around. If you fold the heavier mixture into the lighter, there is a greater risk of deflating it.

TEMPERING Tempering ingredients essentially means combining two ingredients that happen to be different textures or of a different temperature. You have to be able to introduce one to the other gently and slowly. For example, when you make a custard, you have to whisk hot milk or cream into room temperature eggs. Adding the liquid all at once would surely shock the eggs into scrambling, leaving your custard lumpy and egg-y tasting. However, if you introduce just a little of the hot liquid into the eggs, whisking gently, and then add a little more and then a little more, the eggs gradually get used to the heat and the mixture is perfectly combined, instead of a cooked mess. The same principle applies when combining a light airy mixture such as whipped egg whites with a heavier mixture such as melted chocolate, At first, just a little of the egg whites is folded (see above) into the chocolate, lightening it and making it easier to fold in the remainder of the egg whites without losing any volume. Tempering chocolate is another matter altogether and not addressed in this book.

WHIPPING EGG WHITES Just like overmixing can turn the most luxurious of batters into a stubborn mess, overbeating egg whites can spell the difference between a gossamer-textured angel food cake and one that is, well, meh. The secret to beating egg whites is to beat them long enough so that the (unwound or denatured) proteins join together with other proteins. Perfectly beaten, the walls of the egg cells are not stretched to their max, but remain pliable enough so that they can continue to expand in the heat of the oven until they coagulate and set. Overbeaten egg whites have already expanded to their potential so, although the evaporation of the water in the egg whites (egg whites are essentially protein and water) may create steam and thus some natural leavening, the dessert you're making won't rise as much as it could or should.

Properly beaten egg whites will always look supple and moist. The whites should look glossy and billowy, not grainy or matte looking. I remember being in cooking school in San Francisco and having an exam just on beating egg whites properly. The other students and I were handed a copper bowl, a balloon whisk and a cupful of egg whites. We were then instructed to go into an adjoining room and whip the egg whites to soft peaks. Our instructor, from the other room (!!), could tell from the way the whisk brushed against the sides of the copper bowl if we were beating the egg whites properly. After the whites had reached the desired peaks, we had to march into the first room and hold the copper bowl over our heads. If the beaten egg whites spilled out unceremoniously, we failed (and had to go home with really sticky hair). If, on the other hand, the egg whites stayed where they were, we were golden.

Eggs separate better when they're fresh out of the refrigerator but room temperature egg whites will beat to a higher volume, incorporating more air. Some pastry chefs prefer to use older egg whites to beat into a meringue. This is because the coils of protein will have relaxed slightly and will expand more easily. The truth is that while older egg whites do whip faster and to a slightly higher volume, fresh egg whites result in a more stable foam, one that will hold up better in a meringue-based cake.

Egg whites beaten with granulated sugar are the most stable egg whites of all. Scientifically speaking, the sugar strengthens the protein network by pulling some water out of the whites. It also forms a sugar syrup that prevents the developing foam from drying out. If there is not a lot of sugar called for in a recipe, beat the egg whites just until they reach soft peaks. If only a small amount of sugar is added, the whites will simply not be able to be whipped until they are stiff and glossy, no matter how long you wait. This is the easiest type of meringue to overwhip, since some sugar will help stretch the proteins in the egg whites, enabling you to beat them longer. But don't be fooled, whip these egg whites only to stiff peaks or you will dry them out. The more sugar you add, the more stable the foam and the longer you can whip the egg whites without risking dryness. The most stable type of meringue is considered to be the Italian meringue since the sugar is double the weight of the eggs.

When you add the sugar to beaten egg whites is just as important as how long you beat the egg whites for. Sugar, to achieve the greatest volume, should be added gradually once the egg whites reach soft peaks. Don't be tempted to wait any longer or the egg foam will start to dry out. If unsure, err on the side of caution and add the sugar sooner rather than later. You'll just have to beat the foam a little longer this way.

Soft peaks look like floppy mounds that come to a delicate peak. They should be moist and soft. Stiff peaks are characterized by a very white, glossy meringue that remains in a peak when the beater is lifted out of the mixture.

SOME LAST THINGS When whipping meringues, use superfine sugar since it dissolves more quickly and results in a superior texture. Additionally, make sure that the utensils and equipment are scrupulously clean, without a speck of egg yolk or fat. Avoid plastic bowls and instead opt for copper, ceramic or stainless steel. If whipping the whites by hand (really? In this day and age?), use a balloon whisk with lots of tines to catch the air. A mixer with beaters that rotate around the bowl is preferred to one with stationary beaters.

For best results, always fold beaten egg whites into whatever other ingredients are called for and not the other way around. Always lighter into heavier, to avoid deflating those precious air cells. The folding technique is described above. The thing to remember when folding egg whites is to use as broad a stroke with your spatula as possible, covering as much area as you can. Using smaller, more frequent folds will crush the air in the beaten egg whites. The goal here is to suspend the whites in the batter, rather than incorporate them so fully that they lose the air you have worked so meticulously to achieve.

EQUIPMENT

I don't have a lot of fancy gadgetry in my house (my trusty Kitchen Aid mixer is over 25 years old and as solid as they come), but what I do have (often in repetition) is pans that are not warped, an oven that gets a brand new thermometer every couple of months and reliable measuring tools. These tools are essential for trustworthy baking.

But—and it's a huge but—remember that your hands are one of the best tools in your kitchen. They can cut butter into flour for a pie dough just as easily as a pastry cutter. They, more than anything else, can feel if a dough is too moist or too dry. They can detect whether your rolled out pastry is uneven. They can fold up there with the best spatulas. Trust your hands—they come free with the package.

If you've read a few pastry or baking books, then you know the spiel but here goes: Aside from an accurate oven, nothing influences your baking more than measuring. At its heart, baking is science, science is chemistry and chemistry depends on ratios. The amount of flour you're using in relation to the fat and the amount of liquid—be it in the form of yogurt, honey or eggs—as well as the correct level of leavening, are all crucial to successful baking. (See above note about the necessity of being precise as a personality trait for the baker!)

DRY MEASURES These usually come in graduated sets, ¼ cup (60 mL), ⅓ cup (80 mL), ½ cup (125 mL) and 1 cup (250 mL). I prefer to use stainless steel measuring cups; they last longer and tend to be straight sided, which is better for accuracy. I actually have three sets, which you might call overkill, but it means I'm not constantly searching for the right measure.

MEASURING SPOONS These are absolutely essential, especially when you're baking, as an extra ½ tsp (2 mL) of baking powder can entirely throw off a recipe. Again, try to go for stainless steel so they don't warp or crack. They also come in graduated sets, with ¼ tsp (1 mL), ½ tsp (2 mL), 1 tsp (5 mL) and 1 Tbsp (15 mL) being the most common measurements. Try to have at least two sets so that you don't have to wash and dry the spoons you may need for multiple measuring.

LIQUID MEASURING CUPS Buy liquid measuring cups in glass and have at least two 1-cup (250 mL) measures and at least one 2-cup (500 mL) measure.

SCALE Even though you may not yet be weighing your ingredients, it's worthwhile to have a scale in your kitchen. I have three! As I mentioned above, I always weigh my butter and when I make bread, I always weigh my ingredients. If you're going to invest, buy one of the digital scales: they're not that expensive and are the most accurate you can buy.

STAINLESS STEEL BOWLS Have lots and lots of stainless steel bowls, in all sizes. They stack easily and therefore can be stored easily. They are great to use as a double boiler as well. Glass is also good, but tends to be heavier. Avoid plastic mixing bowls.

WOODEN SPOONS These are relatively inexpensive and can be replaced easily. Try to have at least a few handy as they're helpful when making custards and other liquid desserts.

RUBBER SPATULAS Simply put, you can never have too many of these. They're used for scraping down bowls, folding, stirring and many other uses. It doesn't pay to buy cheap spatulas, as sometimes the rubber will wear down and chip off only to be lost in the batter.

WHISKS Whisks are absolutely essential. There are two main kinds of whisks that you can buy. A sauce whisk is long and narrow, with stiff wires that taper off at the bottom. These whisks are designed to blend together two mixtures, so that a minimum of air is incorporated. The tapered end also allows them to get into the stubborn fine edges of a saucepan. The other kind of whisk is referred to as a balloon whisk. It tends to look like a balloon, with its finer steel wires expanding at the bottom. The ballooning feature allows a lot of air to be captured, quite the opposite of the sauce whisk. It is used to beat air into egg whites or into whipping cream.

I also have a variety of smaller whisks which I use all the time, for whisking eggs before beating them into a mixture or for when I make brownies. I tend to use these the most.

STAND MIXER Every serious baker should have one. I have had my Kitchen Aid for over 25 years and it has never once failed me. It has a permanent position of pride on my countertop. The mixer should come with a dough hook, flat paddle and a whisk attachment. If it's in your budget, buy an extra bowl that will come in handy when you're making a cake requiring you to both cream butter with sugar and then beat egg whites.

There is one disadvantage to my Kitchen Aid mixer, however. The paddle and the whisk attachments don't reach all the way to the bottom of the bowl. To rectify this, I lift up the bowl slightly so that the whisk or paddle attachment reaches the bottom and can pick up whatever dry or wet ingredients lurk there. I do this sparingly, since the wires of the whisk attachment can get damaged if you do it too often.

HAND MIXERS These are basically the stand mixer's younger sister, in that they can pretty well do everything that a stand mixer can with the exception of mixing bread doughs. They also have the advantages of being less expensive, easier to store and taking up less counter space. If you're going to invest in a hand-held mixer, buy a powerful model that has at least three speeds.

FOOD PROCESSOR This can make short shrift of chopping nuts, pureeing fruit and mixing some batters. It makes pastry making a breeze. Choose a powerful model with at least a 6- to 8-cup (1.5–2 L) capacity.

TIMER A good and loud timer makes the life of a baker that much easier. Even if you have a pretty good sense of time and can smell when your baked good is nearing completion, it's wise to have a reminder in case you get distracted.

KNIVES Knives are one of the most essential tools in a kitchen, even in baking. Your kitchen should be equipped with at least one 12-inch (30 cm) or 10-inch (25 cm) chef's knife, an 8-inch (20 cm) chef's knife, several small paring knifes and a serrated knife. High carbon no-stain steel is one of the best materials to look for in a knife as it will stay sharp for quite a long time and it will deter rust. Examine the size of your hand, which will determine what size is best for you. Look for heft and balance and make sure that the tang (the blade extension) runs right through from the tip of the blade to the bottom of the handle. If you have a knife where the blade stops at the handle, it will be more insecure and water may get trapped where the two meet. It may even fall out altogether. Never wash your knives in the dishwasher, which dulls the blade and potentially damages the wooden handle. Wash with warm soapy water and store in a wooden knife block or on a magnetic rack, though not in a drawer where the edges can dull. Invest in a steel to keep your knives razor sharp.

CUTTING BOARDS These are essential in any kitchen; in baking they are for chopping chocolate and cutting butter. I have a wooden one that I reserve exclusively for my baking since wood is porous and when I'm cutting chocolate, I don't want it to pick up any other flavours. Durable plastic cutting boards are good too.

BAKING SHEETS Buy heavy, light coloured aluminum rimmed baking sheets, if you can find them. Manufacturers seem to have an ongoing love affair with non-stick sheets, but you can still buy the older fashioned kind at restaurant supply stores. They are relatively inexpensive. Dark ones tend to produce darker coloured baked items. It's also great to have several unrimmed cookie sheets. The flatter surface allows cookies and especially the pastry in the Napoleon Cake (see p. 323) to slide off easily.

WIRE RACKS These are essential for cooling cakes, cookies, scones, pies, you name it. The rack, which should be at least ½ inch (1 cm) high, lifts the baked good up so that the bottom doesn't get soggy and allows air to circulate around the baked good, cooling it evenly. It's helpful to have several and at least one large enough to accommodate a 13- × 9-inch (33 × 23 cm) cake pan.

PARCHMENT PAPER In this day and age, who even wants to bake without parchment? It means that you don't have to grease your cookie or baking sheets and it can be used over and over until it burns or becomes too brittle.

SILICONE MATS An alternative to parchment paper, these are generally shaped to fit right into your rimmed or unrimmed baking sheet and make baking cookies, scones and free-form pies a snap. They can withstand temperatures of up to 500°F (260°C). Although somewhat pricey, they can be used over and over again, so it more than makes up for the cost.

CAKE PANS Here too the non-stick craze seems to have taken hold but if you happen to inherit your family's aluminum cake pans, hold on to those babies. Lighter aluminum reflects the heat, producing a tender crumb. Try to buy lightly coloured metal or aluminum pans. Avoid dark and non-stick cake pans wherever you can. Not all 9-inch (23 cm) pans are actually 9 inches (23 cm) so if you're not sure, measure the pan from the inside, both at the top and at the bottom, inside edge to inside edge.

LAYER CAKE PANS Two or three 8-inch (20 cm) and 9-inch (23 cm) cake pans with sides that are at least 2 inches (5 cm) high. Unlike cake pans, these are measured at the top, from inside edge to inside edge.

SPRINGFORM PANS The most important size of springform pan to have is a 9-inch (23 cm), but if you're feeling swish, buy an 8-inch (20 cm) and a 10-inch (25 cm) one as well.

SQUARE CAKE PANS These pans should be made of metal or aluminum (or at least a light coloured non-stick) with no seams on the inside of the pan. If you can, buy a 9-inch (23 cm), although they are increasingly difficult to find in Canada. You should also have one or two 8-inch (20 cm) pans.

BUNDT PANS The very best pans come from Germany or France, and are made of very heavy aluminum or cast iron. If you can only find non-stick, again, go for the lightest coloured material you can. The 10-cup (2.5 L) and 12-cup (3 L) are the most versatile.

ANGEL FOOD CAKE PAN A 10-inch (25 cm) pan is the ideal size and, optimistically, it should be metal or aluminum or at the very least lightly coloured.

LOAF PANS You should have at least one 8- × 4-inch (20 × 10 cm) loaf pan and one 9- × 5-inch (23 × 13 cm) loaf pan.

LARGER CAKE PANS You should have one or two 13- × 9-inch (33 × 23 cm) baking pans or dishes. (The difference between the two being that a pan is made of metal and a dish refers to glass.)

MUFFIN/CUPCAKE PANS Optimally you should buy aluminum or light coloured muffin tins, or at least lightly coloured non-stick muffin tins. Have at least two regular (12 cup/3 L) sized muffin tins, which are useful for cupcakes, butter tarts and small Bundt cakes. It's also handy to have mini muffin tins that can often be purchased at your local grocery store. They come in either 12- or 24-cup tins.

FRENCH TART TINS This style is a classic European tart tin, made of tinned steel with a removable bottom. They come in a wide range of sizes but if you have to just buy one, buy a 9-inch (23 cm) tart tin. I also have an 8-inch (20 cm), as well as a 10-inch (25 cm) one for variety. Three of my favourites are my 9-inch (23 cm) square pan, and my rectangular 8- × 12-inch (20 × 30 cm) and 4- × 14-inch (10 × 36 cm) pans. The round 4-inch (10 cm) tart tins are a great addition to any baking repertoire. All the tart tins called for in this book have 1-inch (2.5 cm) high sides. There are tart tins with higher sides, but I have not used those. French tart tins should never be washed with soap and water. Like cast iron skillets or rolling pins, the soap strips the tin of its natural patina, built up over several baking episodes. This is also why you don't have to grease a French tart tin. It's naturally protected against sticking by the previous tarts baked in it. Wash them only in hot water.

PIE PLATES   While 9-inch (23 cm) pie plates are the most common, both glass and ceramic pie plates are also excellent choices. I prefer not to use either dark or light coloured metal pie plates. The dark plates will attract heat, making the pastry cook faster than the fruit filling. The lighter pans will simply reflect the heat, resulting in a not fully or evenly baked pastry crust.

ROLLING PINS   There are two different varieties of rolling pins, three if you consider the newer silicone ones. In Europe and among many bakers in North America, the French rolling pin, a thinnish rolling pin with tapered ends, is preferred. More familiar, perhaps, is the two-handled rolling pin—preferably the ball-bearing variety. A good rolling pin should have a smooth finish, with no nicks or gouges that will catch and rip your pastry. It should be at least 14 inches (35 cm) long. And never, ever, submerge your rolling pin in water, or, heaven forbid, soapy water. First, it will ruin the delicate patina that has been built up on the roller, which makes rolling so efficient. Second, it will ruin and rust the ball-bearings if you use that type of rolling pin. It will also leave invisible droplets of water in the wood, which can warp your wood or prevent easy rolling. To clean your rolling pin, simply run a damp cloth over its surface. This will leave the patina intact.

PIE WEIGHTS   These are available in both ceramic and metal forms and will never go bad. Dried beans or rice will also do in a pinch. Dry thoroughly after they've been used.

PASTRY BAGS AND TIPS These are available in canvas and plastic, both of which come in different sizes, and both of which are great. If you buy the canvas-type ones, wash and dry them well, since they can become mouldy and stinky quickly. Have a few 10-inch (25 cm) or 12-inch (30 cm) ones, with different-sized openings so that you can adjust different-sized tips to them. The plastic ones are disposable and you can cut them to whatever size you want, depending on what you're decorating. I find sets of pastry tips burdensome because, unless you decorate cakes for a living, you probably won't even use half of them. To start, buy just a star and rosette tip as well as one medium or large plain tip (½–¾ inch/1–2 cm) and a smaller one (¼ inch/6 mm). See page 312 on how to make small parchment cones for writing on cakes.

PASTRY BRUSHES As I mentioned above, I have several of these, including one restricted to brushing excess flour off of my pastry. They're great for applying glazes or for brushing melted butter. Try to buy brushes with natural bristles, so they don't fall off.

PASTRY CUTTER This tool, which cuts butter into flour to make pastry or biscuits, is a set of curved parallel wires with a rubber or wooden handle. Some pastry cutters come with wires that have a slightly serrated or rough edge while others have smooth wires.

DOUGH SCRAPER OR BENCH KNIFE Whether you buy the plastic variety or the metal kind of dough scraper, these are a life saver. They make clean up a breeze and can be indispensable to cut, turn or even portion out dough.

COOKIE CUTTERS It's really remarkable how many shapes and sizes cookie cutters now come in. I have the standard set of round cookie cutters, which graduate from the smallest ring at ½ inch (1 cm) to the largest at 3½ inches (9 cm). All of my cookie cutter sets are made from stainless steel. And I have quite a few sets—square, crinkled, daisy, heart, star, maple leafs, snowflakes, butterflies and fruit. This is not to mention all of the individual cookie cutters I have. Any of the sets can be used to shape biscuits or pastry as well.

PALETTE KNIFES AND METAL SPATULAS These are really important for evening out batter and of course for icing cakes. Both regular palette knives as well as offset knives are useful. The latter are slightly bent at the midpoint. I find that I like to have at least two long ones, about 8 inches (20 cm) each, and several smaller ones, about 4 inches in length.

CAKE TURNTABLE This is nowhere near essential but great for making short shrift of decorating a cake. Essentially a rotating flat plate set atop a pedestal, there are several forms available. I find the plastic versions too flimsy, but acknowledge that the cast iron one I use is expensive and quite heavy. Whichever you choose, cake turntables take some getting used to. You have to hold your palette knife firmly against the side of the cake while you spin the turntable. Practice makes perfect!

SAUCEPANS Of course you have these in your kitchen but it's good to check that you have a medium-sized one that can do double duty as a double boiler. Ideally, they should an extra thick base, either made from copper or two layers of stainless steel with an inner layer of aluminum. Make sure that the heavy bottom extends all the way to the furthermost edge of the pan.

SKILLET Although a skillet is not used extensively in baking, it's helpful to have a few non-stick skillets around for browning butter and toasting nuts. For Tarte Tatin (see p. 346) it's essential to have a 9-inch (23 cm) or 10-inch (25 cm) cast iron skillet.

COLANDER You probably already have one for spaghetti, but they're helpful for washing fruit for pies.

COFFEE/SPICE GRINDER Owning one is great although not essential for grinding your own spices. I find that getting mine out of a high cabinet is a bit of a nuisance so I frequently opt for my mortar and pestle.

DEEP FRY OR CANDY THERMOMETER These are especially useful when making buttercreams or caramels that only go to a particular stage or temperature.

ICE CREAM SCOOPS These are great for measuring out muffin batter or cookie dough.

JUICER OR REAMER This handy little gadget is extremely helpful when making lemon curd or lemon meringue pie.

MORTAR AND PESTLE Used since ancient times, a mortar and pestle is handy for crushing spices and herbs or making guacamole. Try to buy a pestle (the bowl) that has heft and is not too small. It should have a rough but not porous surface. A granite model with a matte finish is perfect. For best results, the matching mortar (the crusher) should be made of a similar material. Wooden pestles do not have the necessary heft for the job. Also see: spice grinder.

NUTMEG GRATER These are somewhat old fashioned I agree, but I couldn't do without mine. I love the perfume of freshly grated nutmeg. Nutmeg graters are usually available in tin or stainless steel and are characterized by having a slight curve to them. One side is the rasp setting for grating, the other side stores your nutmeg pods.

RAMEKINS For best results, buy ramekins that are straight sided and made from porcelain. They should be about ½ cup (125 mL) in volume.

SAUCE LADLES Ladles are for measuring custards into ramekins or spooning sauces or a ganache over a cake. They are available in plastic and stainless steel. You might be able to find graduated stainless steel sets as well, which can come in handy. My set comes in ¼-cup (60 mL), ½-cup (125 mL) and 1-cup (250 mL) measurements.

SLOTTED SPOON You'll need a slotted spoon, preferably steel, for when you're removing delicate pears from their poaching liquid.

TONGS Stainless steel tongs are a handy tool to have both for cooking and for baking.

WIRE MESH SIEVE Sieves are used to dust with and to sift cocoa powder and cake and pastry flour. Buy durable ones made out of stainless steel—one larger for sifting larger amounts of flour and one smaller to use for dusting icing sugar over cookies or cakes.

ZESTER OR MICROPLANE These now come in thin or wide models and no kitchen should be without one since the zest of citrus fruits can greatly embellish your baking.

COOKIES

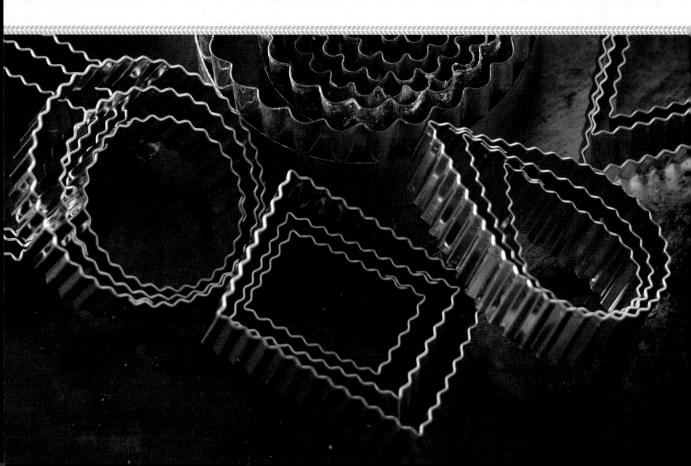

69   CHOCOLATE CHIP COOKIES

71   My Go-To Chocolate Chip Cookie

72   One Damn Good Cookie

74   Chocolate Chip Crispies

75   Passover Chocolate Chip Cookies

76   Add-In All Purpose Cookies

78   Double Trouble Chocolatey Chip Cookies

79   Chocolate Intensities

80   Passover Chocolate Clouds

82   Oatmeal Raisin Cookies

84   Coconut Oatmeal Cookies with Chocolate-Covered Raisins and Almonds

85   Peanut Butter Cookies

87   Oversized Peanut Butter and Oat Cookies (aka Monster Cookies)

88   Ginger Cookies

89   Snickerdoodles

90   Lemon Cornmeal and Currant Cookies

91   Sugar Cookies

93   SHORTBREAD—A FEW TIPS

95   Classic Shortbread

97   Mayan Chocolate Crisps

98   Hazelnut Shortbread Batons

101   Pecan Orange Sandies

102   Toffee Meltaways

103   Lime Basil Meltaways

104   Chai Shortbread

105   Parmesan, Rosemary and Pine Nut Shortbread

106   Blueberry and White Chocolate Shortbread

108   Double Chocolate Shortbread with Pumpkin Seeds and Flax

109   My Favourite Rugelach

112   Five-Spice Butter Cookies

113   Biscotti di Prato

115   Baci di Dama

116   Alfajores

118   Dulce de Leche

119   Cajeta Caramel

120   Almond Tuiles

122   Ladyfingers

123   Tiramisu

ALMOST EVERYBODY loves cookies. In fact, I have yet to meet a person who doesn't like at least one kind of cookie (and I'm not even sure I would want to be friends with someone who doesn't like cookies). Even people who don't bake know how much fun it is to bake cookies. Cookies are just so darn universal. They invite innovation and whimsy, and are so incredibly satisfying to make. Perhaps it's that moment of nostalgia (cookies and milk after school, anyone?), or perhaps it's the fact that even a small morsel will satisfy a sweet craving (without having to commit, for instance, to a whole slice of cake), but cookies are a great way to introduce yourself to baking, to really understand how versatile baking can be and to enter the magical kingdom of your kitchen.

You wouldn't think there was a huge back story to cookies. After all, you cream some butter with sugar, add an egg (or not) then some flour. You may throw in some chocolate chips, raisins or nuts. Then you drop, roll (or shape) and bake. What more is there to the story? Well, actually, quite a lot.

Almost all cookie recipes start out by calling for room temperature butter. This is really important since, for most cookies, the technique of choice is the creaming method. Using a stand mixer or hand-held beaters, the most common method is to cream room temperature butter with some granulated or brown sugar or a combination of both. Professional bakers often call room temperature butter "plastic butter." This means that the butter is soft enough to manipulate or cream easily with sugar, but still firm enough to hold its shape. You definitely don't want squishy butter. For more information on butter and its uses (it's important for cookies!) see page 14.

Having said that, it's also important not to over cream your butter with your sugar. Creaming encourages the development of a vast number of air bubbles that will expand on contact with either baking powder or baking soda and the heat of the oven. Since cookies are baked "free form" on a cookie sheet (as opposed to a cake which is protected by the sides of a cake pan), over-creamed cookies are left with no other option than to expand sideways into flat cookies.

What you bake your cookies on is equally important. Choose sturdy rimless baking sheets that are preferably heavy and shiny. Shiny, light coloured pans will help reflect the heat, resulting in a golden cookie that is not overly dark on the bottom. Darker coloured pans will bake cookies more quickly and run the risk of overbrowned bottoms. Heavy pans are essential as well, since they won't warp or twist upon contact with the heat.

I prefer cookie sheets without rims, which makes sliding the parchment paper off of the sheet or sliding a spatula under the cookies remarkably easy. However, you can use rimmed baking sheets too. Avoid insulated baking sheets. Cookies made on insulated baking sheets will bake more slowly, not brown as effectively and will not yield the golden brown edges that characterize the most scrumptious of cookies.

It's simply not necessary to grease your cookie sheets with butter anymore when baking cookies. This encourages cookies to spread and overbrown on the bottom. Always use parchment paper or a silicone mat. If you use a silicone mat, use a thin one since the thicker ones protect or insulate the cookies from the heat of the oven and prevent them from acquiring a caramelized browned bottom.

While I prefer to bake only one sheet of cookies at a time—I'm a bit of a stickler for this—you can indeed bake more than one sheet of cookies at a time without sacrificing texture or flavour. Simply position your oven racks in the top and bottom third of the oven. Then rotate sheets from top to bottom and from front to back halfway through the baking time. On some of the following recipes, you'll notice that where the results are markedly different, I have suggested baking only one sheet at a time.

If you have only one or two baking sheets, allow the sheets to cool completely between batches. If you put spoonfuls of raw dough on a hot cookie sheet, the cookies will start to melt before they have a chance to bake.

Cookies need space on a cookie sheet to bake evenly, even if they're not the spreading kind. Make sure that they are evenly spaced (no crowding, even if you're short on time), allowing the heat to circulate in between each one. This means that you'll end up with evenly baked cookies, golden on all sides. If you find yourself with only a few cookies left to bake as you work your way through the dough, simply space them evenly around the baking sheet and bake as per usual, checking a minute or two earlier than you normally would.

Shape or mould your cookies into a uniform size to ensure they all bake in the same amount of time. If some spoonfuls of dough are large and some are small, the smaller-sized cookies will be ready before the larger ones are baked through.

Always allow cookies to cool for the first few minutes on their cookie sheet on a wire rack before transferring them off of the pan to the wire rack. This resting period finishes off the baking, allowing the cookies to solidify and set. I have wrecked my fair share of cookies by being impatient and transferring them before they were ready. Cooling them on a rack also prevents the bottoms of the cookies from becoming too soggy. Much like the heat in the oven needs to circulate, the cooler air needs to circulate around and underneath the cookies properly to help them set and cool.

In terms of storing crisp cookies and storing soft, chewy cookies, remember that never the twain shall meet. Always store crisp with crisp and soft with soft or you'll end up with the whole lot being soft and chewy.

Most cookie doughs don't have to be baked off right away and may even benefit from an overnight stay in the refrigerator. If you're in the mood for just a few cookies or don't want your teenaged son to polish off a whole batch in one sitting (believe me, I know of what I speak), bake off what you need and refrigerate the rest of the dough, well wrapped in plastic wrap for up to two or three days. This way you can bake off a batch or two each day and have perfectly fresh cookies at your beck and call. An overnight stay in the refrigerator can benefit cookie dough in a myriad of ways. Resting the dough helps develop its flavour, even out the moisture and relax the gluten, producing tastier cookies that hold their shape.

Most cookie doughs will also freeze well. The lower the amount of sugar in a cookie dough, the better it will freeze. Wrap the dough well in plastic wrap and then overwrap in a freezer bag. Make sure you thaw the cookie dough in the refrigerator. If the cookie is a drop cookie, you can thaw it at room temperature. Or, portion out the cookie dough, and freeze on a parchment paper-lined baking sheet until completely frozen. Then pack the unbaked cookies in a well-sealed freezer bag and freeze for up to 4 months.

And so we arrive at the age old debate. **Chewy vs. Crispy**. It's kind of like the debate on fudgey vs. cakey brownies. Yes, bakers engage in this sort of debate all the time. I personally spend quite a bit of time considering the merits of each and how the temperature of the butter or the amount will affect my cookies. I know, it's a bit weird and won't bring about world peace, but it can make the difference between cookie recipes you prefer, depending on which school you're partial to. Mostly this debate pertains to chocolate chip cookies, but it envelops some other forms of cookies as well. If you prefer soft and chewy cookies, it's crucial to use cooler ingredients and to use a refrigerated dough. (Most cookie doughs will benefit from a stay in the fridge and, at any rate, it will not do the cookie dough any harm.) Using cool ingredients, or dough straight from the refrigerator, means the cookies spread more slowly in the oven since the butter is cold and holds their shape better. This produces a denser, chewier cookie. If the dough is warm or at room temperature, it's apt to spread more quickly in the oven, making the cookies thinner and crisper.

Using more brown sugar will help soften your cookies since it has more moisture than regular granulated sugar. Using honey or a tablespoon or two of corn syrup will achieve the same effect. Both brown sugar and honey are considered to be hygroscopic (with honey being a bit more so than brown sugar) so that cookies made with one or the other will stay soft or soften upon cooling. If you reduce the overall amount of sugar and increase the fat slightly, you'll get the same results.

If, on the other hand, you want crispier cookies, add more granulated sugar.

CHOCOLATE CHIP COOKIES

You could say that I've been reading chocolate chip cookies recipes and making chocolate chip cookies (as well as brownies, but that's another story for another chapter) my whole life. So I have some very strong opinions about them, which you're welcome to agree with or not. I suspect that most young people start their culinary life by making cookies. I also suspect that I started forming these opinions rather early.

In my humble opinion, a good chocolate chip cookie should not have baking powder in it. The addition of baking powder makes the cookie rise too much and produces a slightly cakey cookie. Not one for my cookie jar. Baking soda is the leavener of choice here.

Most chocolate chip cookie recipes have basically the same proportions: 2–2¾ cups (500–680 mL) of flour to either ¾ cup (180 mL) or 1 cup (250 mL) of butter, anywhere between 1¼–2 cups (310–500 mL) of sugar (mixed brown and granulated sugar) and 2 eggs. I've opted to go with one egg for my basic chocolate chip cookie, making it less doughy, and mostly brown sugar for its hygroscopic tendencies. I don't care for crispy chocolate chip cookies but if you prefer your cookies crisp, use 1 cup (250 mL) granulated sugar and ¼ cup (60 mL) brown sugar.

You can use the mixer on low speed to mix the flour into the butter and egg mixture, but since I am a bit of a perfectionist I always remove the bowl from the mixer and use a wooden spoon (or my hands) to mix in the flour. This prevents any gluten from forming and prevents overmixing and toughness as well.

The recipe for One Damn Good Cookie (see p. 72) chills the dough before it is baked, producing soft, chewy cookies. The use of cake flour is uncommon for chocolate chip cookies but the lower protein content of the flour guarantees the cookies' moist and chewy texture. It does contain baking powder, as a result of including cake and pastry flour.

And lastly, the MOST important thing to remember about chocolate chip cookies is in their name—they should contain lots of chocolate chips or shavings. Go for the gusto. Make sure that there are numerous chocolate chips in every bite. I guarantee you'll have a winner.

The two recipes that follow are two of my favourite chocolate chip cookies.

My Go-To Chocolate Chip Cookie

To me, this is the ultimate chocolate chip cookie, slightly crisp and golden brown around the edges, soft and chewy in the middle. Tucked away in an airtight container, they'll stay chewy and delicious for up to 4 or 5 days. Although I am not a proponent of nuts in chocolate chip cookies myself (why ruin a perfectly good chocolate chip cookie?), feel free to add 1 cup (250 mL) of chopped walnuts to the batter along with the chopped chocolate and chocolate chips. Since the nuts may not be directly exposed to the heat of the oven, toast them first in a dry skillet set over medium heat for about 5 minutes, remembering to shake the skillet often.

I find that the chopped chocolate disperses throughout the batter really thoroughly. With the addition of the semisweet chocolate chips, you're guaranteed a chocolatey bite each and every time.

2 cups (500 mL) all-purpose flour

1 tsp (5 mL) baking soda

¼ tsp (1 mL) salt

1 cup (250 mL) unsalted butter, softened (8 oz/250 g)

1 cup (250 mL) packed light brown sugar

¼ cup (60 mL) granulated sugar

1 large egg, at room temperature

1 tsp (5 mL) vanilla

1 cup (250 mL) semisweet chocolate chips

1⅓ cups (330 mL) coarsely chopped semisweet chocolate

Preheat the oven to 375°F (190°C). Line 2 cookie sheets with parchment paper; set aside.

Whisk together the flour, baking soda and salt in a bowl; set aside.

In the bowl of a stand mixer fitted with the paddle attachment, or using a hand-held mixer, beat the butter for 1 minute. Beat in the sugars until the mixture is quite light, 3–5 minutes. Scrape down the dough. Beat in the egg. Beat in the vanilla. Remove the bowl from the stand.

Using a wooden spoon, stir the flour mixture into the butter mixture, in 2 additions. Stir in the chocolate chips and chopped chocolate.

Drop batter in heaping tablespoonfuls onto the prepared cookie sheets, spacing them about 2 inches (5 cm) apart. You should be able to get about 12 blobs on a regular-sized cookie sheet. Flatten slightly.

Bake in the centre of the preheated oven until set and lightly browned around the edges, 8–10 minutes. Cool the cookie sheet on a wire rack for 2 minutes. Transfer the cookies to the wire rack to cool completely. Repeat with the remaining cookie dough, cooling the pans slightly before adding unbaked cookie dough to them. (Cookies can be stored in an airtight container at room temperature for up to 5 days.)

One Damn Good Cookie

2 cups (500 mL) cake and pastry flour, sifted

1⅓ cups (330 mL) all-purpose flour

1½ tsp (7 mL) baking powder

1 tsp (5 mL) baking soda

1 tsp (5 mL) sea salt + more to taste (optional)

1 cup (250 mL) unsalted butter, softened (8 oz/250 g)

1 cup (250 mL) packed light brown sugar

1 cup (250 mL) granulated sugar

2 large eggs, at room temperature

2 tsp (10 mL) vanilla

1½ Tbsp (22 mL) instant espresso powder

2 cups (500 mL) semisweet chocolate chips

1 cup (250 mL) coarsely chopped Skor bars (about three 39 g bars)

I WAS going to call this cookie Salted Coffee Toffee Chocolate Chip Cookie. A bit of a mouthful (no pun intended). However, I was giving a series of cooking classes to three women and at the last class, one focused on cookies and squares, I premiered this cookie. One of the students, Fran Grundman, a dessert lover like myself and a funny, generous woman, sat at my kitchen table, munching away at the cookie, and then finally pronounced, "This is one damn fine cookie. Yes, this is one damn good cookie!" My two other students concurred and I figured I just had to rechristen the cookie.

Because the cookie dough has been chilled, the cookies don't spread much and you have to press down slightly on the balls of dough before they go into the oven. As the dough comes to room temperature, and the butter in the dough softens, they will spread a bit more, so there's no need to flatten them with the palm of your hand.

These cookies have a slightly darker colour to them because of the addition of the coffee, which is what also imparts that wonderful mocha flavour. Try to use the best quality chocolate you can find.

———

Whisk together the flours, baking powder, baking soda and salt in a bowl; set aside.

In the bowl of a stand mixer fitted with the paddle attachment, or using a hand-held mixer, beat the butter for 1 minute. Beat in the sugars until the mixture is quite light, 3–5 minutes. Scrape down the dough. One at a time, beat in the eggs, beating well after the first egg before adding the second. Beat in the vanilla. Beat in the espresso powder.

With the mixer on the lowest speed, mix in the flour mixture until almost incorporated. (I know I've said that with cookies you should always add the flour with a wooden spoon, but there is an awful lot of flour here so I've decided to add it in the machine.) Add the chocolate chips and Skor bars, mixing just until completely incorporated. Cover the dough with plastic wrap and refrigerate for at least 24 hours.

Preheat the oven to 375°F (190°C). Line 2 cookie sheets with parchment paper; set aside.

Drop the batter in large spoonfuls onto the prepared cookie sheets, spacing them about 2 inches (5 cm) apart. You should be able to get about 9–12 blobs on a regular-sized cookie sheet. Flatten slightly. If desired, sprinkle the top of the cookies with more sea salt.

Bake in the centre of the preheated oven until set and lightly browned around the edges, 9–10 minutes. Cool the cookie sheet on a wire rack for 2 minutes. Transfer the cookies to the wire rack to cool completely. Repeat with the remaining cookie dough, cooling the pans slightly before adding unbaked cookie dough to them. (Cookies can be stored in an airtight container at room temperature for up to 5 days.)

HISTORY NOTE

Cookies probably derive from "small cakes" made as long ago as the Roman Empire. Those cakes were usually fried and then topped with honey and pepper. There are records showing that "small cakes" were made in Mesopotamia, using dates as a filling. The cookie, as we know it today, came to us via Dutch settlers: the word "cookie" is a derivative of the Dutch word *"koekje,"* or small cake. Apparently, it was sweetness born from necessity. Bakers in medieval Europe, needing to test the heat of their ovens before bread was baked or meat was cooked, threw in small portions of dough. Once they observed how long it took for these morsels to bake, these "little cakes" were given to children, only too happy to gobble them up.

Chocolate Chip Crispies

1¾ cups (430 mL) all-purpose
    flour

1 tsp (5 mL) baking powder

1 tsp (5 mL) baking soda

¾ tsp (4 mL) salt

1 cup (250 mL) unsalted butter,
    softened (8 oz/250 g)

1 cup (250 mL) packed light brown
    sugar

½ cup (125 mL) granulated sugar

2 large eggs, at room temperature

2 tsp (10 mL) vanilla

1 cup (250 mL) large flake
    rolled oats

1 cup (250 mL) puffed rice cereal

½ cup (125 mL) wheat germ

1½ cups (375 mL) semisweet
    chocolate chips

¾ cup (180 mL) chopped pecans

I'VE INCLUDED this version of chocolate chip cookies for a few reasons. First, they're more child's play than the previous sophisticated chocolate chip cookies. The cereal adds a note of crunchiness, and you can feel a bit better about serving cookies to your youngster since they contain oats and wheat germ.

Preheat the oven to 350°F (180°C). Line 2 cookie sheets with parchment paper; set aside.

Whisk together the flour, baking powder, baking soda and salt in a bowl; set aside.

In the bowl of a stand mixer fitted with the paddle attachment, or using a hand-held mixer, beat the butter for 1 minute. Beat in the sugars until the mixture is quite light, 3–5 minutes. Scrape down the dough. One at a time, beat in the eggs, beating well after the first egg before adding the second. Beat in the vanilla. Remove the bowl from the stand.

Using a wooden spoon, stir in the dry mixture just until combined. Stir in the oats, cereal and wheat germ. Stir in the chocolate chips and pecans.

Drop the batter in heaping tablespoonfuls onto the prepared cookie sheets, spacing them about 2 inches (5 cm) apart. You should be able to get about 12 blobs on a regular-sized cookie sheet.

One sheet at a time, bake in the centre of the preheated oven until set and lightly browned around the edges, 9–11 minutes. Cool the cookie sheet on a wire rack for 5 minutes. Transfer the cookies to the wire rack to cool completely. Repeat with the remaining cookie dough, cooling the pans slightly before adding unbaked cookie dough to them. (Cookies can be stored in an airtight container at room temperature for up to 5 days.)

Passover Chocolate Chip Cookies

ALTHOUGH I never felt deprived during Passover when I was a kid, when I became a mother myself, I felt compelled to develop a chocolate chip cookie without flour so that my son (God forbid) didn't have to go without for the eight days of Passover. I have served these with tea at my seders for several years with great success. This past year, upon tasting them, my cousin Carolyn Murphy thought I had forgotten about the holiday's dietary restrictions and simply made regular chocolate chip cookies—they were that good.

¾ cup (180 mL) matzah cake meal

¼ cup (60 mL) potato starch

½ tsp (2 mL) kosher for Passover baking soda

½ tsp (2 mL) kosher salt

½ cup (125 mL) unsalted butter or margarine, softened (4 oz/125 g)

½ cup (125 mL) packed light brown sugar

¼ cup (60 mL) granulated sugar

1 large egg, at room temperature

2 tsp (10 mL) vanilla powder

1½ cups (375 mL) semisweet chocolate chips

Preheat the oven to 350°F (180°C). Line 2 cookie sheets with parchment paper; set aside.

Whisk together the cake meal, potato starch, baking soda and salt in a bowl; set aside.

In the bowl of a stand mixer fitted with the paddle attachment, or using a hand-held mixer, beat the butter for 1 minute. Beat in the sugars until the mixture is quite light, about 3 minutes. Scrape down the dough. Beat in the egg and the vanilla powder. Remove the bowl from the stand.

Using a wooden spoon, stir in the cake meal mixture and then the chocolate chips.

Drop heaping tablespoonfuls of the batter onto the prepared cookie sheets. One sheet at a time, bake in the centre of the preheated oven until the cookies are set and JUST starting to turn golden around the edges, 8–9 minutes. Cool the cookie sheet on a wire rack for 5 minutes. Transfer the cookies to the wire rack to cool completely. Repeat with the remaining cookie dough, cooling the pans slightly before adding unbaked cookie dough to them. (Cookies can be stored in an airtight container at room temperature for up to 8 days.)

Add-In All-Purpose Cookies

2½ cups (625 mL) all-purpose
flour

1 tsp (5 mL) baking powder

¼ tsp (1 mL) salt

1 cup (250 mL) unsalted butter,
softened (8 oz/250 g)

1 cup (250 mL) packed light brown
sugar

¼ cup (60 mL) granulated sugar

2 large eggs, at room temperature

2 tsp (10 mL) vanilla

ONE BASIC dough, hundreds of variations, what could be better? This all-purpose batter is a reason to play in the kitchen and never get bored with the same cookie. Feel like peanut butter? Add peanut butter chips or chopped up miniature Reese's Pieces. Prefer a cookie within a cookie? Fold in chopped up vanilla cream cookies. Your wish is this cookie's command.

Preheat the oven to 350°F (180°C). Line 2 cookie sheets with parchment paper; set aside.

Whisk together the flour, baking powder and salt in a bowl; set aside.

In the bowl of a stand mixer fitted with the paddle attachment, or using a hand-held mixer, beat the butter for 1 minute. Beat in the sugars until the mixture is quite light, 3–5 minutes. Scrape down the dough. One at a time, beat in the eggs, beating well after the first egg before adding the second. Beat in the vanilla. Remove the bowl from the stand.

Using a wooden spoon, stir the flour mixture into the butter mixture, in two additions. Stir in the additions of your choice.

Drop batter in heaping tablespoonfuls onto the prepared cookie sheets, spacing them about 2 inches (5 cm) apart. You should be able to get about 12 blobs on a regular-sized cookie sheet. Flatten slightly.

Bake in the centre of the preheated oven until set and lightly browned around the edges, 9–11 minutes. Cool the cookie sheet on a wire rack for 2 minutes. Transfer the cookies to the wire rack to cool completely. Repeat with the remaining cookie dough, cooling the pans slightly before adding unbaked cookie dough to them. (Cookies can be stored in an airtight container at room temperature for up to 5 days.)

VARIATIONS

ALMOND PEANUT BUTTER CHIP COOKIES Add 1 pkg (10½ oz/300 g) peanut butter–flavoured chips and 1 cup (250 mL) toasted sliced or slivered almonds.

S'MORE COOKIES Add one 3½-oz (100 g) bar of dark chocolate and one 3½-oz (100 g) bar of milk chocolate, both coarsely chopped. Add 9 graham crackers, coarsely chopped, and as many mini marshmallows as you see fit.

BROWNIE COOKIES Add in 1½ cups (375 mL) of cut up store bought or homemade brownies.

COOKIE-FILLED COOKIES Add in 1½–2 cups (375–500 mL) chopped crème-filled sandwich cookies.

WHITE CHOCOLATE CHERRY COOKIES Add in 1 cup (250 mL) white chocolate chips and 1 cup (250 mL) dried cherries.

CHOCOLATE BAR COOKIES Add 2 cups (500 mL) of chopped up chocolate bars of your choice.

BAKER'S TIP

To revive crisp cookies that have gone a bit soft, "refresh" them by heating them in a 300°F (150°C) oven for 5–10 minutes. Alternatively, to keep soft cookies moist and supple, tuck a ceramic brown sugar softener into the airtight container or a piece of apple or fresh bread.

Double Trouble Chocolatey Chip Cookies

2 cups (500 mL) all-purpose flour

¾ cup (180 mL) unsweetened Dutch-processed cocoa powder, sifted

1 tsp (5 mL) baking soda

½ tsp (2 mL) salt

1 cup (250 mL) unsalted butter, softened (8 oz/250 g)

1 cup (250 mL) packed light brown sugar

⅓ cup (80 mL) granulated sugar

2 Tbsp (30 mL) corn syrup

2 large eggs, at room temperature

2 tsp (10 mL) vanilla

2 cups (500 mL) white chocolate chips

½ cup (125 mL) semisweet chocolate chips

DOUBLE TROUBLE because this delicious, moist and soft cookie contains both white and semisweet chocolate chips. Double trouble because they're in-your-face, rich and chocolatey. Double trouble because your kids or friends will be begging you to bake more, pronto.

Preheat the oven to 350°F (180°C). Line 2 cookie sheets with parchment paper; set aside.

Whisk together the flour, cocoa powder, baking soda and salt in a bowl; set aside.

In the bowl of a stand mixer fitted with the paddle attachment, or using a hand-held mixer, beat the butter for 1 minute. Beat in the sugars until the mixture is quite light, 3–5 minutes. Beat in the corn syrup. Scrape down the dough. One at a time, add the eggs, beating well after the first egg before adding the second. Beat in the vanilla. Remove the bowl from the stand.

Using a wooden spoon, stir the flour mixture into the butter mixture, in two additions. Stir in the white and semisweet chocolate chips.

Drop the batter in heaping tablespoonfuls onto the prepared cookie sheets, spacing them about 2 inches (5 cm) apart. You should be able to get about 12 blobs on a regular-sized cookie sheet. Flatten slightly.

One sheet at a time, bake in the centre of the preheated oven until cookies are puffed and centres are set but still soft, 9–11 minutes. Cool the cookie sheet on a wire rack for 2 minutes. Transfer the cookies to the wire rack to cool completely. Repeat with the remaining cookie dough, cooling the pans slightly before adding unbaked cookie dough to them. (Cookies can be stored in an airtight container at room temperature for up to 5 days.)

NAPOLOGETICALLY AND

Chocolate Intensities

NAPOLOGETICALLY AND unabashedly chocolatey, these cookies explode in your mouth, just as quickly as they melt. I used to make these cookies with more sugar, but after much trial and error I realized that I could significantly decrease the amount of sugar without betraying their integrity. The decreased amount of sugar highlights the coffee flavour and the exquisite, serially special chocolate intensity, hence the name! The recipe also calls for cake and pastry flour, a soft flour that ensures a tender texture. With a full 1 lb (500 g) of chocolate and just ½ cup (125 mL) of cake and pastry flour, there's just enough flour to hold it together and a smidgen of butter for enrichment. Once you try it, there's no going back.

1 lb (500 g) bittersweet chocolate, coarsely chopped
¼ cup (60 mL) unsalted butter, softened (2 oz/60 g)
½ cup (125 mL) cake and pastry flour, sifted
1 tsp (5 mL) baking powder
¼ tsp (1 mL) salt
4 large eggs, at room temperature
1⅔ cup (410 mL) granulated sugar
2 tsp (10 mL) vanilla
1 tsp (5 mL) instant espresso powder
2 cups (500 mL) bittersweet chocolate chips

In the top of a double boiler set over hot, not boiling water, melt the chocolate with the butter. Remove from the heat and let cool slightly.

Whisk together the flour, baking powder and salt in a bowl; set aside.

In the bowl of a stand mixer fitted with the paddle attachment, or using a hand-held mixer, beat the eggs with the sugar until thick and pale in colour, about 5 minutes. Beat in the melted chocolate, vanilla and espresso powder. Remove the bowl from the stand.

Using a wooden spoon, stir in the flour mixture. Stir in the chocolate chips. Cover the surface of the dough with plastic wrap and refrigerate for about 1 hour or until firm.

Preheat the oven to 350°F (180°C). Line 2 cookie sheets with parchment paper.

Drop the dough in heaping tablespoonfuls onto the prepared cookie sheets. Press down on each cookie lightly. Bake in the centre of the preheated oven until the tops look crinkly and appear dry, about 15 minutes. DO NOT OVER-BAKE. Cool the cookie sheet on a wire rack for 2 minutes. Transfer the cookies to the wire rack to cool completely. Repeat with the remaining cookie dough, cooling the pans slightly before adding unbaked cookie dough to them. (Cookies can be stored in an airtight container at room temperature for up to 5 days.)

Passover Chocolate Clouds

½ cup (125 mL) ground almonds

½ cup (125 mL) unsweetened Dutch-processed cocoa powder, sifted

1 tsp (5 mL) kosher for Passover baking powder

Pinch of salt

¼ cup (60 mL) unsalted butter or margarine, softened (2 oz/60 g)

⅔ cup (160 mL) packed light brown sugar

1 large egg, at room temperature

4 oz (125 g) semisweet chocolate, coarsely chopped and melted

¼ cup (60 mL) granulated sugar

½ cup (125 mL) icing sugar

M Y VERY favourite Passover cookie, these are actually more akin to a brownie or confection than to a cookie. The almonds provide a sandy texture but the lack of flour makes them super fudgey. They are super simple to make and keep extremely well in an airtight container for up to 1 week. After a robust meal, such as the Seder, they are the perfect size for dessert, their richness tempered by fruit salad or a cup of coffee or tea.

Stir together the almonds, cocoa powder, baking powder and salt in a bowl; set aside.

In the bowl of a stand mixer fitted with the paddle attachment, or using a hand-held mixer, beat the butter for 1 minute. Beat in the brown sugar until well combined. Beat in the egg. Scrape down the dough. Remove the bowl from the stand.

Using a wooden spoon, stir in the melted chocolate. Stir in the almond-cocoa mixture. Cover the surface of the dough with plastic wrap and let stand at room temperature for 1 hour or until firm enough to roll into balls.

Place the granulated and icing sugars in separate bowls. Preheat the oven to 350°F (180°C). Line 2 cookie sheets with parchment paper.

Scoop small balls of the dough and roll between the palms of your hands into 1-inch (2.5 cm) balls. Roll each ball in the granulated sugar and then in the icing sugar until completely coated. Place 1 inch (2.5 cm) apart on the prepared baking sheets; flatten slightly.

One sheet at a time, bake in the centre of the preheated oven until just set around the edges, 10–12 minutes. Cool the cookie sheet on a wire rack for 2 minutes. Transfer the cookies to the wire rack to cool completely. Repeat with the remaining cookie dough, cooling the pans slightly before adding uncooked cookie dough to them. (Cookies can be stored in an airtight container at room temperature for up to 5 days.)

It's the granulated sugar on the outside that generates the crackly top on these cookies. Make sure you roll them first in the granulated sugar and then the icing sugar. Specially designed kosher for Passover icing sugar—that doesn't contain cornstarch—can be found in most grocery stores.

Many people frown on using chemical leaveners during Passover. They feel it goes against the spirit and the integrity of the holiday. Every individual has to follow their own set of ethics, but I do point out that baking powder itself does not leaven baked goods, it merely acts on the gas already trapped by the creaming process.

Oatmeal Raisin Cookies

1 cup (250 mL) all-purpose flour

1 tsp (5 mL) cinnamon

½ tsp (2 mL) baking powder

½ tsp (2 mL) baking soda

¼ tsp (1 mL) salt

¾ cup (180 mL) unsalted butter, softened (6 oz/175 g)

1 cup (250 mL) packed light brown sugar

1 large egg, at room temperature

2 tsp (10 mL) vanilla

1½ cups (375 mL) large flake rolled oats

½ cup (125 mL) quick-cooking (not instant) rolled oats

1 cup (250 mL) raisins

½ cup (125 mL) dried cranberries

I PREFER soft oatmeal cookies thickish in the middle and only very slightly crispy around the edges. If you prefer them flatter and somewhat crispier, omit the baking powder and increase the baking soda to 1 tsp (5 mL). To help maintain that soft texture, plump your raisins in a little warm water for 10 minutes before you start making your cookies. Dry them extensively before you add them to the batter. Raisins typically draw moisture from baked goods, so plumping them first robs them of this dirty little habit. I also found that due to the inclusion of both raisins and dried cranberries, I could omit the granulated sugar entirely from my cookie, making it a less sweet than other oatmeal cookies (although it's still plenty sweet).

Preheat the oven to 350°F (180°C). Line 2 cookie sheets with parchment paper; set aside.

Whisk together the flour, cinnamon, baking powder, baking soda and salt in a bowl; set aside.

In the bowl of a stand mixer fitted with the paddle attachment, or using a hand-held mixer, beat the butter for 1 minute. Beat in the brown sugar until the mixture is quite light, 3–5 minutes. Scrape down the dough. Beat in the egg until thoroughly incorporated. Beat in the vanilla.

With the mixer on the lowest speed, mix the flour mixture into the butter mixture just until most of it is incorporated. Add the oats, and mix lightly. Add the raisins and dried cranberries. Mix just until the cookie dough holds together. Let the dough rest at room temperature for 15 minutes.

Using heaping spoonfuls of the dough, roll into 1- to 1½-inch (2.5–4 cm) balls. Place on the prepared cookie sheets. Flatten each ball slightly.

One sheet at a time, bake in the centre of the preheated oven for 9 minutes for a softer cookie or 11 minutes for a crunchier cookie. Cool the cookie sheet on a wire rack for 2 minutes. Transfer the cookies to the wire rack to cool completely. Repeat with the remaining cookie dough, cooling the pans slightly before adding unbaked cookie dough to them. (Cookies can be stored in an airtight container at room temperature for up to 5 days.)

OATS Baking with oats adds texture as well as fibre. Use old fashioned or large flake oats when no size is called for in a recipe. These do not absorb as much moisture as quick-cooking or instant oats, making your cookies and muffins moister. I call for a combination in this recipe to make sure the edges are crisp and that you also get a good chew from the large flake oats.

RAISINS When I was growing up, my mother added raisins to all sorts of things: salads, couscous, brownies, cookies, breads, you name it. Accordingly, I have grown up with a serious predilection for raisins. I too tuck them into anything that welcomes them. Raisins happen to be one of the most nutritious dried fruits in the world! Yes, they're definitely sweet and perhaps a dentist's nightmare, but they also contain fibre, vitamins, antioxidants, certain B vitamins and they lend an earthy sweetness to baked goods. Thompson or sultana raisins are primarily used in baking but I like to mix things up and sometimes use golden raisins (unfortunately treated with small amounts of sulphur dioxide), Lexia raisins or if I can find them, plain uncoated muscats.

Coconut Oatmeal Cookies *with* Chocolate-Covered Raisins *and* Almonds

1 cup (250 mL) all-purpose flour

1½ cups (375 mL) large flake rolled oats

½ cup (125 mL) shredded sweetened coconut

½ tsp (2 mL) baking powder

½ tsp (2 mL) baking soda

¼ tsp (1 mL) salt

¾ cup (180 mL) unsalted butter, softened (6 oz/175 g)

1 cup (250 mL) packed light brown sugar

1 large egg, at room temperature

1 tsp (5 mL) vanilla

1½ cups (375 mL) chocolate-covered raisins

¾ cup (180 mL) coarsely chopped blanched almonds

THESE CRAGGLY cookies call for old fashioned oats, so there's some serious chewiness to them. The chocolate-covered raisins poke through the surface of the cookie, as if erupting from the cookie. They're old fashioned looking but spectacular and delicious.

Preheat the oven to 350°F (180°C). Line 2 cookie sheets with parchment paper; set aside.

Stir together the flour, rolled oats, coconut, baking powder, baking soda and salt in a bowl; set aside.

In the bowl of a stand mixer fitted with the paddle attachment, or using a hand-held mixer, beat the butter for 1 minute. Beat in the brown sugar until the mixture is quite light, 3–5 minutes. Scrape down the dough. Beat in the egg and then the vanilla.

With the mixer on the lowest speed, mix the flour mixture into the butter mixture just until most of it is incorporated. Remove the bowl from the stand. Stir in the chocolate-covered raisins and almonds, mixing just until the cookie dough holds together.

Using heaping spoonfuls, roll the dough into 1- to 1½-inch (2.5–4 cm) balls. Place on the prepared cookie sheets. Flatten each ball slightly.

One sheet at a time, bake in the centre of the preheated oven for 9 minutes. Cool the cookie sheet on a wire rack for 2 minutes. Transfer the cookies to the wire rack to cool completely. Repeat with the remaining cookie dough, cooling the pans slightly before adding unbaked cookie dough to them. (Cookies can be stored in an airtight container at room temperature for up to 5 days.)

HISTORY NOTE

It wasn't until the Middle Ages that bakers began to expand their horizons. Eggs, ground nuts and spices started to find their way into baked goods. Suddenly, bakers realized that egg whites could be beaten into a billowy mass and used to lighten their creations. Sugar became more available and more affordable, and soon the sponge and meringue were invented.

Peanut Butter Cookies

A CLASSIC if there ever was one. These cookies, somewhat soft in the middle, with a lot of crunch from the salted peanuts, are perfect for showcasing in an upright glass container. If you want a thinner, crispier cookie, flatten the balls of dough before you bake them. Without flattening, you will get a thicker, chewier but still crunchy-on-the-edges cookie.

Preheat the oven to 350°F (180°C). Line 2 cookie sheets with parchment paper; set aside.

Whisk together the flour, baking soda, baking powder and salt in a bowl; set aside.

In the bowl of a stand mixer fitted with the paddle attachment, or using a hand-held mixer, beat the butter with the peanut butter for 1 minute. Beat in the sugars until the mixture is quite light, 3–5 minutes. Scrape down the dough. One at a time, add the eggs, beating well after the first egg before adding the second. Beat in the vanilla.

With the mixer on the lowest speed, mix the flour mixture into the butter mixture just until most of it is incorporated. Add the peanuts; mix just until the cookie dough comes together.

Using heaping spoonfuls of the dough, roll into 1- to 1½-inch (2.5–4 cm) balls. Place on the prepared cookie sheets. If you wish, dip the tines of a fork in some granulated sugar and press the fork tines against the surface of each cookie, once in one direction and then in a perpendicular position. This is fun to do with young kids.

One sheet at a time, bake in the centre of the preheated oven until crisp and starting to turn golden around the edges, 9–11 minutes. Cool the cookie sheet on a wire rack for 2 minutes. Transfer the cookies to the wire rack to cool completely. Repeat with the remaining cookie dough, cooling the pans slightly before adding unbaked cookie dough to them. (Cookies can be stored in an airtight container at room temperature for up to 5 days.)

2½ cups (625 mL) all-purpose flour

1 tsp (5 mL) baking soda

½ tsp (2 mL) baking powder

¼ tsp (1 mL) salt

1 cup (250 mL) unsalted butter, softened (8 oz/250 g)

1½ cups (375 mL) smooth or chunky peanut butter

1 cup (250 mL) packed light brown sugar

1 cup (250 mL) granulated sugar

2 large eggs, at room temperature

2 tsp (10 mL) vanilla

1¼ cups (310 mL) salted peanuts

BAKER'S TIP

It's important to use the commercially available peanut butter for these cookies and not a natural peanut butter. Unfortunately, natural peanut butter tends to produce a crumbly dry texture. Say what you will about the fats and extra sugars found in mainstream peanut butter, they really do help to develop the taste and texture of a homemade peanut butter cookie.

Oversized Peanut Butter *and* Oat Cookies (*aka* Monster Cookies)

F THERE'S a cookie monster lurking inside of you or inside your house, this is the cookie for you. It's amazing how much fun stuff this cookie can hold—peanut butter, oats, toffee bits, chocolate chips and M&M's. I like to make them rather large, much like the oversized cookies you buy at the coffee shop or cinema. You can, however, make them any size you prefer simply by adjusting the baking time accordingly. Sometimes, I even mix the oats up, using mostly quick-cooking rolled oats but a little of the larger flake oats as well.

Preheat the oven to 350°F (180°C). Line 2 cookie sheets with parchment paper; set aside.

Stir together the oats, flour, baking soda and salt in a bowl; set aside.

In the bowl of a stand mixer fitted with the paddle attachment, or using a hand-held mixer, beat the butter and peanut butter for 1 minute. Beat in the sugars until the mixture is quite light, 3–5 minutes. Scrape down the dough. One at a time, add the eggs, beating well after each addition before adding the next. Beat in the vanilla.

With the mixer on the lowest speed, mix the oat mixture into the butter mixture. Remove the bowl from the stand. Stir in the chocolate chips, candies and Skor bits. Cover the top of the bowl with plastic wrap and refrigerate the dough for 30 minutes.

Using an ice cream scoop, mound cookies on the prepared baking sheets. You should have room for about 6 cookies per tray. Flatten each mound so that it resembles a puck. Refrigerate the remaining batter while you bake the first 2 batches.

One sheet at a time, bake in the centre of the preheated oven until light golden around the edges but still soft in the centres, about 10 minutes. Cool the cookie sheet on a wire rack for 2 minutes. Transfer the cookies to the wire rack to cool completely. Repeat with the remaining cookie dough, cooling the pans slightly before adding unbaked cookie dough to them. (Cookies can be stored in an airtight container at room temperature for up to 4 days.)

4½ cups (1.125 L) quick-cooking rolled oats

⅓ cup (80 mL) all-purpose flour

2 tsp (10 mL) baking soda

¼ tsp (1 mL) salt

½ cup (125 mL) unsalted butter, softened (4 oz/125 g)

1½ cups (375 mL) smooth peanut butter

1 cup (250 mL) packed light brown sugar

1 cup (250 mL) granulated sugar

3 large eggs, at room temperature

2 tsp (10 mL) vanilla

1 cup (250 mL) semisweet chocolate chips

1 cup (250 mL) M&M's or Smarties

½ cup (125 mL) Skor bits

Ginger Cookies

2¼ cups (560 mL) all-purpose
flour

2 tsp (10 mL) baking soda

1 Tbsp (15 mL) ground ginger

½ tsp (2 mL) cinnamon

¼ tsp (1 mL) salt

¼ tsp (1 mL) pepper

⅛ tsp (0.5 mL) allspice

¾ cup (180 mL) unsalted butter,
softened (6 oz/175 g)

1 cup (250 mL) packed light brown
sugar

⅓ cup (80 mL) fancy molasses

1 large egg, at room temperature

1 tsp (5 mL) vanilla

½ cup (125 mL) granulated sugar

THERE'S NO snap in these cookies. They're soft and pliable, and a bit puffy. They're buttery without being overly sweet. They have a little bite although I've been known, when expecting guests whom I know adore ginger, to increase the ginger to 4 or 5 tsp (20–25 mL). Definitely use a fancy molasses here as the other kinds will overwhelm the spices and the lovely overtones of the brown sugar.

Preheat the oven to 350°F (180°C). Line 2 cookie sheets with parchment paper; set aside.

Whisk together the flour, baking soda, ginger, cinnamon, salt, pepper and allspice in a bowl; set aside.

In the bowl of a stand mixer fitted with the paddle attachment, or using a hand-held mixer, beat the butter for 1 minute. Beat in the brown sugar and molasses for 3 minutes. Scrape down the dough. Beat in the egg and then the vanilla.

With the mixer on the lowest speed, mix the flour mixture into the butter mixture just until incorporated.

Using heaping tablespoonfuls, roll the dough into 1- to 1½-inch (2.5–4 cm) balls. Roll each in the granulated sugar until completely coated. Transfer to the prepared cookie sheets. (Do not flatten the cookies.)

One sheet at a time, bake in the centre of the preheated oven until cookies have puffed and are starting to crisp around the edges and beginning to deflate, 9–10 minutes. Cool the cookie sheet on a wire rack for 2 minutes. Transfer the cookies to the wire rack to cool completely. Repeat with the remaining cookie dough, cooling the pans slightly before adding unbaked cookie dough to them. (Cookies can be stored in an airtight container at room temperature for up to 5 days.)

HISTORY NOTE

Whereas once all "cookies" and "small cakes" were boiled and then usually fried, over time baking in enclosed ovens replaced those techniques. It was a slow and long transition. In medieval times, a village would be lucky to have a baker in their midst, supplying them with rough breads and the like. By the Middle Ages, grand homes had ovens within their dwellings. It wasn't until the 18th century, however, that ovens became the norm for most common folk.

Snickerdoodles

SNICKERDOODLES HAVE a long and illustrious history. The first mention of these nutmeg-scented cookies is said to be in the state of Maine, sometime in the early 1800s. However, most food historians believe that the name "snickerdoodle" actually derives from the German word, "schneckennudeln," which means "crinkly dough." The combination of the cream of tartar and baking soda allows the cookies to puff up in the oven and then collapse, cloaking them with their characteristic crinkliness (abetted by the cinnamon sugar with which they're coated). Tradition-ally, snickerdoodles are made with a combination of butter and vegetable shortening that encourages the crispy edges. I've opted to use all-butter here, not only to enhance the flavour but to prevent any overbrowning on the bottom of the cookie. I've also reduced the classic oven temperature of 400°F (200°C) to 350°F (180°C), to help prevent overbrowning and to keep the middle of the cookie soft and chewy.

2½ cups (625 mL) all-purpose flour

2 tsp (10 mL) cream of tartar

1 tsp (5 mL) baking soda

¼ tsp (1 mL) salt

¼ tsp (1 mL) nutmeg

1 cup (250 mL) unsalted butter, softened (8 oz/250 g)

1½ cups (375 mL) granulated sugar

1 large egg, at room temperature

1 tsp (5 mL) vanilla

TOPPING

¼ cup (60 mL) granulated sugar

1 Tbsp (15 mL) cinnamon

Whisk together the flour, cream of tartar, baking soda, salt and nutmeg in a bowl; set aside.

In the bowl of a stand mixer fitted with the paddle attachment, or using a hand-held mixer, beat the butter for 1 minute. Beat in the sugar for 3 min-utes. Scrape down the dough. Beat in the egg and then the vanilla.

With the mixer on the lowest speed, mix the flour mixture into the butter mixture just until incorporated. Cover the dough with plastic wrap and refrigerate for 1–24 hours.

Preheat the oven to 350°F (180°C). Line 2 cookie sheets with parch-ment paper. To make the topping, combine the sugar and cinnamon in a small shallow bowl.

Using heaping tablespoonfuls, roll the dough into 1-inch (2.5 cm) balls. Roll each ball in the sugar-cinnamon mixture until completely coated. Transfer to the prepared cookie sheets. Flatten each cookie slightly.

One sheet at a time, bake in the centre of the preheated oven until cookies are puffed and starting to crisp around the edges, about 12 min-utes. Cool the cookie sheet on a wire rack for 2 minutes. Transfer the cookies to the wire rack to cool completely. Repeat with the remaining cookie dough, cooling the pans slightly before adding unbaked cookie dough to them. (Cookies can be stored in an airtight container at room temperature for up to 5 days.)

Lemon Cornmeal *and* Currant Cookies

1½ cups (375 mL) all-purpose flour

½ cup (125 mL) yellow cornmeal

1 tsp (5 mL) baking powder

¼ tsp (1 mL) salt

¾ cup (180 mL) unsalted butter, softened (6 oz/175 g)

¾ cup (180 mL) granulated sugar

1 large egg, at room temperature

1 Tbsp (15 mL) finely grated lemon zest

1 tsp (5 mL) vanilla

1 cup (250 mL) currants

TOPPING

¼ cup (60 mL) granulated sugar

I WAS inspired to make these cookies by a packaged cookie! I saw a package of cookies at the grocery store, boasting currants (as well as a lower fat content) and immediately thought, gee, I can make those at home. So home I went and the cookies I did make! I decided to add cornmeal for some texture and some lemon zest to bring out the fruitiness of the currants. Crisp and toothsome like their packaged counterpart, these cookies are brilliant with a cup of very lightly sweetened tea.

Preheat the oven to 350°F (180°C). Line 2 cookie sheets with parchment paper.

Whisk together the flour, cornmeal, baking powder and salt; set aside.

In the bowl of a stand mixer fitted with the paddle attachment, or using a hand-held mixer, beat the butter for 1 minute. Beat in the sugar for 3 minutes. Scrape down the dough. Beat in the egg. Beat in the lemon zest and then the vanilla.

With the mixer on the lowest speed, mix the flour mixture into the butter mixture just until crumbly. Add the currants; beat just until the dough holds together.

Place the sugar for the topping in a small bowl.

Using tablespoonfuls, roll the dough into 1-inch (2.5 cm) balls. Roll each in the sugar until completely coated. Transfer to the prepared cookie sheets. With the base of a glass also dipped in the sugar, flatten each cookie to a ¼-inch (6 mm) thickness.

One sheet at a time, bake in the centre of the preheated oven until cookies are golden around the edges, about 15 minutes. Cool the pan on a wire rack for 2 minutes. Transfer the cookies to the wire rack to cool completely. Repeat with the remaining cookie dough, cooling the pans slightly before adding unbaked cookie dough to them. (Cookies can be stored in an airtight container at room temperature for up to 5 days.)

BAKER'S TIP

When I develop a recipe that calls for lemon or orange zest, I prefer to add it in with the butter so that the essential oils get released through the butter, which itself is a distributor of flavour. You don't get quite as much of a citrus hit when you add the zest to the batter along with the flour mixture.

Sugar Cookies

Tender and timeless, these cookies are the workhorse of a baking repertoire. They're buttery with just the right hint of vanilla. By workhorse, I mean that they're the cookies you make when you want to decorate. They're the cookies you use to make stained-glass cookies. And they're the cookies you'll turn to when you and your family want to bake cookies for the holidays and go wild with different coloured sprinkles.

Whisk together the flour, baking powder and salt in a bowl; set aside.

Scrape the seeds from the vanilla bean and stir into the sugar, making sure the seeds are distributed evenly; let stand for 5 minutes. Discard the empty vanilla pod or place in your sugar canister, along with the remaining quarter of the vanilla bean.

In the bowl of a stand mixer fitted with the paddle attachment, or using a hand-held mixer, beat the butter for 1 minute. Beat in the sugar for 3 minutes. Scrape down the dough. Beat in the egg. Remove the bowl from the stand.

With a wooden spoon, stir the flour mixture into the butter mixture just until incorporated. Remove the dough to a work surface. Divide the dough in half. Wrap each half in plastic wrap; flatten into a disc. Refrigerate for 1–24 hours.

Preheat the oven to 350°F (180°C). Line 2 cookie sheets with parchment paper.

Lightly flour your work surface. Working with one disc of dough at a time, roll out each disc to ¼-inch (6 mm) thickness. Cut out desired shapes. Transfer the cookies to the prepared cookie sheet.

One sheet at a time, bake in the centre of the preheated oven until just starting to turn golden around the edges, 8–9 minutes. Cool the cookie sheet on a wire rack for 2 minutes. Transfer the cookies to the wire rack to cool completely. Repeat with the remaining cookie dough, rerolling scraps once only and cooling the pans slightly before adding unbaked cookie dough to them. (Cookies can be stored in an airtight container at room temperature for up to 10 days.)

RECIPE CONTINUED . . .

2¼ cups (560 mL) all-purpose flour
½ tsp (2 mL) baking powder
¼ tsp (1 mL) salt
¾ vanilla bean
1 cup (250 mL) unsalted butter, softened (8 oz/250 g)
1 cup (250 mL) granulated sugar
1 large egg, at room temperature

BAKER'S TIPS

Sugar cookies fall under the category of shaped cookies. These doughs are usually chilled in the refrigerator so that the gluten relaxes and the dough can be rolled. Try to handle the dough as little as possible. If the dough becomes too warm, it will not roll out well and the cookies may spread too much in the oven, ruining whatever shape you've lovingly made them into.

After rolling out your dough on a lightly floured work surface, dip your cookie cutters into a bowl of flour as well, so sticking is not an issue.

USING LEFTOVER DOUGH Once all your shapes have been cut out, you may find yourself with leftover dough. You can re-roll this dough (once only) and use it to make more cookies. Bring the dough together, lightly kneading it into a ball. Refrigerate for 30 minutes. Roll as you did for the first rolling.

SHORTBREAD—A FEW TIPS

Classically made from 2 parts flour to 1 part butter, you can see how "short" most shortbread are. And because they are so short, they need careful handling and much tender loving care. First, make sure the butter is at the appropriate temperature. It should be at room temperature and not overly mushy. If the butter is too soft, you're going to sacrifice some of the tenderness that is so closely associated with good shortbread. Unlike other cookies, you don't need to beat the butter or the butter and sugar together for too long. The point is NOT to incorporate too much air. Likewise, if the recipe contains an egg or egg yolk (most do not), you will only need to mix briefly.

Always use a wooden spoon when you add the flour. Overmixing is anathema to delicate shortbread. Add the flour all at once or in two additions, work with a gentle hand and stir only until the flour disappears into the dough.

Most shortbread benefits from a rest in the refrigerator. It improves the flavour of the cookies and helps them retain their shape while being baked.

BAKER'S TIP

When mixing dry ingredients into the butter base, always use a wooden spoon and not a spatula. Ingredients adhere better to the wood, which means you'll need fewer strokes to combine the dough.

Classic Shortbread

THE USE of rice flour or cornstarch is common for shortbread. The lower protein content of these flours ensures that the shortbread is melt-in-your-mouth tender. This is the kind of cookie that you can add almost anything to, although it needs no embellishment.

Preheat the oven to 300°F (150°C). Line 2 cookie sheets with parchment paper; set aside.

Whisk together the flours and salt; set aside.

In the bowl of a stand mixer fitted with the paddle attachment, or using a hand-held mixer, beat the butter for 1 minute. Beat in the sugar for 2 minutes. Scrape down the dough. Beat in the vanilla. Remove the bowl from the stand.

Using a wooden spoon, stir in the flour mixture in 2 additions, stirring until a dough is formed.

Transfer the dough to a lightly floured work surface. With a lightly floured rolling pin, roll out the dough to ¼-inch (6 mm) thickness. Using a scalloped cookie cutter, cut out cookies. Transfer shapes to the prepared cookie sheets. Refrigerate for 30 minutes.

One sheet at a time (keeping the other sheet refrigerated), bake in the centre of the preheated oven until cookies are just starting to turn lightly golden around the edges, 25–30 minutes. Cool the cookie sheet on a wire rack for 2 minutes. Transfer the cookies to the wire rack to cool completely. Repeat with the chilled cookie shapes. (Cookies can be stored in an airtight container at room temperature for up to 5 days.)

VARIATIONS

GINGER SHORTBREAD Add 3 Tbsp (45 mL) finely chopped crystallized ginger while beating together the butter and sugar.

ORANGE CHOCOLATE SHORTBREAD Add 2 Tbsp (30 mL) finely grated orange zest along with the sugar to the butter and ½ cup (125 mL) mini chocolate chips along with the flour.

1½ cups (375 mL) all-purpose flour
½ cup (125 mL) rice flour or cornstarch
Pinch of salt
1 cup (250 mL) unsalted butter, softened (8 oz/250 g)
⅔ cup (160 mL) icing sugar, sifted (or superfine sugar)
1 Tbsp (15 mL) vanilla

RECIPE CONTINUED . . .

ESPRESSO SHORTBREAD Add 2 Tbsp (30 mL) finely ground coffee beans.

SAGE SHORTBREAD Add 2 tsp (10 mL) crumbled dried (not ground) sage along with the flour.

ROSEMARY LEMON SHORTBREAD Add 1 Tbsp (15 mL) finely grated lemon zest along with the sugar to the butter and 1½ tsp (7 mL) dried rosemary, crumbled, along with the flour.

M&M'S SHORTBREAD Add ½ cup (125 mL) mini M&M's along with the flour.

GREEN TEA SHORTBREAD Add 1 Tbsp (15 mL) matcha (green tea powder) along with the flour.

HISTORY NOTE

The story of cookies and shortbread is one of evolution. In medieval times, leftover dough, it is said, was dried out in the hearth until it became hardened and became more like a rusk or hearty cracker. Later, pieces of dough were baked once, placed in storage, and then baked again to harden for use as food for sailors on long voyages. Thus, the biscuit was born. The word is derived from the French *bis* (twice) and *cuit* (cooked). As time went on, yeast was replaced by butter. Under Mary Queen of Scots (16th century), who was very fond of small thin crispy buttery cookies, the Scots' affinity for shortbread was born.

Mayan Chocolate Crisps

THE INDOMITABLE combination of cinnamon, heat and chocolate takes me back to the very small hotel I once stayed in Zihuatanejo, Mexico, affectionately known as Zihua, many many years ago. Back then, it was a small, lazy fishing village, the destination of tourists who visited from the local resort town of Ixtapa. Now, Zihuatanejo is a destination in its own right. When I visited, the effervescent and friendly woman who ran the small hotel made cookies daily for her guests. They were small round cookies, with the distinctive flavour of local vanilla and some spice to liven up the chocolate. This is my ode to her.

Line 3 cookie sheets with parchment paper; set aside. Whisk together the flours in a bowl; set aside.

In the bowl of a stand mixer fitted with the paddle attachment, or using a hand-held mixer, beat the butter for 1 minute. Beat in the brown sugar for 2 minutes. Scrape down the dough. Beat in the cocoa powder, cinnamon, espresso powder, salt and cayenne pepper, if using. Beat for 1 minute. Scrape down the bowl. Beat in the vanilla. Remove the bowl from the stand.

Using wooden spoon, stir in the flour mixture, just until it is incorporated. Stir in the chocolate chips.

Using tablespoonfuls, roll the dough into balls. Roll in the granulated sugar until completely coated. Place cookies about 2 inches (5 cm) apart on the prepared cookie sheets. Dip the bottom of a glass into the sugar and flatten each cookie. Refrigerate the cookies for 1 hour.

Preheat the oven to 350°F (180°C).

One sheet at a time, bake in the centre of the preheated oven until the cookies appear firm and dry, 8–12 minutes. Cool the cookie sheet on a wire rack for 2 minutes. Transfer the cookies to the wire rack to cool completely. (Cookies can be stored in an airtight container at room temperature for up to 5 days.)

1¾ cups (430 mL) all-purpose flour

¼ cup (60 mL) rice flour

1 cup (250 mL) unsalted butter, softened (8 oz/250 g)

1 cup (250 mL) packed light brown sugar

½ cup (125 mL) unsweetened Dutch-processed cocoa powder, sifted

½ tsp (2 mL) cinnamon

¼ tsp (1 mL) instant espresso powder

¼ tsp (1 mL) salt

¼ tsp (1 mL) cayenne pepper (optional)

1 tsp (5 mL) vanilla

½ cup (125 mL) mini semisweet chocolate chips

TOPPING

½ cup (125 mL) granulated sugar

Hazelnut Shortbread Batons

1 cup (250 mL) all-purpose flour

½ cup (125 mL) finely chopped
toasted hazelnuts

½ tsp (2 mL) baking powder

¼ tsp (1 mL) salt

½ cup (125 mL) unsalted butter,
softened (4 oz/125 g)

½ cup (125 mL) granulated or
superfine sugar

½ tsp (2 mL) vanilla

GARNISH

6 oz (175 g) semisweet chocolate,
coarsely chopped

½ cup (125 mL) finely chopped
toasted hazelnuts

I WILL never tire of the magical combination of hazelnuts and chocolate. They work so hard to bring out the best in each other. The addition of baking powder to the shortbread (heavens! Is that what you might call blasphemy!?!) lightens the dough for an exceptional texture.

Preheat the oven to 325°F (160°C). Line 2 cookie sheets with parchment paper; set aside.

Whisk together the flour, hazelnuts, baking powder and salt in a bowl; set aside.

In the bowl of a stand mixer fitted with the paddle attachment, or using a hand-held mixer, beat the butter for 1 minute. Beat in the sugar for 2 minutes. Scrape down the dough. Beat in the vanilla. Remove the bowl from the stand.

Using a wooden spoon, stir half of the flour into the butter mixture. Stir in the remaining flour just until incorporated.

Using tablespoonfuls, roll the dough into 3-inch (8 cm) logs on your work surface. Spacing the cookies about 1 inch (2.5 cm) apart, transfer them to the prepared cookie sheets.

One sheet at a time, bake in the centre of the preheated oven until the cookies start to turn golden around the edges, about 20 minutes. Cool the cookie sheet on a wire rack for 2 minutes. Transfer the cookies to the wire rack to cool completely. Repeat with the remaining cookie dough, cooling the pans slightly before adding unbaked cookie dough to them.

GARNISH Melt the chocolate in the top of a double boiler set over hot, not boiling water. Cool slightly. Dip one end of each cookie into the melted chocolate, lightly shaking off any excess. Dip the chocolate end into the chopped hazelnuts until coated. Transfer to a wire rack until the chocolate is set. (Cookies can be stored in an airtight container at room temperature for up to 3 days.)

Pecan Orange Sandies

SANDIES, SABLES, shortbread, whichever name you choose, the result is the same: tender, buttery cookies that almost fall apart in your mouth. Including the orange zest in the butter-sugar mixture ensures it gets distributed throughout the batter.

¾ cup (180 mL) unsalted butter, softened (6 oz/175 g)

½ cup (125 mL) icing sugar, sifted

1 Tbsp (15 mL) finely grated orange zest

1 tsp (5 mL) vanilla

1½ cups (375 mL) cake and pastry flour, sifted

¾ cup (180 mL) finely chopped toasted pecans

1 cup (250 mL) mini chocolate chips (optional)

Preheat the oven to 325°F (160°C). Line 2 cookie sheets with parchment paper; set aside.

In the bowl of a stand mixer fitted with the paddle attachment, or using a hand-held mixer, beat the butter for 2 minutes. Beat in the icing sugar for 2 minutes. Beat in the orange zest and then the vanilla.

With the mixer on the lowest speed, mix in the flour just until crumbly. Add the pecans and the chocolate chips, if using. Beat on the lowest speed just until the dough starts to come together.

Using tablespoonfuls, roll the dough into balls. Transfer to the prepared cookie sheets, spacing the cookies about 2 inches (10 cm) apart. Flatten the cookies slightly.

One sheet at a time, bake in the centre of the preheated oven until the cookies start to turn golden around the edges, about 15 minutes. Cool the cookie sheet on a wire rack for 2 minutes. Transfer the cookies to the wire rack to cool completely. Repeat with the remaining cookie dough, cooling the pans slightly before adding unbaked cookie dough to them. (Cookies can be stored in an airtight container at room temperature for up to 4 days.)

HISTORY NOTE

The word "cookie" (then "cookey") first made its appearance in Scotland—home of shortbread—as early as the 1700s. It referred to a small, soft and chewy baked good.

Toffee Meltaways

1¾ cups (430 mL) all-purpose
flour

⅓ cup (80 mL) cornstarch

¾ tsp (4 mL) baking powder

¼ tsp (1 mL) salt

1 cup (250 mL) unsalted butter,
softened (8 oz/250 g)

½ cup (125 mL) icing sugar

1 tsp (5 mL) vanilla

1 cup (250 mL) Skor bits

THANK GOODNESS these endearingly tender cookies don't have to be chilled. I'd be hard pressed to wait for them any longer than I absolutely had to. The toffee bits start to melt as they bake, creating little holes of oozing goodness. The toffee flavour is also a wonderful counterpoint to the butter's natural flavour. Even though these cookies go into the oven perfectly round, they do tend to flatten a bit on the bottom.

Preheat the oven to 325°F (160°C). Line 2 cookie sheets with parchment paper; set aside.

Whisk together the flour, cornstarch, baking powder and salt; set aside.

In the bowl of a stand mixer fitted with the paddle attachment, or using a hand-held mixer, beat the butter for 2 minutes. Beat in the icing sugar for 2 minutes. Beat in the vanilla. Remove the bowl from the stand.

Using a wooden spoon, stir in half of the flour mixture, mixing until thoroughly incorporated. Stir in the remaining flour mixture and the Skor bits, mixing just until incorporated, bringing the dough together with your hands if necessary.

Roll heaping tablespoonfuls of the dough into 1-inch (2.5 cm) balls. Transfer to the prepared cookie sheets.

One sheet at a time, bake in the centre of the preheated oven until just starting to turn golden around the bottom edges, 15–17 minutes. The tops of the cookies should still look pale. Cool pan on a wire rack for 2 minutes. Transfer the cookies to the wire rack to cool completely. Repeat with the remaining cookie dough, cooling the pans slightly before adding unbaked cookie dough to them. (Cookies can be stored in an airtight container at room temperature for up to 5 days.)

Lime Basil Meltaways

THEY'RE NOT called meltaways for nothing. With just 2 Tbsp (30 mL) of butter over the 2 to 1 ratio that is the hallmark of great shortbread, these literally start to melt once you bite into them. The surprise is the combination of lime and basil, which, once introduced to each other, are a completely natural couple.

1⅔ cups (410 mL) all-purpose flour

⅓ cup (80 mL) rice flour

Pinch of salt

1 cup (250 mL) unsalted butter, softened (8 oz/250 g)

½ cup (125 mL) icing sugar, sifted

1 Tbsp (15 mL) honey

3 Tbsp (45 mL) finely grated lime zest (about 3 limes)

2 tsp (10 mL) dried basil

1 tsp (5 mL) vanilla

Whisk together the flours and salt in a bowl; set aside.

In the bowl of a stand mixer fitted with the paddle attachment, or using a hand-held mixer, beat the butter for 2 minutes. Beat in the icing sugar until light and fluffy, about 2 minutes. Beat in the honey. Beat in the lime zest, basil and vanilla. Remove the bowl from the stand.

In 2 additions and using a wooden spoon, stir the flour mixture into the butter mixture just until it comes together as a dough. Transfer the dough to a lightly floured work surface. Divide dough in half. Shape each half into a 9-inch (23 cm) long log. Wrap each log in plastic wrap and refrigerate for 1–24 hours.

Preheat the oven to 325°F (160°C). Line 2 cookie sheets with parchment paper.

Slice the log into ¼-inch (6 mm) thick slices. Transfer the slices to the prepared baking sheets.

One sheet at a time, bake in the centre of the preheated oven until starting to turn golden around the edges, 15–18 minutes. Cool the cookie sheet on a wire rack for 2 minutes. Transfer the cookies to the wire rack to cool completely. Repeat with the remaining cookie dough, cooling the pans slightly before adding unbaked cookie dough to them. (Cookies can be stored in an airtight container for up to 4 days.)

VARIATION

LIME SHORTBREAD Substitute freshly squeezed lime juice for the 1 Tbsp (15 mL) of honey. Omit the basil.

Chai Shortbread

2 cups (500 mL) all-purpose flour

2 Tbsp (30 mL) finely chopped
crystallized ginger

1 tsp (5 mL) ground cardamom

1 tsp (5 mL) ground ginger

1 tsp (5 mL) ground cinnamon

¼ tsp (1 mL) ground nutmeg

¼ tsp (1 mL) salt

Pinch of ground cloves

1 cup (250 mL) unsalted butter,
softened (8 oz/250 g)

½ cup (125 mL) icing sugar, sifted

1 Tbsp (15 mL) finely grated
orange zest

1 tsp (5 mL) vanilla

MY MOTHER still teases me, saying that when I finally grow up, I will develop a liking for coffee and tea. It's true I don't like the flavour of brewed coffee or tea, which is not to say that I don't relish the taste of either in my baked goods. In fact, sometimes I crave one or the other. These cookies fill that craving with all the spices and nuances that make a great cup of chai tea.

Stir together the flour, crystallized ginger, cardamom, ginger, cinnamon, nutmeg, salt and cloves in a bowl; set aside.

In the bowl of a stand mixer fitted with the paddle attachment, or using a hand-held mixer, beat the butter for 2 minutes. Beat in the icing sugar for 2 minutes. Beat in the orange zest and vanilla.

With the mixer on the lowest speed, mix the flour mixture into the butter mixture just until it comes together in a dough. Transfer the dough to a lightly floured work surface. Divide the dough in half. Shape each half into a 9-inch (23 cm) long log. Wrap each log in plastic wrap and refrigerate for 1–24 hours.

Preheat the oven to 325°F (160°C). Line 2 cookie sheets with parchment paper.

Slice the log into ¼-inch (6 mm) thick slices. Transfer the slices to the prepared baking sheets.

One sheet at a time, bake in the centre of the preheated oven until starting to turn golden around the edges, 15–18 minutes. Cool the cookie sheet on a wire rack for 2 minutes. Transfer the cookies to the wire rack to cool completely. Repeat with the remaining cookie dough, cooling the pans slightly before adding unbaked cookie dough to them. (Cookies can be stored in an airtight container for up to 4 days.)

VARIATION

LAVENDER SHORTBREAD Omit the crystallized ginger, orange zest, cardamom, ginger, cinnamon, nutmeg and cloves. Add 1 Tbsp (15 mL) dried culinary grade lavender to the flour mixture. For an extra fillip of flavour, heat 3 Tbsp (45 mL) of honey in the microwave for 20 seconds. Brush the liquefied honey over the just-baked cookies.

Parmesan, Rosemary *and* Pine Nut Shortbread

W<small>HY DO</small> sweet shortbread get all the glory? I love to make savoury shortbreads to serve as appetizers or to place alongside a cheese tray. I've also been known to smear a savoury spread on them or even to top them with a paper-thin slice of prosciutto. You can serve them warm, when the aroma still dances around the room and the seductive texture of the cookie will make you swoon, or at room temperature, when they will still enchant you with their élan.

½ cup (125 mL) unsalted butter, softened (4 oz/125 g)

⅔ cup + ¼ cup (220 mL) all-purpose flour

¼ cup (60 mL) grated Parmigiano Reggiano cheese

1½ tsp (7 mL) dried rosemary

Pinch of pepper

¼ cup (60 mL) toasted pine nuts

In the bowl of a stand mixer fitted with the paddle attachment, or using a hand-held mixer, beat the butter until very soft, about 2 minutes. Add the flour, cheese, rosemary and pepper. With the machine on the lowest speed, beat together until a dough is almost formed. Transfer the mixture to a work surface. Sprinkle the pine nuts over the mixture. Knead gently, incorporating the nuts into the dough, until it forms a ball. Shape the dough into a 1½-inch (4 cm) round log. Wrap in plastic wrap and refrigerate for 1–24 hours.

Preheat the oven to 350°F (180°C). Line 2 cookie sheets with parchment paper.

Slice the log into ¼-inch (6 mm) thick slices. Transfer the slices to the prepared cookie sheets.

One sheet at a time, bake in the centre of the preheated oven for 10 minutes. Cool the cookie sheet on a wire rack for 2 minutes. Transfer the cookies to the wire rack to cool completely. Repeat with the remaining cookie sheet. (Cookies can be stored in an airtight container at room temperature for 1 day.)

BAKER'S TIP

Since I like to serve these warm, I make the cookie dough the morning of my soiree and let it chill. About 2 hours before my guests are set to arrive, I slice and arrange the dough on the cookie sheets and tuck it back into the refrigerator. About 10 minutes before the festivities begin, I simply slide the sheets into the oven—they perfume the house and are charmingly warm as the guests mingle and nibble.

Blueberry *and* White Chocolate Shortbread

1¾ cups (430 mL) all-purpose flour

¼ cup (60 mL) rice flour

½ tsp (2 mL) salt

1 cup (250 mL) unsalted butter, softened (8 oz/250 g)

¾ cup (180 mL) icing sugar, sifted

1 Tbsp (15 mL) finely grated lemon zest

1½ tsp (7 mL) vanilla

3 oz (90 g) white chocolate, coarsely chopped

½ cup (125 mL) dried blueberries

I REMEMBER once taking a baking course in Toronto with Jim Dodge, with whom I had also studied in San Francisco. He made a tart with white chocolate and lemon, a combination of which I was a bit leery at first. Not surprisingly, if you're at all familiar with the desserts that Jim Dodge so famously makes, the combo was inspired. I had to pay homage to him and his unfailing sense of taste by developing this recipe for shortbread.

Whisk together the flours and salt in a bowl; set aside.

In the bowl of a stand mixer fitted with paddle attachment, or using a hand-held mixer, beat the butter for 2 minutes. Beat in the icing sugar for 2 minutes. Beat in the lemon zest and vanilla. Remove the bowl from the stand.

Using a wooden spoon, stir in half of the flour mixture, mixing until thoroughly incorporated. Mix in the remaining flour mixture, the white chocolate and blueberries, mixing just until incorporated, bringing the dough together with your hands if necessary.

Divide the dough in half. Press firmly but gently into a ball and then flatten into a disc. Wrap each ball in plastic wrap and refrigerate for 15–30 minutes or until chilled.

Preheat the oven to 300°F (150°C). Line 2 cookie sheets with parchment paper.

Working with one disc at a time and lightly sprinkling your work surface with some extra flour, roll or flatten the dough into an 8-inch (20 cm) square. Cut into 16 equal-sized squares. Transfer to one of the prepared cookie sheets.

Baking one sheet at a time, bake in the centre of the preheated oven until the cookies are browned on the bottom, 10–14 minutes. Repeat with the remaining baking sheet of cookies. (Cookies can be stored in an airtight container at room temperature for up to 5 days.)

CRANBERRY SHORTBREAD Substitute dried cranberries for the dried blue-berries and reduce the lemon zest to 1 tsp (5 mL).

———

BAKER'S TIP

RICE FLOUR Made simply from white or brown rice that has been finely ground, rice flour lends a tenderness to sweet goods, most particularly shortbread. Since it lacks the higher proteins associated with wheat flour, you should be cautious when substituting white flour with rice flour. Start off by substituting about 15% and working your way up to 25%. If you prefer brown rice flour, expect a somewhat coarser grained shortbread with a somewhat nuttier flavour.

Double Chocolate Shortbread *with* Pumpkin Seeds *and* Flax

1 cup (250 mL) unsalted butter, softened (8 oz/250 g)

1 cup (250 mL) icing sugar, sifted

1¾ cups (430 mL) all-purpose flour

Pinch of salt

1 cup (250 mL) semisweet chocolate chips

1 cup (250 mL) milk chocolate chips

½ cup (125 mL) unsalted sunflower seeds

½ cup (125 mL) shelled pumpkin seeds

¼ cup (60 mL) whole flax seeds

Hmmm, chocolate chips AND flax seeds AND pumpkin seeds AND sunflower seeds? All in one cookie? Too earnest? Not really. These are amazing cookies. I adore the way the milk and semisweet chocolate chips taste next to the crunch of the pumpkin, flax and sunflower seeds. You can use either unsalted or salted sunflower seeds, the salt of the latter adding an extra punch to these sensational morsels. There's just enough dough to hold the inclusions together and what dough there is, is meltingly tender.

Preheat the oven to 300°F (150°C). Line 2 cookie sheets with parchment paper; set aside.

In the bowl of a stand mixer fitted with the paddle attachment, or using a hand-held mixer, beat the butter for 2 minutes. Beat in the icing sugar; beat until the mixture is quite light, about 3 minutes.

Reduce the mixer speed to low. Add the flour and salt and mix just until combined. Remove the bowl from the stand. With a wooden spoon, stir in the chocolate chips and seeds. The mixture will seem as though it cannot incorporate all of the inclusions, and it may be a bit crumbly, but don't worry.

Working with one tablespoonful at a time, knead the dough gently in the palm of your hand until it forms a ball. Place on the prepared baking sheet. Repeat with remaining dough, spacing the balls about 1 inch (2.5 cm) apart.

Baking one sheet at a time, bake in the centre of the preheated oven until cookies look dry and are browned on the bottom, 18–22 minutes. Cool the cookie sheet on a wire rack for 2 minutes. Transfer the cookies to the wire rack to cool completely. Repeat with the remaining cookie dough, cooling the pans slightly before adding unbaked cookie dough to them. (Cookies can be stored in an airtight container at room temperature for up to 5 days.)

My Favourite Rugelach

WHAT I'D really like to know is why I didn't grow up with rugelach. Perhaps my mom thought that what was available wasn't good enough to serve or maybe there just weren't any around. I'll never really know. In any case, once I did discover rugelach and how easy they were to make, I just kept on making them.

Rugelach dough is extremely simple to make. While some rugelach doughs are yeast based, I have chosen to go with the simpler non-yeasted version. This is the one I make at home all the time. Some rugelach doughs contain an egg or even include some sour cream for extra richness. I've added a little sweetener and some lemon zest for flavour. The zest tickles the tang inherent in the cream cheese, bringing it to the forefront. It's better to use the brick-style cream cheese for making rugelach and to make sure it's at room temperature. If it's too cold, it simply won't combine well with the butter.

There are no rules or hard and fast formulas when it comes to the filling. The jam or spread is meant to act as a glue for the nuts or chips, so you're free to choose whatever you want. Same goes for the combination of nuts and other goodies. The two necessary ingredients are some sugar and cinnamon to fully qualify for rugelach status.

You may find that as you roll each triangle into a crescent, some of the inclusions fall out. There's no need to panic. Simply tuck them into the folds in the pastry. This is one place where you definitely want to use parchment, otherwise jam can ooze out of the dough, making the crescents stick to the pan. Just remember to transfer the rugelach to a separate wire rack while they're still warm, or else they will stick to the parchment.

In the bowl of a stand mixer fitted with the paddle attachment, or using a hand-held mixer, beat the butter with the cream cheese for 3 minutes or until light and fluffy. Beat in the sugar; beat for another 2 minutes. Beat in the lemon zest.

Reduce the mixer speed to low. Add the flour and salt and mix just until combined and a dough is formed.

RECIPE CONTINUED . . .

---

1 cup (250 mL) unsalted butter, softened (8 oz/250 g)

8 oz (250 g) cream cheese, softened

3 Tbsp (45 mL) icing sugar

2 tsp (10 mL) finely grated lemon zest

2 cups (500 mL) all-purpose flour

Pinch of salt

1 large egg, lightly beaten, at room temperature

3 Tbsp (45 mL) coarse sugar (optional)

FILLINGS

APRICOT WALNUT FILLING

1⅓ cups (330 mL) finely chopped walnuts

1 cup (250 mL) golden raisins

¾ cup (180 mL) granulated sugar

1½ tsp (7 mL) cinnamon

¾ cup (180 mL) apricot jam

PEACH MACADAMIA NUT FILLING

¾ cup (180 mL) chopped toasted macadamia nuts (or almonds)

½ cup (125 mL) golden raisins

½ cup (125 mL) granulated sugar

1 tsp (5 mL) cinnamon

¾ cup (180 mL) peach jam

RASPBERRY CHOCOLATE FILLING

1 cup (250 mL) chopped pecans

INGREDIENTS CONTINUED . . .

Transfer the dough to a lightly floured work surface and knead very lightly into a ball. Cut the ball into quarters; shape each quarter into a ball and flatten into discs.

Wrap each disc in plastic wrap; refrigerate for at least 2 hours or for up to 2 days. Let the dough stand at room temperature for 20 minutes before rolling.

Preheat the oven to 350°F (180°C). Line 2 cookie sheets with parchment paper; set aside.

FILLING In a small bowl, combine all the ingredients of your chosen filling, except for the jam or peanut butter.

On a lightly floured surface, roll out one of the discs to a 10-inch (25 cm) or 11-inch (28 cm) circle. Spread 3 Tbsp (45 mL) jam or peanut butter evenly over the surface. Sprinkle with one-quarter of the filling. Cut the dough into 12 pie-shaped wedges.

Starting from the wide end, roll up each wedge to form a crescent shape. Transfer to the prepared cookie sheets, spacing each rugelach about 2 inches (5 cm) apart. Repeat with remaining dough and filling.

Brush egg over 1 tray of rugelach. Sprinkle with coarse sugar, if desired. One sheet at a time, bake in the centre of the preheated oven until golden brown, 20–25 minutes. Cool the cookie sheet on a wire rack for a while. Transfer the cookies to the wire rack to cool completely. Repeat with remaining trays of rugelach, cooling the pans slightly before adding unbaked crescents to them. (Cookies can be stored in an airtight container at room temperature for up to 5 days.)

½ cup (125 mL) miniature semi-sweet chocolate chips
⅓ cup (80 mL) packed light brown sugar
1 tsp (5 mL) cinnamon
¾ cup (180 mL) seedless pure raspberry jam

CHERRY WHITE CHOCOLATE FILLING

1 cup (250 mL) chopped toasted hazelnuts
½ cup (125 mL) coarsely chopped white chocolate
½ cup (125 mL) dried sour cherries
½ cup (125 mL) granulated sugar
1 tsp (5 mL) cinnamon
¾ cup (180 mL) cherry jam

PEANUT BUTTER, CHOCOLATE AND CARAMEL FILLING

1 cup (250 mL) chopped unsalted peanuts
¾ cup (180 mL) miniature semi-sweet chocolate chips
½ cup (125 mL) Skor bits
⅓ cup (80 mL) packed light brown sugar
1 tsp (5 mL) cinnamon
½ cup (125 mL) smooth peanut butter

MARMALADE AND ALMOND FILLING

¾ cup (180 mL) chopped blanched almonds
½ cup (125 mL) currants
½ cup (125 mL) packed light brown sugar
1 tsp (5 mL) cinnamon
¾ cup (180 mL) orange marmalade

Five-Spice Butter Cookies

1½ cups (375 mL) all-purpose
    flour
½ tsp (2 mL) five-spice powder
¼ tsp (1 mL) salt
¾ cup (180 mL) unsalted butter,
    softened (6 oz/175 g)
½ cup (125 mL) granulated sugar
1 large egg yolk, at room
    temperature
1 tsp (5 mL) vanilla

TOPPING
4 oz (125 g) semisweet chocolate,
    coarsely chopped

FIVE-SPICE powder is most typically used in Asian cuisine but I love the scent and flavour it imparts to butter cookies. It's a clean, straightforward flavour, uninhibited and unencumbered here by the addition of any self-aggrandizing or superfluous ingredients. Just butter, sugar, egg and the remarkable floral scent and mild spiciness of five-spice powder.

Preheat the oven to 350°F (180°C). Line 2 cookie sheets with parchment paper; set aside.

Whisk together the flour, five-spice powder and salt in a bowl; set aside.

In the bowl of a stand mixer fitted with the paddle attachment, or using a hand-held mixer, beat the butter for 1 minute. Beat in the sugar; beat for 3 minutes. Beat in the egg yolk. Beat in the vanilla.

Reduce the mixer speed to low. Add the flour mixture; mix just until combined.

Transfer the dough to a pastry bag fitted with a ½-inch (1 cm) star tip. Pipe the dough into 1-inch (2.5 cm) shells or rosettes on the prepared cookie sheets, spacing the shells about 1 inch (5 cm) apart.

Baking one sheet at a time, bake in the centre of the preheated oven until the edges are golden, about 12 minutes. Cool the cookie sheet on a wire rack for 2 minutes. Transfer the cookies to the wire rack to cool completely. Repeat with the second cookie sheet.

TOPPING Melt the semisweet chocolate in the top of a double boiler set over hot, not boiling water, until melted and smooth. Remove from the heat. Dip the end of each cookie shell into the melted chocolate; return to the wire rack to cool. (Cookies can be stored in an airtight container separated between layers of waxed paper at room temperature for up to 5 days.)

VARIATION

CARDAMOM-CINNAMON BUTTER COOKIES Substitute ½ tsp (2 mL) ground cardamom and ¼ tsp (1 mL) cinnamon for the five-spice powder.

BAKER'S TIP
Five-spice powder is made up of cinnamon, cloves, fennel seed, star anise and Szechuan peppercorns.

Biscotti di Prato

W HEN I worked and lived in Italy, biscotti had yet to become the rage or grow to the near foot-long size they've become today. Then, the more popular everyday cookie was biscotti di Prato, or cantuccini. They were small, only about 1½ inches (4 cm) in length, served with dessert and dipped in vin santo (an Italian dessert wine). My boss Lorenza de Medici, who ran the Badia a Coltibuono in Tuscany with her husband and sons, used to buy them but she also taught me how to make them. Lorenza was a striking woman who was once food editor for *Italian Vogue* magazine and authored too many Italian cookbooks as well. Daunted by the historical resonance of her name, it took a while before my hands stopped shaking as I followed her instructions, but I soon learned the technique, which is the same as the traditional method for making biscotti.

1¾ cups + 2 Tbsp (460 mL) all-purpose flour

1¼ cups (310 mL) granulated sugar

½ tsp (2 mL) baking powder

Pinch of salt

2 large eggs, at room temperature

1 large egg yolk, at room temperature

1 tsp (5 mL) vanilla

¾ cup (180 mL) coarsely chopped almonds (skin on)

Preheat the oven to 350°F (180°C). Line 2 cookie sheets with parchment paper; set aside.

Dump the flour, sugar, baking powder and salt in a mound on a work surface. Using a spoon, mix together the ingredients and then make a large well in the centre. Place the 2 eggs, egg yolk and vanilla in the well. Using a fork, stir together the wet ingredients until the eggs are broken up. In a circular motion, gradually work the dry ingredients into the egg mixture until a dough is almost formed. Add the almonds. Knead the dough gently until a dough is formed and the almonds are fully incorporated.

Divide the dough into quarters. Roll each quarter into a short log that is about 2 inches (5 cm) wide. Transfer 2 of the logs to one of the prepared cookie sheets. Bake in the centre of the preheated oven until golden and firm, 25–30 minutes. Transfer to a cutting board. Repeat with the remaining 2 logs.

Cut the baked logs diagonally into 1-inch (2.5 cm) slices. Lay them cut side up on the cookie sheet. Repeat with the last 2 logs once they are baked. Reduce the oven temperature to 325°F (160°C). Bake the cookies, one sheet at a time, for 15 minutes.

(Cookies can be stored in an airtight container at room temperature for up to 4 weeks.)

RECIPE CONTINUED . . .

BAKER'S TIP

The key to making cantuccini is to keep them small. They should be no longer than 1–1½ inches (2.5–4 cm) long and no wider than 1 inch (2.5 cm). They're most typically dipped in vin santo, so they should only be one or two mouthfuls. Keeping the skins on the almonds is for visual effect.

Baci di Dama

ANOTHER FABULOUS and small cookie that I learned during my year-long stay in Italy. Literally, the title translates to "ladies kisses," which the sandwiched cookies are said to resemble. Originally from Northern Italy and almost always made with ground hazelnuts, I've messed with history a bit here and made my cookies with almonds and used a ganache for the filling instead of just melted chocolate. I think they're just as good, but if you prefer, feel free to replace the almonds with coarsely ground hazelnuts.

½ cup (125 mL) unsalted butter, softened (4 oz/125 g)
1 cup (250 mL) granulated sugar
1½ cups (375 mL) ground almonds
1 tsp (5 mL) vanilla
1 cup (250 mL) all-purpose flour
Pinch of salt

FILLING

4 oz (125 g) semisweet chocolate, coarsely chopped
3 Tbsp (45 mL) whipping cream, room temperature

Preheat the oven to 350°F (180°C). Line 2 cookie sheets with parchment paper; set aside.

In the bowl of a stand mixer fitted with the paddle attachment, or using a hand-held mixer, beat the butter for 1 minute. Beat in the sugar until well combined. Beat in the almonds. Beat in the vanilla.

Reduce the speed mixer to low. Add the flour and salt and mix just until a dough starts to come together.

Working with rounded teaspoonfuls, roll the dough into balls. The size of each ball should resemble a small marble. Transfer the balls to the prepared cookie sheets, spacing the cookies about 1 inch (2.5 cm) apart.

One sheet at a time, bake in the centre of the preheated oven until golden brown on the edges, about 10 minutes. Cool the cookie sheet on a wire rack for 2 minutes. Transfer the cookies to the wire rack to cool completely. Repeat with the remaining cookie dough, cooling the pans slightly before adding unbaked cookie dough to them.

FILLING Melt the chocolate in the top of a double boiler set over hot, not boiling water. Remove from the heat. Stir in the cream until smooth and thickened. Spread some of the filling evenly over 1 cookie. Sandwich with a same-sized cookie. Repeat until all of the filling and all of the cookies are used. (Cookies can be stored in an airtight container at room temperature separated by pieces of waxed paper for up to 3 days.)

Alfajores

1½ cups (375 mL) all-purpose
flour

¾ cup (180 mL) cornstarch

1½ tsp (7 mL) baking powder

¼ tsp (1 mL) baking soda

¼ tsp (1 mL) salt

1 cup (250 mL) unsalted butter,
softened (8 oz/250 g)

⅔ cup (160 mL) granulated sugar

1 Tbsp (15 mL) finely grated orange
zest

3 large egg yolks, at room
temperature

2 Tbsp (30 mL) milk, at room
temperature

1 tsp (5 mL) vanilla

FILLING

1¼ cups (310 mL) Dulce de Leche
(see p. 118) or Cajeta Caramel
(see p. 118)

TOPPING

2 oz (60 g) white chocolate,
coarsely chopped

1 oz (30 g) semisweet chocolate,
coarsely chopped

ALFAJORES ACTUALLY mean different things in different countries. In Spain, they are an oblong confection, made with honey, almonds and spices. These cookies, which hail from Argentina, are orange-flavoured discs with a rich and creamy dulce de leche filling. Yes, they can be a bit messy to eat. But hey, that's half the fun.

Combine the flour, cornstarch, baking powder, baking soda and salt in a bowl; set aside.

In the bowl of a stand mixer fitted with the paddle attachment, or using a hand-held mixer, beat the butter for 1 minute. Add the sugar and orange zest and beat until light and fluffy, about 3 minutes. One at a time, beat in the egg yolks, scraping down the bowl in between additions. Beat in the milk and vanilla.

Reduce the mixer speed to low. Add the flour mixture, mixing just until a dough is formed. Transfer the dough to a lightly floured work surface. Knead very gently into a ball. Divide the ball in half and press into discs. Wrap each half in plastic wrap and refrigerate for at least 3 hours or up to 2 days. Bring the dough to room temperature for 30 minutes before rolling.

Preheat the oven to 350°F (180°C). Line 2 cookie sheets with parchment paper; set aside.

On a lightly floured surface, roll out 1 disc to a ⅛-inch (3 mm) thickness. Using a 2-inch (5 cm) cookie cutter, cut out rounds. Transfer the rounds to the prepared cookie sheets.

One sheet at a time, bake in the centre of the preheated oven until golden around the edges, about 9 minutes. Cool the cookie sheet on a wire rack for 3 minutes. Transfer the cookies to the wire rack to cool completely. Repeat with the remaining cookie dough, cooling the pans slightly before adding unbaked cookie dough to them.

In the top of a double boiler set over hot, not boiling water, melt the white chocolate; set aside. Melt the semisweet chocolate over the double boiler as well.

Spread a generous amount of the Dulce de Leche or Cajeta Caramel on the flat side of half of the cookies. Sandwich with the remaining cookies. Drizzle with the white and semisweet melted chocolate. (Cookies can be stored in an airtight container at room temperature separated by pieces of waxed paper for up to 3 days.)

Dulce de Leche

THERE ARE two ways to make dulce de leche sauce at home, one using whole or homogenized milk and the other using canned sweetened condensed milk. I tend to use whole milk, although it does require a time commitment on the baker's part. The 2 versions using sweetened condensed milk provide a similar sweetness although they result in a sauce that's a bit lighter in colour.

Classic Version

4 cups (1 L) whole milk

1⅓ cups (310 mL) granulated sugar

¼ tsp (1 mL) baking soda

1 tsp (5 mL) vanilla

Whisk together the milk and sugar in a heavy-bottomed saucepan. Cook over medium heat, stirring occasionally, until the sugar has dissolved. Whisk in the baking soda; the mixture will foam up a bit. Reduce the heat to low and simmer, uncovered and stirring occasionally, until the mixture has caramelized and thickened, 1½–1¾ hours, stirring more frequently near the end of the cooking time. Stir in the vanilla. Transfer to a jar to cool. Makes about 1⅓ cups (310 mL).

Condensed Milk Version (Oven Method)

1 can (310 mL) sweetened condensed milk

Preheat the oven to 425°F (220°C). Scrape the sweetened condensed milk into a round 9-inch (23 cm) glass pie plate. Cover the pie plate with foil. Place the plate in a large roasting pan. Fill the roasting pan with enough hot water to come halfway up the sides of the pie plate. Cook in the middle of the preheated oven, filling the pan with water as necessary to keep it at the halfway point, until the mixture is thickened and golden, about 1½ hours. Makes about 1 cup (250 mL).

Condensed Milk Version (Microwave Method)

1 can (310 mL) sweetened condensed milk

Scrape the sweetened condensed milk into an 8 cup (2 L) glass measuring cup. Cook on medium (50% power) for 2 minutes. Stir the milk. Microwave for another 2 minutes. Cook on medium-low heat (30% power) for 14–16 minutes, stirring every 2 minutes, until thickened and golden. Makes about 1 cup (250 mL).

BAKER'S TIP

Dulce de leche will keep for 2 weeks in a sealed airtight jar in the refrigerator.

Cajeta Caramel

½ tsp (2 mL) baking soda

1 Tbsp (15 mL) water

3 cups (750 mL) goat's milk or
  sweetened condensed milk

1 cup (250 mL) whole milk

2 cups (500 mL) granulated sugar

Pinch of salt

1 cinnamon stick

CAJETA CARAMEL is another wonderful sauce, made with goat's milk. Delicious over ice creams, the use of goat's milk and a cinnamon stick lends a tangy deliciousness to this Mexican caramel.

Dissolve the baking soda in water; set aside.

Combine the goat's milk, whole milk, sugar, salt and cinnamon stick in a heavy-bottomed saucepan.

Cook over medium heat, stirring until the mixture reaches a simmer. Remove the saucepan from the heat. Remove the cinnamon stick. Stirring constantly, stir in the dissolved baking soda. Once the foam has subsided, return the saucepan to the heat. Cook, stirring occasionally, over medium-high heat until the mixture turns pale golden, about 50 minutes. At this point, the bubbles will enlarge and start to look glassy. Now you need to start stirring frequently, as the mixture will turn from a pale gold to a rich caramel brown. It may also start to stick to the bottom edges of the saucepan so stirring is essential. Check the caramel by spooning some of the mixture onto a white plate. It should be medium thick—it will also thicken as it cools. Immediately strain the cajeta through a wire mesh sieve sitting on top of a bowl. Transfer to a jar to cool. Cajeta will keep for 2 weeks in a sealed glass jar in the refrigerator.

Almond Tuiles

⅓ cup (80 mL) sliced almonds

2 large egg whites, at room temperature

½ cup (125 mL) granulated sugar

⅓ cup (80 mL) all-purpose flour

¼ cup (60 mL) unsalted butter, melted and cooled (2 oz/60 g)

1½ tsp (7 mL) water

½ tsp (2 mL) vanilla

ALSO KNOWN as langues de chat, these cookies are really more of a garnish than an eat-out-of-hand cookie. They have a cv that attests to their versatility. They can be flat, shaped into a cigarillo shape, curved to act as a wide spoon or placed inside a muffin cup to resemble a petal container. Classically, they are curved so that they resembles the tile (hence the name tuiles) that lines the rooftops of homes in Southern France.

Preheat the oven to 375°F (190°C). Line 2 cookie sheets with parchment paper. Trace six 4-inch (10 cm) circles on each piece of parchment. Turn the parchment over so that the pen marks are on the bottom side, but still visible.

Spread the almonds on a separate cookie or rimmed baking sheet. Bake in the preheated oven until just starting to turn golden, about 5 minutes. Let cool slightly. (You can also do this in a dry skillet over medium heat, shaking the pan often, until golden, also about 5 minutes.)

Whisk together the egg whites in a bowl, until frothy. Gradually add the sugar, whisking continuously. You do not want to make a meringue. The sugar should just be well incorporated. Add the flour, the melted butter, water and vanilla, whisking until the ingredients are incorporated.

Drop a heaping tablespoon of the batter into each of the pre-drawn circles. With a small offset spatula or plastic spatula, spread the batter so that it fills in the circle. Sprinkle some of the almonds over the batter.

Bake one sheet at a time (do not worry about the sheet of cookies that is not being baked—it will hold very well waiting for its turn), until golden around the edges and baked through, 7–9 minutes. Remove the tray from the oven.

Working very quickly, slide a small offset spatula under one of the cookies and shape into desired shape (see next page). Repeat with remaining cookies. Repeat baking with the remaining batter. Store for up to 2 days in an air tight container.

BAKER'S TIPS

To form a petal cup, press each warm cookie into a muffin tin, pressing it in with the bottom of a cup to hold its shape. This can also be done in a small bowl.

To form a cigarillo, roll up each warm cookie tightly into a cylinder.

To form a curved shape, lay each cookie over a rolling pin, moulding it to the rolling pin to take on a curved shape. Let set for a minute and then let cool completely on a wire rack.

Tuiles are especially susceptible to moisture and humidity so it's important to store them once they're cooled in an air tight container kept at room temperature.

Ladyfingers

4 large eggs, separated, at room
temperature

¾ cup (180 mL) granulated sugar,
divided

1 tsp (5 mL) vanilla

¼ tsp (1 mL) cream of tartar

Pinch of salt

⅔ cup + ¼ cup (220 mL) sifted
cake and pastry flour

¼ cup (60 mL) icing sugar

T HERE SEEMS to be a shroud of inapproachability to homemade ladyfingers. In truth, they're not that difficult to make. They're easier to
make if you have an extra bowl for your stand mixer, but it's not absolutely
necessary. Once you've tasted homemade ladyfingers, there's no going
back to store-bought. This recipe also doubles and triples beautifully in
case you're having a crowd. I'll let you in on a secret, though, ladyfingers
are really just an excuse to make Tiramisu, a recipe I've included on the
next page.

Preheat the oven to 325°F (160°C). Line 2 cookie sheets with parchment
paper; set aside.

In the bowl of a stand mixer fitted with the whisk attachment, or using
hand-held beaters, beat the egg yolks with ¼ cup (60 mL) of the sugar
until very pale and thick, about 5 minutes. Stir in the vanilla; set aside.

In a separate, clean bowl, again using the whisk attachment or a hand-
held mixer, beat the egg whites with the cream of tartar and salt until soft
peaks form. Gradually add the remaining ½ cup (125 mL) of sugar in a
thin stream and beat to firm but not stiff peaks.

Place one-third of the egg whites on top of the egg yolks. Sift one-
third of the cake and pastry flour over top. Gently fold the 3 ingredients
together. Repeat 2 more times. Transfer the mixture to a pastry bag with a
½-inch (1 cm) opening. Pipe 3½-inch (9 cm) batons on the prepared baking sheet, spacing them about 2 inches (5 cm) apart. Dust the icing sugar
over top of the ladyfingers.

Bake, one sheet at a time (don't worry about the waiting ladyfingers,
they will be just as wonderful as the ones that go directly into the oven),
until puffed, firm and very slightly golden, 13–15 minutes. Cool the baking sheet on a rack until completely cool. Repeat with the second baking
sheet.

Tiramisu

Tⁱʳᵃᵐⁱˢᵘ (Italian for "pick me up") has, for reasons unfathomable to me, become dessert non grata in the culinary world. Once ubiquitous on dessert menus, it was run out of town by molten chocolate cakes, or lava cakes (so named because of the warm chocolate liquid that oozes out of the cake once it's cut). It's fascinating to me how food trends and fads come and go.

This recipe comes to me courtesy of Romola, the everyday cook at the Badia a Coltibuono in Italy, who had been cooking for the Medicis for years. I still have the notebook where I wrote her recipe, word-for-word, in Italian. Romola used store-bought savoiardi, hard oval-shaped cookies that soaked up the coffee. I use homemade lady fingers, but otherwise remain true to her original recipe. I've included it here to wrap up the cookie chapter as it uses the cookies in the previous recipe. Because this recipe uses raw eggs, buy the freshest eggs you can.

1 Tbsp (15 mL) instant coffee granules

5 large eggs, separated, at room temperature

5 Tbsp (75 mL) granulated sugar

1 pkg (500 g) mascarpone, at room temperature

5 Tbsp (75 mL) cognac or brandy

3 Tbsp (45 mL) unsweetened Dutch-processed cocoa powder

Place the instant coffee granules in a 1-cup (250 mL) wet measure. Pour in enough boiling water to make ⅓ cup (80 mL). Set aside to cool.

In the bowl of a stand mixer fitted with the whisk attachment, or using hand-held beaters, whisk the egg yolks with the sugar until very pale and thick, about 5 minutes. Add the mascarpone. On low speed, whisk together the eggs and mascarpone until well mixed and homogenous. Whisk in the cognac or brandy.

In a separate, clean bowl, using a clean whisk attachment or hand-held beaters, whisk the egg whites until soft peaks form. In 2 additions, fold the egg whites into the yolk-mascarpone mixture.

ASSEMBLY Place 6 ladyfingers in a single layer on the bottom of a small 8-cup (2 L) capacity trifle bowl. Brush the cooled coffee over the ladyfingers. Spoon and then spread one-quarter of the mascarpone filling over the ladyfingers, making sure that the filling goes right to the edge of the bowl. Using a fine mesh sieve, sprinkle some of the cocoa powder directly on top of the mascarpone. Repeat this layering 3 more times, making sure the final layer is one of mascarpone. Sprinkle some cocoa on top of the mascarpone. Making sure that the plastic wrap does not touch the cocoa, cover the bowl and refrigerate for 6–24 hours. Bring the tiramisu to room temperature for 30 minutes before serving.

Garnish with shaved chocolate, if desired.

BARS AND SQUARES

127 BROWNIES

130 My Fudgey Brownies

133 Bittersweet Brownies

134 Cocoa Brownies

135 Espresso Brownies

136 Orange Cranberry Brownies

137 Dulce de Leche Cream Cheese Brownies

140 S'more Brownies

141 Double Chocolate Ganache Brownies with Fleur de Sel

143 Just for the Fun of It Blondies

145 Coconut and Toffee Blondies

146 Peanutty Peanut Butter Bars

147 Caramelita Bars

150 COOKING SUGAR

152 Chocolate Chip Cookie Bars

153 Caffe Latte Chocolate Chip Squares

154 Three Nut Brittle Squares

157 Pecan Pie Bars

158 Pecan Toffee Bars

159 Caramel Almond Cherry Shortbread Bars

161 Seven Layer Bars with Marshmallows and Dried Cranberries

162 Pucker Up Bars

164 Crumble Bumble Bars

165 Apple Cheesecake Bars

166 Extra Thick Date Squares

167 Nanaimo Bars

169 Chocolate-Filled Nanaimo Bars

170 Caramel Shortbread Bars

BARS AND squares are exquisite wonders to which bakers often gravitate. Like precious family heirlooms, they can be whipped out (or whipped up, as the case may be) at a moment's notice, their sentimentality and familiarity a welcome comfort. In some ways, they're even easier than cookies, since you don't have to bake them a batch at a time. You bake an 8-inch (20 cm) or 13- × 9-inch (33 × 23 cm) pan of whatever goody you're attracted to and then cut that into whatever sized pieces you're in the mood for. No waiting 10 minutes for the first batch and then another 10 minutes for a second batch. You can make three dozen servings in one fell swoop.

BROWNIES

When it comes to comfort intermingled with sweetness, brownies rank way up there. You think bakers compare the merits of soft vs. crispy chocolate chip cookies? Those conversations pale beside the raging debate that focuses on cakey vs. fudgey brownies. I wouldn't be surprised if some bakers came perilously close to a fistfight, they're that passionate. You either fall into one camp or the other and I have yet to meet a person who straddles the divide. Cakey brownies are best described as brownies that have a light crumb and a slightly fluffy interior. Fudgey brownies, accordingly, are brownies that are dense, moist and intensely chocolatey. Some people claim there's a third category, namely chewy, and I would hazard to agree, since chewy is different from both fudgey and cakelike, but the debate rarely stoops to including it. Although I do enjoy a chewy brownie from time to time, my die is cast solidly in the fudgey, dense camp. (Which is not to say that they should be wet, requiring time in the refrigerator to set them.)

It's easy to tell from reading a recipe which type of brownie you're going to end up with. If the recipe calls for creaming the butter with the sugar, chances are it's a cakey brownie. Similarly, if the recipe includes baking powder, it's likely a cakey brownie. Most recipes that call for cocoa powder are also indicative of a cakey brownie since cocoa powder is a drying agent. All fudgey recipes, on the other hand, start off by melting the chocolate with the butter and typically do not contain as much flour as is called for in a cakier brownie recipe. The ratio of butter to flour also tends to be higher in fudgey brownies and there is usually no chemical leavening whatsoever. The chewy variety takes the conservative (some might snipe, commitment phobic) middle ground, with more flour than a fudgey brownie but less flour than a cakey brownie.

Whether you believe that the original brownie sprung from a Bangor, Maine housewife's dismay when she forgot to put baking powder in her chocolate cake, or from a chef in Chicago who developed them for a client who wanted small, crumbless cakes to take to a picnic, the truth is that the first brownie didn't contain chocolate at all. It was a molasses cake that appeared in an 1896 cookbook and more closely resembled a blondie. It wasn't until Fannie Merritt Farmer came out with her revised cookbook in 1906 that it contained chocolate. It's also worth noting that the chocolate version at that time did not contain any baking powder at all (a fact that I use without reservation and without any compunction to argue that a fudgey brownie is the superior way to go).

Since brownies don't require a lot of ingredients, this is the time and place to invest in really good (but NOT high cocoa content) chocolate. Yes, I know, they're JUST brownies. But THEY ARE BROWNIES, and as such, I say, are due some element of reverence.

As most fudgey brownies require you to melt chopped chocolate with butter, it's helpful to cut the butter into pieces as well. This way the butter melts in about the same time as the chocolate and more easily coats the chocolate, protecting it from overheating. Always melt the chocolate about four-fifths of the way through and then take the saucepan off of the heat, stirring the mixture until all of the chocolate is melted and smooth. This also hastens the cooling down of the chocolate. The addition of sugar will cool down the mixture but if the chocolate is still too hot, the eggs will cook and not blend into the mixture smoothly. You might also be alarmed by how grainy the chocolate looks after the sugar is whisked in. No need to panic. The mixture will regain its soft and silky texture once the eggs are gently whisked in too.

It's fascinating to watch the various stages that brownies undergo while baking. The top gets shiny, then perhaps looks puffy, and then has a matte look to it. The more sugar you add, the more the brownies will develop a light shiny skin on their surface. You can also achieve that shiny skin by switching to cold eggs. Add the cold eggs right after the sugar has been whisked into the melted chocolate, then beat vigorously until the shiny batter pulls away from the side of the bowl. Baking expert Alice Medrich also suggests that refrigerating the batter in the pan for 24 hours results in that crinkly paper-thin crust.

Fudgey, decadent brownies do not mean under-baked brownies. Yes, of course, when making brownies it's best to err on the side of caution, since over-baked brownies are even worse than under-baked brownies. Always follow the guidelines spelled out in the recipe and use the cake tester method for testing doneness. Texture trumps time in this case. Brownies are underdone when a cake tester or toothpick comes out with wet smudges of batter clinging to the tester. If the same tester comes out perfectly clean, your brownies are probably overdone. Brownies are baked perfectly when the cake tester comes out with a few moist to fudgey crumbs clinging to it. Brownies, like cookies, will continue to bake even when they're taken out of the oven, which provides even more reason not to over bake them.

As I mention on page 11, trust your nose as well as your kitchen timer. I'll never forget the time I was meeting my friend Purdy Mackenzie in Saint-Adolph-d'Howard in the Laurentians, and as we walked into the house from the driveway, I took a sniff, recognized that sweet intoxicating perfume of chocolate and said, "I think your brownies are ready." Lo and behold, the timer went off at that exact second. I kid you not.

When you crave brownies, it's the brownie you're craving, not the white chocolate chips along with Skor bar bits and raspberry-flavoured candies that you've stirred into the batter. Brownies are best accompanied by only one or two other flavourings, flavourings that enhance, not lay siege to, the primary flavour of chocolate.

There's very rarely a chance of overmixing brownies since the amount of flour called for is minimal. However, the type of pan you use can make a difference. All of my brownies were made in a metal pan. If you only have an 8-inch (20 cm) glass pan, reduce the oven temperature by 25°F and bake the brownies for slightly less time. Glass is one of the worst conductors of heat so precautions must be taken.

One final note: please, please, wait until your brownies have cooled before you cut into them. I know it's hard. Believe me, I know. But cooling them down helps develop their flavour. They will also cut much more easily and have a chance to set properly.

Okay, one more thing. I have included about 6 different brownie recipes, each of them fabulous in their own right, each one highlighting a specific chocolate or a delightful combination. How could I just limit myself to one when my love affair with this sublime goody knows no bounds? You be the judge, and I'll bet any sum that you'll fall in love with more than one too.

My Fudgey Brownies

4 oz (125 g) unsweetened
chocolate, coarsely chopped

¾ cup (180 mL) unsalted butter,
softened and cut into pieces
(6 oz/175 g)

1½ cups (375 mL) granulated
sugar

3 large eggs, at room temperature

1 tsp (5 mL) vanilla

¾ cup (180 mL) all-purpose flour

¼ tsp (1 mL) salt

I HAVE been making brownies for a very long time—first with my mom and then throughout college—to bring as hostess gifts or to stem the all-night essay-writing munchies. The fascination remains to this day. I have a very good friend and fellow recipe developer, Heather Trim, and she and I have had many remarkable conversations exchanging recipes for brownies, discussing the merits of this kind or that kind of chocolate, debating the fudgey school vs. the cakey school and now her daughters are in on the act too. I don't have a daughter to pass this recipe on to but I can tell you that my 16-year-old son adores this recipe and can polish off a good half of it in one sitting. As with most "classic" recipes, this one calls for only unsweetened chocolate.

Preheat the oven to 350°F (180°C). Grease the sides and bottom of an 8-inch (20 cm) square, metal cake pan. Line with parchment paper so that the bottom is covered and there is a 2-inch (5 cm) overhang on 2 sides (see p. 132).

Even though it's always best to melt chocolate in the top of a double boiler set over hot, not boiling water, I find that for these brownies, if you melt the chocolate and the butter together over an extremely low heat, stirring often with a stainless steel spoon, you'll be okay. If you're at all cautious about doing this, feel free to do it in the top of a double boiler—it will be just fine.

That being said, combine the unsweetened chocolate and the butter in a heavy-bottomed saucepan set over very low heat. Cook, stirring often with a spoon, until about three-quarters melted.

Remove from the heat. Continue stirring until both the chocolate and the butter are completely melted. Whisk in the sugar. The mixture should have cooled down quite a bit at this point. One at a time, whisk in the eggs, not too vigorously because you don't want to add too much air. Whisk in the vanilla. Switching to a wooden spoon, stir in the flour and the salt. Transfer the mixture to the prepared cake pan.

Bake in the centre of the preheated oven just until set, 28–30 minutes. Let the brownies cool in the pan on a wire rack for at least 2 hours. Cut into bars (or cut what you need, cover the pan with plastic wrap and store at room temperature for up to 4 days).

RECIPE CONTINUED . . .

VARIATION

FRUIT AND NUT BROWNIES Stir ½ cup (125 mL) golden raisins, ⅓ cup (80 mL) chopped dried apricots and ⅓ cup (80 mL) chopped walnuts into the batter along with the flour. Bake as directed.

BAKER'S TIP

LINING PANS FOR BARS AND SQUARES When making brownies and other bars, always line your pans with enough parchment paper so that some of the parchment paper hangs over on two of the sides by at least 2 inches (5 cm). This leaves you with "handles" to grip when releasing the brownies. I don't like the hassle of making hospital corners to tuck excess parchment paper into the edges of the pan, so I always cut my parchment paper the width of the pan with a good 3-inches (8 cm) excess in length for overhang. I also tend to lightly grease the pan before I put in the parchment, just to be on the safe side. Always let your brownies or bars cool completely before attempting to release them from the pan. Run a knife around the two edges that do not have parchment paper and they will lift out easily.

Bittersweet Brownies

BROWNIES, LIKE almost everything else, change and evolve as time goes on, as tastes mature and become more sophisticated. Brownie recipes from about 15 years ago called for quite a bit more flour. It wasn't at all unusual to see over one cup of all-purpose flour called for in a recipe that only had 4 ounces of semisweet chocolate in it (bittersweet chocolate not even being available at that time). As a result, there was great admonition not to over mix when adding the flour (always with a spoon and heaven's forbid, NEVER a whisk) since any undue action would toughen the brownie batter. This is less true today since the trend of late has been to decrease the amount of flour required, as you will notice in the recipe below. For good measure (no pun intended!), it's still wise to not be too aggressive in your mixing.

8 oz (250 g) bittersweet or semisweet chocolate, coarsely chopped

⅓ cup (80 mL) unsalted butter, softened and cut into pieces (3 oz/90 g)

¾ cup (180 mL) granulated sugar

2 large eggs, at room temperature

1 tsp (5 mL) vanilla

⅓ cup (80 mL) all-purpose flour

¼ tsp (1 mL) salt

Preheat the oven to 350°F (180°C). Grease the sides and bottom of an 8-inch (20 cm) square metal cake pan. Line with parchment paper so that the bottom is covered and there is a 2-inch (5 cm) overhang on 2 sides.

Combine the chocolate and the butter in a heavy-bottomed saucepan set over very low heat or in the top of a double boiler set over hot, not boiling water. Cook, stirring often with a stainless steel spoon, until about three-quarters melted.

Remove from the heat. Continue stirring until both the chocolate and the butter are completely melted. Whisk in the sugar. The mixture should have cooled down quite a bit by this point. One at a time, whisk in the eggs, not too vigorously because you don't want to add too much air. Whisk in the vanilla. Switching to a clean wooden spoon, stir in the flour and the salt. Transfer the mixture to the prepared cake pan.

Bake in the centre of the preheated oven until the centre of the brownies feels almost set, 25–30 minutes. Let the brownies cool in the pan on a wire rack for at least 2 hours. Cut into bars (or cut what you need, cover the pan with plastic wrap and store at room temperature for up to 4 days).

Cocoa Brownies

¾ cup (180 mL) unsalted butter, softened and cut into pieces (6 oz/175 g)

⅔ cup (160 mL) unsweetened Dutch-processed cocoa powder, sifted

1⅓ cups (330 mL) granulated sugar

3 large eggs, at room temperature

2 tsp (10 mL) vanilla

⅓ cup (80 mL) all-purpose flour

¼ tsp (1 mL) salt

I HAVE been such a die-hard chocolate brownie fan that it's taken me years to come up with a cocoa brownie that I can enjoy, let alone one of which I can be proud. This is the one. It is densely chocolate, with no bitter aftertaste and you know the old saw—it pairs beautifully with a cold glass of milk.

Preheat the oven to 325°F (160°C). Grease the sides and bottom of an 8-inch (20 cm) square metal cake pan. Line with parchment paper so that the bottom is covered and there is a 2-inch (5 cm) overhang on 2 sides.

Melt the butter in a heavy-bottomed saucepan set over medium heat until melted and very hot. Remove from the heat. Whisk in the cocoa powder until completely incorporated and smooth. Let the mixture cool slightly.

Whisk the sugar into the cocoa mixture. One at a time, whisk in the eggs, not too vigorously because you don't want to add too much air. Whisk in the vanilla. Switching to a clean wooden spoon, stir in the flour and the salt. Transfer the mixture to the prepared cake pan.

Bake in the centre of the preheated oven until the centre of the brownies feels almost set, 25–30 minutes. Let the brownies cool in the pan on a wire rack for at least 2 hours. Cut into bars (or cut what you need, cover the pan with plastic wrap and store at room temperature for up to 3 days).

BAKER'S TIP

As mentioned on page 36, there are two different kinds of cocoa powder, alkalized and non-alkalized. For most of the recipes in this book, including the Cocoa Brownies, I used an alkalized cocoa powder, namely Fry's cocoa powder, since it is widely available. I would not recommend switching to the natural cocoa powder for this recipe.

Espresso Brownies

IF YOU'RE like me, then you find the combination of chocolate and coffee irresistible. I adore the way the coffee can stand alone, while simultaneously paying homage to its brethren, the chocolate in the recipe. The vanilla also aids in encouraging the essence of both to develop, resulting in a perfect ménage-a-trois. These brownies are dense and fudgey like the first one in this collection.

8 oz (250 g) bittersweet chocolate, coarsely chopped

½ cup (125 mL) unsalted butter, softened and cut into pieces (4 oz/125 g)

1 cup (250 mL) granulated sugar

3 large eggs, at room temperature

2 tsp (10 mL) vanilla

½ cup (125 mL) all-purpose flour

1 Tbsp (15 mL) instant espresso powder

¼ tsp (1 mL) salt

Preheat the oven to 350°F (180°C). Grease the sides and bottom of an 8-inch (20 cm) square metal cake pan. Line with parchment paper so that the bottom is covered and there is a 2-inch (5 cm) overhang on 2 sides.

Combine the chocolate and the butter in a heavy-bottomed saucepan set over very low heat or in the top of a double boiler set over hot, not boiling water. Cook, stirring often with a stainless steel spoon, until about three-quarters melted.

Remove from the heat. Continue stirring until both the chocolate and the butter are completely melted. Whisk in the sugar. The mixture should have cooled down quite a bit by this point. One at a time, whisk in the eggs, not too vigorously because you don't want to add too much air. Whisk in the vanilla. Switching to a clean wooden spoon, stir in the flour, espresso powder and salt. Transfer the mixture to the prepared cake pan.

Bake in the centre of the preheated oven until the centre of the brownies feels almost set, about 25 minutes. Let the brownies cool in the pan on a wire rack for at least 2 hours. Cut into bars (or cut what you need, cover the pan with plastic wrap and store at room temperature for up to 4 days).

BAKER'S TIP

HIGHER PERCENTAGE CHOCOLATES For brownies, excluding unsweetened chocolate, the best percentage for bittersweet chocolate is between 58 and 68%. The higher the percentage of cocoa content, the more sugar you will have to add. You'll also have to adjust the butter. You might find that the brownies ooze a bit of butter on the surface or don't set as much but with experimentation, you'll find your way.

Orange Cranberry Brownies

7 oz (210 g) semisweet chocolate, coarsely chopped

¾ cup (180 mL) unsalted butter, softened and cut into pieces (6 oz/175 g)

1 cup (250 mL) granulated sugar

3 large eggs, at room temperature

1 Tbsp (15 mL) finely grated orange zest (zest of 1 orange)

½ cup (125 mL) all-purpose flour

Pinch of salt

⅔ cup (160 mL) dried cranberries

LIKE RASPBERRIES and chocolate or coffee and chocolate, orange and chocolate is a match that stands the test of time. The orange jazzes up the flavour of the chocolate while the tart cranberries counterweigh its sweetness.

Preheat the oven to 350°F (180°C). Grease the sides and bottom of an 8-inch (20 cm) square metal cake pan. Line with parchment paper so that the bottom is covered and there is a 2-inch (5 cm) overhang on 2 sides.

Combine the chocolate and the butter in a heavy-bottomed saucepan set over very low heat, or in the top of a double boiler set over hot, not boiling water. Cook, stirring often with a stainless steel spoon, until about three-quarters melted.

Remove from the heat. Continue stirring until both the chocolate and the butter are completely melted. Whisk in the sugar. The mixture should have cooled down quite a bit by this point. One at a time, whisk in the eggs, not too vigorously because you don't want to add too much air. Whisk in the orange zest. Switching to a clean wooden spoon, stir in the flour, salt and dried cranberries. Transfer the mixture to the prepared cake pan.

Bake in the centre of the preheated oven until the centre of the brownies feels almost set, 25–28 minutes. Let the brownies cool in the pan on a wire rack for at least 2 hours. Cut into bars (or cut what you need, cover the pan with plastic wrap and store at room temperature for up to 4 days).

Dulce de Leche Cream Cheese Brownies

Unlike the previous recipes, this brownie starts off by creaming the butter with the sugar, a sure sign that it is a cakier brownie—and, yes, it is. However, the method and the proportions of the ingredients also make for a sturdier brownie, one well able to structurally hold up the topping. Although I fall squarely in the fudgey camp in the brownie debate, I make an exception for this tantalizing confection of a dessert.

* * *

Preheat the oven to 350°F (180°C). Grease the sides and bottom of a 13- × 9-inch (33 × 23 cm) square metal cake pan. Line with parchment paper so that the bottom is covered and there is a 2-inch (5 cm) overhang on the 2 long sides.

CREAM CHEESE LAYER In the bowl of a stand mixer fitted with the paddle attachment or using hand-held beaters, beat the cream cheese until fluffy. Scrape down the bowl. Gradually beat in the sugar. Beat, scraping down the sides of the bowl occasionally, until very fluffy, about 3 minutes. Beat in the egg and then the vanilla. Set aside.

BROWNIE LAYER In the top of a double boiler set over hot, not boiling water, melt the semisweet and unsweetened chocolate. Set aside to cool slightly.

In the bowl of a stand mixer fitted with the paddle attachment or using a hand-held mixer, beat the butter with the sugar until light and fluffy, about 3 minutes. One at a time, beat in the eggs, beating well after each egg before adding the next. Beat in the vanilla. Switching to a wooden spoon, stir in the melted and cooled chocolate. Gently stir in the flour and salt. Set aside 1 cup (250 mL) of the batter.

Spread the remaining batter in the prepared pan. Dollop the cream cheese filling evenly over the brownie layer. Evenly pour or dollop (depending on the thickness of your sauce) the dulce de leche sauce over the cream cheese. Dollop the reserved 1 cup (250 mL) of brownie batter over the sauce. Using the blunt edge of a knife, draw the knife gently through the cream cheese, sauce and brownie to make a marbled effect and to even out the layers if necessary.

RECIPE CONTINUED . . .

CREAM CHEESE LAYER

1 lb (500 g) cream cheese, softened (two 250 g pkgs)

⅓ cup (80 mL) granulated sugar

1 large egg, at room temperature

1 tsp (5 mL) vanilla

BROWNIE LAYER

6 oz (175 g) semisweet or bittersweet chocolate, coarsely chopped

3 oz (90 g) unsweetened chocolate, coarsely chopped

1 cup (250 mL) unsalted butter, softened (8 oz/250 g)

1⅔ cups (410 mL) granulated sugar

3 large eggs, at room temperature

2 tsp (10 mL) vanilla

1 cup (250 mL) all-purpose flour

¼ tsp (1 mL) salt

⅓ cup (80 mL) Dulce de Leche (see p. 118)

Bake in the centre of the preheated oven until a cake tester inserted in the centre of the brownies comes out with just a few moist crumbs clinging to it, 30–35 minutes. Let the brownies cool in the pan on a wire rack for at least 2 hours. Refrigerate until firm. Cut into bars (or cut what you need, cover the pan with plastic wrap and store in the refrigerator for up to 3 days).

VARIATION

RASPBERRY JAM CREAM CHEESE BROWNIES Replace the dulce de leche sauce with ½ cup (125 mL) of raspberry jam.

S'more Brownies

CRUST

1⅓ cups (330 mL) graham cracker
   crumbs

⅓ cup (80 mL) unsalted butter,
   melted and cooled (3 oz/90 g)

BROWNIES

6 oz (175 g) semisweet or bittersweet chocolate, coarsely
   chopped

2 oz (60 g) unsweetened chocolate, coarsely chopped

⅓ cup (80 mL) unsalted butter,
   softened and cut into pieces
   (3 oz/90 g)

1 cup (250 mL) granulated sugar

3 large eggs, at room temperature

1 tsp (5 mL) vanilla

⅔ cup (160 mL) all-purpose flour

¼ tsp (1 mL) salt

1 cup (250 mL) mini
   marshmallows

¼ cup (60 mL) milk chocolate or
   semisweet chocolate chips

A HYBRID that combines the best of brownies with the campfire treat, this brownie is not for the faint of heart. I really like the way the graham cracker base melds into the chocolate brownie. The crowning glory, of course, is the sticky, gooey topping that browns ever so slightly in the heat of the oven.

———

Preheat the oven to 325°F (160°C). Grease the sides and bottom of an 8-inch (20 cm) square metal cake pan. Line with parchment paper so that the bottom is covered and there is a 2-inch (5 cm) overhang on 2 sides.

CRUST Place the graham cracker crumbs in a bowl. Drizzle the butter over, tossing with a small fork until the crumbs are thoroughly moistened. Pat evenly onto the bottom of the prepared pan. Bake for 12 minutes or until golden. Let cool slightly

BROWNIES Combine both of the chocolates and the butter in a heavy-bottomed saucepan set over very low heat or in the top of a double boiler set over hot, not boiling water. Cook, stirring often with a stainless steel spoon, until about three-quarters melted.

Remove from the heat. Continue stirring until both the chocolates and the butter are completely melted. Whisk in the sugar. The mixture should have cooled down quite a bit by this point. One at a time, whisk in the eggs, not too vigorously because you don't want to add too much air. Whisk in the vanilla. Switching to a clean wooden spoon, stir in the flour and salt. Transfer the mixture to the prepared cake pan. Sprinkle the marshmallows over the batter and then the chocolate chips.

Bake in the centre of the preheated oven until the centre of the brownies feels almost set, about 35 minutes. Let the brownies cool in the pan on a wire rack for at least 2 hours. Cut into bars (or cut what you need, cover the pan with plastic wrap and store at room temperature for up to 5 days).

VARIATION

SIMPLE S'MORE BROWNIES For an easier version, omit the crust and fold 1 cup (250 mL) of coarsely broken graham crackers into the brownie batter just after folding in the flour and salt. Bake as directed.

Double Chocolate Ganache Brownies *with* Fleur de Sel

YOU COULD, with enough time, goad me into admitting that this brownie recipe gilds the proverbial lily. It's got both semisweet chocolate and cocoa powder, boasts chunks of bittersweet chocolate suspended in the fudgey batter and has a ganache topping, as if all of that chocolate wasn't enough. In my defense, I would say that this brownie is a wonderful study in how one ingredient can fully transform a dessert. The fleur de sel arouses the senses, surprises the taste buds and so cleanly envelops and promotes the chocolate taste that it almost defies belief. Really quite memorable, these brownies will have you converted as soon as you taste them.

Preheat the oven to 350°F (180°C). Grease the sides and bottom of an 8-inch (20 cm) square metal cake pan. Line with parchment paper so that the bottom is covered and there is a 2-inch (5 cm) overhang on 2 sides.

Combine the chocolate, butter and the unsweetened cocoa powder in a heavy-bottomed saucepan set over very low heat or in the top of a double boiler set over hot, not boiling water. Cook, stirring often with a stainless spoon, until about three-quarters melted.

Remove from the heat. Continue stirring until the chocolate, butter and cocoa powder are completely melted. Whisk in the sugar. The mixture should have cooled down quite a bit by this point. One at a time, whisk in the eggs and the egg yolk, not too vigorously because you don't want to add too much air. Whisk in the vanilla. Switching to a clean wooden spoon, stir in the flour, salt and the chocolate chips. Transfer the mixture to the prepared cake pan.

Bake in the centre of the preheated oven until the centre of the brownies feels almost set, about 30 minutes. Let the brownies cool in the pan on a wire rack for at least 2 hours.

GANACHE Once the brownies are completely cooled, bring the whipping cream to a boil in a saucepan set over medium-high heat. Remove from the heat. Immediately add the chopped chocolate. Let stand for 1 minute, then whisk gently until the chocolate is completely melted. Let cool for 5 minutes. Pour the ganache over the brownies, spreading gently so that the brownies are completely covered. Sprinkle with the fleur de sel. Refrigerate for at least 1 hour or for up to 3 days.

RECIPE CONTINUED . . .

6 oz (175 g) semisweet or bittersweet chocolate, coarsely chopped

⅓ cup (80 mL) unsalted butter, softened and cut into pieces (3 oz/90 g)

2 Tbsp (30 mL) unsweetened Dutch-processed cocoa powder, sifted

1 cup (250 mL) granulated sugar

2 large eggs, at room temperature

1 large egg yolk, at room temperature

2 tsp (10 mL) vanilla

⅔ cup (160 mL) all-purpose flour

½ tsp (2 mL) fleur de sel

½ cup (125 mL) chopped bittersweet chocolate or chocolate chips

GANACHE

½ cup (125 mL) whipping cream, at room temperature

4 oz (125 g) bittersweet chocolate, coarsely chopped

¼ tsp (1 mL) fleur de sel or sea salt

BAKER'S TIPS

Brownies freeze exceptionally well. It's best to freeze them whole, however, and not in individual bars. Remove the whole bars from the 8-inch (20 cm) or 13- × 8-inch (33 × 20 cm) pan (which you can cut in half for ease). Wrap the entire brownies in TWO layers of plastic wrap. Then place the whole thing in a freezer bag. Try to find a place in your freezer where the brownies can lay flat. To thaw, place in the refrigerator for at least 8 hours or overnight. Don't forget to bring them to room temperature before you eat them to let the chocolate flavour shine through.

FLEUR DE SEL Fleur de sel is typically used as a finishing salt because of its high cost. Fleur de sel salt is a delicate white salt harvested from the northern Atlantic coast off of France (although some comes from Spain, Portugal and even parts of the United Kingdom). It is usually harvested by hand and only in certain weather conditions (hence the high price tag). Fleur de sel is produced by collecting the thin top layer of salt in shallow pools of sea water or salt marshes. Its name, literally translated as "flower of salt," comes from the aroma of violets that emanates from the salt as it dries. Fleur de sel can be a little moist so it is usually sold in jars. It also dissolves fairly rapidly which is why it's usually added just before serving.

Just for the Fun of It Blondies

BRIMMING WITH goodies, this proves that blondes (oops, I mean blondies) have more fun.

Light golden brown, with a sheer, paper-thin skin on top, these blondies have just enough batter to encase a cup and a half of chocolate bars. They're also great for smaller families like mine, yielding fewer bars than the recipe on page 145. You'll still be tempted in the middle of the night (or the morning or the afternoon for that matter) to sneak down to the kitchen and shave small slivers off the blondie, 'til almost a whole row is gone, telling yourself all the while, "Well, a sliver doesn't really count, a sliver has no calories, does it." We all do it, so it must be true!

The other great thing about this blondie is that it's malleable. It can hold its own against candy bars, chocolate chips, cranberries, chocolate-covered pretzels and the like. To get your imaginative juices flowing, I've listed a few specific variations, but be sure to join in the fun and create your own signature blondie.

Preheat the oven to 350°F (180°C). Lightly grease the sides and bottom of an 8-inch (20 cm) metal cake pan. Line with parchment paper so that the bottom is covered and there is a 2-inch (5 cm) overhang on 2 sides.

Whisk together the flour, baking powder, salt and baking soda in a bowl; set aside.

Melt the butter in a medium saucepan. Remove the pan from the heat and whisk in the sugar until smooth. Whisk in the egg and then the vanilla. Make sure the mixture is not too hot. If it's warm or tepid, you can proceed. If it's really hot, which it shouldn't be, let it cool for 1 or 2 minutes. Using a wooden spoon, stir the flour mixture into the butter mixture, mixing until JUST combined. Fold in the chocolate bars. Scrape the batter—it will be quite thick—into the prepared pan, smoothing the top with the back of a knife

Bake in the centre of the preheated oven until the top is golden brown, sheathed in a papery skin, and a cake tester comes out relatively clean, 25–28 minutes. Cool the bars completely in the pan on a wire rack. Cut into bars (or cut what you need, cover the pan with plastic wrap and store at room temperature for up to 5 days).

1 cup (250 mL) all-purpose flour
½ tsp (2 mL) baking powder
¼ tsp (1 mL) salt
⅛ tsp (0.5 mL) baking soda
½ cup (125 mL) unsalted butter (4 oz/125 g)
1 cup (250 mL) packed light brown sugar
1 large egg, at room temperature
2 tsp (10 mL) vanilla
1½ cups (375 mL) chopped up chocolate bars (whatever your favourite is)

VARIATIONS

THREE CHOCOLATE FUN BLONDIES Replace the chocolate bars with ½ cup (125 mL) semisweet chocolate chips, ½ cup (125 mL) milk chocolate chips and ½ cup (125 mL) white chocolate chips.

FRUIT AND CHOCOLATE FUN BLONDIES Replace the chocolate bars with ¾ cup (180 mL) semisweet chocolate chips and ¾ cup (180 mL) dried cranberries.

CRUNCHY FUN BLONDIES Replace the chocolate bars with 1 cup (250 mL) broken-up chocolate covered pretzels and ½ cup (125 mL) semisweet chocolate chips.

Coconut and Toffee Blondies

I**T TOOK** me some time to really get acquainted with blondies and to appreciate their chewy, brown sugar goodness. I suppose it was because of my devotion to brownies. I just didn't think that a chocolate-less brownie—as sometimes a blondie is known—was worth my time, let alone any effort. How wrong I was. Soft, rich and moist, a blondie is a cross between a pan-baked chocolate chip cookie and a sweet bar made sultry by the inclusion of butter and brown sugar, and it is open to suggestions when it comes to add ins. Because they're so moist and soft, they're good keepers: store them packed between layers of waxed paper in an airtight container at room temperature and you'll be enjoying their comforts for as long as 5 days. However, if you find yourself carving away at them in the middle of the night, they're equally happy tucked away in the freezer, contentedly waiting your next visit. In this rendition, I've opted to substitute some of the brown sugar with granulated sugar to make it a little less sweet and a little less gooey. Let's face it, I'm a total convert.

2 cups (500 mL) all-purpose flour

1 tsp (5 mL) baking powder

½ tsp (2 mL) salt

1 cup (250 mL) unsalted butter, softened (8 oz/250 g)

1 cup (250 mL) packed light brown sugar

⅔ cup (160 mL) granulated sugar

2 large eggs, at room temperature

2 tsp (10 mL) vanilla

1 cup (250 mL) semisweet chocolate chips

1 cup (250 mL) Skor bits

¾ cup (180 mL) shredded coconut or coarsely chopped peanuts

½ cup (125 mL) white chocolate chips

Preheat the oven to 325°F (160°C). Lightly grease the sides and bottom of a 13- × 9-inch (33 × 23 cm) metal cake pan. Line with parchment paper so that the bottom is covered and there is a 2-inch (5 cm) overhang on the 2 long sides.

Whisk together the flour, baking powder and salt in a bowl; set aside.

In the bowl of a stand mixer fitted with the paddle attachment, or using a hand-held mixer, cream the butter with the sugars until light and fluffy. Scrape down the bowl. One at a time, beat in the eggs, making sure the first one is incorporated before adding the second. Scrape down the bowl. Beat in the vanilla.

Add the flour mixture, semisweet chocolate chips, Skor bits, coconut (or peanuts) and white chocolate chips. Mix on low speed just until all of the additions are incorporated. Scrape the mixture into the prepared pan, smoothing the top.

Bake in the centre of the preheated oven until a cake tester inserted in the centre of the blondies comes out clean, about 35 minutes. Let the blondies cool in the pan on a wire rack for at least 2 hours. Cut into bars (or cut what you need, cover the pan with plastic wrap and store at room temperature for up to 5 days).

Peanutty Peanut Butter Bars

1 cup + 3 Tbsp (295 mL)
    all-purpose flour

¾ tsp (4 mL) baking powder

Pinch of salt

½ cup (125 mL) unsalted butter,
    softened (4 oz/125 g)

⅓ cup (80 mL) smooth peanut
    butter (not natural)

1 cup (250 mL) packed light brown
    sugar

1 large egg, at room temperature

1 large egg yolk, at room
    temperature

1 tsp (5 mL) vanilla

4 bars (46 g each) Reese's Peanut
    Butter Cups, cut into pieces (or
    16 mini cups, kept whole)

⅓ cup (80 mL) Skor bits

⅓ cup (80 mL) coarsely chopped
    roasted salted peanuts

THESE CHEWY bars are generously endowed with all things peanut butter—the real McCoy (as in peanut butter), chocolate-covered peanut butter cups and salted peanuts. I've thrown in some caramel bits for crunch, too.

Preheat the oven to 350°F (180°C). Grease the sides and bottom of an 8-inch (20 cm) square metal cake pan. Line with parchment paper so that the bottom is covered and there is a 2-inch (5 cm) overhang on 2 sides.

Whisk together the flour, baking powder and salt in a small bowl; set aside.

In the bowl of a stand mixer fitted with the paddle attachment, or using a hand-held mixer, beat together the butter, peanut butter and brown sugar until light and fluffy. Beat in the egg and then the egg yolk, scraping down the bowl in between. Beat in the vanilla.

Add the flour mixture to the butter mixture along with the chunks of peanut butter cups, Skor bits and peanuts. Mix on low speed just until incorporated. Scrape the mixture into the prepared pan, smoothing the top.

Bake in the centre of the preheated oven until golden brown and set, 30–35 minutes. Let the bars cool in the pan on a wire rack for at least 2 hours. Cut into bars (or cut what you need, cover the pan with plastic wrap and store at room temperature for up to 4 days).

Caramelita Bars

I KNOW mothers and authors are not supposed to play favourites, but if I'm perfectly honest, this is one of my very favourite bars. I love the oatiness of the base and topping, revel in the richness of the caramel filling and swoon when I think of how the chocolate melts into the amber coloured caramel. I made these bars for my friend, Cindy Nathan, who was having a party for her husband's 50th birthday. Unfortunately, my husband and I couldn't make the party, but the day after, Cindy called me and said that her guests, who virtually ignored all the other desserts arranged decoratively on her dessert table, devoured these treats and then promptly spent the night discussing how good they were. Now I know my friend Cindy and she might have exaggerated a teensy bit, but they really are that good.

The caramel in this recipe yields about 2 cups (500 mL). Yes, of course, you can buy readymade caramel and use it as an alternative, but the homemade version is so luxurious and sublime that I urge you to try your hand at making it. Don't be tempted to bake these bars longer than 15 minutes, the filling should ooze ever so slightly.

Quick oats or a combination of large flake (old fashioned) and quick oats are fine.

CARAMEL Make the caramel first. In a heavy-bottomed saucepan set over low heat, combine the sugar and corn syrup with ½ cup (125 mL) water. Cook gently until the sugar dissolves. Increase the heat to medium-high and bring to a boil. Reduce heat to medium and boil without stirring but brushing down the sides of the pan with a brush dipped in cold water, until the mixture turns a deep amber colour, 5–8 minutes. Averting your face (to avoid any sputtering caramel), pour the cream into the saucepan. Add in the butter. Cook, stirring constantly, until the mixture stops boiling and the caramel is smooth. Remove from the heat and let cool at room temperature for at least 1 hour or until thickened.

Meanwhile, preheat the oven to 350°F (180°C). Lightly grease the sides and bottom of a 13- × 9-inch (33 ×23 cm) metal cake pan. Line with parchment paper so that the bottom is covered and there is a 2-inch (5 cm) overhang on the 2 long sides.

RECIPE CONTINUED . . .

CARAMEL

2 cups (500 mL) granulated sugar

1 Tbsp (15 mL) light corn syrup

½ cup (125 mL) water

¾ cup (180 mL) whipping cream, at room temperature

2 Tbsp (30 mL) unsalted butter, softened (1 oz/30 g)

CRUST AND TOPPING

2 cups (500 mL) rolled oats

1⅔ cups (410 mL) all-purpose flour

¾ cup (180 mL) packed light brown sugar

½ tsp (2 mL) baking soda

¼ tsp (1 mL) salt

¾ cup (180 mL) unsalted butter, melted and cooled (6 oz/175 g)

1 cup (250 mL) semisweet chocolate chips

1 cup (250 mL) chopped walnuts

CRUST AND TOPPING In a large bowl, combine the oats, flour, sugar, baking soda and salt. Pour the melted butter over the dry mixture, stirring with a fork until the mixture is thoroughly moistened and starts to clump together. Transfer 1 heaping cup (250+ mL) of the mixture to a separate bowl; set aside.

Press the remainder of the oat mixture evenly into the base of the prepared cake pan. Bake in the centre of the preheated oven until the crust is golden, 20–25 minutes. Remove the pan from the oven. Spread the cooled caramel over the base without disturbing it too much. Sprinkle with the chocolate chips and the walnuts. Sprinkle the reserved oat mixture over the surface.

Bake for an additional 15 minutes or until the topping is JUST starting to turn golden. Let the bars cool in the pan on a wire rack for at least 2 hours. Run a small paring knife around the edges of the pan to loosen. Lift out using the parchment paper. Cut into bars (or cut what you need, cover the pan with plastic wrap and store at room temperature for up to 5 days).

BAKER'S TIPS
Adding corn syrup (or some lemon juice) to the caramelizing sugar helps prevent crystallization.

This recipe is a good example of how introducing other ingredients changes the nature of caramelized sugar. Add some whipping cream and you have a caramel sauce. Add some butter and whipping cream, and you have a butterscotch sauce.

COOKING SUGAR

Armed with a candy thermometer and nimble fingers, you can tell when the sugar reaches different stages:

1. Thread Stage (223–234°F/106–112°C): At this stage not very much of the water has evaporated and it is mostly a syrup, the kind you might use to make an Italian meringue or use as the base of lemonade. When you drop a little of this syrup into cold water, it will form liquid threads. It will not yet ball up.

2. Soft Ball Stage (235–240°F/113–116°C): A lot more of the water has cooked off by now, so that when you pinch together some of the sugar between your fingers or drop some on some cold water, it will form a soft, flexible ball. If you hold it for a few minutes longer, it will actually flatten in the palm of your hand.

3. Firm Ball Stage (242–248°F/117–120°C): At this temperature, a small amount of sugar should form a firm ball, one that doesn't flatten into a pancake after a few minutes of holding it.

4. Hard Ball Stage (250–268°F/121–131°C): Just a little hotter and the sugar forms ropy threads if you hold a wooden spoon covered with the sugar above the saucepan. If you drop some of the sugar into cold water it will form a hard ball and, although hard, you will still be able to manipulate its shape.

5. Soft Crack Stage (270–290°F/132–143°C): Sugar brought to this stage can be used for salt water taffy and butterscotch. Sugar dropped into water will at this stage solidify into flexible strands or threads.

6. Hard Crack Stage (295–310°F/146–154°C): the highest temperature you are likely to need, sugar at this stage will form hard brittle threads or balls. Typically used for making lollipops and other hard candies.

7. Caramel Stage (320–360°F/160–182°C): At this stage, the sugar will start to change colour, starting with a light golden brown and progressing to a dark amber.

Chocolate Chip Cookie Bars

2 cups (500 mL) all-purpose flour

½ tsp (2 mL) baking soda

½ tsp (2 mL) salt

¾ cup (180 mL) unsalted butter, softened (6 oz/175 g)

1 cup (250 mL) packed light brown sugar

½ cup (125 mL) granulated sugar

1 large egg, at room temperature

1 large egg yolk, at room temperature

1 tsp (5 mL) vanilla

2⅓ (580 mL) cups semisweet chocolate chips

DID YOU know that the original chocolate chip cookie is said to have been baked in 1937 in Massachusetts by Ruth Wakefield? Ruth and her husband owned a lodge called the Toll House Inn. She made cookies for her guests and one day chopped up a Nestle chocolate bar to add to her cookie dough. The story is that Mrs. Wakefield expected the chocolate to melt in the cookie. Instead it held its shape and a star was born. As the popularity of the cookie grew, demand for Nestle chocolate bars soared. Ruth Wakefield sold the rights to the recipe to Nestle and received free chocolate for life. Can you imagine? Free chocolate for life? What I wouldn't give for that kind of trade. But I digress.

What I really love about this recipe is that it's a cross between a moist and chewy blondie and a chocolate chip cookie. What shape you cut them into or how you serve them is entirely up to you. I have been known to cut out pieces in the shape of hearts, letters and even butterflies. The best part of cutting them into shapes is that there are tons of irregularly shaped pieces lying around just dying to be eaten. Regardless of the shape, they never last very long in my house.

Preheat the oven to 325°F (160°C). Line a 13- × 9-inch (33 × 23 cm) metal cake pan with parchment paper so that the bottom is covered and there is a 2-inch (5 cm) overhang on the 2 long sides.

Whisk together the flour, baking soda and salt in a bowl; set aside.

In the bowl of a stand mixer fitted with the paddle attachment, or using a hand-held mixer, beat the butter for 1 minute. Beat in the sugars until the mixture is quite light, about 3 minutes. Scrape down the dough. Beat in the egg, egg yolk and vanilla. Remove the bowl from the stand.

Using a wooden spoon, stir the flour mixture into the butter mixture, in 2 additions. Stir in the chocolate chips.

Flouring your hands if necessary, pat the dough into the prepared baking pan, making it as even as possible.

Bake in the centre of the preheated oven until lightly golden and set around the edges, 28–30 minutes. Let the bars cool in the pan on a wire rack for at least 1 hour. Cut into bars (or cut what you need, cover the pan with plastic wrap and store at room temperature for up to 5 days).

Caffe Latte Chocolate Chip Squares

EVEN THOUGH the name may suggest that this recipe is simply the recipe that precedes it with some coffee thrown in, that's not the case. These bars are thinner, crispier and meant more for adults and a cup of tea or java than for kids and a cup of milk. Since it's so crisp you might anticipate the recipe calling for granulated sugar or at least a combination of white and brown sugar. Yet, I have called for only the latter since it pairs so beautifully with the coffee and the chocolate. I don't crush the instant coffee granules as I admire the way they fleck the squares. In this instance, it's not wise to substitute espresso powder which is much finer.

2 cups (500 mL) all-purpose flour

½ tsp (2 mL) baking powder

¼ tsp (1 mL) salt

1 cup (250 mL) unsalted butter, softened (8 oz/250 g)

1 cup (250 mL) packed light brown sugar

1 tsp (5 mL) vanilla

2 Tbsp (30 mL) instant coffee granules (not espresso)

¼ tsp (1 mL) cinnamon

1¼ cups (310 mL) semisweet chocolate chips

Preheat the oven to 350°F (180°C). Line a 13- × 9-inch (33 × 23 cm) metal cake pan with parchment paper so that the bottom is covered and there is a 2-inch (5 cm) overhang on the 2 long sides.

Whisk together the flour, baking powder and salt in a bowl; set aside.

In the bowl of a stand mixer fitted with the paddle attachment, or using a hand-held mixer, beat the butter for 1 minute. Beat in the brown sugar until quite light. Beat in the vanilla, coffee granules and cinnamon, beating until the granules are well broken up and the mixture is a light mocha colour.

Reduce the mixer speed to low. Add the flour mixture and mix just until almost all of it is incorporated. Add the chocolate chips; mix until just incorporated and no flour streaks remain.

By handfuls, flouring your hands if necessary, pat the mixture into the prepared pan.

Bake in the centre of the preheated oven until golden brown all over and firm to the touch, 20–25 minutes. Let the bars cool in the pan on a wire rack. Cut while still warm into squares. (These actually store better layered between sheets of waxed paper in a cookie tin at room temperature, for up to 4 days.)

Three Nut Brittle Squares

BASE

½ cup (125 mL) unsalted butter, softened (4 oz/125 g)

½ cup (125 mL) packed light brown sugar

1 large egg, at room temperature

1 egg yolk, at room temperature

1 tsp (5 mL) vanilla

2¼ cups (560 mL) all-purpose flour

BRITTLE TOPPING

⅓ cup (80 mL) clear corn syrup

½ cup (125 mL) packed light brown sugar

¼ cup (60 mL) unsalted butter, cubed (2 oz/60 g)

¼ cup (60 mL) whipping cream, at room temperature

1¼ cups (310 mL) roasted salted peanuts

½ cup (125 mL) whole cashews

½ cup (125 mL) shelled salted pistachios

1 tsp (5 mL) vanilla

GLAZE

6 oz (175 g) semisweet chocolate, coarsely chopped

2 Tbsp (30 mL) butter (1 oz/30 g)

W HEN I was attending chef's school, living in San Fransisco was like a dream writ large, a veritable smorgasbord of new experiences and new challenges. At school, I learned the intricacies of building a masterful soufflé and the depth of a dish made with a browned roux. In my free time, I explored incredible restaurants and the nooks and crannies of the grande dame of a city, finding hidden vistas, remarkable architecture and the history of Cuban immigration in a two block radius. Then, as now, San Francisco was a mecca of gastronomy, leading the focus on local, seasonal and regional. There was a bakery near where I lived, at the intersection of Polk and Union, that exclusively sold baked goods with nuts in them, and what a tempting variety they were. My roommate, Cathy Byrd, and I would drop in at the bakery every weekend and come away with boxes of nut sables, rum-drenched raisin and nut tarts and almond-filled danishes. With longing, I remember their nut bars, sweet and salty, so I simply had to develop a recipe that comes close to the ones they perfected.

Preheat the oven to 350°F (180°C). Lightly grease the sides and bottom of a 13- × 9-inch (33 × 23 cm) metal cake pan with parchment paper so that the bottom is covered and there is a 2-inch (5 cm) overhang on the 2 long sides.

BASE In the bowl of a stand mixer fitted with the paddle attachment, or using a hand-held mixer, beat the butter for 1 minute. Beat in the brown sugar until quite light, about 3 minutes. Beat in the egg, beating until fully incorporated before adding the egg yolk. Beat in the vanilla. Remove the bowl from the stand.

Using a wooden spoon, stir in the flour just until a dough is formed.

Press the dough into the bottom of the prepared pan. Refrigerate for 15 minutes.

Prick the entire surface of the dough with the tines of a fork. Bake in the centre of the preheated oven until the pastry is lightly golden, about 20 minutes.

RECIPE CONTINUED . . .

BRITTLE TOPPING Meanwhile, combine the corn syrup and brown sugar in a heavy saucepan. Heat over low heat, stirring, until the brown sugar is dissolved. Stir in the butter and cream. Increase the heat to high. Bring to a rolling boil. Boil for 30 seconds. Immediately remove the pot from the heat. Stir in the peanuts, cashews, pistachios and vanilla, stirring until all of the nuts are well coated. Pour the mixture over the still warm crust, spreading it evenly.

Bake until bubbly and golden, 15–20 minutes. Let the bars cool in the pan on a wire rack until completely cool.

GLAZE Once the bars are cool, melt the chocolate and butter together in the top of a double boiler set over hot, not boiling water, until melted and smooth. Cut the bars on the long side into eighths, and then across into fourths for a total of 24 pieces. Dip each bar into the warm chocolate mixture, coating it about one-third of the way up. Let cool on parchment paper–lined cooling rack. (Bars can be stored at room temperature, separated by pieces of waxed paper, in a cookie tin for up to 4 days.)

Pecan Pie Bars

THERE USED to be a commercial for a candy bar that sang, "Sometimes you feel like a nut, sometimes you don't." Now that I think of it, I suppose it was Almond Joy and Mounds, apparently one coming with nuts and one without. I don't know, I've never tasted them, but for some reason, the tune has always stuck with me. I found myself humming it when I created this recipe. Obviously, you can't take the pecans out of this bar or there would be no point. Rather, the jingle made me think, sometimes you feel like a piece of pie, sometimes you don't. When you don't, a smaller piece of this delectable bar fits the bill perfectly.

Preheat the oven to 350°F (180°C). Grease the sides and bottom of a 13- × 9-inch (33 × 23 cm) metal cake pan. Line with parchment paper so that the bottom is covered and there is a 2-inch (5 cm) overhang on the 2 long sides.

CRUST In the bowl of a stand mixer fitted with the paddle attachment, or using a hand-held mixer, beat the butter for 1 minute. Beat in the icing sugar until quite light, about 3 minutes. On the lowest possible speed, add the flour, baking powder and salt, mixing just until incorporated. Grab a handful of dough and knead slightly, if necessary, until it comes together; pat evenly into the bottom of the prepared pan. Repeat until all of the dough is used. Bake in the centre of the preheated oven until the pastry is lightly golden, about 20 minutes. Let cool for 15 minutes.

FILLING Meanwhile, whisk together the brown sugar, corn syrup, butter, eggs and vanilla in a bowl. Whisk in the pecans. Pour the mixture over the cooled crust, tilting the pan so that the filling evens out and the nuts are evenly distributed.

Bake until bubbly and golden, 25–30 minutes. Let the bars cool in the pan on a wire rack for at least 2 hours. Cut into bars (or cut what you need, cover the pan with plastic wrap and store at room temperature for up to 4 days).

CRUST

1 cup (250 mL) unsalted butter, softened (8 oz/250 g)
⅔ cup (160 mL) icing sugar
2 cups (500 mL) all-purpose flour
¼ tsp (1 mL) baking powder
¼ tsp (1 mL) salt

FILLING

1 cup (250 mL) packed light brown sugar
⅔ cup (160 mL) clear corn syrup
⅓ cup (80 mL) melted unsalted butter (3 oz/90 g)
2 large eggs, at room temperature
2 tsp (10 mL) vanilla
2 cups (500 mL) pecan pieces

Pecan Toffee Bars

CRUST

2 cups (500 mL) all-purpose flour

½ cup (125 mL) granulated sugar

Pinch of salt

¾ cup (180 mL) cold unsalted
butter, in pieces (6 oz/175 g)

3 Tbsp (45 mL) cold water

FILLING

4 large eggs, at room temperature

1 cup (250 mL) granulated sugar

1 cup (250 mL) golden corn syrup

¼ cup (60 mL) unsalted butter,
melted and cooled (2 oz/60 g)

1 pkg (225 g) chocolate-covered
caramels, halved if very large
(about 1¼ cups/310 mL)

1½ cups (375 mL) coarsely chopped
pecans

A GOOD friend of mine, Heather Trim, tested all of the recipes in this chapter to make sure that they worked in her kitchen and that I hadn't inadvertently left out any of the major ingredients. As a matter of a fact, she made so many bars that her family actually got tired of eating sweets—can you imagine? So she roped in some of her neighbours, handing out treats with a few pointed questions. The results? This bar came back with a roar of approval. I cut the chocolate-covered caramels in half so they would be better distributed, but that's optional.

Preheat the oven to 350°F (180°C). Grease the sides and bottom of a 13- × 9-inch (33 × 23 cm) metal cake pan. Line with parchment paper so that the bottom is covered and there is a 2-inch (5 cm) overhang on the 2 long sides.

CRUST Whisk together the flour, sugar and salt in a large bowl. With a pastry cutter or 2 knives, cut the butter in until the mixture resembles coarse meal. Drizzle 3 Tbsp (45 mL) cold water over the mixture, stirring with a fork just until the mixture is thoroughly moistened. Working with handfuls of dough at a time, knead the dough gently until it comes together. Pat evenly onto the bottom of the prepared pan.

Bake in the centre of the preheated oven until golden, about 20 minutes.

FILLING Meanwhile, whisk together the eggs, sugar, corn syrup and butter. Stir in the caramels and pecans, lightly spreading them so the mixture is even.

Pour the filling over the baked crust. Return to the oven and bake until the filling has started to turn golden and is set, 30–35 minutes. Let the bars cool in the pan on a wire rack for at least 2 hours. Cut into bars (or cut what you need, cover the pan with plastic wrap and store at room temperature for up to 5 days).

Caramel Almond Cherry Shortbread Bars

THE BUTTERY shortbread crust is tender, yet still strong enough to support the honey-based caramel that encases the cherries and almonds. I love making these as hostess gifts around the holidays. They cut beautifully and look gorgeous nestled together in a gift box.

Preheat the oven to 350°F (180°C). Lightly grease the sides and bottom of a 13- × 9-inch (33 × 23 cm) metal cake pan. Line with parchment paper so that the bottom is covered and there is a 2-inch (5 cm) overhang on the 2 long sides.

CRUST In the bowl of a stand mixer fitted with the paddle attachment, or using a hand-held mixer, beat the butter for 1 minute. Beat in the brown sugar until fluffy. On the lowest possible speed, add the flour and salt, mixing just until incorporated. Working with handfuls of dough at a time, knead the dough gently until it comes together. Pat evenly onto the bottom of the prepared pan.

Bake in the centre of the preheated oven for 20 minutes.

FILLING In a heavy-bottomed saucepan set over medium-high heat, combine the sugar and honey with ¼ cup (60 mL) water; bring to a boil. Reduce heat to medium and boil, without stirring but brushing down the sides of the pan with a brush dipped in cold water, until the mixture turns a deep amber colour, 5–8 minutes. Averting your face (to avoid any sputtering caramel), pour the cream and butter into the saucepan. Cook, stirring constantly, over low heat until the mixture stops boiling and the caramel is smooth.

Remove from the heat. Stir in the almonds, cherries and orange zest, if using. Pour the mixture over the crust, lightly spreading it so that it is even.

Bake until bubbling and golden, about 20 minutes. Let the bars cool in the pan on a wire rack for at least 2 hours. Cut into bars (or cut what you need, cover the pan with plastic wrap and store at room temperature for up to 4 days).

CRUST

1 cup (250 mL) unsalted butter, softened (8 oz/250 g)
⅔ cup (160 mL) packed light brown sugar
2¼ cups (560 mL) all-purpose flour
Pinch of salt

FILLING

1¼ cups (310 mL) granulated sugar
¼ cup (60 mL) honey
1 cup (250 mL) whipping cream, at room temperature
2 Tbsp (30 mL) unsalted butter, softened (1 oz/30 g)
2 cups (500 mL) sliced almonds
1 cup (250 mL) dried cherries
1 Tbsp (15 mL) finely grated orange zest (optional)

Seven-Layer Bars
with Marshmallows *and* Dried Cranberries

THESE BARS have been around forever, and are sometimes called magic bars, Hello Dolly bars or seven-layer bars. This particular variation sports marshmallows—which melt into a gooey, sticky crater—as well as tart dried cranberries and coconut. It's an extravaganza in your mouth. What is even more impressive is that they're incredibly quick to assemble and bake. These are the reason I always have sweetened condensed milk in my pantry.

Preheat the oven to 350°F (180°C). Lightly grease the sides and bottom of a 13- ×9-inch (33 ×23 cm) metal cake pan. Line with parchment paper so that the bottom is covered and there is a 2-inch (5 cm) overhang on the 2 long sides.

Place the graham cracker crumbs into a bowl. Pour the melted butter over the crumbs, stirring with a fork until thoroughly combined. Pat the moistened crumbs into an even layer on the bottom of the prepared cake pan.

Drizzle one-third of the sweetened condensed milk over the base. Then sprinkle with the marshmallows, pecans, cranberries, chocolate chips and coconut, in that order. Drizzle the remainder of the sweetened condensed milk over top.

Bake in the centre of the preheated oven until lightly browned, about 25–30 minutes. Let the bars cool in the pan on a wire rack for at least 2 hours. Cut into bars (or cut what you need, cover the pan with plastic wrap and store at room temperature for up to 5 days).

2½ cups (625 mL) graham wafer crumbs

¾ cup (180 mL) unsalted butter, melted (6 oz/175 g)

1 can (300 mL) sweetened condensed milk

1 cup (250 mL) mini marshmallows

1 cup (250 mL) coarsely chopped pecans

1 cup (250 mL) dried cranberries

¾ cup (180 mL) semisweet chocolate chips

¾ cup (180 mL) shredded sweetened coconut

Pucker Up Bars

CRUST

1 cup (250 mL) all-purpose flour

⅓ cup (80 mL) granulated sugar

Pinch of salt

½ cup (125 mL) cold unsalted
   butter, in pieces (4 oz/125 g)

FILLING

4 large eggs, at room temperature

1 cup (250 mL) granulated sugar

1 Tbsp (15 mL) finely grated lemon
   zest

¼ cup (60 mL) freshly squeezed
   lemon juice (about 1 lemon)

1 tsp (5 mL) finely grated lime zest

¼ cup (60 mL) freshly squeezed
   lime juice (about 2 limes)

Pinch of salt

3 Tbsp (45 mL) all-purpose flour

TOPPING

2 Tbsp (30 mL) icing sugar

MANY LEMON bars call for you to make curd but I prefer the way this baked lemon filling contrasts with the buttery shortbread crust in your mouth. A microplane or zester comes in really handy here; grate the zest only and try not to get any of white pith underneath, it's bitter. If you have any bars left, don't let the plastic wrap touch the lemon filling while you store the bars or it will pull some of it away.

Preheat the oven to 350°F (180°C). Grease the sides and bottom of an 8-inch (20 cm) square metal cake pan. Line with parchment paper so that the bottom is covered and there is a 2-inch (5 cm) overhang on 2 sides.

CRUST Combine the flour, sugar and salt in a bowl. Using a pastry cutter or 2 knives, cut in the butter until the mixture resembles coarse meal. Gathering bits of the dough together in your hands and kneading gently, press the dough into the bottom of the prepared pan. Chill for 20 minutes. This step is quite important not only to relax the gluten but to make sure that your base doesn't shrink. If it shrinks, then some of the lemon filling will flow underneath the crust, meaning you have less on top.

Bake in the centre of the preheated oven until golden, 15–18 minutes.

FILLING Meanwhile, in the bowl of an electric mixer fitted with the whisk attachment, or using a hand-held mixer, beat together the eggs, sugar, lemon zest and juice, lime zest and juice and salt for about 5 minutes or until somewhat pale. On low speed, beat in the flour. Pour over the hot crust, making sure you include whatever zest has stuck to the beaters.

Bake in the centre of the oven until the filling is just set, 25–30 minutes. Let the bars cool in the pan on a wire rack for at least 2 hours. Once cooled, dust with icing sugar. Cut into bars (or cut what you need, cover the pan with plastic wrap and store at room temperature for up to 3 days).

Crumble Bumble Bar

FILLING

2½ cups (625 mL) fresh blueberries, divided

½ cup (125 mL) granulated sugar

⅓ cup (80 mL) freshly squeezed
 lime juice

1 Tbsp (15 mL) cornstarch

1 cup (250 mL) fresh raspberries

2 tsp (10 mL) finely grated lime
 zest

BASE AND TOPPING

2 cups (500 mL) large flake
 rolled oats

¾ cup (180 mL) all-purpose flour

⅔ cup (160 mL) packed light
 brown sugar

¼ tsp (1 mL) salt

¾ cup (180 mL) unsalted butter,
 melted and cooled (6 oz/175 g)

I MIGHT be stretching the definition a bit by calling this a bar, because you really have to plate it and eat it with a fork, but these kind of bars rank right up there for me. If it's got fruit and an oat-y topping, I'm going to love it. I had actually intended to call these the rather boring and non-descript Blueberry Raspberry Lime Bars. After I made them, though, my sister Noni and I were plowing our way through a portion and laughing about how I kept calling it a crumble and the filling a bubble or bumble of freshness, and she said, that's what you should call it. So I did.

FILLING Combine 2 cups (500 mL) of the blueberries, sugar, lime juice and cornstarch in a saucepan. Set the saucepan over medium-high heat and bring to a boil, stirring often. Reduce the heat and simmer, stirring often, for about 5 minutes or until the mixture is thickened. Remove from the heat. Stir in the remainder of the blueberries, the raspberries and lime zest. Transfer the mixture to a bowl and refrigerate until thoroughly chilled, about 1 hour.

Meanwhile, preheat the oven to 350°F (180°C). Grease the sides and bottom of an 8-inch (20 cm) square metal cake pan. Line with parchment paper so that the bottom is covered and there is a 2-inch (5 cm) overhang on 2 sides.

BASE In a large bowl, stir together the oats, flour, sugar and salt. Drizzle the melted butter over the dry ingredients, stirring with a fork until thoroughly moistened. Pat just a bit more than half of the mixture into the bottom of the prepared pan. Spread the filling evenly over the crust. Sprinkle with the remaining oat mixture.

Bake in the centre of the preheated oven until the filling is bubbling and the topping is golden, about 30 minutes. Let the bars cool in the pan on a wire rack for at least 2 hours. Refrigerate for at least 1 hour. Cut into bars (or cut what you need, cover the pan with plastic wrap and keep refrigerated for up to 3 days).

Apple Cheesecake Bars

THIS IS a type of bar you can nibble on using your hands or even serve as a more sophisticated plated dessert. You probably didn't know that you needed this chameleon bar in your repertoire, but once you've tried it, you'll find that you keep on making it.

The crust has more sugar than you might expect, but the brown sugar helps tone down the slight tang of the cream cheese and bring out the flavour of the apples. I like to use an apple that will hold its shape but still has some tartness.

Preheat the oven to 350°F (180°C). Grease the sides and bottom of an 8-inch (20 cm) square metal cake pan. Line with parchment paper so that the bottom is covered and there is a 2-inch (5 cm) overhang on 2 sides.

CRUST In the bowl of a stand mixer fitted with the paddle attachment, or using a hand-held mixer, beat the butter with the sugars until light and fluffy. Add the flour and salt; on low speed, beat until the mixture is just crumbly.

Transfer a heaping ½ cup (125+ mL) of the crumbly dough to a separate bowl; set aside.

Gathering bits of the dough together in your hands and kneading gently, press the dough into the bottom of the prepared pan. Bake in the centre of the preheated oven until golden, 15–18 minutes. Let cool slightly on a wire rack. Reduce the oven heat to 325°F (160°C).

FILLING In a clean bowl of a stand mixer fitted with the paddle attachment, or using a hand-held mixer, beat the cream cheese with the granulated sugar and cinnamon until very fluffy. Scrape down the bowl well, so that there are no unbeaten clumps of cream cheese on the bottom. Beat in the egg. Scrape down the bowl; beat in the vanilla. Remove the bowl from the stand. Stir in the flour.

Arrange the apple slices, slightly overlapping, on top of the warm crust. Pour the cream cheese mixture evenly over the apples. Stir the 2 Tbsp (30 mL) of brown sugar for topping into the reserved ½ cup (125 mL) of crumbly dough. Sprinkle over the cheesecake filling.

Bake in the centre of the oven until the cheesecake is just set in the centre, about 30 minutes. Let the bars cool completely in the pan on a wire rack for at least 2 hours. Refrigerate for at least 2 hours or for up to 24 hours before cutting into bars.

CRUST

½ cup (125 mL) unsalted butter, softened (4 oz/125 g)
¼ cup (60 mL) granulated sugar
¼ cup (60 mL) packed light brown sugar
1¼ cups (310 mL) all-purpose flour
Pinch of salt

FILLING

12 oz (350 g) cream cheese, softened
⅔ cup (160 mL) granulated sugar
¼ tsp (1 mL) cinnamon
1 large egg, at room temperature
1 tsp (5 mL) vanilla
1 tsp (5 mL) all-purpose flour
1 apple, peeled, cut into quarters and thinly sliced

TOPPING

2 Tbsp (30 mL) light brown sugar

Extra Thick Date Squares

FILLING

2 cups (500 mL) packed pitted
  Medjool dates
  (about 10 oz/300 g)

½ cup (125 mL) water

½ cup (125 mL) freshly squeezed
  orange juice

2 Tbsp (30 mL) light brown sugar

1 Tbsp (15 mL) finely grated
  orange zest

1 tsp (5 mL) vanilla

BASE AND TOPPING

2 cups (500 mL) large flake
  rolled oats

1 cup (250 mL) all-purpose flour

1 cup (250 mL) packed light brown
  sugar

1 tsp (5 mL) baking soda

Pinch of salt

1 cup (250 mL) unsalted butter,
  softened, cubed (8 oz/250 g)

I HAVE tasted my fair share of date squares, ones with almost no filling but tons of crumb, ones that are too sweet and ones that are not sweet enough. My overriding feeling about date squares, though, is that if there's not a rockin' thick layer of pureed dates in the centre, why bother? Cooking the dates with orange juice lends a subtle trace of citrus to the filling and prevents too much sweetness.

———

FILLING Combine the dates, water, orange juice, and sugar in a heavy-bottomed saucepan set over medium-high heat. Bring to a boil, stirring. Reduce heat and simmer, stirring occasionally to break down the dates, until the filling is very thick, 10–20 minutes depending on the freshness of your dates. Remove from the heat; stir in the orange zest and vanilla. Set aside to cool for 30 minutes.

Meanwhile, preheat the oven to 350°F (180°C). Grease the sides and bottom of an 8-inch (20 cm) square metal cake pan. Line with parchment paper so that the bottom is covered and there is a 2-inch (5 cm) overhang on 2 sides.

BASE AND TOPPING Combine the oats, flour, sugar, soda and salt in a large bowl. Add the butter, working it into the mixture with your fingertips until the mixture is thoroughly moistened and starting to clump together. Press just over half of the mixture into the bottom of the prepared pan. Spread the date filling evenly over the base. Sprinkle the remaining oat mixture evenly over top.

Bake in the centre of the preheated oven until the topping is golden, about 30 minutes. Let the bars cool in the pan on a wire rack for at least 2 hours. Cut into bars (or cut what you need, cover the pan with plastic wrap and store at room temperature for up to 4 days).

Nanaimo Bars

THESE BARS are as Canadian as they come and no Canadian baking book worth its salt (sugar?) should be without one. Although there is some mystery as to its origins, Nanaimo, British Columbia has officially adopted it as their own. The city's website even has a prize winning recipe posted. There's really not a whole lot of difference between one Nanaimo bar and another one. Although I am a purist 99% of the time, I've played around with the ingredients by adding miniature chocolate chips to the base.

Preheat the oven to 350°F (180°C). Lightly grease the sides and bottom of a 13- × 9-inch (33 × 23 cm) metal cake pan. Line with parchment paper so that the bottom is covered and there is a 2-inch (5 cm) overhang on the 2 long sides.

BASE In a large bowl, stir together the graham cracker crumbs, coconut, walnuts (if using), sugar, chocolate chips and cocoa powder. In a separate bowl, whisk together the butter and egg. Pour the egg mixture over the graham cracker mixture, stirring with a fork until evenly moistened. Transfer the mixture to the prepared pan, patting it evenly onto the bottom of the pan. Bake in the centre of the preheated oven for 10 minutes. Let cool completely on a wire rack.

FILLING In the bowl of a stand mixer fitted with the paddle attachment, or using a hand-held mixer, beat the butter with the custard powder and vanilla until well combined. Scrape down the sides of the bowl. Beat in half of the icing sugar and half of the milk. Add remaining icing sugar and remaining milk, scraping down the sides of the bowl. Scrape the mixture onto the cooled crust, spreading it evenly. Refrigerate until the filling is set and hardened, about 30 minutes.

TOPPING In the top of a double boiler set over hot, not boiling water, melt the chocolate with the butter until smooth. Pour over the cooled base, spreading evenly. Refrigerate until the chocolate is set, about 30 minutes. Cut into bars (or cut what you need, cover the pan and store in the refrigerator for up to 5 days).

RECIPE CONTINUED . . .

BASE

1 cup (250 mL) graham cracker crumbs
⅔ cup (160 mL) shredded sweetened coconut
⅓ cup (80 mL) finely chopped walnuts (optional)
¼ cup (60 mL) granulated sugar
¼ cup (60 mL) miniature chocolate chips
¼ cup (60 mL) unsweetened cocoa powder, sifted
⅓ cup (80 mL) unsalted butter, melted and cooled (3 oz/90 g)
1 large egg, at room temperature

FILLING

⅓ cup (80 mL) unsalted butter, softened (3 oz/90 g)
2 Tbsp (30 mL) custard powder
1 tsp (5 mL) vanilla
2 cups (500 mL) icing sugar
2 Tbsp (30 mL) milk, at room temperature

TOPPING

6 oz (180 g) semisweet chocolate, coarsely chopped
1 Tbsp (15 mL) unsalted butter, softened (0.5 oz/15 g)

BAKER'S TIPS

If you happen to be out of graham cracker crumbs, but have graham crackers, place about 18 in the bowl of a food processor fitted with the metal "S" blade. Grind the cookies until they are in fine crumbs. Add the rest of the base ingredients and pulse until well combined. Proceed with the recipe.

Beware of graham cracker crumbs getting old and stale, which they will do if you store them for longer than 6 months. Always sniff the crumbs before you use them. If too old, they will start to smell off or rancid. Throw them out immediately and buy a new package. There's no point in ruining your entire dessert.

Chocolate-Filled Nanaimo Bars

As GOOD as the original Nanaimo bar but with pecans instead of the usual walnuts and a chocolate middle that doesn't require you to go out and buy a tin of custard powder.

Preheat the oven to 350°F (180°C). Lightly grease the bottom and sides of a 13- × 9-inch (33 × 23 cm) metal cake pan. Line with parchment paper so that the bottom is covered and there is a 2-inch (5 cm) overhang on the 2 long sides.

BASE In a large bowl, stir together the graham cracker crumbs, coconut, pecans and sugar. In a separate bowl, whisk together the butter and egg. Pour the egg mixture over the graham cracker mixture, stirring with a fork until evenly moistened. Transfer the mixture to the prepared pan, patting it evenly onto the bottom of the pan. Bake in the centre of the preheated oven for 10 minutes. Let cool completely on rack.

FILLING Dissolve the espresso powder in the very hot water to make espresso. Let cool slightly.

In the bowl of a stand mixer fitted with the paddle attachment, or using a hand-held mixer, beat the butter with the cocoa powder until well combined. Scrape down the sides of the bowl. Beat in half of the icing sugar and half of the espresso. Beat in the remaining icing sugar, the remainder of the espresso, the milk and vanilla. Scrape the mixture onto the cooled crust, spreading it evenly. Refrigerate until the filling is set and hardened, about 30 minutes.

TOPPING In the top of a double boiler set over hot, not boiling water, melt the white chocolate until smooth. Pour over the cooled base, spreading evenly. Refrigerate until the chocolate is set, about 30 minutes. Cut into bars (or cut what you need, cover the pan and store in the refrigerator for up to 5 days).

BASE
- 1⅓ cups (330 mL) graham cracker crumbs
- ⅔ cup (160 mL) shredded sweetened coconut
- ⅓ cup (80 mL) chopped pecans
- 2 Tbsp (30 mL) granulated sugar
- ⅓ cup (80 mL) unsalted butter, melted and cooled (3 oz/90 g)
- 1 large egg, at room temperature

FILLING
- 1 tsp (5 mL) instant espresso powder
- 3 Tbsp (45 mL) very hot water
- ⅓ cup (80 mL) unsalted butter, softened (3 oz/90 g)
- ⅔ cup (160 mL) unsweetened cocoa powder, sifted
- 1½ cups (375 mL) icing sugar
- 1 Tbsp (15 mL) milk, at room temperature
- 1 tsp (5 mL) vanilla

TOPPING
- 8 oz (250 g) white chocolate, coarsely chopped

Caramel Shortbread Bars

SHORTBREAD

½ cup (125 mL) unsalted butter,
softened (4 oz/125 g)
⅓ cup (80 mL) granulated sugar
1 cup (250 mL) all-purpose flour
Pinch of salt

FILLING

½ cup (125 mL) unsalted butter,
cubed (4 oz/125 g)
½ cup (125 mL) granulated sugar
1 can (300 mL) sweetened
condensed milk

TOPPING

4 oz (125 g) bittersweet chocolate,
coarsely chopped
1 tsp (5 mL) clear corn syrup
2 Tbsp (30 mL) unsalted butter,
cubed (1 oz/30 g)
1 tsp (5 mL) fleur de sel (optional)

THESE DECADENT bars, with their buttery gooey centres and their suave dark chocolate toppings, are also known as Millionaire Bars, perhaps because they're so rich. Incredibly simple to assemble, it's the combination of the shortbread base, the caramel filling and the chocolate topping—all three flavours in one bite—that make them so irresistible. I've upped the ante by sprinkling the bars with a little fleur de sel, so that the sweetness is cut somewhat by the salt. It's still a match worth a million bucks.

Preheat the oven to 350°F (180°C). Grease the sides and bottom of an 8-inch (20 cm) square metal cake pan. Line with parchment paper so that the bottom is covered and there is a 2-inch (5 cm) overhang on 2 sides.

SHORTBREAD In the bowl of a stand mixer fitted with the paddle attachment, or using a hand-held mixer, beat the butter with the sugar until light and fluffy. On low speed, add the flour and salt, mixing until a crumbly dough forms. Working with floured hands, gently press the dough into an even layer in the prepared pan. Bake in the centre of the preheated oven or until just starting to turn golden, about 20 minutes. Let the base cool in the pan on a wire rack.

FILLING In a saucepan set over medium heat, melt the butter and sugar together. Add the condensed milk. Bring to a boil over medium-high heat. Reduce the heat slightly; simmer, stirring often, until thick and a light caramel colour, 20–25 minutes. Immediately pour over the shortbread layer, smoothing the top. Refrigerate until the filling is set, about 2 hours.

TOPPING In the top of a double boiler set over hot, not boiling water, melt the chocolate, corn syrup and butter until smooth. Pour the chocolate evenly over the caramel layer, smoothing the top. Sprinkle with the salt, if using. Cover and chill until set, about 2 hours. Cut into bars (or cut what you need, cover the pan with plastic wrap and store in the refrigerator for up to 5 days).

ALL THINGS CHOCOLATE

174   CHOCOLATE—TAKE TWO

179   Chocolate Devil's Food Cake with Chocolate Buttercream

181   BUTTERCREAMS

182   Dairy-Free Chocolate Coconut Milk Cake

185   Chocolate Blackout Cake

187   ICING CAKES: THE FINISHING TOUCHES

190   Chocolate Bundt Cake

192   Chocolate Crater Cake

193   Chocolate Pound Cake with Chocolate Tres Leches

195   Chocolate Gateau with White Chocolate Cream Cheese Swirl

197   Chocolate Cheesecake

199   Chocolate Chip Meringue Kisses

200   Peek-A-Boo Chocolate Cupcakes

202   All-Occasion Chocolate Cupcakes with French Buttercream

204   Fudge Truffle Tart

207   Chocolate Truffle Pecan Tart with Spun Sugar Dome

209   Chocolate Pots de Crème

210   My Head's in the Clouds Chocolate Cream Pie

212   Truffle Hazelnut Petits Four Bars

214   Cocoa Cinnamon Meringue

216   Triple Chocolate Almond Biscotti

CHOCOLATE—TAKE TWO

I've already said rather a lot about chocolate (see p. 33–39) but there's still so much to say. I can recall when I was a co-host (along with Elizabeth Baird and Emily Richards) on Canadian Living Cooks, on the Food Network. We had a floor manager named Dave who had a sign, reserved exclusively (and embarrassingly) for me, that read, "Stop talking, start cooking!" So bear with me a while longer as I rant some more about chocolate before we get to the actual chapter's recipes.

I come from a long line of chocolate lovers; my father adores really good chocolate and in fact insists on a chocolate dessert when we organize major events. My mother can still recall the chocolates her mother bought for her at a small confectionary store called Chocolats Andrée tucked away on Park Avenue in Montreal, between St. Viateur and Fairmount. Run by three sisters (my grandmother used to call them "maiden sisters"), each chocolate was handmade and lovingly arranged in a small display case. My grandmother was such a devotee of their products that she would make special requests for some of their chocolate and sprinkles when she herself made cookies. So you see I come by my love quite naturally. Chocolate and I understand each other. Having worked so much with chocolate over the years, chocolate and I have settled into a comfortable and dependable relationship: I keep buying it and making wonderful baked goods with it and it has committed to never turning its back on me!

One of the questions I often get asked is, "How do you know which chocolate to use when?" Another is, "How do you know if it's better to use chocolate or cocoa powder?" Answering the first question is straightforward. Generally, if you're making a dessert where chocolate is to be the primary flavour, the chocolate itself should be as unctuous and wonderful as possible. Take a simple chocolate sauce for example. A good chocolate sauce is essentially chocolate, milk or cream, perhaps a pat of butter and a dash of vanilla or corn syrup. Accordingly, the chocolate is the primary flavour and the sauce will reflect all of the nuances and qualities of the chocolate you choose. Buy a bittersweet chocolate you love and you will love your chocolate sauce. Really distinctive, exquisite chocolate hates being overshadowed by too many ingredients or pushed out of the limelight by an excess of cream, sugar or butter. Complex chocolates tend to do best in rich desserts and tortes where they can deliver a pure chocolate flavour.

Following this line of reasoning, a superb bittersweet chocolate may be too intense for the chocolate pudding you want to serve on a regular Wednesday night. In that case, a subtler chocolate is called for. Likewise, if the chocolate in a recipe is only one of many ingredients, it similarly should not be that intense.

Answering the second question requires more consideration. Again, if you're making a dessert such as a mousse, chocolate sauce or custard, chocolate is better than cocoa powder. These desserts rely on a silkiness that only cocoa butter can provide. Cocoa butter melts at a temperature almost exactly that of our body temperature. Chocolate, unlike cocoa powder, melts on our tongue, lingering there a while before we swallow it. For desserts that depend on that kind of mouth feel, chocolate is preferable.

In cakes, the choice is a bit more complicated. It can depend on the type of fat being used, what kind of milk products are called for and the texture you ultimately want to achieve. For my Chocolate Devil's Food Cake on page 179, I wanted a really dark, moist, chocolate-flavoured cake. I opted to go with cocoa powder and oil, a combination that ensures a moist texture. Omitting milk or butter also ensures a deep flavour since dairy products tend to dilute the pure flavour of cocoa. This is also why many chocolate cake recipes that call for cocoa powder have hot water in them, used either to reconstitute the cocoa powder or as part of the liquids. Hot or boiling water causes cocoa powder to swell and release is flavour. Milk simply doesn't do that. Oil is the fat of choice here too since vegetable oil is liquid at room temperature, unlike butter and cocoa butter, which are solid. This means that even if you serve the Chocolate Devil's Food Cake straight from the refrigerator, it will still be moist.

Cakes made with chocolate, on the other hand, tend to be more sensitive to temperature. Remember that cocoa butter and butter (with which it's almost always paired) are solid fats, hard even at room temperature. Because the cocoa butter is the conduit that carries the chocolate flavour, the colder it is, the longer it takes to melt on your tongue and for you to experience its flavour. That's not to say to avoid making cakes with chocolate. Just be sure to serve them at room temperature.

The same rules apply when making bars or cookies. You need to consider the fats inherent in the chocolate and in the recipe. Cocoa powder has no fat in it and butter is soft at room temperature. So brownies or cookies made with cocoa powder plus butter will have a soft, chewy texture. The cocoa provides a deeply rich chocolate experience heightened by a lingering buttery aftertaste. By contrast, if you make the same brownies or cookies with melted chocolate and butter, the baked good will be firmer, almost fudge-like. Again, it goes back to the fact that the cocoa butter is a solid fat.

Chocolate Devil's Food Cake *with* Chocolate Buttercream

T HIS CAKE does the grand tradition of chocolate devil's food cake proud. There are an awful lot of recipes out there for devil's food cake. The origin of the cake seems to be in the early 1900s and the lore is that it was once made with beets, which explained the dark, almost reddish colour of the cake. Another explanation cites it was called "devil's food" to differentiate it from the starkly white "angel food cake." What *is* known about the cake is that it is a deep dark colour with an equally deep and rich flavour. Devil's food cake should always be velvety moist and really chocolatey. Most often it is made only with cocoa powder, buttermilk or water as a liquid and baking soda as the sole leavener. Unlike regular chocolate cakes, it is almost never made with butter. Coming up with this recipe, I poured over older recipes, researched its ingredients and make just under a dozen cakes. I knew I wanted to omit butter and milk, as dairy ingredients tend to dull the flavour of chocolate. I knew I wanted to use oil as the fat, but I wasn't as confident that I could get away with only using baking soda. American bakers tend to use natural cocoa powder, hence the use of baking soda in so many of their recipes for this cake. I also felt that adding a bit of chocolate as well as coffee would help augment the intensity of the cocoa. Switching to brown sugar heightened the flavour of the chocolate and increased the moisture of the cake. In the end, I was happy to build this cake using cocoa powder and chocolate, coffee, brown sugar, buttermilk, oil and baking soda with just a smidgen of baking powder to set its structure. It's wickedly chocolatey, incomparably moist and a fine specimen of its birthright. Make sure you use Dutch-processed cocoa powder to get the full extent of its colour.

Preheat the oven to 325°F (160°C). Lightly grease the bottoms and sides of two 9-inch (23 cm) metal cake pans. Line the bottoms with a circle of parchment paper.

Place the chopped chocolate in a large bowl. Pour the hot coffee over the chocolate, whisking until the chocolate is completely melted and the mixture is smooth; set aside.

In a separate large bowl, whisk together the flour, sugars, cocoa powder, baking soda, baking powder and salt, until the dry ingredients are thoroughly combined. You want to make sure that there are no cocoa or brown sugar lumps. If there are, break them up with your fingertips.

In a separate bowl, whisk together the buttermilk, oil, eggs and vanilla.

3 oz (90 g) bittersweet chocolate, coarsely chopped

1 cup (250 mL) hot brewed coffee (regular coffee, not espresso)

1¾ cups (430 mL) all-purpose flour

1⅓ cups (330 mL) granulated sugar

⅔ cup (160 mL) packed light brown sugar

½ cup (125 mL) unsweetened Dutch-processed cocoa powder, sifted

1¼ tsp (6 mL) baking soda

½ tsp (2 mL) baking powder

¾ tsp (4 mL) salt

1 cup (250 mL) buttermilk, at room temperature

½ cup (125 mL) vegetable oil

2 large eggs, at room temperature

1 tsp (5 mL) vanilla

BUTTERCREAM

4 oz (125 g) semisweet chocolate, coarsely chopped

3 large egg whites, at room temperature

⅔ cup (160 mL) granulated sugar

1¼ cup (310 mL) unsalted butter, very soft (10 oz /300 g)

RECIPE CONTINUED . . .

Make a well in the centre of the dry ingredients. Pour the buttermilk mixture and the chocolate mixture into the well. Gently whisk until a smooth batter is formed, with no streaks of flour remaining. Divide the batter evenly between the 2 pans.

Bake in the centre of the preheated oven until the top of each cake springs back when very lightly pressed, 35–45 minutes. Cool the cakes in the pans on a wire rack for at least 30 minutes. Run a small knife around the edge of the cake pans to loosen the cakes from the pan. Remove the cakes from the pans and cool completely on the wire racks, parchment side down.

BUTTERCREAM Melt the chocolate in the top of a double boiler set over hot, not boiling water; set aside.

Whisk together the egg whites and sugar in a large bowl. Place over a saucepan of simmering water. Cook, whisking frequently, until the mixture is very hot (about 120°F/50°C) on a candy thermometer or until your finger cannot remain in the mixture for longer than 10 seconds. Immediately transfer the mixture to a stand mixer fitted with the whisk attachment. Whisk on medium to medium-high speed for about 10 minutes or until the mixture is completely cool and quite thick. Switch to the paddle attachment. A bit at a time, about ¼ cup (60 mL), add in the butter, beating well in between each addition, and making sure that each addition is fully incorporated before adding the next, until all of the butter is used. It may start to look a bit curdled once about two-thirds of the butter has been added but keep going. Add the melted and cooled chocolate, beating just until fully incorporated.

ASSEMBLY Remove the parchment from the bottom of one of the cake layers. Place on a cake plate or a decorating turntable. If the cake has domed significantly, use a serrated knife to even it off. Using a long metal palette knife, spread about 1 cup (250 mL) of the buttercream over the top of this layer. Remove the parchment paper from the second layer. Again, if it has crowned significantly, even it off with a serrated knife. Invert the cake and place on top of the buttercream, so that what was previously the bottom of the cake is now actually the top. This will ensure that you have a flat, even surface to ice. Spread the top and sides with the remaining buttercream. Refrigerate for at least 1 hour before serving. Remember, buttercream has the same properties as butter. It will harden upon refrigeration and then soften when brought to room temperature. So bring the cake to room temperature for at least 30 minutes before serving.

BUTTERCREAMS

There are basically three different kinds of buttercream (and I'm totally ignoring icings that masquerade as buttercream but only call for butter, flavouring and icing sugar. Icing sugar does not an authentic buttercream make, although it can make a really good icing). There is Italian buttercream, Swiss buttercream and French buttercream.

Swiss meringue buttercream is the one used with the Chocolate Devil's Food Cake (see p. 179). Basically, eggs whites are combined with granulated sugar and cooked over a hot water bath to a temperature of between 120–130°F (49–53°C). They are then transferred to the bowl of a stand mixer and beaten until stiff glossy peaks form. At this point, room temperature butter is slowly beaten into the egg whites to create a soft and silken textured buttercream. There are Swiss meringue buttercreams that call for you to fold the meringue into already beaten butter, but I find that more troublesome and less stable.

Italian meringue buttercreams also use egg whites but in this instance they are beaten, usually with some cream of tartar, until the egg whites reach soft peaks. At the same time, you make a sugar syrup by cooking some granulated sugar and water until it reaches 240–248°F (115–120°C). The hot syrup is then poured into the beaten egg whites, with the machine running. The meringue is beaten until it is cool, at which point you gradually add the softened butter.

A French meringue, unlike the previous two, uses whole eggs or egg yolks. Here too a sugar syrup is made until it reaches 230°F (110°C). This mixture is poured into the beaten eggs, egg yolks or a combination of the two, beaten to the ribbon stage then beaten until stiff and cool. The butter is then added gradually.

The buttercream used on the Chocolate Devil's Food Cake is the base that I use for all of my buttercreams. It's extremely versatile and takes to almost any flavouring. It also triples and quadruples brilliantly. Buttercream, because it has all the properties of butter, refrigerates and freezes extremely well. It can be refrigerated for up to 1 week or frozen for up to 3 months. If refrigerated, bring it completely to room temperature and then, using a paddle attachment, beat until aerated and fluffy. If frozen, thaw completely in the refrigerator, then bring to room temperature and beat with a paddle attachment until aerated and fluffy.

Dairy-Free Chocolate Coconut Milk Cake

CAKE

2 cups (500 mL) all-purpose flour

1⅔ cups (410 mL) granulated
   sugar

¾ cup (180 mL) unsweetened
   Dutch-processed cocoa powder,
   sifted

2 tsp (10 mL) baking powder

¾ tsp (4 mL) baking soda

½ tsp (2 mL) salt

¾ cup (180 mL) vegetable oil

¾ cup (180 mL) coconut milk
   (not light)

¾ cup (180 mL) water

3 large eggs, at room temperature

2 tsp (10 mL) vanilla

FROSTING

12 oz (360 g) semisweet chocolate, coarsely chopped

2 cups (500 mL) non-dairy whip
   or whipping cream, cold, divided

2 Tbsp (30 mL) light corn syrup

I URGE you to try this cake. It's an incredibly moist, darling of a chocolate cake that just happens to use coconut milk instead of cow's milk.
I developed it for those who are lactose intolerant or who keep kosher and
want a chocolate cake with their meat meal. You won't even notice the
coconut milk, which is a stand in for buttermilk. The fat used is again
oil, which makes it super-duper moist. Because Dutch-processed cocoa
powder is used, there is both baking powder and baking soda in the
cake. Another wonderful thing about this cake is that it doesn't really
dome, making icing a breeze. Non-dairy whip topping is usually found
in the kosher section of the supermarket, in the freezer or with the milk
products.

———

Preheat the oven to 350°F (180°C). Lightly grease the bottoms and sides
of two 9-inch (23 cm) metal cake pans. Line the bottoms with a circle of
parchment paper.

Whisk together the flour, sugar, cocoa powder, baking powder, baking soda and salt in a bowl, until the dry ingredients are thoroughly
combined. In a separate bowl, whisk together the vegetable oil, coconut
milk, water, eggs and vanilla. Pour the coconut milk–oil mixture over the
flour mixture; whisk gently until thoroughly combined. Divide the batter
evenly between the 2 prepared pans.

Bake in the centre of the preheated oven until the top of the cake
springs back when lightly pressed, 25–30 minutes. Cool the cakes in the
pans on a wire rack for 30 minutes. Run a small knife around the edge of
the cake pans to loosen the cakes from the pan. Remove the cakes from
the pans and cool completely on the wire racks, parchment side down.

FROSTING In the top of a double boiler set over hot, not boiling water, melt
the chocolate. Remove from the heat. Stir in 1 cup (250 mL) of the non-
dairy whip and the corn syrup. Set aside momentarily. In the bowl of a
stand mixer fitted with the whisk attachment, or using hand-held beaters,
beat the remaining non-dairy whip until peaks form. Replace the whisk
attachment with the paddle attachment. Add the chocolate mixture to
the mixer. Beat until thoroughly combined and smooth.

ASSEMBLY Remove the parchment paper from the bottom of one of the cake layers. Place directly on a cake plate or a decorating turntable. If the cake has domed significantly, use a serrated knife to even it off. Using a long metal palette knife, spread about 1 heaping cup (250+ mL) of the icing over the top of the cake layer. Remove the parchment paper from the second cake layer. Again, if it has crowned significantly, use a serrated knife to even it out. Invert and place on top of the icing, so that what was previously the bottom the cake is now actually the top. This will ensure that you have a flat, even surface to ice. Ice the sides and top of the cake with the remaining icing. Bring to room temperature before serving. (Cake can be made ahead and stored at room temperature for up to 4 days.)

BAKER'S TIPS

ICING WITHOUT A TURNTABLE You can turn out a beautifully iced and garnished cake without a cake decorating turntable. Place your first cake layer on a flat plate or the serving plate you're going to use. Lay a rectangular strip of waxed or parchment paper under each side of the cake. Spread some of the icing on top of this first layer. Invert the second layer on top of the first, so that the underside is now the top. Remove the parchment paper if it's still attached to the underside of the cake. Ice the sides, letting any excess icing set up a bit higher than the top of the cake. Ice the top of the cake, levelling off the excess from the sides. Garnish as desired. Remove the 4 strips of parchment and you have a gorgeous looking cake and no messy remnants on the plate. Place thin toothpicks into the surface of the cake and cover lightly with plastic wrap until you're ready to serve your masterpiece.

Most butter- or oil-based cakes freeze well. Wrap each layer tightly and well in plastic wrap to avoid moisture loss and odour absorption. I like the extra precaution of then rewrapping them in a freezer bag. If freezing an iced cake, make room in the freezer for the entire cake. Once the icing is frozen, and the outside cannot be marred in any way, wrap and rewrap and freeze.

Chocolate Blackout Cake

I**F YOU'VE** been baking for as long as I have, then you've probably heard of blackout cake. It originated in Brooklyn, New York, at a bakery chain called Ebinger's. The cake, so named after the blackout drills performed by the Civilian Defense Corps (ostensibly to prevent ships sailing at night from being detected), became famous, drawing other bakeries to try their hand at the three-layered cake. Locals will still tell you that the competition never matched the original. When the company declared bankruptcy in 1972 (it was founded in 1898), lore has it that only Entenmann's had a version that came close. Below you'll find my rendition, with a creamy pudding filling, a luxe chocolate icing and one layer of the cake devoted to making the crumbs for garnishing the exterior of the cake.

PUDDING FILLING In the bowl of a stand mixer fitted with the paddle attachment, or using a hand-held mixer, beat the egg yolks with the sugar, cornstarch and salt until lightly coloured and thickened.

Meanwhile, in a saucepan set over medium heat, bring the water and cream to a boil. Remove the saucepan from the heat. Whisk about one-third of the hot liquid into the egg mixture along with the cocoa powder. Whisk another third of the liquid into the egg mixture. Whisk the warm egg mixture into the remaining liquid in the saucepan. Cook over medium heat, whisking constantly, until boiling and thickened, 2–3 minutes. Remove from the heat. Whisk in the melted chocolate. Stir in the vanilla. Transfer the mixture to a bowl. Place plastic wrap directly on the surface. Refrigerate until completely chilled, about 2 hours.

CAKE Preheat the oven to 350°F (180°C). Lightly grease the bottoms and sides of two 8-inch (20 cm) metal cake pans. Line the bottoms with a circle of parchment paper.

Melt the chocolate in the top of a double boiler set over hot, not boiling water. Set aside to cool slightly.

Whisk together the flour, baking powder, baking soda and salt in a bowl, whisking until the dry ingredients are thoroughly combined.

In the bowl of a stand mixer fitted with the paddle attachment, or using a hand-held mixer, beat the butter for 1 minute. Add the sugars and

PUDDING FILLING

3 large egg yolks, at room temperature

½ cup (125 mL) granulated sugar

2 Tbsp (30 mL) cornstarch

Pinch of salt

⅔ cup (160 mL) water

½ cup (125 mL) whipping cream, at room temperature

2 Tbsp (30 mL) unsweetened Dutch-processed cocoa powder, sifted

3 oz (90 g) bittersweet chocolate, melted

1 tsp (5 mL) vanilla

CAKE

3 oz (90 g) semisweet chocolate, coarsely chopped

1½ cups (375 mL) all-purpose flour

¾ tsp (4 mL) baking powder

¾ tsp (4 mL) baking soda

½ tsp (2 mL) salt

⅔ cup (160 mL) unsalted butter, softened (5 oz/150 g)

½ cup (125 mL) granulated sugar

½ cup (125 mL) packed light brown sugar

3 large eggs, at room temperature

2 tsp (10 mL) vanilla

½ cup (125 mL) unsweetened Dutch-processed cocoa powder, sifted

1 cup (250 mL) buttermilk, at room temperature

RECIPE CONTINUED . . .

INGREDIENTS CONTINUED . . .

⅓ cup (80 mL) very hot water

ICING

4 oz (125 g) unsweetened chocolate, coarsely chopped

2 oz (60 g) bittersweet chocolate,
coarsely chopped

¾ cup (180 mL) unsalted butter,
softened (6 oz/175 g)

1¾ cup (430 mL) icing sugar

¼ cup (60 mL) whipping cream, at
room temperature

1 tsp (5 mL) vanilla

beat until light and fluffy, about 3 minutes. One at a time, beat in the eggs, beating well after each egg before adding the next. Beat in the vanilla. Beat in the cocoa powder and the melted chocolate. Alternately, beat in the flour mixture with the buttermilk, making 3 additions of the flour and 2 of the buttermilk. Stir in the hot water.

Divide the batter evenly between the 2 prepared pans. Bake in the centre of the preheated oven until the top of the cake springs back when lightly pressed, 25–30 minutes. Cool the cakes in the pans on a wire rack for 20 minutes. Run a small knife around the edge of the cake pans to loosen the cakes from the pan. Remove the cakes from the pans and cool completely on the wire racks, parchment side down.

ICING Melt the unsweetened and bittersweet chocolate in the top of a double boiler set over hot, not boiling water, until smooth. Set aside to cool slightly.

In the bowl of a stand mixer fitted with the paddle attachment, beat the butter for 1 minute. In 3 additions, add the icing sugar, adding 3 Tbsp (45 mL) of the whipping cream between the second and third addition. Beat in the melted and cooled chocolate. Beat in the vanilla and the remaining 1 Tbsp (15 mL) of whipping cream.

ASSEMBLY Remove the parchment paper from the cake layers. Cut each cake layer in half horizontally. Crumble one of the cake layers and set the crumbs aside in a bowl.

Place one of the cake layers on a cake plate or a decorating turntable. Using a long metal palette knife, spread half of the pudding over the cake's surface. Top with a second cake layer. Spread with the remaining pudding. Top with a third cake layer. Ice the sides and top of the cake with the chocolate icing.

Gently press the reserved cake crumbs over the sides and top of the cake. Refrigerate the cake for about 1 hour before serving. If refrigerated for longer, bring to room termperature before serving.

ICING CAKES:
THE FINISHING TOUCHES

When icing cakes, most professional pastry chefs apply what is called a "crumb coat," which ensures that the icing goes on smoothly, spotless and crumb free. It's easy to do at home. Place the first cake layer on a regular plate. Spread some of the icing on top and then layer with the second layer of cake. Using an offset spatula and as little icing as possible, spread as thin a layer of frosting on top of the cake and on the sides of the cake, again spreading it as thinly as you can. You'll be able to see the cake through the icing and that's okay. This is what is called the crumb coating. It actually has nothing to do with crumbs. What it means is that this thin layer prevents any crumbs from adhering to the final layer of icing. Then place the cake on the plate in the refrigerator for at least 20 minutes or until the crumb coat is set. Remove the cake from the refrigerator, transfer it to a cake turntable and ice thoroughly. You'll be surprised to see how smoothly and evenly the top and final coating of icing can be applied.

If not applying the crumb coat, place the cake on a decorating turntable, ready to be iced. If the cake is domed slightly, use a serrated knife to level off the surface of the cake. Cut the cake horizontally into two if making a four-layer cake and set aside one of the layers. Place some icing on top of the first layer. Icing in the middle of a cake, whether it's a two-layer cake or a four-layer cake, should be about ¼ inch (6 mm) or a mite shorter for a four-layer cake. Using a palette knife (a long flat metal spatula), and using a back and forth motion, spread the icing over the surface of the first layer. Try to use as fluid a movement as possible, without lifting up the palette knife that will pull away crumbs from your cake and ruin the smoothness of the icing. To ensure that you have a nice, even and flat layer of icing, place the palette knife halfway across the icing. Angle the blade of the knife so that it is almost flat against the icing. Holding your palette knife firmly in place, rotate the turntable or plate one full turn. This will level out the icing. Place any excess icing back in the bowl. Place the next layer of cake, flat side up, on top of the icing. Repeat for all layers, but ice the top and sides following the instructions below.

The best way to ice the outside of a cake is to start with the sides. Using the same palette knife, scoop out a good mound of icing from the bowl. With your knife at a strict 90 degree angle, parallel to the side of the

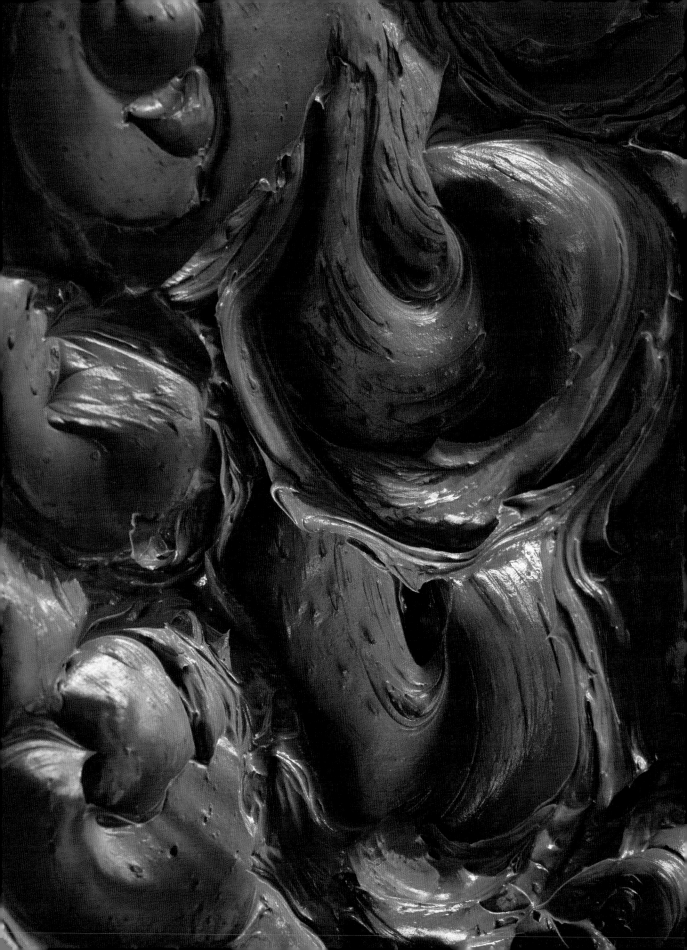

cake, press the frosting onto the side of the cake. Again, try not to lift your knife from the side of the cake. Continue this same motion all around the cake, adding more icing as necessary, and allowing any excess icing to rise about ¼ inch (6 mm) above the top of the cake. Ice the top of the cake in the same way—scoop out some icing and press against the top surface of the cake. When the top of the cake is iced, angle the blade of the knife so that it is almost flat against the icing. Holding your palette knife firmly in place, rotate the turntable or plate one full turn. Then, to straighten the edge of the cake and remove any excess icing, place your palette knife, at a 90 degree angle, right against the side of the cake and rotate the plate one full circle. With a clean palette knife or one dipped in hot water and dried, level off the top by drawing onto the top of the cake the excess icings on the side.

Chocolate Bundt Cake

3 cups (725 mL) all-purpose flour

3 cups (725 mL) granulated sugar

1 cup (250 mL) unsweetened Dutch-processed cocoa powder, sifted

1 Tbsp (15 mL) baking powder

1 tsp (5 mL) salt

¼ tsp (1 mL) baking soda

1 cup (250 mL) unsalted butter, very soft (8 oz/250 g)

1½ cups (375 mL) milk, at room temperature

1 Tbsp (15 mL) vanilla

3 large eggs, at room temperature

½ cup (125 mL) whipping cream, at room temperature

THIS IS the chocolate cake I grew up with. My mom used to make it for our Friday night dinners and my sisters and I couldn't wait to finish our main course so that we could tuck into a piece of this heavenly cake. What fascinates me is that years before another of my dessert goddesses, Rose Levy Beranbaum, published *The Cake Bible* cookbook, my mom used the same method that Rose espouses—adding milk and butter to dry ingredients before adding the eggs—without ever knowing why. The reason you add the butter and some of the liquid to the dry ingredients is to help distribute the butter throughout the batter and to help set the cake's structure and foundation. This is very different from creaming, which results in a densish cake with a soft but compact crumb. The eggs are added to the batter last so that they do not get overworked and start to flex their leavening muscles.

I have only called for a hand-held mixer in this recipe because of its volume. Unless you have an old fashioned stand mixer with a wide, low round bowl, most modern stand mixers won't work as well for this recipe.

Preheat the oven to 325°F (160°C). Grease a 12-cup (3 L) Bundt pan; set aside.

In a large bowl, whisk together the flour, sugar, cocoa powder, baking powder, salt and baking soda, whisking until the dry ingredients are thoroughly combined.

Make a well in the centre of the dry ingredients. Add the butter, milk and vanilla. Using a hand-held mixer, beat the mixture for 5 minutes. One at a time, beat in the eggs, beating well after each egg before adding the next one. Beat in the cream.

Using a spatula, transfer the mixture to the prepared Bundt pan. Bake in the centre of the preheated oven until the top of the cake springs back when lightly pressed, about 70 minutes. Let the cake cool in the pan on a wire rack for 30 minutes. Remove the cake from the pan and cool completely on a wire rack. Serve at room temperature.

VARIATION

SOUR CREAM CHOCOLATE BUNDT CAKE Replace the ½ cup (125 mL) whipping cream with ½ cup (125 mL) sour cream.

Chocolate Crater Cake

1 lb (500 g) semisweet chocolate, coarsely chopped

½ cup (125 mL) unsalted butter, in pieces (4 oz/125 g)

4 large eggs, at room temperature

2 Tbsp (30 mL) granulated sugar

1 Tbsp (15 mL) all-purpose flour or potato starch

Pinch of salt

TOPPING

1 cup (250 mL) whipping cream, softly whipped

1½ cups (375 mL) raspberry coulis

2 cups (500 mL) fresh raspberries

SOMETIMES CALLED earthquake cake, sometimes called San Francisco cake (earthquakes, get it?), this is a dense chocolate cake supported (for a while) by beaten whole eggs. Since there is so little flour in it and so much chocolate, the cake has nowhere to go but down once it comes out of the oven. It falls into itself, looking like an earthquake hit it. Or reflecting the moniker I've chosen, like a chocolate crater. You'll often see these kinds of recipes call for separated eggs, and that is indeed what I have done for my Passover Chocolate Cake (see p. 327). For this recipe, however, I have opted to keep the eggs whole to keep matters simple. To help the eggs achieve their full volume, make sure they're at room temperature before you start.

Preheat the oven to 400°F (200°C). Grease the sides and bottom of an 8½-inch (22 cm) springform pan. Line the bottom with a round of parchment paper.

In the top of a double boiler set over hot, not boiling water, melt the chocolate and butter together, until smooth. Remove from the heat and let cool slightly.

In the bowl of a stand mixer fitted with the whisk attachment, or using a hand-held mixer, beat the eggs with the sugar until very light coloured and about tripled in volume, about 5 minutes. Fold one-third of the beaten eggs into the melted chocolate to lighten it. Fold in the remaining eggs, flour and salt. Scrape the mixture into the prepared pan.

Bake in the centre of the preheated oven until the sides look set and dull and a cake tester inserted in the centre of the cake comes out with some moist crumbs still clinging to it, 15–18 minutes. Let the cake cool completely in the pan set on a wire rack. Remove the springform pan and gently transfer the cake to a cake plate. Serve at room temperature with whipping cream, raspberry coulis and fresh raspberries.

Chocolate Pound Cake *with* Chocolate Tres Leches

W HEN I worked as a pastry chef, I had a 14- × 4-foot (4.3 ×1.2m) deep pastry case to fill. Early in the week, we didn't need to fill it since Monday and Tuesday were relatively slow days. By Thursday, however, I knew that people were starting to think about the weekend and to dial up their entertaining. That's when my team and I flew into action, and by Friday there wasn't an inch of space uncovered. Do you know how much pastry you need to fill a 14-foot (4.3 m) long pastry case? A dazzling amount, I have to tell you. What shocked me at the time was how much room I had to devote to chocolate desserts only—at least 60%. I'm sure if you talk to professional pastry chefs these days, they would concur that when it comes to chocolate, its popularity has never been greater.

Tres leches is a South American specialty, a cake soaked in a sauce made from condensed milk, whipping cream and goat's milk. I've replaced goat's milk with the easier to find coconut milk and swathed the whole dessert in a toothsome wrapping of chocolate.

CHOCOLATE POUND CAKE Preheat the oven to 350°F (180°C). Lightly grease an 8- × 4- or 5-inch (20 × 10 or 13 cm) loaf pan; set aside.

Whisk together the flour, cocoa powder, baking soda and salt in a bowl until the dry ingredients are thoroughly combined; set aside.

In a stand mixer fitted with the paddle attachment, or using a hand-held mixer, beat the butter for 1 minute or until fluffy. Add the sugar and beat until quite light, about 3 minutes. One at a time, beat in the eggs, scraping down the mixture in between the addition of the first and the second egg. Beat in the vanilla. Remove the bowl from the stand. Starting with the flour, alternately stir in the flour mixture and the buttermilk, making 3 additions of the flour mixture and 2 additions of the buttermilk. Using a plastic spatula, scrape the mixture into the prepared loaf pan.

Bake in the centre of the preheated oven until the top of the cake springs back when lightly pressed, 55–65 minutes. Let the cake cool in the pan on a wire rack. Run a small knife around the edges of the pan to loosen the cake from the pan. Unmould and cool completely. (Cake can be prepared up to 24 hours in advance. Be sure to wrap it in plastic wrap and store at room temperature.)

RECIPE CONTINUED . . .

CHOCOLATE POUND CAKE

1¾ cups (430 mL) all-purpose flour

½ cup (125 mL) natural unsweetened cocoa powder, sifted

1 tsp (5 mL) baking soda

½ tsp (2 mL) salt

¾ cup (180 mL) unsalted butter, softened (6 oz/175 g)

1 cup (250 mL) granulated sugar

2 large eggs, at room temperature

1½ tsp (7 mL) vanilla

¾ cup (180 mL) buttermilk, at room temperature

CHOCOLATE TRES LECHES

1 can (300 mL) sweetened condensed milk

¾ cup (180 mL) whipping cream, at room temperature

¾ cup (180 mL) coconut milk

¼ cup (60 mL) unsweetened cocoa powder, sifted

½ tsp (2 mL) instant espresso powder

½ tsp (2 mL) vanilla

¼ tsp (1 mL) cinnamon

CHOCOLATE TRES LECHES In a large bowl or wet measure, whisk together the sweetened condensed milk, whipping cream and coconut milk. Remove about ⅓ cup (80 mL) of the mixture to a separate bowl. Whisk in the cocoa powder, espresso powder, vanilla and cinnamon until smooth. Whisk back into the rest of the milk mixture. (The sauce can be covered with plastic wrap and refrigerated for up to 2 days. Bring to room temperature before serving.)

To serve, slice the pound cake into thickish slices. Place on a dessert plate, and pour the tres leches sauce generously over.

Chocolate Gateau *with* White Chocolate Cream Cheese Swirl

THIS ALMOST flourless cake is devilishly chocolatey, with a ribbon of tangy sweet white chocolate swirled through it. It's dense and unctuous, more like a piece of fudge with a swirl of sweetened cream cheese. Like many flourless cakes, it calls for a lot of chocolate and some butter. This gateau is about as far away from a shy wallflower as you can get, and it can serve a crowd since all you need is a thin sliver.

Preheat the oven to 300°F (150°C). Lightly grease the bottom of a 9-inch (23 cm) metal cake pan. Line the bottom with a circle of parchment paper; set aside.

CREAM CHEESE LAYER In the top of a double boiler set over hot, not boiling water, melt the chocolate. Set aside to cool slightly.

In the bowl of a stand mixer fitted with the paddle attachment, or using hand-held beaters, beat the cream cheese until very soft. Scrape down the sides of the bowl. Beat in the sugar for 2 minutes. Scrape down the sides of the bowl. Beat in the egg, scraping down the side of the bowl to make sure that there are no clumps of cream cheese. Remove the bowl from the stand. Stir in the white chocolate and the vanilla; set aside.

CHOCOLATE CAKE LAYER In the top of a double boiler set over hot, not boiling water, melt the chocolate with the butter until three-quarters melted. Remove from the heat; stir until both the chocolate and butter are completely melted and smooth. Cool slightly.

In the clean bowl of a stand mixer fitted with the whisk attachment, beat the eggs with the sugar for about 4 minutes, until the mixture has thickened and turned a pale yellow colour. Remove the bowl from the stand. With a spatula, fold in the melted chocolate mixture and the vanilla. Fold in the flour.

Pour about two-thirds of the chocolate mixture into the prepared pan. Top with two-thirds of the white chocolate mixture. Swirl the two together. Top with the remaining chocolate batter and the remaining white chocolate cheese mixture. Marble the two together.

RECIPE CONTINUED . . .

CREAM CHEESE LAYER

2 oz (60 g) white chocolate, coarsely chopped

6 oz (175 g) cream cheese, softened

½ cup (125 mL) granulated sugar

1 large egg, at room temperature

1 tsp (5 mL) vanilla

CHOCOLATE CAKE LAYER

8 oz (250 g) bittersweet chocolate, coarsely chopped

½ cup (125 mL) unsalted butter, in pieces (4 oz/125 g)

3 large eggs, at room temperature

¼ cup (60 mL) granulated sugar

2 tsp (10 mL) vanilla

2 Tbsp (30 mL) all-purpose flour

Bake in the centre of the preheated oven until the sides of the cake seem set but the centre still jiggles slightly, 35–40 minutes. Cool the cake in the pan on a wire rack—the cake will deflate slightly and may crack. This is completely normal. It's important to keep the cake in the pan during the whole cooling process. Refrigerate for 8–24 hours. Remove the cake from the pan and remove the parchment. Serve chilled in very thin wedges.

BAKER'S TIP

I find that using a metal skewer to create the marble patterns is the best way to go. A wooden skewer is too thin and the back of a spoon or the tip of a knife can be too thick.

Chocolate Cheesecake

THIS CHEESECAKE owes a certain amount of its genesis to the New York cheesecake. Dense, rich and tall, New York cheesecake is replete with cream cheese, sour cream or whipping cream, eggs and sometimes an extra egg yolk or two for richness. My cheesecake is not quite as tall as a New York cheesecake, but it is dense, creamy and thoroughly luxurious. I always bake my cheesecakes in a water bath (see p. 388) and have even been accused of taking cheesecakes way too seriously. Perhaps so, but I am a big proponent of adding sour cream to the batter to act as a counterpoint to its sweetness and to provide the sensuous mouth feel that should accompany a great cheesecake.

Preheat the oven to 325°F (160°C).

In a bowl, whisk together the cookie crumbs and the sugar. Pour the melted butter over and stir until the crumbs are thoroughly moistened. With the back of a spoon, press the cookie mixture onto the bottom of an 8½-inch (22 cm) springform pan. Bake in the centre of the preheated oven for 10 minutes. Let the pan cool slightly on a wire rack. Place the cooled pan on a large piece of aluminum foil. Press or scrunch up the aluminum so that it creates a solid basket or barrier around the springform. This will help prevent any water from the water bath from seeping into the cheesecake. Place the springform pan into a larger roasting pan so that there are at least 1–2 inches (2.5–5 cm) of space around the springform pan.

FILLING In the top of a double boiler set over hot, not boiling water, melt the chocolate. Set aside to cool slightly.

In the bowl of a stand mixer fitted with the paddle attachment, or using a hand-held mixer, beat the cream cheese until very smooth, about 3 minutes. Beat in the sugar, scraping down the sides of the bowl occasionally to ensure that there are no clumps of cream cheese. On low speed, add the eggs, one at a time, beating well after each egg before adding the next. Scrape down the bowl. Beat in the vanilla. Remove the bowl from the stand. Gently stir in the melted and cooled chocolate and then the sour cream.

RECIPE CONTINUED . . .

1½ cups (375 mL) chocolate wafer
  cookie crumbs
2 Tbsp (30 mL) granulated sugar
⅓ cup (80 mL) unsalted butter,
  melted and cooled (3 oz/90 g)

FILLING

8 oz (250 g) semisweet chocolate,
  coarsely chopped
1 lb (500 g) cream cheese,
  softened (two 250 g pkgs)
¾ cup (180 mL) granulated sugar
3 large eggs, at room temperature
2 tsp (10 mL) vanilla
1 cup (250 mL) sour cream, at
  room temperature

Transfer the mixture to the springform, levelling the surface. Pour enough hot water into the pan, avoiding getting any into the springform or between the springform and the aluminum foil, so that the water comes 1 inch (2.5 cm) up the side of the pan.

Bake the cheesecake in the centre of the preheated oven until the edges are set but the centre still jiggles, 65–75 minutes. Turn the oven off but keep the cheesecake in the water bath in the turned-off oven for 1 hour. Remove the cheesecake from the water bath, remove the foil and let cool completely in the pan on a wire rack. Refrigerate for 8–24 hours.

Remove the cake from the springform; bring to room temperature for 20–30 minutes before servings.

BAKER'S TIP
Refer to page 388 for cheesecake guidelines.

Chocolate Chip Meringue Kisses

THESE MERINGUES cookies LITERALLY melt in your mouth. The minute these babies hit the roof of your mouth, they start to instantly dissolve, the crunch of the meringue melding with the soft centre and the texture of the chocolate chips. They should be baked until just very lightly golden on the outside. They should not be rock hard. If kept at room temperature for too long they will start to soften, so try to eat them up quickly. I'm fairly confident you won't have any trouble.

3 egg whites, at room temperature

⅛ tsp (0.5 mL) cream of tartar

⅛ tsp (0.5 mL) salt

¾ cup (180 mL) granulated sugar

1 tsp (5 mL) vanilla

1 cup (250 mL) mini semisweet chocolate chips

½ cup (125 mL) regular-sized semisweet chocolate chips

Preheat the oven to 300°F (150°C). Line 2 cookie sheets with parchment paper; set aside.

In the bowl of a stand mixer fitted with the whisk attachment, or using hand-held beaters, whisk the egg whites with the cream of tartar and salt until the whites reach soft but deliberate peaks. Very gradually, add the sugar, beating until the egg whites form stiff but shiny peaks.

Gently fold in the vanilla and both chocolate chips.

Using a large rubber spatula, transfer half of the mixture into a pastry bag with a 1-inch (2.5 cm) opening. Pipe 1-inch (2.5 cm) kisses on each sheet. You should be able to get about 22 kisses per cookie sheet.

You can bake both sheets at the same time, if you wish, positioning the oven racks in the top and bottom third of the oven. Bake until the tips and edges of the kisses are just beginning to brown, 25–30 minutes. I prefer to bake them one sheet at a time, in the centre of the oven for the same amount of time. The second tray of cookies, which will have to wait until the first tray bakes, will not suffer in the least for having to wait its turn.

Allow the cookies to cool on the pan on a wire rack until completely cool. The meringues can be stored in an airtight container at room temperature for up to 4 days.

Peek-A-Boo Chocolate Cupcakes

CREAM CHEESE FILLING

8 oz (250 g) cream cheese, softened
½ cup (125 mL) granulated sugar
1 large egg, at room temperature
Pinch of salt

CUPCAKES

3 cups (725 mL) all-purpose flour
2 cups (500 mL) granulated sugar
½ cup (125 mL) unsweetened Dutch-processed cocoa powder, sifted
2 tsp (10 mL) baking soda
2 cups (500 mL) very warm water
⅔ cup (160 mL) canola or vegetable oil
2 Tbsp (30 mL) white vinegar
1 Tbsp (15 mL) vanilla
⅓ cup (80 mL) mini semisweet chocolate chips

THE DEEP and delightful chocolatey flavour of these cupcakes comes from the fact that they use very warm water as the main liquid. The warm water intensifies the flavour of the cocoa powder, allowing it to swell and release all of its essential properties. I have heard this type of chocolate cake batter referred to as a "wacky" cake. Why wacky I'm not sure, but a wacky cake is all made within one bowl and it's wacky good. It's equally good without the cream cheese filling.

Preheat the oven to 350°F (180°C). Lightly grease 2 muffin tins so that you have enough for 18 cupcakes. Line with muffin cups.

CREAM CHEESE FILLING In the bowl of a stand mixer fitted with the paddle attachment, or using a hand-held mixer, beat the cream cheese until fluffy, about 1 minute. Scrape down the sides of the bowl. Add the sugar; beat until smooth, 2–3 minutes. Scrape down the sides of the bowl. Beat in the egg and the salt, scraping down the sides of the bowl as needed to make sure the filling is as smooth as possible, but not liquid; set aside.

CUPCAKES In a large bowl, whisk together the flour, sugar, cocoa powder and baking soda until the dry ingredients are thoroughly combined. In a separate bowl, whisk together the water, oil, vinegar and vanilla. Make a well in the centre of the dry ingredients. Whisk in the wet ingredients until a smooth batter is formed.

Evenly divide the cupcake batter among 18 muffin cups, filling each three-quarters full. Evenly spoon the cream cheese filling over the cupcakes. Sprinkle the chocolate chips over the cream cheese filling.

Bake in the centre of the preheated oven until the top of the cake springs back when lightly pressed, about 20 minutes. Cool the cupcakes in the pans on a wire rack for at least 15 minutes. Remove cupcakes to the wire rack to cool completely.

All-Occasion Chocolate Cupcakes *with* French Buttercream

2 cups (500 mL) granulated sugar

1¾ cups (430 mL) all-purpose flour

¾ cup (180 mL) unsweetened Dutch-processed cocoa powder, sifted

1½ tsp (7 mL) baking powder

1½ tsp (7 mL) baking soda

½ tsp (2 mL) salt

1 cup (250 mL) milk, at room temperature

½ cup (125 mL) unsalted butter, melted and cooled (4 oz/125 g)

2 large eggs, at room temperature

1 Tbsp (15 mL) vanilla

1 cup (250 mL) very hot water

FRENCH BUTTERCREAM

6 oz (175 g) semisweet chocolate, coarsely chopped

1 cup + 2 Tbsp (280 mL) granulated sugar

⅓ cup (80 mL) water

3 large eggs, at room temperature

1½ cups (375 mL) unsalted butter, softened (12 oz/350 g)

1 tsp (5 mL) vanilla

AFTER ALL I've said, you might think it hypocritical of me to offer a recipe for chocolate cupcakes that features butter. After all, aren't dairy products supposed to moderate the intense flavour of chocolate? Well, yes, they are, but I like the flavour of butter here. Once again, I've used the technique of adding hot water to help release all of the wonderful elements from the cocoa powder. This buttercream, which uses a French meringue at its base, is captivating but if your children or family find it too rich, you can easily swap it out for the chocolate fudge icing on page 317. It also makes 3¼ cups (810 mL) of icing and will be plenty for 18 cupcakes.

Preheat the oven to 350°F (180°C). Lightly grease 2 muffin tins so that you have enough for 18 cupcakes. Line with muffin cups.

In a large bowl, whisk together the sugar, flour, cocoa powder, baking powder, baking soda and salt until the dry ingredients are thoroughly combined. In a separate bowl, whisk together the milk, butter, eggs and vanilla.

Pour the wet ingredients over the dry ingredients and whisk until well combined with no evidence of any flour. Pour in the hot water and whisk until well blended. The batter will be quite thin.

Using a ladle or wet measure with a spout, pour the batter evenly among the 18 muffin cups, filling each cup almost to the top. These cupcakes don't rise that much so there's no need to fear spillover.

Bake in the centre of the preheated oven until the tops of the cupcakes spring back when lightly pressed, 25–30 minutes. Cool the cupcakes in the pans on a wire rack for 20 minutes. Remove the cupcakes to the wire rack to cool completely.

FRENCH BUTTERCREAM In the top of a double boiler set over hot, not boiling water, melt the chocolate; set aside to cool slightly. Stir together the sugar and water in a small heavy-bottomed saucepan set over medium heat. Cook, stirring occasionally, until the sugar has dissolved.

In the bowl of a stand mixer fitted with the whisk attachment, beat the eggs on medium speed. You can keep the mixer going while the sugar is reaching its correct temperature. They should be light and billowy and tripled in volume by the time the sugar syrup is ready to be added.

Increase the heat under the sugar mixture to high. Boil, without stirring, until the mixture reaches 238°F (114°C) on a candy thermometer. Immediately remove from the heat. Turn off the mixer. Pour about one-quarter of the sugar syrup into the eggs. Immediately turn the mixer on to high and beat for about 10 seconds. Turn the mixer off, then resume beating for another 10 seconds. Repeat until you have used up the entire sugar syrup. Continue to beat the mixture until it is completely cool, about 10 minutes.

There are many recipes that call for you to add the sugar syrup while the machine is running, but I find this method to be much more practical. The first method may be more authentic but I find invariably that half of the sugar mixture ends up on the sides of the mixer rather than incorporated into the egg mixture and it's hellish trying to clean the mixer afterward.

Once the mixture has cooled, start adding the butter, 2 Tbsp (30 mL) at a time, with the machine on medium speed. It may not look as though it will come together but do persevere, it will! Add the vanilla. Once all the butter has been added, increase the speed to high and beat until a buttercream consistency is formed, about 3 minutes.

Fold the cooled chocolate into the buttercream.

Transfer the buttercream to a piping bag fitted with a star tip. Pipe the top of each cupcake with icing. The icing will yield just over 3 cups (750 mL) which will be plenty to ice 18 cupcakes or one 9-inch (23 cm) layer cake.

BAKER'S TIP

CHOCOLATE BUTTERCREAM Just like you add air the more you cream butter and sugar together, the same is true the more you beat your buttercream. This is fine—you want an ethereal and airy buttercream. It adds to its allure. Once you've added the chocolate, however, stop beating if you want a deep chocolatey colour. If you prefer a lighter milk chocolate colour, beat until that colour is achieved.

Please make sure that your melted chocolate is cooled but still liquid. If the chocolate is still hot when you add it to the buttercream or icing, the chocolate may very well melt the buttercream, leaving you with soup. Alternately, it could solidify upon contact with the cooler buttercream, meaning you'll have shards of chocolate in what otherwise should be a satiny buttercream.

Fudge Truffle Tart

SHELL

2 cups (500 mL) chocolate cookie
wafer crumbs

⅓ cup (80 mL) unsalted butter,
melted and cooled (3 oz/90 g)

FILLING

1 Tbsp (15 mL) instant coffee
granules

¼ cup (60 mL) hot water

8 oz (250 g) semisweet chocolate,
coarsely chopped

¾ cup (180 mL) granulated sugar

⅔ cup (160 mL) unsalted butter,
cubed (5 oz/150 g)

6 large egg yolks, at room
temperature

¾ cup (180 mL) cold whipping
cream

TOPPING

½ cup (125 mL) cold whipping
cream

I ACTUALLY developed this recipe many years ago for a chocolate article I wrote for *Canadian Living Magazine*. Some time has passed since then but this three-layer tart is as alluring now as it was back then. My friend Cindy's husband, Michael Zahavi, a true chocoholic if there ever was one, adores this tart. In fact, when I visited their cottage up in Muskoka, Ontario one summer and brought this along as a treat, he got up in the middle of the night to nosh away at it, leaving us sleepyheads with nary a crumb the next day.

It's important to use a chocolate with a 65% or lower cocoa content for this tart. Any higher and the proportions will be off and the middle cream layer will not set properly.

SHELL Preheat the oven to 350°F (180°C). Place the cookie crumbs in a bowl. Pour the melted butter over, stirring with a fork until the crumbs are thoroughly moistened. Using a regular spoon, pat the mixture onto the bottom and sides of a 9-inch (23 cm) round French tart tin with a removable bottom. Bake in the centre of the preheated oven for 10 minutes. Let the crust cool completely in the pan set on a wire rack.

FILLING Meanwhile, dissolve the coffee granules in the hot water. Place the chocolate in a saucepan set over very low heat. Stirring often, melt the chocolate. Remove from the heat. Whisk in the sugar, butter and coffee, whisking until smooth. Whisk in the yolks all at once. Return to a very low heat and cook, whisking constantly, until thickened, about 3 minutes. Immediately scrape the mixture into a clean bowl. Cover the bowl with plastic wrap and refrigerate for about 1 hour or until cooled and thickened but still spreadable.

Spread half of the chocolate mixture onto the cooled crust. Whip the cream to soft peaks. Fold one-third of the whipped cream into the remaining chocolate mixture in order to lighten it. Gently fold the remaining cream into the chocolate. Spread this mixture over the dark chocolate mixture. Cover without disturbing the dark chocolate filling and refrigerate for 4–12 hours.

Remove the tart from the tin and transfer to a serving platter.

TOPPING Whip the cream to soft peaks. Scrape the mixture into a pastry bag fitted with a rosette tip. Pipe rosettes of whipped cream around the border of the tart. Serve slightly chilled.

BAKER'S TIP

FOLDING There's a basic rule in baking when you're folding ingredients together—lighter into heavier. Always. So when you're folding beaten egg whites, egg yolks or whipping cream, consider the density of both entities. Take chocolate for example: melted chocolate will always be heavier than say beaten egg whites or whipping cream. Accordingly, you need to fold the lighter into the heavier to avoid deflating whatever air you've whipped into the eggs or cream. To facilitate this, you also do it gradually. Start off by folding one-third of the lighter mixture into the heavier mixture to lighten the heavier mixture and to prime it so that it can accept the remainder of the lighter mixture. This goes for a flour mixture or batter as well, since by weight they will always be heavier than the beaten whites or cream.

Chocolate Truffle Pecan Tart *with* Spun Sugar Dome

THIS SPECTACULAR tart was originally developed for the website Kosher Scoop, run by the very talented and lovely Estee Kafra. Gorgeous and sophisticated, the filling is a cinch to make since it's not much more than a ganache enriched by egg yolks, and it's perfectly wonderful without the spun sugar dome. If you do try your hand at the spun sugar, be armed with patience. It takes a little practice but in the end you'll get it. Even if your dome cracks a bit, keep going. In the worst case scenario—at least the first time you make it—you can always pretend that you meant to use shards in the first place.

CRUST Preheat the oven to 350°F (180°C).

Place the pecans, sugar and flour into the bowl of a food processor fitted with the metal "S" blade. Pulse together until the pecans are finely ground. Pour in the melted butter and pulse again until the mixture is thoroughly moistened. Press the pecan mixture onto the bottom and up the sides of a 9-inch (23 cm) or 10-inch (25 cm) French tart pan with a removable bottom.

Place the tart pan on a baking sheet and bake in the centre of the preheated oven for 15 minutes. Transfer to a wire rack to cool completely.

FILLING Heat the cream in a saucepan just until bubbles appear around the edge. Pour just under ¼ cup (60 mL) of the mixture into the egg yolks, whisking constantly. Whisk the egg mixture and the remaining cream over the chocolate, whisking until the chocolate is completely melted and smooth. Whisk in the vanilla. Pour into the cooled shell. Cover lightly and refrigerate for at least 8 hours or for up to 2 days. Remove the tart from the tart pan and place on a serving plate.

SPUN SUGAR Lightly grease a stainless steel bowl with outer rims that match the edges of whatever tart tin size you've chosen. Fill a large bowl with water and ice cubes. Combine the sugar and ¼ cup (60 mL) water in a heavy-bottomed saucepan set over medium-high heat. Cook, without stirring, until the sugar is dissolved. Continue to cook, brushing down the sides of the pan with a brush dipped in cold water, for 5–8 minutes until

CRUST

2 cups (500 mL) pecan halves

½ cup (125 mL) granulated sugar

2 Tbsp (30 mL) all-purpose flour or potato starch

⅓ cup (80 mL) unsalted butter, melted and cooled (3 oz/90 g)

FILLING

1 cup (250 mL) whipping cream, at room temperature

2 large egg yolks, at room temperature

9 oz (275 g) bittersweet chocolate, coarsely chopped

1 tsp (5 mL) vanilla

SPUN SUGAR

⅔ cup (160 mL) granulated sugar

¼ cup (60 mL) water

RECIPE CONTINUED . . .

the mixture turns a deep golden colour. Immediately immerse the bottom of the pan in the bowl filled with ice water for 5 seconds. This will stop the cooking process. Dip a fork or spoon into the caramelized sugar. Allow the excess to drip back into the pan. Once you have a thread going, move the fork in a circular pattern over the greased bowl, so that the threads start to encircle the bowl. Repeat with the caramel, until a dome or bowl shape is achieved. If the caramel becomes too hard to use, very briefly rewarm it over low heat—it will reliquelify and you will be able to proceed. Allow the sugar dome to cool. Using a small paring knife, release the sugar dome from the bowl and gently place atop the tart. Caramelized sugar doesn't hold very well. If there is any moisture in the air, it will start to soften so that this part can only be done 1–2 hours before you serve the tart. Serve slightly chilled.

BAKER'S TIPS

It's well near impossible to remove caramel from a saucepan by washing it, so give your hands a break and use this foolproof method. Fill the saucepan with water and place it back on the stove over high heat. Bring the water to a boil, which will melt any cooked sugar that has stuck to the saucepan. Once it's all melted, just drain the saucepan.

CARING FOR TART TINS French tart tins are expensive so it's imperative to handle them properly. Once you've baked a tart in a French tart tin, it starts to develop a patina, much like a cast iron skillet does. This patina helps prevent later tarts, be they made from crumbs or pastry, from sticking to the pan, once you remove the sides from the bottom. Washing them in soapy water would rob the tart tin of its patina. Make sure you wash them only with very hot water and dry them thoroughly to avoid rust spots.

Chocolate Pots de Crème

THIS FRENCH dessert is creamy, comforting and classic. Bearing no relation to its American cousin, pudding, this is a cooked custard made rich by the addition of heavy cream and egg yolks. Its interior is silky smooth and pleasure on a spoon.

Preheat the oven to 325°F (160°C). Place six ¾-cup (180 mL) ramekins inside a large roasting pan.

Stir the 2 creams together in a saucepan. Place over medium-high heat and bring to a boil. Remove the saucepan from the heat. Add the chopped chocolate to the saucepan and let the chocolate sit in the hot cream for 1 minute. Whisk the chocolate and cream together until the chocolate is completely melted and the mixture is smooth.

Whisk the egg yolks with the sugar in a small bowl. Gradually whisk in about ¼ cup (60 mL) of the chocolate mixture. Whisk in another ¼ cup (60 mL). Gradually add the egg mixture back into the saucepan, whisking constantly. Whisk in the espresso powder and vanilla. Stir the mixture gently to remove as much of the foam as possible.

Divide the mixture evenly among the prepared ramekins. Pour hot water into the roasting pan so that the water reaches halfway up the sides of the ramekins.

Bake in the centre of the preheated oven until the custard is set but still a little jiggly, 25–30 minutes. Remove the roasting pan from the oven. Using a towel or tongs, remove each ramekin to a wire rack to cool completely.

Cover each ramekin with plastic wrap and refrigerate for at least 8 hours or up to 2 days. Bring to room temperature for 30 minutes before serving.

1 cup (250 mL) whipping cream

1 cup (250 mL) 18% cream

4 oz (125 g) semisweet or bittersweet chocolate, coarsely chopped

6 large egg yolks, at room temperature

⅓ cup (80 mL) granulated sugar

½ tsp (2 mL) instant espresso powder

½ tsp (2 mL) vanilla

My Head's in the Clouds Chocolate Cream Pie

CRUST

2 cups (500 mL) chocolate cookie wafer crumbs

⅓ cup (80 mL) unsalted butter, melted and cooled (3 oz/90 g)

FILLING

12 oz (375 g) semisweet chocolate, coarsely chopped

¼ cup (60 mL) unsalted butter, softened (2 oz/60 g)

4 large egg whites, at room temperature

1 cup (250 mL) granulated sugar

2 cups (500 mL) whipping cream, cold

TOPPING

1 cup (250 mL) cold whipping cream

IF THERE ever was a dessert destined for a diner, this is the one—and this is the one I imagine I would have if I ever ate at a diner. Terrifically high and voluptuous, this chocolate cream pie gets a boost from an abbreviated Swiss meringue that lends an incredible smoothness to the filling. Although it might be a diner staple, there's absolutely nothing old fashioned about this rich, satisfying pie.

CRUST Preheat the oven to 350°F (180°C). Place the cookie crumbs in a bowl. Pour the melted butter over, stirring with a fork until the crumbs are thoroughly moistened. Using a regular spoon, pat the mixture onto the bottom and sides of a 9-inch (23 cm) deep dish glass pie plate. Bake in the centre of the preheated oven for 10 minutes. Let the crust cool completely in the pie plate set on a wire rack.

FILLING In the top of a double boiler set over hot, not boiling water, melt the chocolate and butter until melted and smooth; set aside.

Whisk the egg whites and sugar together in a separate stainless steel bowl. Set over the saucepan of hot, not boiling water. Cook, whisking frequently, until the eggs are warm but not hot, about 3 minutes. Immediately transfer the mixture to a stand up mixer fitted with the whisk attachment. Beat on medium-high speed until completely cool; set aside.

In a clean bowl with a clean whisk attachment, beat the cream to soft peaks. Fold one-third of the beaten egg whites into the warm melted chocolate. Fold in the remaining egg whites. Fold one-third of the whipped cream into the chocolate mixture. Fold in the remaining whipped cream. Scrape the chocolate mixture into the cooled pie shell without deflating the mixture. Refrigerate the pie for 4–24 hours.

TOPPING Whip the 1 cup (250 mL) of cream to soft peaks. Mound on top of the chocolate filling, covering it completely. Serve slightly chilled.

BAKER'S TIP
Even though it doesn't really need any more chocolate, I often garnish this pie with either shaved bittersweet chocolate, chocolate butterflies or musical notes. To make these, melt some bittersweet chocolate and make a paper cone (see p. 312). Fill the cone with the melted chocolate. Snip off the tip of the cone. Working on parchment paper, trace a heart, butterflies or musical notes, whatever your pleasure may be. Let the chocolate cool completely. Once cool, slide a small offset spatula knife under the decoration and place it decoratively on top of the whipped cream. Let the chocolate set at room temperature and not in the refrigerator where it may bloom.

Truffle Hazelnut Petits Four Bars

½ cup (125 mL) hazelnuts, skin on

½ cup (125 mL) macadamia nuts

¾ cup (180 mL) all-purpose flour

½ cup (125 mL) granulated sugar

¼ tsp (1 mL) salt

¼ cup (60 mL) unsalted butter
(2 oz/60 g)

6 oz (175 g) bittersweet chocolate,
coarsely chopped

2 large eggs, at room temperature

TRUFFLE TOPPING

1 cup (250 mL) whipping cream, at
room temperature

2 Tbsp (30 mL) unsalted butter
(1 oz/30 g)

12 oz (375 g) bittersweet chocolate, coarsely chopped

2 Tbsp (30 mL) hazelnut liqueur
(optional)

Pinch of salt

THIS IS a deeply engaging bar, basically a chocolate and nut base with a deeply soulful ganache topping; this truffle-based confection is sure to win accolades from your guests. Because they're so rich, a little piece goes a long way. I almost didn't include this recipe because it is so very rich. I did though, since one of my mantras is (to spin Dorothy Parker's quote) "You can never bake too much or eat enough chocolate."

⬤————

Preheat the oven to 350°F (180°C). Lightly grease the sides and bottom of an 8-inch (20 cm) square metal cake pan. Line with parchment paper so that the bottom is covered and there is a 2-inch (5 cm) overhang on 2 sides.

Place the hazelnuts and macadamia nuts on an unlined baking sheet. Bake in the centre of the preheated oven for 5–8 minutes or until fragrant and golden. Let cool for 5 minutes.

In the bowl of food processor fitted with the metal "S" blade, combine the hazelnuts, macadamia nuts, flour, sugar and salt; pulse until finely ground and set aside.

In a saucepan set over very low heat, melt the butter and chocolate together, whisking until melted and smooth. Remove from the heat. One at a time, whisk in the eggs. Stir in hazelnut mixture just until combined.

Scrape the mixture into the prepared pan, patting it evenly into the bottom. Bake in the centre of the preheated oven until a cake tester inserted in the centre comes out with just a few dry crumbs clinging to it, 15–20 minutes. Let the bars cool completely in the pan on a wire rack.

TRUFFLE TOPPING In a saucepan, bring the cream and butter to a boil. Remove from the heat. Add the chocolate and whisk until all of the chocolate is melted and the mixture is completely smooth. (At this point, if you're serving this to adults, feel free to add 2 Tbsp/30 mL hazelnut liqueur!) Pour the ganache over the cooled base, tilting the pan so that it is completely covered and even. Cover with plastic wrap; refrigerate until firm, about 3 hours.

Bring to room temperature before cutting and serving (or cut what you need, cover the pan with plastic wrap and store in the refrigerator for up to 7 days).

GANACHE Basic chocolate ganache is classically made of equal parts semi-sweet or bittersweet chocolate and whipping cream. Melting 4 oz (125 g) of chocolate with ½ cup (125 mL) of just boiling whipping cream is creamy and pourable when warm, but still solid enough to make truffles. Depending on what you want to make, the formula can have many variations. If you want a runnier sauce to pour over ice cream or even poached pears (where a classic ganache might overwhelm the delicate texture and flavour of the pears), for example, you might increase the whipping cream and keep the amount of chocolate the same. Conversely, if you want a much richer texture, you would decrease the whipping cream and keep the amount of chocolate the same.

HAZELNUTS Also known as filberts, hazelnuts and chocolate make a perfect marriage. They tend to be quite robust in flavour and should be toasted before using. Toasting also loosens the skin on hazelnuts, which should be removed as much as possible before baking (the skins tend to have a slightly bitter aftertaste).

Cocoa Cinnamon Meringue

5 egg whites, at room temperature

1½ cups (375 mL) superfine sugar

¼ cup (60 mL) water

1 tsp (5 mL) pure vanilla extract

Pinch of salt

2 Tbsp (30 mL) unsweetened
   cocoa powder

1 Tbsp (15 mL) cinnamon

TOPPING

1 cup (250 mL) whipping cream

1½ cups (375 mL) mixed berries
   or fruit

1 tsp (5 mL) cocoa powder
   (optional)

ALTHOUGH NOT strictly a pavlova, given that it's actually a Swiss meringue (so named because of the sugar syrup), let's not quibble over nomenclature. Suffice it to say, this meringue is just plain delicious. The cinnamon–cocoa powder combo is addictive and the sugar-syrup method ensures a crisp exterior with a soft, marshmallow-like interior.

Preheat the oven to 225°F (105°C). Line a cookie sheet with parchment paper. Trace a 9-inch (23 cm) circle on the paper. Turn the paper over.

In the bowl of an electric mixer fitted with the whisk, start to slowly whip the egg whites until soft peaks appear.

Simultaneously, stir together the sugar and water in a small saucepan set over medium-high heat. Boil gently, stirring only once or twice, until the mixture boils and reaches 175°F (79°C) on a candy thermometer or until the bubbles start to thicken slightly and the mixture appears "sticky." This should only take about 5 minutes.

With the machine running, slowly pour the sugar mixture into the egg whites. Whisk on high speed for 5–7 minutes or until the mixture is stiff and glossy white. Whisk in the vanilla and salt.

In a small bowl, stir together the cocoa powder and cinnamon. With a rubber spatula, fold the cocoa mixture into the egg whites, allowing some streaks to remain.

Mound the meringue mixture inside the outlined circle. Bake in the centre of the preheated oven for 2–2½ hours or until dry and crisp on the outside. Let cool completely. (Meringue can be made up to 2 days ahead. Store in a cool, dry place.)

TOPPING Transfer meringue to a serving plate. Mound the cream over the top of the meringue in decorative swirls. Garnish with fresh fruit. For extra garnish, sprinkle 1 tsp (5 mL) sifted cocoa powder on top.

VARIATION

INDIVIDUAL PAVLOVAS Trace nine 4-inch (10 cm) circles on the parchment paper. Mound meringue mixture in each and bake as directed.

Triple Chocolate Almond Biscotti

1½ cups (375 mL) all-purpose flour

½ cup (125 mL) unsweetened cocoa powder, sifted

½ cup (125 mL) granulated sugar

½ cup (125 mL) packed light brown sugar

2 tsp (10 mL) baking soda

⅛ tsp (0.5 mL) salt

3 large eggs, at room temperature

2 Tbsp (30 mL) unsalted butter, melted and cooled (1 oz/30 g)

2 tsp (10 mL) vanilla

3 oz (90 g) semisweet or bitter-sweet chocolate, coarsely chopped

2 oz (60 g) white chocolate, coarsely chopped

⅓ cup (80 mL) chopped whole (unskinned) almonds

A DDING BUTTER to biscotti is pretty well blasphemous in Italy. Biscotti are meant to be crunchy and hard, their very solidity making them the perfect vehicle to dip into a cuppa java or some vin santo. So you'll have to excuse me for adding some of the aforementioned butter to this recipe. I prefer my biscotti to fall just under the really crunchy mark, for them to give a bit. You can certainly omit the butter if you want. There is also a fair bit of soda in this recipe. You won't actually taste it but it does cause the cookies to spread.

Preheat the oven to 350°F (180°C). Line a large cookie sheet with parchment paper; set aside.

Place the flour, cocoa powder, granulated and brown sugars, baking soda and salt in the bowl of a stand mixer fitted with the paddle attachment. This can also be done with a hand-held mixer and a regular bowl. Mix the dry mixture until well combined.

In a separate bowl whisk together the eggs, butter and vanilla. Pour the wet mixture directly into the flour mixture. Beat on low speed until the mixture is thoroughly combined. Beat in the dark and white chocolate and the almonds.

Transfer the dough to a clean work surface. Divide the dough into 3 equal pieces. Working with lightly floured hands to prevent the dough from sticking, roll each piece of dough into a 7½-inch long, 1½-inch wide and ¾-inch high log (19 × 4 × 2 cm). Transfer the logs to the prepared cookie sheet, spacing them at least 3–4 inches (8–10 cm) apart (they will spread quite a bit).

Bake in the centre of the preheated oven for 20 minutes. Remove the pan to a wire rack to cool for 15 minutes. One at a time, transfer the logs to a cutting board. Slice each log diagonally, into about ½-inch (1 cm) pieces. Return to the baking sheet, cut side up. You might need another parchment paper–covered cookie sheet at this point (actually, if you don't bake them again, you have a really tasty soft cookie).

Bake again until the cookies are firm, 12–15 minutes. Let the cookies cool on the cookie sheet on a wire rack for 10 minutes. Remove the cookies to the wire rack to cool completely. (The biscotti can be stored at room temperature in an airtight container for up to 10 days.)

MUFFINS, BISCUITS AND SCONES

221   MUFFINS

222   Incredibly Moist Bran Muffins

223   Oh So Chocolatey Chip Muffins

224   Morning Glory Hallelujah Muffins

226   Banana Wheat Muffins

227   Coffee Cake Muffins

229   Pear Cranberry Muffins with Crunchy Almond Topping

230   Sour Cream Bluebaby Muffins

233   Nutella Swirl Muffins

235   Golden Corn Muffins

236   Double Apple Muffins

237   Zucchini Cheese Muffins with Sun-Dried Tomatoes

239   Orange Vanilla Muffins with Marmalade Glaze

240   Triple Ginger Muffins

241   BISCUITS

244   Everyday Buttery Biscuits

246   Buttermilk Biscuits

248   Sour Cream Biscuits with Cinnamon

249   Tender Flaky Biscuits

250   Citrus Sunshine Biscuits

251   Parmesan Thyme Biscuits

252   SCONES

253   Classic Cream Scones

254   Orange Kissed Scones with Vanilla-Roasted Plums

256   Gingerbread Scones

257   Morning Oatmeal Scones with Dried Fruit Pear Compote

259   Black Forest Scones

260   Cherry Sauce

261   Tweed Scones

263   Strawberry Almond Scones

264   Double Blueberry Scones

265   A Peach of a Scone

266   Gruyère, Prosciutto and Chive Scones

268   Feta, Olive and Rosemary Scones

269   Sun-Dried Tomato Scones with Asiago and Basil

BREAKFAST IS a funny time, absolutely necessary to start your day off right (personally, I wake up hungry everyday so breakfast is a must), but it's always a bit rushed, and often eaten on the fly. I think people yearn for something warm and delicious in the morning, only to have their fantasies dashed and replaced by something less than delicious at the local coffee shop. It's too bad because morning baking can be gratifying and expedient. Muffins are a snap to put together, especially if you organize the dry ingredients in a bowl the night before and whisk together your wet ingredients and stash them in the refrigerator. In the morning, wake up 5 minutes earlier than usual, preheat the oven, mix everything together and 20 minutes later, after your shower, teeth, make-up, what have you, breakfast is ready. The same is true of biscuits and scones. Cut your butter into the dry ingredients the night before and refrigerate overnight. The next morning, add the wet ingredients, form and bake. And, no, I'm not living in a fantasy land or suggesting anyone return to the June Cleaver household. What I am saying is that it's possible and worth every mouthful. Muffins and scones also freeze extremely well, so they can be enjoyed as an afternoon treat or as part of a light lunch or more filling dinner.

MUFFINS

In the world of baking, muffins are actually considered to be part of the quick bread category, which basically covers three methods.

The most popular is what is called the muffin method. Essentially, this is where the baker whisks or blends together the dry ingredients in one bowl and whisks the liquid ingredients together in another bowl. The liquid ingredients are poured over the dry ingredients (and not the other way around), and the baker gently stirs or whisks them together into a somewhat lumpy batter. The point is to mix the two together just until no streaks of flour remain or there is no unmixed liquid, and no more. It's actually a good sign if there is some lumpiness in the batter—it's a surefire sign that the baker has not overmixed the batter. The lumps will disappear during baking. Overmixing muffins makes them tough and chewy and may even contribute to tunnels, those nasty holes in the crumb that make slices unseemly.

Baking soda is typically used in muffins that contain an acid, such as buttermilk, molasses, sour cream or cocoa powder. Baking powder is used in recipes that include milk, whipping cream, vanilla and other non-acidic ingredients. Sometimes, both are called for. However, a word of caution, these leaveners are NOT interchangeable.

The second method is the creaming method, discussed more fully in the sugar section (see p. 16) and the cakes chapter (see p. 305), and the third is the biscuit method, discussed on page 241.

Even though you may think that muffins are a no brainer, it's still important to do your mise en place and to have all your ingredients ready before you start to assemble the muffins. Muffins should go together quickly and then go into the oven, pronto. If you're looking around for that box of baking soda or aren't sure you actually measured out the sugar (as I most memorably did once when making banana muffins) then your muffin batter is going to mournfully be sitting around while you get the ingredients together. Mix quickly, without hesitation, and try not to overmix. If the recipe calls for melted butter, you can always substitute canola or a flavourless oil, but you may miss the buttery flavour.

Muffins are typically baked in a 375°F (190°C) oven, to ensure domed tops and a quick bake. You can bake muffins with muffin liners or without. Some say that you use less batter with a muffin liner but after several tests I have found this not to be true. What is different though is the golden colour you get when you bake muffins without liners. Whichever method you choose, if there is not enough batter to fill all 12 cups, fill the unused cups halfway with water to prevent the muffin tin from overheating.

Incredibly Moist Bran Muffins

DATE PURÉE
2 cups (500 mL) pitted dates
¾ cup (180 mL) very hot water

MUFFINS
2 cups (500 mL) all-purpose flour
½ cup (125 mL) whole-wheat flour
4 tsp (20 mL) baking powder
½ tsp (2 mL) baking soda
½ tsp (2 mL) cinnamon
½ tsp (2 mL) salt
1½ cups (375 mL) natural bran
1 cup (250 mL) buttermilk, at
    room temperature
¾ cup (180 mL) fancy molasses
½ cup (125 mL) canola or vege-
    table oil
½ cup (125 mL) packed light
    brown sugar
1 large egg, at room temperature
2 tsp (10 mL) vanilla
1½ cups (375 mL) raisins

I KNOW it's just a muffin, but I am absurdly proud of this recipe. I tried several different versions of bran muffin before I settled on this one. Moist, a little molassesy, full of raisins and well, full of bran and fibre to get the job done, so to speak (ahem). The date purée adds sweetness and moistness while the molasses imparts that wonderful earthy brown that should accompany all bran muffins. Like all the muffins in this chapter, they freeze extremely well and are great for lunch alongside a salad or a bowl of soup.

DATE PURÉE Soak the dates in the hot water for 30 minutes. Transfer the dates and water to the bowl of a food processor fitted with the metal "S" blade. Purée until smooth. Set aside to cool slightly. Purée can be made ahead and refrigerated for up to 1 week.

MUFFINS Preheat the oven to 375°F (190°C). Get out a 12-cup muffin tin and lightly grease or line with muffin cups; set aside.

Whisk together the flours, baking powder, baking soda, cinnamon and salt in a bowl until the dry ingredients are thoroughly combined; set aside.

In a separate large bowl, whisk together the bran, date purée, buttermilk, molasses, oil, brown sugar, egg and vanilla until well combined. Pour the buttermilk-date mixture over the dry ingredients along with the raisins. Using a wooden spoon, quickly stir together until just moistened and a thick batter is created.

Divide the batter evenly amongst the prepared muffin cups—the cups will be very full to overflowing.

Bake in the centre of the preheated oven until the tops of the muffins spring back when lightly pressed, 25–30 minutes. Cool the muffins in the pan on a wire rack for 10 minutes. Remove the muffins from the pan, transferring to the wire rack to cool completely.

BAKER'S TIP
You'll notice, especially when a muffin calls for oil as its fat, that the sugar is added to the liquid ingredients. The sugar becomes part of the liquid and increases the volume of the mixture, creating more liquid to blend with the dry ingredients.

Oh So Chocolatey Chip Muffins

THIS IS my son's favourite muffin. Jacob, like me, has a serious penchant for chocolate and likes nothing better than waking up to these muffins coming out of the oven. He also has a discerning palate—at least for all things chocolate. I remember once making a chocolate sauce with corn syrup in it to give it some shine. Jacob tasted it, smelled it, tasted it again, and then pronounced, "Good, Mom, but just a touch greasy." Because this muffin contains both chopped chocolate as well as larger chocolate chips, it positively bursts with chocolate inflections.

Preheat the oven to 375°F (190°C). Get out a 12-cup muffin tin and lightly grease or line with muffin cups; set aside.

Whisk together the all-purpose flour, baking powder, baking soda and salt in a bowl until the dry ingredients are thoroughly combined; set aside.

In a separate large bowl, whisk together the buttermilk, oil, sugar, eggs and vanilla until well combined. Pour the buttermilk mixture over the dry ingredients along with the chocolate chips and chopped chocolate. Using a wooden spoon, quickly stir together until just moistened and a thick batter is created.

Divide the batter evenly among the prepared muffin cups.

Bake in the centre of the preheated oven until the tops of the muffins spring back when lightly pressed, about 25 minutes. Cool the muffins in the pan on a wire rack for 10 minutes. Remove the muffins from the pan, transferring to the wire rack to cool completely.

2½ cups (625 mL) all-purpose flour

1 Tbsp (15 mL) baking powder

¼ tsp (1 mL) baking soda

¼ tsp (1 mL) salt

1 cup (250 mL) buttermilk, at room temperature

½ cup (125 mL) canola or vegetable oil

1 cup (250 mL) granulated sugar

2 large eggs, at room temperature

2 tsp (10 mL) vanilla

1 cup (250 mL) semisweet chocolate chips

4 oz (125 g) semisweet chocolate, finely chopped

BAKER'S TIP

If you want to see a golden crust on your muffin sides, avoid using paper cups but grease and flour the muffin tin well and don't forget, especially if you're making oversized muffin tops, to grease the top of the muffin tin too. In general, you want to fill the muffin cups two-thirds to three-quarters full. If any of the cups are empty, fill them up halfway with water to prevent the pan from getting too hot. Most muffins are baked at 375°F (190°C) or 400°F (200°C) to ensure a fast rise, nicely rounded tops and a quick bake.

Morning Glory Hallelujah Muffins

2½ cups (625 mL) all-purpose
   flour

1 Tbsp (15 mL) baking powder

1 tsp (5 mL) baking soda

2 tsp (10 mL) cinnamon

¾ tsp (4 mL) salt

1½ cups (375 mL) grated carrots

1 cup (250 mL) buttermilk, at
   room temperature

1 cup (250 mL) packed light brown
   sugar

1 cup (250 mL) shredded apple

½ cup (125 mL) canola or vegetable oil

2 large eggs, at room temperature

⅓ cup (80 mL) raisins, plumped
   (see below)

⅓ cup (80 mL) pumpkin seeds

⅓ cup (80 mL) sunflower seeds

¼ cup (60 mL) flax seeds

YOU MAY or may not know this but whether you shred or grate your carrots can make a big difference to a muffin. I actually prefer grating my carrots, which I do the night before, either in my food processor or using the coarse side of a box grater. Grated carrot is very small, much like grated Parmesan cheese, and keeps for up to 5 days in the refrigerator covered in plastic wrap. Shredded carrot, on the other hand, comes out as long shreds or pieces. It takes up more room and doesn't lend as much moisture to the muffin. The shredded apple (this you can shred!) also contributes to the moistness of this breakfast treat.

Preheat the oven to 375°F (190°C). Get out a 12-cup muffin tin and lightly grease or line with muffin cups; set aside.

Whisk together the all-purpose flour, baking powder, baking soda, cinnamon and salt in a bowl until the dry ingredients are thoroughly combined; set aside.

In a separate large bowl, whisk together the carrots, buttermilk, sugar, apple, oil and eggs until well combined. Pour the buttermilk mixture over the dry ingredients along with the raisins, pumpkin, sunflower and flax seeds. Using a wooden spoon, quickly stir together until just moistened and a thick batter is created.

Divide the batter evenly among the prepared muffin cups. The cups will be very full.

Bake in the centre of the preheated oven until the tops of the muffins spring back when lightly pressed, about 25 minutes. Cool the muffins in the pan on a wire rack for 10 minutes. Remove the muffins from the pan, transferring to the wire rack to cool completely.

BAKER'S TIPS

Sprinkle some more pumpkin, flax and sunflower on top of each muffin before baking for an extra special touch.

Dried fruit can actually dry out biscuits and scones because it acts as a magnet for moisture. To avoid this, plump your dried fruit in hot water for 10–15 minutes before draining and then adding to the mixture.

Banana Wheat Muffins

1 cup (250 mL) all-purpose flour

½ cup (125 mL) whole-wheat flour

2 Tbsp (30 mL) toasted wheat germ

1 tsp (5 mL) baking powder

1 tsp (5 mL) baking soda

¼ tsp (1 mL) salt

3 large bananas, mashed

¾ cup (180 mL) packed light brown sugar

⅓ cup (80 mL) unsalted butter, melted and cooled (3 oz/90 g)

1 large egg, at room temperature

1 tsp (5 mL) vanilla

½ cup (125 mL) mini chocolate chips or chopped walnuts (optional)

I ALWAYS buy bananas with the best of intentions. Before I know it, though, I find the bananas sitting on my kitchen counter, browning, no longer yellow and no longer attractive enough for my family members to notice them. So into my freezer they go. I'm sure the same has happened to you. Ripe bananas are always the best for baking and freezing them renders them juicy and soft when they defrost, ideal for muffins and cakes. As a result, I'm never lacking for bananas to bake with. If you don't happen to have whole-wheat flour tucked away in your freezer—where it should be stored—simply use white flour.

———

Preheat the oven to 375°F (190°C). Get out a 12-cup muffin tin and lightly grease or line with muffin cups; set aside.

Whisk together the all-purpose flour, whole-wheat flour, wheat germ, baking powder, baking soda and salt in a bowl until the dry ingredients are thoroughly combined; set aside.

In a separate large bowl, whisk together the bananas, sugar, butter, egg and vanilla until well combined. Pour the banana mixture over the dry ingredients along with the chocolate chips, if using. Using a wooden spoon, quickly stir together until thoroughly moistened and a thick batter is created.

Divide the batter evenly among the prepared muffin cups.

Bake in the centre of the preheated oven until the tops of the muffins spring back when lightly pressed, about 20 minutes. Cool the muffins in the pan on a wire rack for 10 minutes. Remove the muffins from the pan, transferring to the wire rack to cool completely.

BAKER'S TIP

QUICK MUFFINS When you want to make muffins first thing in the morning, you don't always have time to let melted butter rest until it is room temperature or to bring cold ingredients to room temperature. You can use the cold temperature of other liquids to bring hot melted butter to room temperature quickly with this tried and true method. Melt the butter in a medium-sized skillet set over medium heat. Once the butter is melted, turn off the heat and slowly pour in the milk or whatever liquid is called for. Cool the milk-butter mixture slightly and then whisk in the eggs. The milk, butter and eggs should be at room temperature at this point.

Coffee Cake Muffins

THIS CAKE-LIKE muffin is perfect for a mid-morning snack or an afternoon coffee. Somewhat flat-topped, they're best fresh, right out of the oven or at least still warm.

Preheat the oven to 375°F (190°C). Line a 12-cup muffin tin with muffin cups. It's important to use liners here because the filling tends to seep out a bit, which can cause the muffins to stick to the pan and make removing them very difficult. Set aside.

CINNAMON COFFEE RIPPLE Stir together the brown sugar, flour, espresso powder, cinnamon and chocolate chips. Remove ¼ cup (60 mL) of this to another bowl and reserve for the topping. Stir the melted butter into the remaining ripple until well moistened; set aside.

BATTER Whisk together the all-purpose flour, baking powder, baking soda and salt in a bowl until the dry ingredients are thoroughly combined; set aside.

In a separate large bowl, whisk together the buttermilk, butter, sugar, eggs and vanilla until well combined. Pour the buttermilk mixture over the dry ingredients. Using a wooden spoon, stir together until just moistened and a thick batter is created.

Fill the muffin cups about one-third full. Sprinkle the cinnamon coffee ripple evenly over. Top with the remaining batter. Sprinkle with reserved topping.

Bake in the centre of the preheated oven until the tops of the muffins of spring back when lightly pressed, 20–25 minutes. Cool the muffins in the pan on a wire rack for 10 minutes. Remove the muffins from the pan, transferring to the wire rack to cool completely.

CINNAMON COFFEE RIPPLE

½ cup (125 mL) packed light brown sugar

1 Tbsp (15 mL) all-purpose flour

2 tsp (10 mL) instant espresso powder

1½ tsp (7 mL) cinnamon

½ cup (125 mL) mini chocolate chips

2 Tbsp (30 mL) butter, melted and cooled (1 oz/30 g)

BATTER

2½ cups (625 mL) all-purpose flour

2 tsp (10 mL) baking powder

1 tsp (5 mL) baking soda

¼ tsp (1 mL) salt

1¼ cups (310 mL) buttermilk, at room temperature

½ cup (125 mL) unsalted butter, melted and cooled (4 oz/125 g)

½ cup (125 mL) packed light brown sugar

2 large eggs, at room temperature

1 tsp (5 mL) vanilla

Pear Cranberry Muffins *with* Crunchy Almond Topping

THERE ARE just so many reasons why you will adore these muffins. One reason is that buttermilk, like sour cream, imparts a wonderfully moist and tender texture. The combination of the sweet pear with the tangy red cranberries is another. The fact that they bake up large and grand is another. The most compelling reason, though, is the crunchy, addictive topping that crowns them.

Preheat the oven to 375°F (190°C). Get out a 15-cup muffin tin and lightly grease or line with muffin cups; set aside.

TOPPING Whisk together the brown sugar, flour and cinnamon until the dry ingredients are thoroughly combined. With your fingertips, work the butter into the flour mixture until it's crumbly and starting to chunk together. Mix in the almonds; set aside.

BATTER Whisk together the all-purpose flour, baking soda, baking powder, cinnamon, ginger and salt in a bowl until the dry ingredients are thoroughly combined; set aside.

In a separate large bowl, whisk together the buttermilk, sugar, oil, egg and vanilla until well combined. Pour the buttermilk mixture over the dry ingredients along with the pear and cranberries. Using a wooden spoon, quickly stir together until just moistened and a thick batter is created.

Divide the batter evenly among the prepared muffin cups. The cups should be very full. Sprinkle the topping evenly over the batter.

Bake in the centre of the preheated oven until the tops of the muffins spring back when lightly pressed, 25–30 minutes. Cool the muffins in the pan on a wire rack for 10 minutes. Remove the muffins from the pan, transferring to the wire rack to cool completely.

TOPPING

½ cup (125 mL) packed light brown sugar

½ cup (125 mL) all-purpose flour

½ tsp (2 mL) cinnamon

¼ cup (60 mL) unsalted butter, softened (2 oz/60 g)

⅓ cup (80 mL) sliced almonds

BATTER

2½ cups (625 mL) all-purpose flour

1 tsp (5 mL) baking soda

½ tsp (2 mL) baking powder

½ tsp (2 mL) cinnamon

½ tsp (2 mL) ground ginger

½ tsp (2 mL) salt

1 cup (250 mL) buttermilk, at room temperature

1½ cups (375 mL) packed light brown sugar

⅔ cup (160 mL) canola or vegetable oil

1 large egg, at room temperature

1 tsp (5 mL) vanilla

1½ cups (375 mL) chopped peeled pear

¾ cup (180 mL) frozen cranberries, roughly chopped

BAKER'S TIP

Muffin batter can hold in the refrigerator overnight, with a moderate decrease in volume or height. Leaveners get right to work once the batter is mixed together, so they won't be at full strength the next morning. The batter will be full of air bubbles so it's important not to stir it and risk more loss of volume. Scoop out the batter, as it is, into a prepared muffin tin and get it right into the oven. Or better yet, fill the muffin tin the night before and then all you have to do is pop the entire tray into the oven.

Sour Cream Bluebaby Muffins

2 cups (500 mL) all-purpose flour
  (+ 2 Tbsp/30 mL extra if using
  frozen blueberries)

¾ tsp (4 mL) baking powder

1 tsp (5 mL) baking soda

½ tsp (2 mL) salt

1¼ cups (310 mL) granulated
  sugar

⅔ cup (160 mL) sour cream, at
  room temperature

½ cup (125 mL) unsalted butter,
  melted and cooled (4 oz/125 g)

2 large eggs, at room temperature

2 Tbsp (30 mL) finely grated
  lemon zest

1½ cups (375 mL) fresh or frozen
  wild blueberries

WHEN MY son Jacob was a mere toddler, we used to spend a month in the summer up at our cottage in the Laurentians in Quebec. We made weekly (sometimes daily) pilgrimages to a field down the dirt road that the cottagers colloquially dubbed "Blueberry Hill," since it was covered with wild blueberry bushes. Jacob (who is now a strapping teenager and prefers to go by Jake) and I would pick and eat pails of blueberries. Then we would go back to the cottage and make muffins. For some reason, however, my son took to calling blueberries "bluebabies," a moniker my whole family has now adopted. In his honour and in memory of those sun-drenched afternoons on blueberry hill, I christen these tender and berry-filled muffins Bluebaby Muffins.

If you don't happen to have fresh blueberries, or they're out of season, you can use frozen blueberries. Don't take them out of the freezer until you're just about to fold them in. I measure them and then stick them back in the freezer. If they thaw, they'll bleed (a pastry term meaning their juices will run throughout the batter), turning your lovely muffin batter a greenish blue. Tossing the frozen blueberries in all-purpose flour helps prevent this and keep the blueberries separate as you fold them into the batter. The sour cream in the batter helps bring out the subtle notes of citrus and highlights the tang of the blueberries.

Preheat the oven to 375°F (190°C). Get out a 12-cup muffin tin and lightly grease or line with muffin cups; set aside.

Whisk together the all-purpose flour, baking powder, baking soda and salt in a bowl in a bowl until the dry ingredients are thoroughly combined; set aside.

In a separate large bowl, whisk together the sugar, sour cream, butter, eggs and lemon zest until well combined. Pour the sour cream mixture over the dry ingredients. Using a wooden spoon, quickly stir together until just moistened. If using frozen blueberries, toss them in 2 Tbsp (30 mL) flour. Quickly and gently fold in the blueberries.

Divide the batter evenly among the prepared muffin cups. The cups should be quite full.

RECIPE CONTINUED . . .

Bake in the centre of the preheated oven until the tops of the muffins spring back when lightly pressed, about 20 minutes. Cool the muffins in the pan on a wire rack for 10 minutes. Remove the muffins from the pan, transferring to the wire rack to cool completely.

VARIATION

OVERSIZED BUTTERMILK BLUEBERRY MUFFINS Increase the flour to 3 cups (750 mL). Combine with 4 tsp (20 mL) baking powder and 1 tsp (5 mL) baking soda. Substitute the sour cream with 1¼ cups (310 mL) room temperature buttermilk. Fill the 12 muffin cups until they are overflowing. Bake as directed.

BAKER'S TIP

If you like your blueberry muffins with a little topping, combine about ¼ cup (60 mL) of granulated sugar in a small bowl with a pinch of ground cinnamon. Sprinkle on top of the muffins just before they go into the oven.

Nutella Swirl Muffins

NUTELLA IS finally enjoying its time in the limelight, and these muffins offer a compelling reason to always have it on hand. Topped with a light sprinkle of sweetness, the attractive and tempting nutella swirl is encased in a tender crumbed vanilla-tickled batter. Let these muffins cool for at least 5 minutes in the pan—they are delicate and you don't want them to fall apart in your haste to taste (do I mean devour?) them.

Preheat the oven to 375°F (190°C). Grease a 12-cup muffin tin well with butter or cooking spray. Line 10 of the muffin cups with paper muffin cups. It's important to use liners here because the swirl can cause the muffins to stick to the pan, making removing them very difficult; set aside.

TOPPING In a small bowl, combine the sugars and cinnamon until well mixed; set aside.

BATTER In a separate bowl, whisk together the flour, baking powder, baking soda and salt until the dry ingredients are thoroughly combined; set aside.

In the bowl of a stand mixer fitted with the paddle attachment, or using hand-held beaters, beat the butter for 1 minute. In a thin stream, gradually add the sugar and beat until very light, about 3 minutes. One at a time, beat in the eggs, beating well after the first egg before adding the second, and scraping down the bowl with a plastic spatula in between the 2 additions. Beat in the vanilla. Remove the bowl from the stand.

Using a wooden spoon, quickly stir in half of the flour mixture. Stir in the sour cream and then the remaining flour mixture. Dollop the Nutella all over the batter. Gently swirl the Nutella through the batter with the handle of a spoon. Spoon the mixture evenly among the prepared cups. Sprinkle the topping evenly over the batter. Pour water halfway up the unfilled and unlined cups.

Bake in the centre of the preheated oven until the tops of the muffins spring back when lightly pressed, 20–25 minutes. Cool the muffins in the pan on a wire rack for 10 minutes. Remove the muffins from the pan, transferring to the wire rack to cool completely.

TOPPING

2 Tbsp (30 mL) granulated sugar

2 Tbsp (30 mL) light brown sugar

½ tsp (2 mL) cinnamon

BATTER

1½ cups (375 mL) all-purpose flour

¾ tsp (4 mL) baking powder

¼ tsp (1 mL) baking soda

¼ tsp (1 mL) salt

½ cup (125 mL) unsalted butter, softened (4 oz/125 g)

1 cup (250 mL) granulated sugar

2 large eggs, at room temperature

2 tsp (10 mL) vanilla

½ cup (125 mL) sour cream, at room temperature

¼ heaping cup (60+mL) Nutella

Golden Corn Muffins

I FIRST gained knowledge of corn muffins, a specialty of the southern United States, while I was studying in San Francisco. A guest teacher, Beth Hensperger, was teaching that day and she made an outlandishly delicious corn muffin with fresh corn kernels, chives and habanero peppers. I was blown away. Beth was an incredible teacher and I will never forget the way she taught us to make bread; she taught us to spend the necessary time, and to never rush it. In my head, I still hear her say, "You have to love your bread and give it warmth." I still heed those words. And I still love her muffins, although I have altered the heat somewhat by calling for chipotle instead of a habanero, and I've changed the chives to green onions. I hope she would approve.

Preheat the oven to 375°F (190°C). Get out a 12-cup muffin tin and lightly grease or line with muffin cups; set aside.

Whisk together the flour, cornmeal, baking powder, baking soda, pepper, salt and chipotle chili powder in a bowl until the dry ingredients are thoroughly combined; set aside.

In a separate large bowl, whisk together the buttermilk, sugar, butter and eggs until well combined. Pour the buttermilk mixture over the dry ingredients. Add the corn and green onion. Using a wooden spoon, quickly stir together until just moistened.

Divide the batter evenly among the prepared muffin cups. Bake in the centre of the preheated oven until the tops of the muffins spring back when lightly pressed, about 18 minutes. Cool the muffins in the pan on a wire rack for 10 minutes. Remove the muffins from the pan, transferring to the wire rack to cool completely.

1 cup (250 mL) all-purpose flour

1 cup (250 mL) yellow cornmeal

2 tsp (10 mL) baking powder

1 tsp (5 mL) baking soda

1 tsp (5 mL) ground black pepper

½ tsp (2 mL) salt

¼ tsp (1 mL) chipotle chili powder (or 1 tsp/5 mL regular chili powder)

1 cup (250 mL) buttermilk, at room temperature

½ cup (125 mL) granulated sugar

⅓ cup (80 mL) unsalted butter, melted and cooled (3 oz/90 g)

2 large eggs, at room temperature

1 cup (250 mL) roasted corn kernels (or frozen corn niblets)

¼ cup (60 mL) chopped green onion

Double Apple Muffins

TOPPING
2 Tbsp (30 mL) granulated sugar

½ tsp (2 mL) cinnamon

BATTER
2 cups (500 mL) all-purpose flour

1 Tbsp (15 mL) baking powder

½ tsp (2 mL) cinnamon

Pinch of salt

¾ cup (180 mL) unsweetened
   applesauce

¾ cup (180 mL) granulated sugar

⅓ cup (80 mL) unsalted butter,
   melted and cooled (3 oz/90 g)

1 large egg, at room temperature

1 tsp (5 mL) vanilla

1 cup (250 mL) diced peeled apple
   (about 1 apple)

PERFECTLY DOMED, dainty and a little craggly, I like to think of these muffins as reminiscent of days gone by. I would actually call them quaint and can perfectly picture my grandmother eating them with her friends while drinking tea in her living room. If she had been a grander woman, I might say her parlour, but indeed it would have been her living room. My grandmother, as did many women of her generation, collected Rosenthal and other high brow tea cups, each one with a different design, most often floral. I have those same tea cups on display in my dining room, and occasionally take them out to serve tea along with these muffins.

Preheat the oven to 375°F (190°C). Get out a 12-cup muffin tin and lightly grease or line with muffin cups; set aside.

TOPPING Stir together the sugar and cinnamon until well mixed; set aside.

BATTER Whisk together the flour, baking powder, cinnamon and salt in a bowl until the dry ingredients are thoroughly combined; set aside.

In a separate large bowl, whisk together the applesauce, sugar, butter, egg and vanilla until well combined. Pour the applesauce mixture over the dry ingredients along with the diced apple. Using a wooden spoon, quickly stir together until just moistened.

Divide the batter evenly among the prepared muffin cups. Evenly sprinkle the topping over the batter.

Bake in the centre of the preheated oven until the tops of the muffins spring back when lightly pressed, about 25 minutes. Cool the muffins in the pan on a wire rack for 10 minutes. Remove the muffins from the pan, transferring to the wire rack to cool completely.

Zucchini Cheese Muffins *with* Sun-Dried Tomatoes

IN GENERAL, I like to keep sweet things sweet and savoury things savoury. However, muffins don't always have to be sweet (nor do scones) to be enjoyed. Muffins are great and efficient transmitters of flavour and can make the leap from breakfast to lunch to dinner without so much as a backward glance. They're great for lunch with a side salad and can travel to a park or a hiking trail comfortably in a picnic basket or backpack. Just don't get me to endorse chocolate chip bagels—my flexibility only goes so far.

Preheat the oven to 375°F (190°C). Get out a 12-cup muffin tin and lightly grease or line with muffin cups; set aside.

Whisk together the flour, cheese, baking powder, baking soda, basil, pepper and salt in a bowl until the dry ingredients are thoroughly combined; set aside.

In a separate large bowl, whisk together the milk, zucchini, tomatoes, oil and eggs until well combined. Pour the zucchini mixture over the dry ingredients. Using a wooden spoon, quickly stir together until just moistened.

Divide the batter evenly among the prepared muffin cups. Sprinkle the cheese evenly over the top of each muffin.

Bake in the centre of the preheated oven until the tops of the muffins spring back when lightly pressed, 18–20 minutes. Cool the muffins in the pan on a wire rack for 10 minutes. Remove the muffins from the pan, transferring to the wire rack to cool completely.

VARIATION

RED PEPPER AND FETA MUFFINS Replace the sun-dried tomatoes with ½ cup (125 mL) julienned roasted red peppers (patted dry), the dried basil with 3 Tbsp (45 mL) finely chopped fresh basil and the Fontina with ½ cup (125 mL) crumbled feta cheese.

RECIPE CONTINUED . . .

2½ cups (625 mL) all-purpose flour
½ cup (125 mL) grated Parmigiano Reggiano cheese
2 tsp (10 mL) baking powder
1 tsp (5 mL) baking soda
1½ tsp (7 mL) dried basil leaves
1 tsp (5 mL) ground black pepper
½ tsp (2 mL) salt
1¼ cups (310 mL) milk, at room temperature
1 cup (250 mL) shredded zucchini
⅓ cup (80 mL) chopped packed in oil sun-dried tomatoes
⅓ cup (80 mL) canola or vegetable oil
2 large eggs, at room temperature
½ cup (125 mL) shredded Fontina or Gruyère cheese

BAKER'S TIP

When using Parmesan cheese, look for the real McCoy: Parmesan sold in wheels with the words Parmigiano Reggiano stenciled on the side. This way, you're guaranteed it was produced in the very strictly controlled regions in Italy that are allowed to make real Parmesan. Imposters abound. Avoid buying cheese labeled Grana Padano or any product that contains non-dairy fillers. If you buy your cheese at a store that has a high turnover, you're more likely to get a freshly cut piece that hasn't been on the shelves for who knows how long. Good Parmesan is aged for at least a year, better if it's two. Try to buy a piece with the rind still attached; it helps the cheese stay fresh. And if at all possible, buy it as soon as it's cut. The more it is cut up, the more moisture it loses. The cheese's interior should be scaly or flaky when broken, with white dots resembling grain kernels. The colour should be as uniform as possible with no whitish haze around the rind (if there is, it means the cheese has been stored improperly and is beginning to dry out). The colour should range from a pale cream to a deep yellow straw. Holes in Parmesan are a deep flaw.

Orange Vanilla Muffins *with* Marmalade Glaze

REQUIRING NOTHING more than two bowls and a sturdy hand, these muffins are quick to put together and ideal for those who kind of stumble into the kitchen in the morning. To make things even easier, you can combine the sugar, orange zest and vanilla bean the night before.

Preheat the oven to 375°F (190°C). Get out a 12-cup muffin tin and lightly grease or line with muffin cups; set aside.

Toss together the sugar and orange zest until the zest is well distributed. With the pointy tip of a small knife, scrape out the seeds from both halves of the vanilla bean. Add to the sugar and stir until well distributed. Let stand while you prepare the other ingredients.

Whisk together the all-purpose flour, baking powder, baking soda, cardamom and salt in a bowl until the dry ingredients are thoroughly combined; set aside.

In a separate large bowl, whisk together the sour cream, butter, orange juice and eggs until well combined. Whisk in the flavoured sugar. Pour the sour cream mixture over the dry ingredients. Using a wooden spoon, quickly stir together until just moistened.

Divide the batter evenly among the prepared muffin cups.

Bake in the centre of the preheated oven until the tops of the muffins spring back when lightly pressed, 18–20 minutes. In a small saucepan, heat the marmalade with 1 Tbsp (15 mL) water just until heated through. Brush over the tops of each muffin. Cool the muffins in the pan on a wire rack for 10 minutes. Remove the muffins from the pan, transferring to the wire rack to cool completely.

⅔ cup (160 mL) granulated sugar

2 Tbsp (30 mL) finely grated orange zest

1 large vanilla bean, split lengthwise

2 cups (500 mL) all-purpose flour

2 tsp (10 mL) baking powder

½ tsp (2 mL) baking soda

½ tsp (2 mL) ground cardamom

¼ tsp (1 mL) salt

1 cup (250 mL) sour cream, at room temperature

⅓ cup (80 mL) unsalted butter, melted and cooled (3 oz/90 g)

¼ cup (60 mL) freshly squeezed orange juice

2 large eggs, at room temperature

¼ cup (60 mL) orange marmalade

1 Tbsp (15 mL) water

BAKER'S TIP
The vanilla bean in this recipe can be replaced with 1 tsp (5 mL) vanilla extract.

Triple Ginger Muffins

TOPPING

⅓ cup (80 mL) packed light brown sugar

⅓ cup (80 mL) all-purpose flour

¼ tsp (1 mL) ground ginger

Pinch of cinnamon

3 Tbsp (45 mL) unsalted butter, melted and cooled (1.5 oz/45 g)

BATTER

2 cups (500 mL) all-purpose flour

1 tsp (5 mL) baking powder

1 tsp (5 mL) ground ginger

½ tsp (2 mL) baking soda

½ tsp (2 mL) salt

⅔ cup (160 mL) packed light brown sugar

½ cup (125 mL) sour cream, at room temperature

½ cup (125 mL) buttermilk, at room temperature

½ cup (125 mL) unsalted butter, melted and cooled (4 oz/125 g)

2 large eggs, at room temperature

1 tsp (5 mL) vanilla

¼ cup (60 mL) diced crystallized ginger

3 Tbsp (45 mL) minced fresh ginger

CALLING ALL ginger lovers. These are the muffins for you. With ground ginger, crystallized ginger and fresh ginger, these will perk up your taste buds and bring a smile to your face. They call for both buttermilk and sour cream, so a tender crumb is guaranteed.

Preheat the oven to 375°F (190°C). Get out a 12-cup muffin tin and lightly grease or line with muffin cups; set aside.

TOPPING Stir together the sugar, flour, ginger and cinnamon. Drizzle the melted butter over, tossing with your fingertips or a fork until well moistened; set aside.

BATTER Whisk together the flour, baking powder, ground ginger, baking soda and salt in a bowl until the dry ingredients are thoroughly combined; set aside.

In a separate large bowl, whisk together the sugar, sour cream, buttermilk, butter, eggs and vanilla until well combined. Pour the sour cream mixture over the dry ingredients along with the crystallized and fresh ginger. Using a wooden spoon, quickly stir together until just moistened.

Divide the batter evenly among the prepared muffin cups. Evenly sprinkle the topping over the batter.

Bake in the centre of the preheated oven until the tops of the muffins spring back when lightly pressed, about 18 minutes. Cool the muffins in the pan on a wire rack for 10 minutes. Remove the muffins from the pan, transferring to the wire rack to cool completely.

BISCUITS

The third technique in the quick bread category, used for most biscuits and scones—as well as pies—is the cut-in method or pie method. This method relies on cold unsalted butter being cut, either using a food processor, pastry blender, two knives or your fingers, into a bowl of flour, sugar and some kind of leavener. The butter is cut into smaller and smaller pieces until finally it resembles the size and shape of small peas with a few larger pieces mixed in. Liquid is then poured into the mixture and fluffed or stirred until a shaggy dough is formed. The dough is kneaded ever so slightly before being cut or shaped into biscuits.

HOW DO YOU GET THE FLAKY INTO FLAKY BISCUITS AND SCONES?

Basically the answer is threefold: the temperature of the butter, the cutting in of the butter and the temperature of the oven. First, the butter has to be very cold. Then it is cut in. Some of the butter coats the flour, tenderizing it and discouraging gluten development, while the majority of it gets cut up into pieces about the size of peas (the butter pieces need to be the right size or they won't melt properly). The pea-sized pieces of butter have to stay distinct from the flour so that when they melt in the heat of the oven, they leave a gap between where they were and the surrounding dough, creating a flake or a flaky texture. If the butter is too enmeshed into the dough, you will lose this opportunity for flakiness. Likewise, if the size of the butter is too big, the dough will break or tear and you still lose flakiness.

To achieve these spaces, the oven has to be very hot, generally around 400°F (200°C). The high heat causes the proteins and starches in the dough to set quickly, before the butter has a chance to melt. This is also why the butter has to be cold—to ensure that the dough sets before the butter has a chance to melt.

Minimal handling is key to making good scones and biscuits. Too much handling of the dough translates to increased gluten formation, while the butter tends to get warmer and warmer, ruining your chances for the "flake." This is one reason why so many people prefer to use a food processor, myself included. It eliminates handling the dough too much and minimizes the opportunity for the butter to warm up. A word of caution, however. Food processors work very quickly and there is a very fine line between cutting in butter that's the size of peas and going just a bit too far, at which point your butter more closely remembers grains of sand. Definitely not optimal. Your biscuits will still turn out delicious, just not as flaky. Pulse, rather than keeping the machine running, and start to "listen" to your food processor. You will hear a distinct difference in how the machine sounds when it is first cutting the butter and when the butter has reached the small-pea stage. It takes some time to get used to but you will find a distinction. The butter can be uneven, just not overall too small or too large. And even though most biscuits contain chemical leaveners that will ensure a good rise, they do not create the flakiness, they simply rise.

As you can see, I take this kind of seriously. I'm biased because I like my biscuits and scones nice and tall. I also advocate, as I do when making pastry, that you add the liquid to the dry mixture all at once. If you add it a bit at a time, the gluten in the dough gets developed unevenly. If you're not sure how much to add or even of the humidity in your kitchen (which can affect the outcome) add the least amount of liquid called for. That way, you just have to add a tablespoon or two more to get the dough to the right consistency. I do not do this in the food processor because of the speed of the machine. Once you add the liquid you still have to pulse the dough to combine it, which runs the risk of cutting the butter into smaller and smaller pieces, thereby losing your flake. The food processor also brings the dough together quickly, more quickly than you might think, which actually risks it being overdone and ending up more of a homogenous mass than the desired shaggy one.

Everyday Buttery Biscuits

2 cups (500 mL) all-purpose flour

1 Tbsp (15 mL) baking powder

1 Tbsp (15 mL) granulated sugar

¾ tsp (4 mL) salt

¾ cup (180 mL) cold unsalted
butter (6 oz/175 g)

¾ cup (180 mL) cold milk

Biscuits are always best eaten the day they're made. With no cream to weigh it down, these biscuits are genuinely scrumptious, and ideal for serving with a simple week-night supper.

Preheat the oven to 425°F (220°C). Line a baking sheet with parchment paper; set aside.

Combine the flour, baking powder, sugar and salt in the bowl of a food processor fitted with the metal "S" blade. Pulse twice to combine and aerate. Cut the butter into cubes and add to the food processor. Pulse until the butter is cut into pieces the size of small peas, with a few larger pieces. (Conversely, you can do the above in a large bowl, using a pastry cutter or two knives to cut in the butter until it's the size of irregular-shaped peas.)

Transfer the dry ingredients to a bowl. Pour the milk all over the flour-butter mixture. Toss with a fork until the mixture is thoroughly moistened. It may not fully come together; there may be some flour not fully incorporated—don't worry about this.

Transfer the dough to a clean work surface, including the unincorporated bits. Knead gently, about 4 or 5 times, just until the dough forms a moist, cohesive ball. Gently pat the dough down until it's about 1 inch (2.5 cm) thick. Using a 2½-inch (6 cm) cookie cutter, cut out rounds, rerolling scraps only once; any dough remaining after the first re-roll must be discarded as the biscuits will be tough. Transfer the biscuits to the prepared baking sheet.

Bake in the centre of the preheated oven until puffed and golden, about 12 minutes. Cool the biscuits on the pan on a wire rack for at least 5 minutes before serving.

CHEESE BISCUITS Reduce the sugar to 1 tsp (5 mL). After the butter is in pea-sized pieces, add 1 cup (250 mL) shredded old cheddar, 1 cup (250 mL) shredded Gruyère and 1 tsp (5 mL) dried mustard. Proceed with the recipe.

DRIED FRUIT BISCUITS Increase the sugar to 2 Tbsp (30 mL). After the butter is in pea-sized pieces, add either ¾ cup (180 mL) dried currants, ¾ cup (180 mL) dried blueberries or 1 cup (250 mL) raisins. Proceed with the recipe.

CRANBERRY LEMON BISCUITS Increase the sugar to 2 Tbsp (30 mL). After the butter is in pea-sized pieces, add 1 Tbsp (15 mL) finely grated lemon zest and 1 cup (250 mL) chopped fresh or frozen cranberries. Proceed with the recipe.

BAKER'S TIP

Biscuits are meant to be eaten the day they're made and don't hold well. If you must hold them over for another day, the best thing to do is to freeze them and thaw them just before you're going to eat them.

Buttermilk Biscuits

1¾ cups (430 mL) all-purpose flour

1 Tbsp (15 mL) granulated sugar

2 tsp (10 mL) baking powder

½ tsp (2 mL) baking soda

½ tsp (2 mL) salt

½ cup (125 mL) cold unsalted butter (4 oz/125 g)

¾ cup (180 mL) cold buttermilk

So HIGH they resemble a top hat, these are the quintessential brunch biscuits. Eaten while still warm, butter melting on each half, they fairly cry out for jam or crème fraîche. They're equally majestic made slightly smaller or larger.

Preheat the oven to 425°F (220°C). Line a baking sheet with parchment paper; set aside.

Combine the flour, sugar, baking powder, baking soda and salt in the bowl of a food processor fitted with the metal "S" blade. Pulse twice to combine and aerate. Cut the butter into cubes and add to the food processor. Pulse until the butter is cut into pieces the size of small peas, with a few larger pieces. (Conversely, you can do the above in a large bowl, using a pastry cutter or two knives to cut in the butter until it's the size of irregular-shaped peas.)

Transfer the dry ingredients to a bowl. Pour the buttermilk all over the flour-butter mixture. Toss with a fork until the mixture is thoroughly moistened. It may not fully come together; there may be some flour not fully incorporated—don't worry about this.

Transfer the dough to a clean work surface, including the unincorporated bits. Knead gently, about 4 or 5 times, just until the dough forms a moist, cohesive ball. Gently pat the dough down until it's about 1 inch (2.5 cm) thick. Using a 2½-inch (6 cm) cookie cutter, cut out rounds, rerolling scraps only once. Transfer the biscuits to the prepared baking sheet.

Bake in the centre of the preheated oven until puffed and golden, about 12 minutes. Cool the biscuits on the pan on a wire rack for at least 5 minutes before serving.

BAKER'S TIP

Some baking books call for grating frozen butter into their biscuits, as opposed to cutting it in with a pastry cutter or in the food processor. This helps distribute the butter evenly and ensures that the butter stays cold. It's a great and efficient method and helps avoid having to guess if your butter is sufficiently cut in.

Sour Cream Biscuits *with* Cinnamon

SWIRL

2 Tbsp (30 mL) packed light brown
 sugar

1 tsp (5 mL) cinnamon

DOUGH

2 cups (500 mL) all-purpose flour

2 Tbsp (30 mL) granulated sugar

1 Tbsp (15 mL) baking powder

½ tsp (2 mL) salt

⅔ cup (160 mL) cold unsalted
 butter (5 oz/150 g)

½ cup (125 mL) cold sour cream

¼ cup (60 mL) cold milk

I SUPPOSE I'm partial to swirls in my biscuits, muffins and other cakes, because it's a subtle way of enjoying more flavour. A swirl kind of tickles your taste buds without a full on assault. It's more provocative than straightforward. In this case, its subtlety allows the sour cream notes to take centre stage while the cinnamon swirl struts in the background,

Preheat the oven to 425°F (220°C). Line a baking sheet with parchment paper; set aside.

SWIRL In a small bowl, stir together the sugar and cinnamon until well combined; set aside.

DOUGH Combine the flour, sugar, baking powder and salt in the bowl of a food processor fitted with the metal "S" blade. Pulse twice to combine and aerate. Cut the butter into cubes and add to the food processor. Pulse until the butter is cut into pieces the size of small peas, with a few larger pieces. (Conversely, you can do the above in a large bowl, using a pastry cutter or two knives to cut in the butter until it's the size of irregular-shaped peas.)

Transfer the dry ingredients to a bowl. Stir in the cinnamon swirl.

Stir together the sour cream and milk until blended; pour all over the flour-butter mixture. Toss with a fork until the mixture is thoroughly moistened. It may not fully come together; there may be some flour not fully incorporated—don't worry about this.

Transfer the dough to a clean work surface, including the unincorporated bits. Knead gently, about 4 or 5 times, just until the dough forms a moist, cohesive ball. Gently pat the dough down until it's about 1 inch (2.5 cm) thick. Using a 2½-inch (6 cm) cookie cutter, cut out rounds, rerolling scraps only once. Transfer the biscuits to the prepared baking sheet.

Bake in the centre of the preheated oven until puffed and golden, about 12 minutes. Cool the biscuits on the pan on a wire rack for at least 5 minutes before serving.

BAKER'S TIP

Like muffins, biscuits can be made the day before, cut or shaped and held in the refrigerator overnight. There will be a slight loss in height. They will only hold for 1 day, no longer.

Tender Flaky Biscuits

W**HAT GIVES**? Aren't all biscuits flaky? Why specifically call *these* tender and flaky? Yes, all of my biscuits are flaky. What makes a biscuit tender AND flaky depends on the fat you use. Shortening, which is always soft, even when chilled, coats the flour instead of remaining separate from it. This tenderizes the biscuit. The butter does the flaky thing. Together, their combined efforts result in the much heralded tender but flaky biscuit. For a lengthier explanation, see page 241.

2¼ cups (560 mL) all-purpose flour

1 Tbsp (15 mL) baking powder

1 Tbsp (15 mL) granulated sugar

¾ tsp (4 mL) salt

⅓ cup (80 mL) cold unsalted butter (3 oz/90 g)

2 Tbsp (30 mL) cold vegetable shortening (1 oz/30 g)

1 cup (250 mL) cold milk

Preheat the oven to 425°F (220°C). Line a baking sheet with parchment paper; set aside.

Combine the flour, baking powder, sugar and salt in the bowl of a food processor fitted with the metal "S" blade. Pulse twice to combine and aerate. Cut the butter and shortening into cubes and add to the food processor. Pulse until the butter and shortening are cut into pieces the size of small peas, with a few larger pieces. (Conversely, you can do the above in a large bowl, using a pastry cutter or two knives to cut in the butter and shortening until it's the size of irregular-shaped peas.)

Transfer the dry ingredients to a bowl. Pour the milk all over the flour-butter mixture. Toss with a fork until the mixture is thoroughly moistened. It may not fully come together; there may be some flour not fully incorporated—don't worry about this.

Transfer the dough to a clean work surface, including the unincorporated bits. Knead gently, about 4 or 5 times, just until the dough forms a moist, cohesive ball. Gently pat the dough down until it's about 1 inch (2.5 cm) thick. Using a 2½-inch (6 cm) cookie cutter, cut out rounds, rerolling scraps only once. Transfer the biscuits to the prepared baking sheet.

Bake in the centre of the preheated oven until puffed and golden, about 12 minutes. Cool the biscuits on the pan on a wire rack for at least 5 minutes before serving.

BAKER'S TIP

Biscuits and scones are always baked in a hot oven, generally 400°F (200°C) to 425°F (220°C), so that they can bake and rise before they dry out.

Citrus Sunshine Biscuits

2 cups (500 mL) all-purpose flour

2 Tbsp (30 mL) granulated sugar

2¼ tsp (11 mL) baking powder

½ tsp (2 mL) baking soda

½ tsp (2 mL) salt

½ cup (125 mL) cold unsalted
butter (4 oz/125 g)

1 Tbsp (15 mL) finely grated lemon
zest

1 Tbsp (15 mL) finely grated
orange zest

¾ cup (180 mL) cold buttermilk

SPECKLED WITH orange zest and golden surfaced, this biscuit reminds me of sunshine streaming through a morning window.

Preheat the oven to 425°F (220°C). Line a baking sheet with parchment paper; set aside.

Combine the flour, sugar, baking powder, baking soda and salt in the bowl of a food processor fitted with the metal "S" blade. Pulse twice to combine and aerate. Cut the butter into cubes and add to the food processor. Pulse until the butter is cut into pieces the size of small peas, with a few larger pieces. Add the citrus zests; pulse once to combine. (Conversely, you can do the above in a large bowl, using a pastry cutter or two knives to cut in the butter until it's the size of irregular-shaped peas. Stir in the citrus zests.)

Transfer the mixture to a large bowl. Pour the buttermilk all over the flour-butter mixture. Toss with a fork until the mixture is thoroughly moistened. It may not fully come together; there may be some flour not fully incorporated—don't worry about this.

Transfer the dough to a clean work surface, including the unincorporated bits. Knead gently, about 4 or 5 times, just until the dough forms a moist, cohesive ball. Gently pat the dough down until it's about 1 inch (2.5 cm) thick. Using a 2½-inch (6 cm) cookie cutter, cut out rounds, rerolling scraps only once. Transfer the biscuits to the prepared baking sheet.

Bake in the centre of the preheated oven until puffed and golden, about 12 minutes. Cool the biscuits on the pan on a wire rack for at least 5 minutes before serving.

BAKER'S TIP

Placing the biscuits at least 2 inches (5 cm) apart on the baking sheet ensures even heat circulation so that the sides bake to a golden colour and provide the contrasting chew to the tender interiors. If you want the sides of your biscuits to be extra soft, place the biscuits as close as possible to each other on the baking sheet. They'll come out softer that way.

Parmesan Thyme Biscuits

THESE BISCUITS round out the dinner table whether you're serving soup, a stew or just want to spread a little herbed cream cheese on them. They're also great as a miniature sandwich. Cut in half horizontally and pile high with some thinly sliced roast beef or cheese.

Preheat the oven to 425°F (220°C). Line a baking sheet with parchment paper; set aside.

Combine the flour, cheese, baking powder, sugar, thyme, soda, salt and pepper in the bowl of a food processor fitted with the metal "S" blade. Pulse twice to combine and aerate. Cut the butter into cubes and add to the food processor. Pulse until the butter is cut into pieces the size of small peas, with a few larger pieces. (Conversely, you can do the above in a large bowl, using a pastry cutter or two knives to cut in the butter until it's the size of irregular-shaped peas.)

Transfer the mixture to a large bowl. Pour the buttermilk all over the flour-butter mixture. Toss with a fork until the mixture is thoroughly moistened. It may not fully come together; there may be some flour not fully incorporated—don't worry about this.

Transfer the dough to a clean work surface, including the unincorporated bits. Knead gently, about 4 or 5 times, just until the dough forms a moist, cohesive ball. Gently pat the dough down until it's about 1 inch (2.5 cm) thick. Using a 2½-inch (6 cm) cookie cutter, cut out rounds, rerolling scraps once only. Transfer the biscuits to the prepared baking sheet.

Bake in the centre of the preheated oven until puffed and golden, about 12 minutes. Cool the biscuits on the pan on a wire rack for at least 5 minutes before serving.

VARIATIONS

ROMANO SAGE BISCUITS Substitute grated Romano cheese for the Parmesan, and dried rubbed sage (not ground) for the thyme leaves.

2¼ cups (560 mL) all-purpose flour
⅓ cup (80 mL) finely grated Parmigiano Reggiano cheese
2¼ tsp (11 mL) baking powder
1 tsp (5 mL) granulated sugar
1 tsp (5 mL) dried thyme leaves
½ tsp (2 mL) baking soda
¼ tsp (1 mL) salt
¼ tsp (1 mL) ground black pepper
½ cup (125 mL) cold unsalted butter (4 oz/125 g)
¾ cup (180 mL) cold buttermilk

SCONES

Though both scones and biscuits rely on the same basic method, scones are of Scottish descent whereas the biscuit is American through and through, with roots in the Southern states. The scone, in its infancy, used to be oat based and was commonly made in a skillet before being shaped into pie wedges and served with meals. The wedge shape is still the most common shape for scones. Even today, scones in the United Kingdom tend to be less sweet and use less butter. One of the most common explanations for this is that butter is slathered on top, and jam is usually piled on top of the butter, making butter and sugar unnecessary in the dough itself. Scones as we in North America have come to know and love them are sweeter, quite large, use more butter and tend to have inclusions, such as dried fruit, fresh fruit or, of course, cheese. They're eaten with meals, as a snack, or even as a dessert. Once you have the basics down, use your own imagination to dress them up.

Classic Cream Scones

Sweet but not so sweet that they won't welcome some butter and a ruby red berry jam, these scones are welcome any time of the day, although they're best warm.

Preheat the oven to 400°F (200°C). Line a baking sheet with parchment paper; set aside.

Combine the flour, sugar, baking powder and salt in the bowl of a food processor fitted with the metal "S" blade. Pulse twice to combine and aerate. Cut the butter into cubes and add to the food processor. Pulse until the butter is cut into pieces the size of small peas, with a few larger pieces. (Conversely, you can do the above in a large bowl, using a pastry cutter or two knives to cut in the butter until it's the size of irregular-shaped peas.) Transfer the mixture to a large bowl.

Whisk together the whipping cream and egg until thoroughly blended. Pour over the flour-butter mixture along with the currants. Toss with a fork until the mixture is thoroughly moistened. It may not fully come together; there may be some flour not fully incorporated—don't worry about this.

Transfer the dough to a clean work surface, including the unincorporated bits. Knead gently, about 4 or 5 times, just until the dough forms a moist, cohesive ball. Gently pat the dough down into an even rectangle that is about 8 × 5 inches (20 × 12 cm). It should be about 1 inch (2.5 cm) thick.

With a sharp knife or pastry cutter, cut the rectangle in half lengthwise. Then cut each half into 6 triangles. Transfer the scones to the prepared baking sheet.

Bake in the centre of the preheated oven until golden and baked through, 16–18 minutes. Cool the scones on the pan on a wire rack for at least 5 minutes before serving.

2 cups (500 mL) all-purpose flour

⅓ cup (80 mL) granulated sugar

1 Tbsp (15 mL) baking powder

½ tsp (2 mL) salt

⅓ cup (80 mL) cold unsalted butter (3 oz/90 g)

¾ cup (180 mL) cold whipping cream

1 cold large egg

½ cup (125 mL) currants

VARIATIONS

CITRUS SCONES After the butter is in pea-sized pieces, stir in 1 Tbsp (15 mL) finely grated orange or lemon zest along with ⅔ cup (160 mL) chopped fresh or frozen cranberries.

RAISIN SCONES After the butter is in pea-sized pieces, stir in ¾ cup (180 mL) raisins.

CHERRY WHITE CHOCOLATE SCONES After the butter is in pea-sized pieces, stir in ⅔ cup (160 mL) dried cherries and 2 oz (60 g) coarsely chopped white chocolate.

Orange Kissed Scones *with* Vanilla-Roasted Plums

VANILLA ROASTED PLUMS

¾ cup (180 mL) granulated sugar

½ vanilla bean

6 firm ripe plums

SCONES

1¾ cups (430 mL) all-purpose
   flour

3 Tbsp (45 mL) granulated sugar

1 Tbsp (15 mL) baking powder

¼ tsp (1 mL) baking soda

¼ tsp (1 mL) salt

⅓ cup (80 mL) cold unsalted
   butter (3 oz/90 g)

2 Tbsp (30 mL) finely grated
   orange zest

⅔ cup (160 mL) cold buttermilk

1 cold large egg yolk

THESE TWO recipes are marvellous together. The scones are light and airy, happily made tender by the addition of buttermilk. They're made in the classic triangle shape but can just as easily be made in another shape. The vanilla roasted plums are divine. I sometimes make this sauce just to eat it on its own, standing at my counter, spoon in hand, slurping the soft plums and sauce straight from the bowl. Roasting brings out all of the richness of the plums. As the sugar cooks, it melts into a voluptuous sauce, with tantalizing high notes of vanilla. Combined with the scones, this is a plated dessert, one of which the gods would approve, it's that heavenly.

Preheat the oven to 350°F (180°C).

VANILLA ROASTED PLUMS Add the sugar to an 8-inch (20 cm) square glass baking dish. Split the vanilla bean in half horizontally. Scrape the seeds into the sugar, distributing them as evenly as possible.

Cut the plums in half; remove the pits. Cut into thick slices. Stir into the flavoured sugar.

Roast in the centre of the preheated oven for 15 minutes. Stir the plums gently so that all of the sugar is liquefied and the plums are covered. Roast for an additional 10–15 minutes or until the plums are tender. (Plums can be cooled and refrigerated for up to 3 days. Bring to room temperature before serving.)

SCONES Increase the oven heat to 400°F (200°C). Line a baking sheet with parchment; set aside.

Combine the flour, sugar, baking powder, baking soda and salt in the bowl of a food processor fitted with the metal "S" blade. Pulse twice to combine and aerate. Cut the butter into cubes and add to the food processor. Pulse until the butter is cut into pieces the size of small peas, with a few larger pieces. (Conversely, you can do the above in a large bowl, using a pastry cutter or two knives to cut in the butter until it's the size of irregular-shaped peas.) Transfer the mixture to a large bowl. Stir in the orange zest.

Whisk together the buttermilk and egg yolk until thoroughly blended. Pour over the flour-butter mixture. Toss with a fork until the mixture is thoroughly moistened. It may not fully come together; there may be some flour not fully incorporated—don't worry about this.

Transfer the dough to a clean work surface, including the unincorporated bits. Knead gently, about 4 or 5 times, just until the dough forms a moist, cohesive ball. Gently pat the dough down into an even rectangle that is about 7 × 5 inches (18 × 12 cm). It should be about 1 inch (2.5 cm) thick.

With a sharp knife or pastry cutter, cut the rectangle in half lengthwise. Then cut each half into 6 triangles. Transfer the scones to the prepared baking sheet.

Bake in the centre of the preheated oven until golden and baked through, 16–18 minutes. Cool the scones on the pan on a wire rack for at least 5 minutes before serving.

Serve with vanilla roasted plums spooned over top.

Gingerbread Scones

2 cups (500 mL) all-purpose flour

¼ cup (60 mL) packed light brown sugar

2½ tsp (12 mL) baking powder

1 tsp (5 mL) ground ginger

¾ tsp (4 mL) cinnamon

½ tsp (2 mL) baking soda

½ tsp (2 mL) salt

Pinch of ground nutmeg

Pinch of ground black pepper

⅓ cup (80 mL) cold unsalted butter (3 oz/90 g)

⅔ cup (160 mL) cold buttermilk

3 Tbsp (45 mL) fancy molasses

WITH ALL of the spices that make gingerbread special, this light brown scone resembles a thick, cake-like cookie. It's especially good with some maple syrup poured overtop.

Preheat the oven to 400°F (200°C). Line a baking sheet with parchment paper; set aside.

Combine the flour, sugar, baking powder, ginger, cinnamon, baking soda, salt, nutmeg and pepper in the bowl of a food processor fitted with the metal "S" blade. Pulse twice to combine and aerate. Cut the butter into cubes and add to the food processor. Pulse until the butter is cut into pieces the size of small peas, with a few larger pieces. (Conversely, you can do the above in a large bowl, using a pastry cutter or two knives to cut in the butter until it's the size of irregular-shaped peas.) Transfer the mixture to a large bowl.

Whisk together the buttermilk and molasses until thoroughly blended. Pour over the flour-butter mixture. Toss with a fork until the mixture is thoroughly moistened. It may not fully come together; there may be some flour not fully incorporated—don't worry about this.

Transfer the dough to a clean work surface, including the unincorporated bits. Knead gently, about 4 or 5 times, just until the dough forms a moist, cohesive ball. Gently pat the dough down into an even rectangle that is about 8 × 5 inches (20 × 12 cm). It should be about 1 inch (2.5 cm) thick.

With a sharp knife or pastry cutter, cut the rectangle in half lengthwise. Then cut each half into 6 triangles. Transfer the scones to the prepared baking sheet.

Bake in the centre of the preheated oven until golden and baked through, 16–18 minutes. Cool the scones on the pan on a wire rack for at least 5 minutes before serving.

Morning Oatmeal Scones *with* Dried Fruit Pear Compote

Oᴸᴰ ꜰᴀꜱʜɪᴏɴᴇᴅ and craggly, these oat-based scones are not too sweet. The pecans add crunch and accentuate the earthiness. They pair beautifully with the mildly spicy and pear-flavoured compote. Making the compote the day before allows its flavours to develop. You can also combine the dry ingredients the day before (except for the baking powder and salt—add those at the last minute) and stir together the buttermilk and egg right before you bake the scones. All you have to do in the morning is a little stirring, a little bending to get the scones in and out of the oven, and you'll be rewarded with a warm and truly remarkable breakfast.

ᴄᴏᴍᴘᴏᴛᴇ Using a sharp paring knife or a peeler, cut two 3-inch (8 cm) strips of peel from both the lemon and the orange. Juice the lemon to make 2 Tbsp (30 mL) of juice.

Combine the orange and lemon peel, lemon juice, cranberries, raisins, apricots, cinnamon stick, ginger, sugar, pear nectar and 2 cups (500 mL) water in a saucepan set over high heat. Bring to a boil. Reduce the heat and cook, covered, for about 15 minutes or until the dried fruit is tender.

Stir in the apple and pear. Cook, uncovered and stirring occasionally, for 10 more minutes or until all the fruit is soft. Just before serving, remove the orange and lemon peel and the cinnamon stick. (Compote can be refrigerated, covered, for up to 3 days.) Bring to room temperature before serving.

ꜱᴄᴏɴᴇꜱ Preheat the oven to 400°F (200°C). Line a baking sheet with parchment paper; set aside.

Combine the flour, sugar, baking powder, baking soda, salt and cinnamon in the bowl of a food processor fitted with the metal "S" blade. Pulse twice to combine and aerate. Cut the butter into cubes and add to the food processor. Pulse until the butter is cut into pieces the size of small peas, with a few larger ones. (Conversely, you can do the above in a large bowl, using a pastry cutter or two knives to cut in the butter until it's the size of irregular-shaped peas.) Transfer the mixture to a large bowl. Add the rolled oats and pecans.

Whisk together the buttermilk and egg until thoroughly blended. Pour

COMPOTE

2 oranges

1 lemon

½ cup (125 mL) dried cranberries

½ cup (125 mL) golden raisins

½ cup (125 mL) slivered dried apricots

1 cinnamon stick

One 1-inch (2.5 cm) piece peeled fresh ginger

⅓ cup (80 mL) granulated sugar

1 cup (250 mL) pear nectar

2 cups (500 mL) water

1 red-skinned apple, unpeeled, cored and sliced

1 pear, peeled, cored and thinly sliced

SCONES

1⅔ cups (410 mL) all-purpose flour

⅓ cup (80 mL) packed light brown sugar

2½ tsp (12 mL) baking powder

½ tsp (2 mL) baking soda

½ tsp (2 mL) salt

¼ tsp (1 mL) cinnamon

⅓ cup (80 mL) cold unsalted butter (3 oz/90 g)

1⅓ cups (330 mL) large flake (old fashioned) rolled oats

¾ cup (180 mL) chopped toasted pecans

½ cup (125 mL) cold buttermilk

1 cold large egg

RECIPE CONTINUED . . .

over the flour-butter mixture. Toss with a fork until the mixture is thoroughly moistened. It may not fully come together; there may be some flour not fully incorporated—don't worry about this.

Transfer the dough to a clean work surface, including the unincorporated bits. Knead gently, about 4 or 5 times, just until the dough forms a moist, cohesive ball. Gently pat the dough down into an even rectangle that is about 8 × 5 inches (20 × 12 cm). It should be about 1 inch (2.5 cm) thick.

With a sharp knife or pastry cutter, cut the rectangle in half lengthwise. Then cut each half into 6 triangles. Transfer the scones to the prepared baking sheet.

Bake in the centre of the preheated oven until golden and baked through, 16–18 minutes. Cool the scones on the pan on a wire rack for at least 5 minutes before serving.

Serve with the pear compote.

Black Forest Scones

Growing up, my sisters and I knew a special occasion was imminent when my mother started making her Black Forest cake. It was a multi-day affair, so we could tell a few days in advance that something grand was on the horizon. As an adult, I don't much care for the old fashioned versions of Black Forest cake, but I do appreciate the combination of chocolate, cherries and cream. That combination as well as my mother's cake inspired this scone. It's a soft dough, so you will need to flour your work surface. Once baked, the scone is cake-like with a distinctive rustic look. If you prefer to serve these as a dessert, serve with a cherry sauce (recipe follows).

Preheat the oven to 400°F (200°C). Line a baking sheet with parchment paper; set aside.

Combine the flour, cocoa powder, sugar, baking powder, baking soda and salt in the bowl of a food processor fitted with the metal "S" blade. Pulse twice to combine and aerate. Cut the butter into pieces and add to the food processor. Pulse until the butter is cut into pieces the size of small peas, with a few larger pieces. (Conversely, you can do the above in a large bowl, using a pastry cutter or two knives to cut in the butter until it's the size of irregular-shaped peas.) Transfer the mixture to a large bowl. Stir in the chocolate and cherries.

Whisk together the sour cream and egg until thoroughly blended. Pour over the flour-butter mixture. Toss with a fork until the mixture is thoroughly moistened. It may not fully come together; there may be some flour not fully incorporated—don't worry about this.

Transfer the dough to a clean work surface, including the unincorporated bits. Knead gently, about 4 or 5 times, just until the dough forms a moist, cohesive ball. Lightly flour your work surface. Gently pat the dough down into an even rectangle that is about 8 × 5 inches (20 × 12 cm). It should be about 1 inch (2.5 cm) thick.

With a sharp knife or pastry cutter, cut the rectangle in half lengthwise. Then cut each half into 7 large triangles. Transfer the scones to the prepared baking sheet.

1⅔ cups (410 mL) all-purpose flour

⅓ cup (80 mL) unsweetened Dutch-processed cocoa powder, sifted

¼ cup (60 mL) granulated sugar

2 tsp (10 mL) baking powder

½ tsp (2 mL) baking soda

¼ tsp (1 mL) salt

½ cup (125 mL) cold unsalted butter (4 oz/125 g)

4 oz (125 g) bittersweet chocolate, coarsely chopped

½ cup (125 mL) dried cherries

1 cup (250 mL) cold sour cream

1 cold large egg

⅔ cup (175 mL) whipping cream, cold (optional)

1 batch Cherry Sauce (optional; recipe follows)

RECIPE CONTINUED . . .

Bake in the centre of the preheated oven until golden and baked through, 16–18 minutes. Cool the scones on the pan on a wire rack until cool.

Serve with whipped cream and Cherry Sauce, if desired.

VARIATION

FRESH CHERRY BLACK FOREST SCONES If fresh dark cherries are in season, try to get your hands on some and replace the dried in the recipe with the same amount of fresh.

MAKES 2 CUPS (500 ML)

Cherry Sauce

⅓ cup + 1 Tbsp (95 mL) water, divided
½ cup (125 mL) granulated sugar
1 Tbsp (15 mL) fresh lemon juice
1 Tbsp (15 mL) cornstarch
2 cups (500 mL) pitted sour cherries

IN A stainless steel saucepan, combine ⅓ cup (80 mL) water, sugar and lemon juice. Bring to a boil, stirring to dissolve the sugar. Dissolve cornstarch in 1 Tbsp (15 mL) water. Stir into the sugar mixture along with pitted sour cherries. Bring to a boil and cook, stirring, for 2 minutes or until thickened. Sauce can be kept for up to 3 days in the refrigerator.

Tweed Scones

Even scones are fair game when it comes to adding chocolate. The Scots might disapprove but the light airy texture of this scone welcomes the rich and impressive combination of two kinds of chocolate and caramel bits. Dotted throughout the batter, the inclusions make for a tweed-like look. Serve these sweet scones in the afternoon or for dessert.

2 cups (500 mL) all-purpose flour

⅓ cup (80 mL) granulated sugar

1 Tbsp (15 mL) baking powder

½ tsp (2 mL) salt

½ cup (125 mL) cold unsalted butter (4 oz/125 g)

½ cup (125 mL) mini dark chocolate chips

½ cup (125 mL) milk chocolate chips

⅓ cup (80 mL) Skor bits

¾ cup (180 mL) cold whipping cream

2 cold large egg yolks

Preheat the oven to 400°F (200°C). Line a baking sheet with parchment paper; set aside.

Combine the flour, sugar, baking powder and salt in the bowl of a food processor fitted with the metal "S" blade. Pulse twice to combine and aerate. Cut the butter into cubes and add to the food processor. Pulse until the butter is cut into pieces the size of small peas, with a few larger pieces. (Conversely, you can do the above in a large bowl, using a pastry cutter or two knives to cut in the butter until it's the size of irregular-shaped peas.) Transfer the mixture to a large bowl. Stir in the dark chocolate chips, milk chocolate chips and Skor bits.

Whisk together the cream and egg yolks until thoroughly blended. Pour over the flour-butter mixture. Toss with a fork until the mixture is thoroughly moistened. It may not fully come together; there may be some flour not fully incorporated—don't worry about this.

Transfer the dough to a clean work surface, including the unincorporated bits. Knead gently, about 4 or 5 times, just until the dough forms a moist, cohesive ball. Gently pat down into an even rectangle that is about 8 × 5 inches (20 × 12 cm). It should be about 1 inch (2.5 cm) thick.

With a sharp knife or pastry cutter, cut the rectangle in half lengthwise. Then cut each half into 6 triangles. Transfer the scones to the prepared baking sheet.

Bake in the centre of the preheated oven until golden and baked through, 16–18 minutes. Cool the scones on the pan on a wire rack for at least 5 minutes before serving.

Strawberry Almond Scones

THESE SCONES bring to mind the English countryside, sturdy picnic tables festooned with gracious linen and china bowls filled with clotted cream, unsalted locally churned butter and fresh, dewy strawberries. Bite into one and you too will be able to visualize the bucolic scene.

2 cups (500 mL) all-purpose flour

¼ cup (60 mL) granulated sugar

2 Tbsp (30 mL) ground almonds

1 Tbsp (15 mL) baking powder

½ tsp (2 mL) salt

½ cup (125 mL) cold unsalted butter (4 oz/125 g)

¾ cup (180 mL) cold whipping cream

1 tsp (5 mL) almond or vanilla extract

1 cup (250 mL) chopped fresh strawberries

1 large egg, lightly beaten, at room temperature

¼ cup (60 mL) sliced almonds

Preheat the oven to 400°F (200°C). Line a baking sheet with parchment paper; set aside.

Combine the flour, sugar, ground almonds, baking powder and salt in the bowl of a food processor fitted with the metal "S" blade. Pulse twice to combine and aerate. Cut the butter into cubes and add to the food processor. Pulse until the butter is cut into pieces the size of small peas. (Conversely, you can do the above in a large bowl, using a pastry cutter or two knives to cut in the butter until it's the size of irregular-shaped peas.) Transfer the mixture to a large bowl.

Whisk together the cream and extract of your choice until thoroughly blended. Pour over the flour-butter mixture. Add the strawberries. Toss with a fork until the mixture is thoroughly moistened. It may not fully come together; there may be some flour not fully incorporated—don't worry about this.

Transfer the dough to a clean work surface, including the unincorporated bits. Knead gently, about 4 or 5 times, just until the dough forms a moist, cohesive ball. Gently pat the dough down into an even rectangle that is about 8 × 5 inches (20 × 12 cm). It should be about 1 inch (2.5 cm) thick.

With a sharp knife or pastry cutter, cut the rectangle in half lengthwise. Then cut each half into 6 triangles. Transfer the scones to the prepared baking sheet.

Brush the surface of each scone with the beaten egg. Sprinkle the almonds over the scones.

Bake in the centre of the preheated oven until golden and baked through, 16–18 minutes. Cool the scones on the pan on a wire rack for at least 5 minutes before serving.

Double Blueberry Scones

2¼ cups (560 mL) all-purpose
  flour

¼ cup (60 mL) granulated sugar

2 tsp (10 mL) baking powder

½ tsp (2 mL) baking soda

½ tsp (2 mL) salt

½ cup (125 mL) cold unsalted
  butter (4 oz/125 g)

2 tsp (10 mL) grated lemon zest

¾ cup (180 mL) cold buttermilk

1 cold large egg yolk

1 cup (250 mL) fresh blueberries

⅓ cup (80 mL) dried blueberries

WHEN MY niece Hilary was born, my soon to be sister-in-law asked that I make something sweet for her baby naming. I, the new girl-friend, wanted to impress the family and so made scones, cut into the shape of hearts. They were a hit and to this day Hilary is a sweetheart of a young lady.

Preheat the oven to 400°F (200°C). Line a baking sheet with parchment paper; set aside.

Combine the flour, sugar, baking powder, baking soda and salt in the bowl of a food processor fitted with the metal "S" blade. Pulse twice to combine and aerate. Cut the butter into cubes and add to the food processor. Pulse until the butter is cut into pieces the size of small peas, with a few larger pieces. (Conversely, you can do the above in a large bowl, using a pastry cutter or two knives to cut in the butter until it's the size of irregular-shaped peas.) Transfer the mixture to a large bowl. Stir in the lemon zest.

Whisk together the buttermilk and egg yolk until thoroughly blended. Pour over the flour-butter mixture along with the fresh and dried blueberries. Toss with a fork until the mixture is thoroughly moistened. It may not fully come together; there may be some flour not fully incorporated—don't worry about this.

Transfer the dough to a clean work surface, including the unincorporated bits. Knead gently, about 4 or 5 times, just until the dough forms a moist, cohesive ball. Gently pat the dough down into an even rectangle that is about 8 × 5 inches (20 × 12 cm). It should be about 1 inch (2.5 cm) thick.

With a sharp knife or pastry cutter, cut the rectangle in half lengthwise. Then cut each half into 6 triangles. Transfer the scones to the prepared baking sheet.

Bake in the centre of the preheated oven until golden and baked through, 16–18 minutes. Cool the scones on the pan on a wire rack for at least 5 minutes before serving.

BAKER'S TIP

Make these scones when blueberries are in season. Avoid using frozen blueberries, as the moisture from the blueberries will make the scones too soggy and the colour bluish.

A Peach of a Scone

MOST SCONES don't take particularly well to frozen fruit because of the high moisture levels associated with it. Scones baked with frozen peaches or blueberries tend to turn out gummy and a little wet. Use only fresh peaches for this recipe, and when peaches are out of season, opt for fresh mango chunks. Dried mango (albeit usually treated with sulphide) will work in a pinch as well.

Preheat the oven to 400°F (200°C). Line a baking sheet with parchment paper; set aside.

Combine the flour, sugar, baking powder, ginger and salt in the bowl of a food processor fitted with the metal "S" blade. Pulse twice to combine and aerate. Cut the butter into cubes and add to the food processor. Pulse until the butter is cut into pieces the size of small peas, with a few larger pieces. (Conversely, you can do the above in a large bowl, using a pastry cutter or two knives to cut in the butter until it's the size of irregular-shaped peas.) Transfer the mixture to a large bowl. Stir in the crystallized ginger.

Whisk together the cream and egg until thoroughly blended. Pour over the flour-butter mixture along with the peaches. Toss with a fork until the mixture is thoroughly moistened. It may not fully come together; there may be some flour not fully incorporated—don't worry about this.

Transfer the dough to a clean work surface, including the unincorporated bits. Knead gently, about 4 or 5 times, just until the dough forms a moist, cohesive ball. Gently pat the dough down into an even rectangle that is about 8 × 5 inches (20 × 12 cm). It should be about 1 inch (2.5 cm) thick.

With a sharp knife or pastry cutter, cut the rectangle in half lengthwise. Then cut each half into 6 triangles. Transfer the scones to the prepared baking sheet. Sprinkle with 1 Tbsp (15 mL) sugar for topping.

Bake in the centre of the preheated oven until golden and baked through, 16–18 minutes. Cool the scones on the pan on a wire rack for at least 5 minutes before serving.

2 cups (500 mL) all-purpose flour

¼ cup (60 mL) granulated sugar

1 Tbsp (15 mL) baking powder

½ tsp (2 mL) ground ginger

½ tsp (2 mL) salt

⅓ cup (80 mL) cold unsalted butter (3 oz/90 g)

⅓ cup (80 mL) finely chopped crystallized ginger

¾ cup (180 mL) cold whipping cream

1 cold large egg

1 cup (250 mL) chopped fresh peaches

TOPPING

1 Tbsp (15 mL) granulated sugar

Gruyère, Prosciutto *and* Chive Scones

2⅓ cups (580 mL) all-purpose flour

1 Tbsp (15 mL) granulated sugar

1 Tbsp (15 mL) baking powder

½ tsp (2 mL) salt

½ tsp (2 mL) ground black pepper

½ cup (125 mL) cold unsalted butter (4 oz/125 g)

¾ cup (180 mL) cold buttermilk

1 cold large egg

¾ cup (180 mL) shredded Gruyère

½ cup (125 mL) chopped prosciutto (or cooked bacon)

¼ cup (60 mL) chopped chives

SCONES ARE malleable, morphing from sweet to savoury with the switch of an ingredient or two. Luckily, one can play around with the amount of sugar in a scone without destroying its structure. And so play I have, experimenting with different herb and cheese combinations, traversing cuisines, to come up with the following trio of scones.

⸺

Preheat the oven to 400°F (200°C). Line a baking sheet with parchment paper; set aside.

Combine the flour, sugar, baking powder, salt and pepper in the bowl of a food processor fitted with the metal "S" blade. Pulse twice to combine and aerate. Cut the butter into cubes and add to the food processor. Pulse until the butter is cut into pieces the size of small peas, with a few larger pieces. (Conversely, you can do the above in a large bowl, using a pastry cutter or two knives to cut in the butter until it's the size of irregular-shaped peas.) Transfer the mixture to a large bowl.

Whisk together the buttermilk and egg until thoroughly blended. Pour over the flour-butter mixture along with the cheese, prosciutto and chives. Toss with a fork until the mixture is thoroughly moistened. It may not fully come together; there may be some flour not fully incorporated—don't worry about this.

Transfer the dough to a clean work surface, including the unincorporated bits. Knead gently, about 4 or 5 times, just until the dough forms a moist, cohesive ball. Gently pat the dough down into an even rectangle that is about 8 × 5 inches (20 × 12 cm). It should be about 1 inch (2.5 cm) thick.

With a sharp knife or pastry cutter, cut the rectangle in half lengthwise. Then cut each half into 6 triangles. Transfer the scones to the prepared baking sheet.

Bake in the centre of the preheated oven until golden and baked through, 16–18 minutes. Cool the scones on the pan on a wire rack for at least 5 minutes before serving.

Feta, Olive and Rosemary Scones

2¼ cups (560 mL) all-purpose
  flour

2 Tbsp (30 mL) granulated sugar

2½ tsp (12 mL) baking powder

1½ tsp (7 mL) dried rosemary

½ tsp (2 mL) baking soda

½ tsp (2 mL) salt

¼ tsp (1 mL) ground black pepper

½ cup (125 mL) cold unsalted
  butter (4 oz/125 g)

½ cup (125 mL) cold sour cream

3 Tbsp (45 mL) cold milk

1 cold large egg

½ cup (125 mL) crumbled feta
  cheese

½ cup (125 mL) chopped olives

RIGHT AFTER I finished my Bachelor of Arts I took a 3 month long trip around Europe. The vacation started in Greece and I soon found myself on the mystical island of Santorini. Never before had I experienced such beauty, the black sands of its famous beaches, the deeply coloured jade of its olives. I stayed in a local home and everyday made my way to the local bakery. They made a yeasted bun studded with chunks of hard salty feta, chopped up wrinkled olives and a brush of olive oil and rosemary on top. Although this recipe is not for a yeast-based bun, these scones were inspired by that trip and still bring me back to that island.

Preheat the oven to 400°F (200°C). Line a baking sheet with parchment paper; set aside.

Combine the flour, sugar, baking powder, rosemary, baking soda, salt and pepper in the bowl of a food processor fitted with the metal "S" blade. Pulse twice to combine and aerate. Cut the butter into cubes and add to the food processor. Pulse until the butter is cut into pieces the size of small peas, with a few larger pieces. (Conversely, you can do the above in a large bowl, using a pastry cutter or two knives to cut in the butter until it's the size of irregular-shaped peas.) Transfer the mixture to a large bowl.

Whisk together the sour cream, milk and egg until thoroughly blended. Pour over the flour-butter mixture along with the feta and olives. Toss with a fork until the mixture is thoroughly moistened. It may not fully come together; there may be some flour not fully incorporated—don't worry about this.

Transfer the dough to a clean work surface, including the unincorporated bits. Knead gently, about 4 or 5 times, just until the dough forms a moist, cohesive ball. Gently pat the dough down until it's about 1 inch (2.5 cm) thick. Using a 2½-inch (6 cm) cookie cutter, cut out rounds, rerolling scraps only once. Transfer the scones to the prepared baking sheet.

Bake in the centre of the preheated oven until golden and baked through, 16–18 minutes. Cool the scones on the pan on a wire rack for at least 5 minutes before serving.

Sun-Dried Tomato Scones *with* Asiago *and* Basil

I OFTEN make focaccia at home, its dimples filled with olive oil, its surface sprinkled with sun-dried tomatoes or roasted red peppers, with some cheese melted on top. One day as I was making it I thought, you know, these ingredients would be great in a scone. The very next day, I made the scones. The amounts needed tweaking but finally I got the proportions right and it's a wonderful addition to any repast.

Preheat the oven to 400°F (200°C). Line a baking sheet with parchment paper; set aside.

Pat the sun-dried tomatoes until very dry. Chop finely and set aside.

Combine the flour, sugar, baking powder, salt and pepper in the bowl of a food processor fitted with the metal "S" blade. Pulse twice to combine and aerate. Cut the butter into cubes and add to the food processor. Pulse until the butter is cut into pieces the size of small peas, with a few larger pieces. (Conversely, you can do the above in a large bowl, using a pastry cutter or two knives to cut in the butter until it's the size of irregular-shaped peas.) Transfer the mixture to a large bowl.

Pour the buttermilk over the flour-butter mixture along with the sun-dried tomatoes, cheese and basil. Toss with a fork until the mixture is thoroughly moistened. It may not fully come together; there may be some flour not fully incorporated—don't worry about this.

Transfer the dough to a clean work surface, including the unincorporated bits. Knead gently, about 4 or 5 times, just until the dough forms a moist, cohesive ball. Gently pat the dough down until it's about 1 inch (2.5 cm) thick. Using a 2½-inch (6 cm) cookie cutter, cut out rounds, rerolling scraps only once. Transfer the scones to the prepared baking sheet.

Bake in the centre of the preheated oven until golden and baked through, 16–18 minutes. Cool the scones on the pan on a wire rack for at least 5 minutes before serving.

½ cup (125 mL) oil-packed
  sun-dried tomatoes
2⅓ cups (580 mL) all-purpose
  flour
1 Tbsp (15 mL) granulated sugar
1 Tbsp (15 mL) baking powder
½ tsp (2 mL) salt
½ tsp (2 mL) ground black pepper
½ cup (125 mL) cold unsalted
  butter (4 oz/125 g)
1 cup (250 mL) cold buttermilk
¾ cup (180 mL) shredded Asiago
  cheese
¼ cup (60 mL) finely chopped
  fresh basil (or 4 tsp/20 mL
  dried basil)

BAKER'S TIP

Although dried sun-dried tomatoes may have more depth and pungency, I find it easier in baking to use the oil-packed variety. They won't draw any moisture from the baked good and don't require reconstitution.

QUICK AND YEAST BREADS

273   QUICK BREADS

274   Bubbie's Banana Bread

276   My Very Favourite Banana Bread

277   Carrot Loaf with Mascarpone Frosting

279   Blueberry Raspberry Loaf

280   Cornmeal Pear Loaf

281   Spiced Pumpkin Loaf with Maple Drizzle

283   YEAST BREADS

287   Challah

290   Multi-Seed Bread

292   Cinnamon Raisin Whole-Wheat Bread

294   Special Occasion Chocolate Coffee Babka

296   Sticky Cinnamon Buns

300   Cheese Danish

ALTHOUGH BOTH are called bread, quick and yeast breads differ significantly. First, quick breads rely on chemical leaveners such as baking powder or baking soda, while yeast breads rely, of course, on yeast. Quick breads are just that, quick to put together and relatively quick to bake. Yeast breads, on the other hand, require more time for the yeast to proof, for the bread to rise and then to undergo a second rise once shaped. The one constant between quick and yeast breads, however, is the marvelous variety of both that you can create in the warmth of your own kitchen. I've heard so many people argue, "Why make your own bread when there is so much wonderful, artisanal bread to buy?" What you miss is the sheer joy of bread making: the experience of watching yeast proof, of smelling the nascent, pungent and earthy perfume of the growing yeast, the feel of the slightly sticky dough underneath your hands and the enchanting moment when you open the oven to remove that gorgeous golden loaf. There's a reason why people have enjoyed making bread for literally thousands of years. First, it has always been and remains the staff of life. Making bread takes us back to our roots, be it an Irish soda bread, a Hungarian kalac, a French baguette or a challah. Our ancestors made bread by feel, with unreliable ingredients and primitive yeast spores. Now we have reliable formulas and consistent ingredients, but bread is still a culinary adventure because you're working with a live entity—the yeast—that can change course depending on the weather, the mood of the baker and sundry other factors. This isn't a bread book, so I have only included some of my very favourite foolproof recipes. Hopefully they will entice you to step into the chemically magic world of baking breads, quick or otherwise.

QUICK BREADS

Quick breads, as their name implies, are breads that are quickly mixed together and rely on either baking powder or baking soda to rise, not yeast. When "yeast powder" (as baking powder was originally called) was introduced in the middle of the 19th century, it was actually decried as an almost evil invention, as bread bakers worried that their livelihood was in danger. Twas not to be; yeasted breads remained popular as ever now accompanied by sweeter loaves that didn't take hours to rise and bake. In their inception, quick breads were not as sweet as they are today, that was more of a recent invention.

As I mentioned in the introduction to the muffin chapter, quick breads (and muffins) rely on one of two methods, either the muffin method or the creaming method (see pages 221 and 16 respectively). There are a number of other things that differentiate muffins and quick breads. First, of course, is their size. Quick breads are almost always baked in a loaf pan, usually a 9-inch (23 cm) or an 8-inch (20 cm), but sometimes even the miniature 4-inch (10 cm) variety; muffins are always individual. Muffins are also typically broken apart with your hands, whereas quick breads have to be sliced. Likewise, quick breads tend to have more moisture, which means they hold their shape when sliced and have a longer shelf life than most muffins. Unlike muffins, the flavour and texture of a quick bread often improves overnight.

In a pinch, you can turn a muffin batter into a quick bread batter or a quick bread batter into a muffin batter, with a few guidelines. If a muffin recipe calls for dried fruit or whole nuts, cut the fruit or nuts into smaller pieces when baking the same recipe as a quick bread. The larger pieces of fruit will be harder to cut in a loaf shape. Be sure to wrap the loaf in plastic wrap to keep the bread as moist as possible. Heat is another issue. Muffins are better off cooked quickly at a higher heat, generally at 375°F (190°C) for 20–30 minutes, max. Quick breads, on the other hand, are almost always baked at 325°F (160° C) for anywhere from 45–65 minutes. Bake accordingly.

Bubbie's Banana Bread

TOPPING

½ cup (125 mL) shredded sweetened coconut

¼ cup (60 mL) packed light brown
  sugar

¼ tsp (1 mL) ground nutmeg

1 Tbsp (15 mL) all-purpose flour

1 Tbsp (15 mL) unsalted butter,
  softened (0.5 oz/15 g)

BREAD

2 cups (500 mL) all-purpose flour

1 tsp (5 mL) baking powder

1 tsp (5 mL) baking soda

Pinch of salt

½ cup (125 mL) unsalted butter,
  softened (4 oz/125 g)

1 cup (250 mL) packed light brown
  sugar

3 large eggs, at room temperature

1 tsp (5 mL) vanilla

1 cup (250 mL) mashed ripe
  bananas

WHILE I was writing this book, miles away from my editor, Jordie Yow, I was fairly certain I knew what he would say when he made his way to this chapter: "Daphna, why do you have two different banana bread recipes? What makes them so different? Can you just include one?" There's no doubt that one would have sufficed, but that would mean not only shortchanging my mother, who made this bread when I was young, but it would also deprive the reader of a sensational butter-based banana bread with a topping that really rocks. Creaming together the butter and sugar makes this bread fluffier than the oil-based bread, as does the addition of one more egg. What really changes the picture, however, is the brown sugar and coconut-based topping. Even if you're not overly fond of coconut, you will love the crunch and sweetness this topping gives to every slice.

Preheat the oven to 325°F (160°C). Grease a 9- × 5-inch (23 × 13 cm) loaf pan; set aside.

TOPPING In a bowl, combine the coconut, brown sugar, nutmeg, flour and butter, rubbing the butter in with your fingertips until the mixture starts to clump together; set aside.

BREAD Whisk together the all-purpose flour, baking powder, baking soda and salt in a bowl until the dry ingredients are thoroughly combined; set aside.

In the bowl of a stand mixer fitted with the paddle attachment, or using a hand-held mixer, beat the butter for 1 minute. Add the brown sugar and beat until the mixture is light and fluffy. One at a time, beat in the eggs, beating well after each egg before adding the next. Beat in the vanilla.

Remove the bowl from the stand. Using a wooden spoon, stir in half of the flour mixture. Stir in the mashed bananas. Stir in the remaining flour mixture. Turn the mixture into the prepared pan, smoothing the top. Sprinkle with the topping.

Bake in the centre of the preheated oven until a cake tester inserted in the centre comes out clean, 55–65 minutes. Cool the loaf in the pan on a wire rack for 30 minutes. Remove the loaf from the pan and cool completely on the wire rack.

My Very Favourite Banana Bread

4 large very ripe bananas, mashed

1 cup (250 mL) granulated sugar

½ cup (125 mL) vegetable oil

2 large eggs, at room temperature

1 tsp (5 mL) vanilla

2 cups (500 mL) all-purpose flour

2 tsp (10 mL) baking soda

½ tsp (2 mL) baking powder

Pinch of salt

½ cup (125 mL) mini semisweet
   chocolate chips (optional)

THIS IS the banana bread I make regularly. It's super easy, requires no creaming and is moist and dense. Because it's oil based, it also keeps really well—up to a week! It never lasts that long in our house, so I had to make a special one and hide it just so I could gauge how long it would last.

Preheat the oven to 325°F (160°C). Grease a 9- × 5-inch (23 × 13 cm) loaf pan; set aside.

In a large bowl, whisk together the bananas, sugar, oil, eggs and vanilla. In a separate bowl, whisk together the flour, baking soda, baking powder and salt until the dry ingredients are thoroughly combined. Add the wet ingredients to the dry ingredients, stirring together until well combined. Stir in chocolate chips, if using. Turn the batter into the prepared pan.

Bake in the centre of the preheated oven until the top of the cake springs back when lightly pressed, 60–75 minutes. Cool the loaf in the pan on a wire rack for 30 minutes. Remove the loaf from the pan and cool completely on the wire rack.

Carrot Loaf *with* Mascarpone Frosting

IT'S FUNNY how tastes change and recipes evolve over time. When I started out as a pastry chef, it wasn't unusual to see a carrot cake recipe call for 1½ cups (375 mL) of oil. You'd never see that now, it's simply not necessary. In the recipe below, I've substituted pineapple juice for some of the oil and also have been able to reduce the sugar. Even without the original amount of oil and sugar it's sweet and incredibly moist, with just the right spice and carrot overtones. The carrot cake in the next chapter is more solid so that it can be layered, iced and sliced without incident.

Preheat the oven to 325°F (160°C). Grease a 9- × 5-inch (23 × 13 cm) loaf pan; set aside.

Whisk together the flour, baking soda, cinnamon, salt and walnuts in a bowl until the dry ingredients are thoroughly combined; set aside.

In a separate large bowl, whisk together the carrots, sugar, pineapple juice, oil, crushed pineapple, eggs and vanilla. Add the wet ingredients to the dry mixture, whisking until smooth. Turn the batter into the prepared pan.

Bake in the centre of the preheated oven until the top springs back when lightly pressed, about 1 hour. Let the loaf cool in the pan on a wire rack for 30 minutes. Remove the loaf from the pan and cool completely on the wire rack.

FROSTING In the bowl of a stand mixer fitted with the paddle attachment, or using a hand-held mixer, beat the mascarpone until light. Beat in the icing sugar. Add the whipping cream, adding up to an additional 1 Tbsp (15 mL) to get the frosting light and fluffy. With an offset spatula, spread the frosting on the top of the loaf.

VARIATION

CREAM CHEESE FROSTING If you want a more classical or traditional cream cheese frosting, you can replace the frosting in this recipe with the following: beat together ½ cup (125 mL) of softened unsalted butter with ⅓ cup (80 mL) icing sugar until light and fluffy. Beat in ½ cup (125 mL) of softened cream cheese.

2 cups (500 mL) all-purpose flour

2 tsp (10 mL) baking soda

1½ tsp (7 mL) cinnamon

Pinch of salt

½ cup (125 mL) walnut pieces

2 cups (500 mL) grated carrots

1½ cups (375 mL) granulated sugar

⅔ cup (160 mL) pineapple juice (from the can of crushed pineapple)

½ cup (125 mL) canola or vegetable oil

⅓ cup (80 mL) well drained crushed pineapple

3 large eggs, at room temperature

1 tsp (5 mL) vanilla

FROSTING

1 cup (250 mL) mascarpone cheese, softened

⅓ cup (80 mL) icing sugar

1–2 Tbsp (15–30 mL), whipping cream, at room temperature

BAKER'S TIP For this recipe, it's important that your carrots are very finely grated. I peel my carrots, cut them into large chunks and then use the regular steel "S" blade on my food processor to grind them up.

Blueberry Raspberry Loaf

THERE ARE a couple of recipes included in this book that I have been making forever and this is one of them. Much like the Chocolate Truffle Pecan Tart (see p. 207) and the Blueberry Coffee Cream Cheese Cake (see p. 352), both of which I initially developed for *Canadian Living Magazine*, this is a slight riff on the blueberry loaf I developed for them many years ago. The fact that I include it in this collection testifies to its merits, both because it's really simple to make and because it's timelessly delicious.

Preheat the oven to 325°F (160°C). Grease an 8- × 4- or 5-inch (20 × 10 or 13 cm) loaf pan; set aside.

TOPPING In a small bowl, stir together the sugar, flour and butter until the mixture is crumbly; set aside.

BREAD Whisk together the flour, baking powder and salt in a bowl until the dry ingredients are thoroughly combined; set aside.

In the bowl of a stand mixer fitted with the paddle attachment, or using a hand-held mixer, beat the butter for 1 minute. With the machine running, gradually add the sugar in a thin stream. Beat until very light and fluffy, about 3 minutes. One at a time, beat in the eggs, beating well after the first egg before adding the second. Beat in the vanilla and the lemon zest.

Remove the bowl from the stand. Using a wooden spoon, stir in one-third of the flour mixture. Stir in half of the cream. Stir in another third of the flour mixture and then the remaining cream. Stir in the remaining flour mixture. Gently toss the blueberries and raspberries with 1 tsp (5 mL) flour; gently fold into the batter. Turn the mixture into the prepared pan, smoothing the top. Place on 2 baking sheets. Sprinkle the topping over the batter.

Bake in the centre of the preheated oven until the top springs back when lightly pressed, about 1 hour and 15 minutes. Cool the cake in the pan on a wire rack for 30 minutes. Remove the loaf from the pan and cool completely on the wire rack.

TOPPING

¼ cup (60 mL) granulated sugar

¼ cup (60 mL) all-purpose flour

2 Tbsp (30 mL) unsalted butter, melted and cooled (1 oz/30 g)

BREAD

2 cups (500 mL) all-purpose flour
+ 1 tsp (5 mL) for the berries

2 tsp (10 mL) baking powder

½ tsp (2 mL) salt

½ cup (125 mL) unsalted butter, softened (4 oz/125 g)

1 cup (250 mL) granulated sugar

2 large eggs, at room temperature

2 tsp (10 mL) vanilla

1 Tbsp (15 mL) grated lemon zest

⅔ cup (160 mL) 10% cream, at room temperature

1⅓ cups (330 mL) fresh blueberries

½ cup (125 mL) fresh raspberries

Cornmeal Pear Loaf

1 cup (250 mL) all-purpose flour

1 cup (250 mL) yellow cornmeal

½ tsp (2 mL) baking powder

Pinch of salt

1 cup (250 mL) unsalted butter, softened (8 oz/250 g)

1¼ cups (310 mL) granulated sugar

4 large eggs, at room temperature

1 tsp (5 mL) vanilla

¼ cup (60 mL) pear nectar, at room temperature

2 cups (500 mL) chopped peeled pears (about 2 pears)

O**F ALL** of the quick loaves in this chapter, this recipe is the one that I get the most comments about. It's not that the other ones aren't delicious, it's just this quick bread is so unusual and so captivating, that it's an unexpected treat. Try to use only pear nectar and not juice since its viscosity is integral to the recipe.

Preheat the oven to 325°F (160°C). Grease a 9- × 5-inch (23 × 13 cm) loaf pan; set aside.

Whisk together the flour, cornmeal, baking powder and salt in a bowl until the dry ingredients are thoroughly combined; set aside.

In the bowl of a stand mixer fitted with the paddle attachment, or using a hand-held mixer, beat the butter for 1 minute. With the machine running, gradually add the sugar in a thin stream. Beat until very light and fluffy, about 3 minutes. One at a time, beat in the eggs, beating well after each egg before adding the next. Beat in the vanilla.

Remove the bowl from the stand. Using a wooden spoon, stir in half of the flour mixture. Stir in the pear nectar. Stir in the remaining flour mixture. Gently fold in the pears. Turn the mixture into the prepared pan, smoothing the top. Place on 2 baking sheets.

Bake in the centre of the preheated oven until the top springs back when lightly pressed, 65–75 minutes. Cool the cake in the pan on a wire rack for 30 minutes. Remove the loaf from the pan and cool completely on the wire rack.

Spiced Pumpkin Loaf *with* Maple Drizzle

THERE'S A reason why baking magazines start to feature more baking recipes once the autumn hits. Once the air turns crisp, people move indoors and don't mind turning on their oven. The produce available lends itself to comforting baked goods. Just about anything you make with pumpkin is apt to be moist and flavourful (make sure you're using the real McCoy and not pumpkin pie filling which can contain spices and some gums). Mildly spicy, but not overwhelmingly so, the loaf and the drizzle are both sweetened with maple syrup. We're so lucky here in Canada to have world class maple syrup (I should know, I lived in the US and had to ask my mom to send me some Canadian maple syrup). Try to buy the deepest-flavoured maple syrup you can.

Preheat the oven to 325°F (160°C). Grease a 9- × 5-inch (23 × 13 cm) loaf pan; set aside.

Whisk together the flour, baking soda, ginger, cinnamon, nutmeg and salt in a bowl until the dry ingredients are thoroughly combined; set aside.

In the bowl of a stand mixer fitted with the paddle attachment, or using a hand-held mixer, beat the butter for 1 minute. Add the brown sugar. Beat until very light coloured and fluffy, 2–3 minutes. One at a time, beat in the eggs, beating well after the first egg before adding the second. Beat in the maple syrup. The mixture will look curdled at this point but don't worry, it will come together once you start adding the flour.

Remove the bowl from the stand. Using a wooden spoon, stir in half of the flour mixture. Stir in the pumpkin. Stir in the remaining flour mixture. Gently fold in the walnuts. Turn the mixture into the prepared pan, smoothing the top. Place on 2 stacked baking sheets.

Bake in the centre of the preheated oven until the top springs back when lightly pressed, 60–70 minutes. Cool the cake in the pan on a wire rack for 30 minutes. Remove the loaf from the pan and cool completely on the wire rack.

GLAZE To make the glaze, whisk together the icing sugar and maple syrup in a small bowl. Using the tines of a fork or the whisk, drizzle the glaze over the top of the pumpkin loaf.

2¼ cups (560 mL) all-purpose flour
2 tsp (10 mL) baking soda
2 tsp (10 mL) ground ginger
1½ tsp (7 mL) cinnamon
¾ tsp (4 mL) ground nutmeg
¼ tsp (1 mL) salt
½ cup (125 mL) unsalted butter, softened (4 oz/125 g)
½ cup (125 mL) packed light brown sugar
2 large eggs, at room temperature
½ cup (125 mL) pure maple syrup
1⅓ cups (330 mL) packed cooked canned pumpkin
½ cup (125 mL) chopped walnuts

GLAZE
⅓ cup (80 mL) icing sugar
2 Tbsp (30 mL) pure maple syrup

RECIPE CONTINUED . . .

BAKER'S TIP

MAPLE SYRUP GRADES If you're a patron of farmer's markets, then you're well aware that maple syrups come in a variety of colours and grades (it's harder to find anything but one type in most supermarkets), which affects its flavour. Genuine Canadian maple syrup is classified using three grades containing several different levels of colour that are based on its translucence, meaning the amount of light visible through the syrup.

The grades in Canada range from #1 Extra Light, #1 Light, #1 Medium, #2 Amber and #3 Dark. In the United States the classifications would be Grade A for the first three (Extra Light–Medium), Grade B for the #2 Amber and Grade C for #3 Dark. To achieve its grade, a syrup must not ferment, must have a uniform colour and must have a flavour consistent with its flavour. Accordingly, light syrups have a subtler maple flavour and are typically produced at the beginning of the maple season. Amber maple syrup is the most commonly bought maple syrup, with a still-mild but maple-y flavour. As the season progresses, the maple syrup becomes darker and more robust, producing #2 Amber and then the dark category. Many maple syrup experts actually prefer the later sap maple syrup for its stronger flavour (although all of the above maple syrups are equally sweet).

YEAST BREADS

BREAD—THE ABBREVIATED STORY

I'm pretty crazy about bread, any kind of bread. I've been making bread a long time and will never forget the words of one of my first teachers, Beth Hensperger, who said that to make bread is to love your bread. And it's true.

As hokey as that may sound, bread making is an activity to relish and enjoy. You have to put in the time. Love your bread and it will love you back.

To understand bread making, it's important to understand wheat. Wheat is the only grain that contains both glutenin and gliadin, the proteins that, when combined with liquid and exercised (kneaded), form gluten strands. The more the bread dough is kneaded, the more the gluten strands link together and become longer and stronger. As a result, a web of gluten is formed throughout the dough, holding it all together. The web traps the bubbles of carbon dioxide emitted by the yeast feeding on the sugar and flour, and then expands as the bubbles multiply, allowing the bread to rise.

Without this complex and fortifying network of flexible gluten strands, bread cannot rise properly, so it's important to choose the right flour when making breads. While specialty flours may be added to provide texture and flavour, it's essential to use, at least some of, either all-purpose flour or bread flour, with 9–11% or 12–14% protein respectively.

Yeast is what gets the whole marathon going. I mostly use active dry yeast in the recipes that follow, so I will concentrate on that.

Yeast is most often proofed in some hot water with a little bit of sugar added. The water should typically be between 110–120°F (45–55°C), hotter than you might think. Hotter than that and the yeast will die. In most cases, tap water is fine unless it is heavily mineralized, which can slow down the fermentation of your dough. Sugar is added since the yeast feeds on the sugar, helping it get going. Salt, on the other hand, is never stirred into the yeast at this point because it's a surefire way of killing it—it's added later. Once the yeast has proofed (become foamy and practically doubled in volume), other liquid ingredients are added.

Milk and buttermilk, if added, not only contribute lovely flavour but also impart a lovely brown colour to the crust.

Eggs enrich a dough as well as add colour and flavour. Yolks on their own, because of their fat content and their lecithin, add more colour, flavour and moisture than whites, which can dry out a dough. Breads that contain whole eggs will typically also call for milk, sugar, butter or oil, all of which counteract the drying effects of the whites.

At this point, your dry ingredients are stirred in as well as salt and other flavourings or inclusions. Make sure that your salt is well distributed throughout the flour mixture. I also use the word stir intentionally. You never dump the full amount of flour into the liquid-yeast mixture. Too many variables can determine how much flour should be added—the temperature of your water, the temperature of your kitchen, how much liquid has already been added, etc. Always add it gradually, adding enough until a shaggy dough is formed. This is quite different from making pastry because you don't have to worry about the formation of gluten, you want to encourage it. If you're making a sponge or polish, only a very small amount of flour is added.

Kneading is essential to good bread. Try not to over-flour while you're kneading—the end result should still, in most cases, be a bit sticky. Don't over knead either. Over-kneading can over-oxidize the dough, negatively affecting its flavour. It may also cause fermentation to occur too quickly.

To tell if a dough is sufficiently kneaded, press your palm firmly into the dough. If the impression fills in quickly, your dough is ready for its first rise. It should also look elastic and smooth.

The first rise allows the yeast to feed on the starches in the flour, producing carbon dioxide and alcohol. The gluten network created by kneading traps the carbon dioxide, causing the bread to swell and increase in volume. The first rise is when most of the flavour and elasticity is formed. During the first rise, try to use a straight-sided bowl or other vessel so that the strands of gluten develop vertically and not horizontally.

Why do you punch down the dough? To release (gently! No need for violence here!) some of the carbon dioxide that has built up in the dough. Don't knead it again at this point, it's not necessary. In fact, you want your dough as pliable as possible in order to shape it.

The thing to keep in mind when you're shaping your dough, whether it's into a loaf pan, a free form loaf or even buns, is that you need to create a certain amount of tension. The dough needs to be taut enough so that it holds its shape as it undergoes the second rise. To create this type of tension, you have to make sure to tighten the dough at the bottom of the loaf, or bun. At this point, it's important to keep your work surface free and clear of flour so that the dough sticks slightly to the surface as you tighten it, without slipping across the surface.

If the dough becomes too hard to handle, let it rest for 15–20 minutes to relax the gluten and then try again.

After the dough is shaped, it usually needs a second rise to double in size. When you cover the dough with plastic wrap be sure to do so loosely to let the bread grow. Test the dough by poking your finger on one side of the dough. If the hole fills back in slowly or doesn't fill in much, then your bread is ready for baking. If the hole fills in quickly, then more proofing is required. If the dough collapses upon touching it, then it is over-proofed. Over-proofed doughs can be recovered, if they haven't been over-proofed longer than 30–45 minutes. (If they have, they cannot be saved.) Simply punch down the dough and reshape and then proof again for slightly less time.

When a bread is perfectly proofed or even a little under-proofed, there is still enough yeast activity remaining to provide what bakers call an "oven spring," the last burst of growth that occurs once the bread is placed in the oven, producing a dramatic rise.

If the bread is extensively under proofed and placed in the oven, the yeast will have too much say (that is, activity to spend) in the oven and the inside of the dough will burst though the crust, causing a crack or seam to open.

One last thing: salt. Salt is as important in bread as sugar is to defining what a baked dessert is. Without salt, the bread will not taste anything near what it should taste like. It will be sadly flat, without any special nuance or depth. Salt also slows down the fermentation process and a long slow rise means a bread with better flavour and texture. Salt, like sugar, is hygroscopic, meaning it attracts and bonds with water or moisture. This means that bread made with salt (and sugar for that matter) will stay softer and fresher longer by retaining moisture.

Most breads call for some sort of glaze, which in French is called a "dorure." Doughs brushed with whole eggs will result in a warm, golden colour. Glazes with more fat, such as egg yolks or cream, will impart a deeper golden or brown colour. Whites alone will produce more of a sheen.

Challah

Tʜɪs ɪs the challah I make almost every week. Sometimes I make a double batch and make 4–6 challahs at once, either to give some away to friends or to tuck away in the freezer since my son thinks there is only one type of bread worth eating—that is, challah (although he will deign to eat French bread, if forced).

This is not the place to go into the history of challah. There have been several books written on that subject, some containing over a dozen different recipes just for challah. Suffice it to say that to the Jewish community, bread has been of vital importance since the days of the First Temple and even before, as offering bread to guests is mentioned often in the Old Testament. Bread, it can be said, is meant not just to sustain our physical selves but to nourish our soul as well.

The challah I used to make contained butter and honey and I love that one, but I now prefer this one made with regular granulated sugar and oil. It's fairly sweet and cake-like; if you prefer an airier one, reduce the sugar to ½ cup (125 mL). At Rosh Hashanah, when honey is added to symbolize a sweet new year, I use honey in this challah instead of sugar.

Using oil as the fat in the challah means that people who keep kosher can still enjoy this version with a meat meal. It rises beautifully with a distinctive yellow colour, otherwise how would you know it's egg bread? I also call for both all-purpose flour and bread flour because of the elasticity the bread flour imparts. However, you can just use all-purpose flour and still adorn your Friday night table with a delicious challah.

This bread, like most breads, can be started the day before. I often make the dough on Thursday, let it rise for 15 minutes at room temperature then place the bowl in the refrigerator. The next morning, I take the bowl out of the refrigerator, let it come to room temperature and proceed with shaping and the second rise.

In a glass 2-cup (500 mL) wet measure, stir together the water and 1 Tbsp (15 mL) of the sugar. Sprinkle the yeast over top. Let stand for 10 minutes or until foamy. Due to the high proportion of water to yeast here the mixture will not get as foamy as if you had used only ½ cup (125 mL) of hot

1¾ cups (430 mL) quite warm water

⅔ cup (160 mL) granulated sugar, divided

2 Tbsp (30 mL) active dry yeast (just over 2 pkgs)

½ cup (125 mL) canola or vegetable oil

4 large eggs, at room temperature

5 cups (1.25 L) bread flour

1 Tbsp (15 mL) salt

3½ cups (825 mL) all-purpose flour (approx.)

TOPPING

1 large egg, lightly beaten, at room temperature

Poppy or sesame seeds, as many as you like

RECIPE CONTINUED . . .

water, in which case it would get foamy and almost double in volume. I prefer not to use a bowl here because it runs the risk of cooling down the water too much, which might not activate the yeast as effectively.

Pour the yeast mixture into a large bowl. Stir in the remaining sugar, oil and eggs, mixing until well combined. Using a wooden spoon, stir in all of the bread flour and the salt. Starting with 1 cup (250 mL) at a time, stir in the all-purpose flour, until a kneadable dough is formed.

Transfer the dough to a lightly floured work surface. Sprinkling the surface as needed with flour, knead the dough until it is very smooth and elastic, about 10 minutes. It's important that you not over-flour the dough; just use enough to prevent it from sticking to the surface.

Lightly oil a large bowl. Place the dough in the bowl, turning it until the dough is thoroughly coated with the oil. Cover the bowl with plastic wrap and then a kitchen towel. Let the dough rise in a warm, draft-free area for 1 hour or until it's doubled in bulk. The dough is ready when you poke it with a finger and the indentation remains. Punch down the dough.

Transfer the dough to a work surface. Using a sharp knife, divide the dough in half (or in thirds if smaller loaves are desired). Then, divide one-half (or one-third) equally into 6 pieces. Roll each piece into a 14-inch (35 cm) braid. Arrange the 6 ropes together in an inverted "V" and pinch the tops together. Starting with the strand farthest to the left, treat them as strand 1, strand 2, strand 3, all the way up to 6. Then once you start moving them around, the one that is currently farthest to the left will always be strand 1.

Bring strand 6 (the one farthest to the right) over strand 1. Then lay strand 2 over strand 6. Bring strand 1 over strand 3. Lay strand 5 over strand 1. Lay strand 6 over strand 4. Repeat strand 2 over strand 6, strand 1 over 3, strand 5 over 1 and strand 6 over 4 until you reach the end. Pinch the ends together and tuck underneath. Transfer the loaf to a parchment paper–lined baking sheet.

Repeat with the second half of the dough (or, if you've cut into thirds, repeat two more times). Place beside the first loaf on the prepared baking sheet. Cover with plastic wrap and let rise in a warm, draft-free area for 45 minutes to 1 hour, or until the loaves double in bulk.

Preheat the oven to 350°F (180°C).

Brush the beaten egg all over the bread. Sprinkle with the sesame or poppy seeds. Bake in the centre of the preheated oven until deep golden on the outside and the bread sounds hollow when tapped, 35–40 minutes. Let the breads cool on the pan on a wire rack.

VARIATIONS
. . . .

ROUND LOAF FOR ROSH HASHANAH Replace the sugar with honey and knead in ⅔ cup (180 mL) golden raisins after the first rise. Shape the dough into one long rope. Keeping one end in place, wrap the rope around the stationary tip to create a round bread.

ANISE-FLAVOURED CHALLAH Crush 1 Tbsp (15 mL) of anise seeds and add with the first addition of flour. Use ¼ cup (60 mL) honey and ⅓ cup (80 mL) granulated sugar instead of the previous sugar amount. Use 2 egg yolks for the wash instead of an egg.

Multi-Seed Bread

2 cups (500 mL) warm water

½ cup (125 mL) cracked wheat

2 Tbsp (30 mL) active dry yeast
(just over 2 pkgs)

⅓ cup (80 mL) honey

¼ cup (60 mL) canola or
vegetable oil

½ cup (125 mL) sunflower seeds

⅓ cup (80 mL) shelled raw
pumpkin seeds

¼ cup (60 mL) raw flax seeds

1 Tbsp (15 mL) sesame seeds

1 Tbsp (15 mL) poppy seeds

4 cups (1 L) bread flour (approx.)

1 Tbsp (15 mL) salt

TOPPING

1 egg, lightly beaten, at room
temperature

1 Tbsp (15 mL) sesame seeds

THIS IS a crackerjack of a bread. The cracked wheat may seem unusual but it imbues the bread with a chewy, nutty character and I know I'm getting extra grains in my diet. The loaf is sweet, pockmarked with seeds and nuts and ideal for smearing with butter and jam or cream cheese. I swear it's even better toasted. The recipe makes two full-sized loaves because I can tell you right now, one will simply not be enough.

In a large bowl, pour the warm water over the cracked wheat. Let the mixture stand for 15 minutes. Sprinkle the yeast over. Let stand for 15 minutes or until the mixture is frothy.

Using a wooden spoon, stir in the honey, oil, sunflower seeds, pumpkin seeds, flax seeds, sesame seeds and poppy seeds. Stir in 1½ cups (375 mL) of the flour. Gradually stir in the remaining flour, ½ cup (125 mL) at a time, along with the salt, until a soft, slightly sticky dough is formed.

Transfer the dough to a lightly floured work surface. Sprinkling the surface with extra flour as needed to prevent the dough from sticking, knead the dough until it is soft, supple and elastic, 8–10 minutes. Generously oil a large bowl. Place the dough in the bowl, turning the dough to grease it all over. Cover the bowl with plastic wrap and let the dough rise in a warm, draft-free area until it's doubled in size, about 2 hours.

Punch down the dough. Divide the dough in half; shape each half into a rectangle and fit into 2 lightly greased 8½- × 5½-inch (22 × 14 cm) loaf pans. Cover each pan loosely with plastic wrap and let rise in a warm, draft-free area until the dough has doubled in size, about 45 minutes.

Preheat the oven to 375°F (190°C).

Brush the top of each loaf with the lightly beaten egg; sprinkle with sesame seeds.

Bake in the centre of the preheated oven until breads are golden brown and sound hollow when tapped, 35–40 minutes. Cool the breads in the pans on a wire rack. Tap the loaves out of the loaf pan and let them cool completely on the wire rack.

Cinnamon Raisin Whole-Wheat Bread

2 cups (500 mL) all-purpose flour
    (approx.)
2 cups (500 mL) whole-wheat
    flour
2 Tbsp (30 mL) cinnamon
2¼ tsp (11 mL) instant dried yeast
    (1 pkg)
1 Tbsp (15 mL) salt
¾ cup (180 mL) hot water
½ cup (125 mL) milk, at room
    temperature
⅓ cup (80 mL) honey
¼ cup (60 mL) unsalted butter,
    softened (2 oz/60 g)
1 large egg, at room temperature
2 cups (500 mL) raisins

FILLING

3 Tbsp (45 mL) unsalted butter,
    melted and cooled (1.5 oz/45 g)
⅓ cup (80 mL) granulated sugar
3 Tbsp (45 mL) cinnamon

TOPPING

1 large egg, at room temperature

MUCH HAS been written about the cathartic properties of making bread and how it's like therapy—from watching the yeast proof in some water or milk, to the Zen-like state you achieve as you knead the dough and the satisfaction you inevitably get as you cut the first slice of homemade bread. Plus, it leaves the whole house smelling amazing.

While it's true that you can now readily purchase every kind of bread imaginable, and we're incredibly lucky to have such quality breads available, there's still nothing quite as remarkable as making your own artisanal bread. It actually takes much less time than you might imagine. Try to schedule a morning where you have a lot to accomplish while still in the house so that you can devote the rising times to good use. As a general rule, most breads will take about 1–1½ hours for their preliminary rise—just enough time to start, if not finish, another project. The second rise can take anywhere from 30–60 minutes—time enough for a good workout on the treadmill or even a good drama on TV.

I have called for instant yeast in this recipe. Unlike regular dry active yeast, the instant variety has to be combined with the dry ingredients and the water must be hot.

In the bowl of a stand mixer, combine the flours, cinnamon, yeast and salt, not letting the salt touch the yeast. Using the paddle attachment or dough hook, mix for 1 minute or until well combined. Add the water, milk, honey, butter and egg. Mix on low speed until combined and a soft dough is formed. Increase the speed to medium and beat, adding up to ¼ cup (60 mL) more all-purpose flour if necessary. Continue for 8 minutes or until a soft, sticky dough is formed and is clinging to the paddle attachment, not to the sides of the bowl. Scrape the dough away from the paddle or dough hook; transfer to a lightly floured work surface. By hand, knead the raisins in a third at a time. It will seem like a LOT of raisins but you will want to incorporate them all.

Lightly oil a large bowl. Place the dough in the bowl, turning it until it is thoroughly coated with the oil. Cover with plastic wrap and let rise in a warm, draft-free area for 1 hour or until the dough is doubled in bulk.

Transfer the dough to a lightly floured work surface. Cut the dough into 2 equal-sized pieces. Roll 1 piece of dough into a 16- × 8-inch (40 × 20 cm) rectangle. Brush the surface with half of the butter. In a small bowl, combine the sugar and cinnamon. Sprinkle half over the buttered dough. Starting at the short end, tightly roll up the dough, jelly roll–style. Place into a well greased 8- × 5-inch (20 × 12 cm) loaf pan. Repeat the process with the remaining dough and filling. Place into a second well-greased 8- × 5-inch (20 × 12 cm) loaf pan. Cover with plastic wrap and let both doughs rise again in a warm, draft-free area for 1–1½ hours, or until doubled in bulk.

Meanwhile, preheat the oven to 375°F (190°C).

In a small bowl, lightly beat the egg. Brush the egg over the tops of the risen loaves. Bake in the centre of the preheated oven until loaves are golden and sound hollow when tapped, 30–35 minutes. Cool the breads in the pans on a wire rack. Tap the loaves out of the loaf pans and let them cool completely on the wire rack.

Special Occasion Chocolate Coffee Babka

⅓ cup (80 mL) granulated sugar, divided

½ cup (125 mL) warm water

2¼ tsp (11 mL) active dry yeast (1 pkg)

⅓ cup (80 mL) unsalted butter, softened (3 oz/90 g)

¾ cup (180 mL) milk, at room temperatue

2 large eggs, at room temperature

1 large egg yolk, at room temperature

1 tsp (5 mL) salt

1½ tsp (7 mL) vanilla

4½ cups (1.125 L) all-purpose flour (approx.)

FILLING

½ cup (125 mL) granulated sugar

¼ cup (60 mL) unsweetened cocoa powder, sifted

2 tsp (10 mL) coffee granules, crushed

1 tsp (5 mL) cinnamon

4 oz (125 g) semisweet chocolate, coarsely chopped

½ cup (125 mL) raisins

⅓ cup (80 mL) unsalted butter, melted and cooled (3 oz/90 g)

THE WORD "babka" is a Polish word for grandmother or older woman, but also refers to a yeasted coffee cake made with nuts, dried fruit or even chocolate that hails from Eastern Europe. Although many bakers bake their babkas in a loaf pan, I prefer to bake mine in a tube pan. It comes out of the oven majestic and regal. I certainly grew up eating many different kinds of babkas, from ones studded throughout with dried fruit, courtesy of a Russian relative, to densely textured and loaf-shaped ones that had more of a pudding-like swirl. Not all were adorned with a streusel; more often the topping was a blond-looking combination of white flour, white sugar and just a smidgeon of butter. Mine tends to be a bit moister and a bit darker due to the inclusion of brown sugar.

In a large bowl, stir 1 Tbsp (15 mL) of the sugar into warm water. Sprinkle the yeast over the water. Let stand for about 10 minutes or until frothy.

Meanwhile, melt the butter with the remaining sugar and the milk in a small saucepan set over medium heat. Remove from the heat and let the mixture cool slightly. Whisk the warm milk mixture into the yeast mixture along with the eggs, egg yolk, salt and vanilla.

Stir in 4 cups (1 L) of the flour, stirring until a soft, slightly sticky dough is formed. Transfer the dough to a lightly floured work surface. Sprinkling the surface as needed with flour, knead the dough until it is very smooth and elastic, about 10 minutes. It's important that you not over flour the dough; use just enough to prevent it from sticking to the surface.

Lightly oil a large bowl. Place the dough in the bowl, turning it until it the dough is thoroughly coated with the oil. Cover the bowl with plastic wrap and then a kitchen towel. Let the dough rise in a warm, draft-free area for 1 hour or until it's doubled in bulk. The dough is ready when you poke it with a finger and the indentation remains.

FILLING Meanwhile, in a small bowl, whisk together the sugar, cocoa powder, coffee granules and cinnamon. In a separate bowl, stir together the chocolate and raisins. Lightly grease a 10-inch (25 cm) tube pan with a removable bottom; set aside.

TOPPING

¼ cup (60 mL) all-purpose flour

2 Tbsp (30 mL) packed light brown
    sugar

2 Tbsp (30 mL) icing sugar

2 Tbsp (30 mL) unsalted butter,
    softened (1 oz/30 g)

1 large egg, lightly beaten, at room
    temperature

Punch down the dough. On a lightly floured work surface, roll the dough into a 22- × 10-inch (55 × 25 cm) rectangle. Leaving a 1-inch (2.5 cm) border, brush the surface of the dough with the melted butter. Sprinkle the sugar-cocoa filling evenly over the dough. Sprinkle with the chocolate and raisins.

Starting with the long side, roll up the dough jelly roll–style. Pinch the bottom edges to seal. Twist the ends of the roll in opposite directions about 6 times. Place into the prepared tube pan. Cover the tube with plastic wrap and a kitchen towel and let the dough rise in a warm, draft-free area for 1½ hours or until doubled in bulk.

TOPPING For the topping, combine the flour and sugars in a bowl. Using your fingertips, rub the butter into the mixture until crumbly; set aside.

Preheat the oven to 350°F (180°C).

Gently brush the surface of the dough with the beaten egg. Sprinkle the topping evenly over. Bake the babka in the middle of the preheated oven the dough is golden and puffed quite high, about 40 minutes. Let cool in pan on a wire rack for at least 20 minutes. Run a small knife around the edge of the cake pan to loosen the babka. Remove the sides and the bottom of the cake pan; let the babka cool on a wire rack.

Sticky Cinnamon Buns

¼ cup (60 mL) granulated sugar,
  divided

½ cup (125 mL) warm water

1 Tbsp (15 mL) active dry yeast

½ cup (125 mL) sour cream, at
  room temperature

⅓ cup (80 mL) unsalted butter,
  melted and cooled (3 oz/90 g)

2 eggs, at room temperature,
  beaten

2 tsp (10 mL) salt

1 tsp (5 mL) vanilla

1 cup (250 mL) bread flour

3 cups (750 mL) all-purpose flour
  (approx.)

STICKY BOTTOM

¾ cup (180 mL) unsalted butter
  (6 oz/175 g)

1 cup (250 mL) packed light brown
  sugar

¼ cup (60 mL) maple syrup

1 Tbsp (15 mL) light corn syrup

1½ cups (375 mL) pecan halves

FILLING

¾ cup (180 mL) packed light
  brown sugar

1 Tbsp (15 mL) cinnamon

¼ cup (60 mL) unsalted butter,
  melted and cooled (2 oz/60 g),
  divided

1 cup (250 mL) golden raisins

CINNAMON BUNS are crowd pleasers. The yeasted bread should be light and fluffy, the filling sweet and sensational and the sticky topping sinful. Even the most well-bred will be tempted to lick the gooey glaze from their fingertips. Yes, they take time and a lot of butter. But they're so amazing, they will cement your reputation as a baker extraordinaire.

Dissolve 1 tsp (5 mL) of the sugar in warm water. Sprinkle in the yeast; let stand for 10 minutes or until frothy.

Meanwhile, in a large bowl, gently whisk together the sour cream, butter, remaining sugar, eggs, salt and vanilla. Once the yeast is sufficiently proofed, stir it into the sour cream–butter mixture.

Using a wooden spoon, stir in the bread flour and 1 cup (250 mL) of the all-purpose flour until a thickish, somewhat lumpy mixture is formed. Stir in enough of the remaining flour, ½ cup (125 mL) at a time, to make a soft, slightly sticky dough. Transfer the dough to a lightly floured work surface. Sprinkling the surface with extra flour as needed to prevent the dough from sticking, knead the dough until smooth and elastic, about 10 minutes. Generously oil a large bowl. Place the dough in the bowl, turning the dough to grease it all over. Cover the bowl with plastic wrap and let the dough rise in a warm, draft-free area until it's doubled in size, 1–1½ hours.

Meanwhile, prepare the sticky bottom mixture.

STICKY BOTTOM In a saucepan set over medium-low heat, melt the butter, brown sugar, maple syrup and corn syrup together, whisking often until the butter is completely melted and the mixture is smooth and homogenous. Remove from the heat. Pour into the bottom of a 13- × 9-inch (33 × 23 cm) rectangular glass dish. Sprinkle the pecan halves over the mixture.

FILLING Combine the brown sugar and cinnamon.

Punch down the dough. On a lightly floured surface, roll the dough out to a 18- × 15-inch (45 × 38 cm) rectangle. Brush the surface with 3 Tbsp (45 mL) of the melted butter, leaving a 1-inch (2.5 cm) border on all sides.

RECIPE CONTINUED . . .

Sprinkle the surface evenly with the sugar-cinnamon mixture. Sprinkle the raisins evenly over. Starting with a long side, roll up the dough tightly, jelly roll–style. Brush the surface with the remaining 1 Tbsp (15 mL) of melted butter. Cut the log into 12 equal-sized pieces; arrange the rolls, cut side down, in a single layer over the sticky sauce. Cover the dish with plastic wrap and let the dough rise in a warm, draft-free area until it's doubled in bulk, about 1 hour.

Preheat the oven to 375°F (190°C).

Bake in the centre of the preheated oven until the buns are golden and the top sounds hollow when tapped, about 30 minutes. Let the buns stand in the pan on a wire rack for 3 minutes. Invert onto a serving platter, scraping any remaining sticky sauce in the pan onto the top of the buns.

Cheese Danish

¼ cup (60 mL) granulated sugar,
  divided

¼ cup (60 mL) warm water

2 tsp (10 mL) active dry yeast

2½ cups (625 mL) all-purpose
  flour (approx.)

1 cup (250 mL) cold unsalted
  butter (8 oz/250 g)

½ cup (125 mL) milk, at room
  termperature

1 large egg, lightly beaten, at room
  temperature

¾ tsp (4 mL) salt

CHEESE FILLING

12 oz (375 g) cream cheese,
  softened

½ cup (125 mL) granulated sugar

1 large egg yolk, at room
  termperature

2 Tbsp (30 mL) all-purpose flour

½ tsp (2 mL) finely grated lemon
  zest

1 tsp (5 mL) vanilla

GLAZE

1 large egg, lightly beaten, at room
  temperature

I FIRST learned how to make Danish many years ago while I was working under pastry chef Steve Fromm at the Fairmont San Francisco, a swank hotel located in Nob Hill. We used to make it for brunch at the hotel, so you can just imagine how many pounds of butter we used. This recipe is way more manageable and will become the gold standard by which you judge all other Danish.

In a small bowl, sprinkle 1 tsp (5 mL) of the sugar over the warm water. Sprinkle the yeast over; let stand for 10 minutes or until frothy.

Meanwhile, place the flour in the bowl of a food processor fitted with the metal "S" blade. Cut the butter into large cubes and add to the food processor; pulse until the butter is in ¼- to ½-inch (5–10 mm) pieces.

In a large bowl, stir together the remaining sugar, milk, egg and salt; stir in the yeast mixture. Using a wooden spoon, stir the flour mixture into the yeast mixture, stirring just until a rough ball is formed and the dry ingredients are thoroughly moistened. Cover with plastic wrap and refrigerate for 8–24 hours.

Transfer the dough to a lightly floured work surface; sprinkle the dough lightly with flour. Pat the dough into a square, then roll into an 18- × 10-inch (45 × 20 cm) rectangle. Using the short edge closest to you, fold the top third over the middle third of the dough. Fold the bottom third over top, matching the edges. Then turn the dough so that the closed fold is on the left. Repeat rolling out, folding and turning the dough 3 more times. If the dough becomes too soft, simply refrigerate it on a plate covered with plastic wrap for about 5 minutes. Wrap the dough in plastic wrap and refrigerate for 1 hour or up to 2 days. Bring the dough to room temperature for 30 minutes before proceeding.

Roll out the dough on a lightly floured surface to a 14- × 10-inch (35 × 25 cm) rectangle. Cut lengthwise into 15 equal strips. Using your hands, roll each strip into a 16-inch (40 cm) rope. Holding one end of the rope in place, coil the rest of the rope loosely around the anchored end, tucking the end underneath. Repeat with all 15 ropes.

Arrange the coiled circles on 2 parchment paper–lined baking sheets, placing them about 1 inch (2.5 cm) apart. Cover loosely with plastic wrap. Let rise in a warm, draft-free area until lightly puffed, about 40 minutes.

Preheat the oven to 400°F (200°C).

CHEESE FILLING In the bowl of a stand mixer fitted with the paddle attachment, or using a hand-held mixer, beat the cream cheese until fluffy. Beat in the sugar, egg yolk, flour, lemon zest and vanilla.

Using your fingers, make a 2¼-inch (5.5 cm) wide indentation in the centre of each Danish. Spoon or pipe in the cheese filling.

GLAZE Brush each Danish with the egg, being careful not to let the egg touch the filling.

Bake in the centre of the preheated oven until the Danish are puffed and golden, 15–20 minutes. Let cool the on the pan on a wire rack for 15 minutes. Transfer the danish to the wire rack and cool completely.

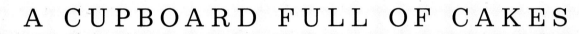

A CUPBOARD FULL OF CAKES

305   CAKE METHODS

308   LAYER CAKES AND CUPCAKES

309   White Cake with Lemon Curd and White Chocolate Whipped Cream

314   Golden Butter Cake with Mocha Buttercream

317   Chocolate Birthday Cake

319   Spiced Layer Cake with Maple Cream Cheese Icing

321   Carrot Cake with Cream Cheese Icing

323   Mom's Napoleon Cake

327   Passover Chocolate Cake

329   Buttery Cupcakes

330   A Palette's Worth of Icings

332   Pavlova Cupcakes with Honey Roasted Strawberries

334   ANGEL FOOD CAKES

335   Classic Angel Food Cake

336   EVERYDAY AND FRUIT-BASED CAKES

337   French Toast Cake

338   Plum Kuchen

341   Banana Bundt Cake

342   Crackle-Topped Peach Cake

344   Individual Plum Cornmeal Cakes with Rosemary

346   Tarte Tatin Cake

348   Apple Cake with Pecan Glaze

349   Apple Honey Cardamom Cake

352   Blueberry Coffee Cream Cheese Cake

355   Blueberry Lime Bundt Cake

356   Roasted Pineapple Cake

358   Gingerbread-Style Sticky Date Pudding Cake

360   Honey Cake

361   Meyer Lemon Pudding Cake

362   Pistachio Lemon Dacquoise

365   Gâteau Breton

366   COFFEE CAKES AND POUND CAKES

367   Ye Olde Fashioned Sour Cream Coffee Cake

368   Chocolate Ribbon Coffee Cake

370   Individual Yeasted Coffee Cakes with Cherries and Almonds

372   Orange Cardamom Coffee Cake with Almond Swirl

374   Sour Cream Pound Cake

376   Almond Crusted Cherry Pound Cake

378   Lemon Pound Cake with Ginger Speckles

380   Orange Cream Cheese Pound Cake

381   FROZEN CAKES

382   Reine de Saba Ice Cream Cake

384   Caffe Latte Chocolate Bar Explosion Ice Cream Cake

386   Coffee Ice Cream

387   Rich Chocolate Ice Cream

388   CHEESECAKES

390   Vanilla Cheesecake

393   Pumpkin Cheesecake

395   Light-as-a-Feather Lemon Mousse Cheesecake

NOTHING SAYS "special" more than a cake. It can be birthday party special, entertaining special, graduation special or simply express that you are special to someone. And nothing says "extra special" more than a home baked cake.

CAKE METHODS

There are basically (with some exceptions) two types of cake: butter-based cakes and foam-based cakes. Butter-based cakes, as the name implies, rely on beating butter and sugar together to create air bubbles (the creaming process), as well as chemical leaveners for their rise. Foam-based cakes, on the other hand, rely on foam produced by beaten whole eggs, egg whites or a mixture of beaten yolks and beaten whites.

There are certainly whole categories of cakes that do not fit into this neat package. Tortes fall out of this purview as do flourless chocolate cakes and cheesecakes. On the whole, though, the two cake categories apply.

When you make a butter cake, such as the White Cake on page 309 or the Golden Butter Cake on page 314, you almost always use the creaming method. When you cream butter together with sugar, it's essential that the butter be at room temperature. An internal temperature of between 65–68°F (18–20°C) means that the butter will be pliable enough to hold the maximum number of air bubbles. The crystalline edges of the sugar provide the friction necessary for those air bubbles to develop. These air bubbles are intrinsic to the rise and the texture of the cake, since the baking powder or soda called for in the recipe actually increases the size of those bubbles, it doesn't create new ones. As the bubbles grow and enlarge, the cake rises. If the butter is too cold, it will not be elastic enough to hold the bubbles, whereas if it's overly soft it won't be able to hold and suspend air bubbles. Too few bubbles can mean a heavy, dense cake and a disappointed baker. So make sure your butter is room temperature and malleable.

As I said on page 17, it's important to cream the butter with the sugar for as long as the recipe indicates to make sure you are creating enough air bubbles. You can usually tell by looking at your butter-sugar mixture. It should be pale, almost white and fluffy. Don't overdo it though, since you run the risk of warming the butter to the point where it can no longer keep the bubbles in suspension, causing them to collapse. Follow the times given by recipes and watch the colour of your butter and you'll have nothing to worry about.

Adding the eggs is an important step. Of course, the eggs should be at room temperature. If cold, the eggs will simply re-solidify the butter, causing the air bubbles or cells to collapse. You probably have had this happen to you, I know I have. The batter starts to curdle and look funny. Sometimes this happens when the number of eggs called for is large or if you add the eggs too quickly. The batter will come together and smooth out when the flour mixture is added, but you may forfeit some height. Always add the eggs one at a time if more than one is called for, and make sure that the first one is thoroughly incorporated before adding the next.

Remember that once you start adding other ingredients (such as eggs) to the creamed butter and sugar mixture you will not develop any more air bubbles.

Sometimes the liquid is added right after the eggs, with the flour last, while in other cases a recipe might call for you to add the flour and liquid is an alternating sequence. This latter method helps retain the delicate emulsion and prevents gluten development. If you had to mix the flour in all at once, you would probably have to stir so hard that an excess amount of gluten would develop. As gluten develops, the leavener has to work harder to penetrate tough cells walls, which can result in a tight grain, peaked top or those unseemly tunnels running throughout your cake. Add the flour first and last with the addition of liquid in between.

Foam cakes rely on air bubbles whipped into whole eggs, egg whites or a combination of the two. Most sponge cakes and genoise fall into the whole-egg category. In these situations, whole eggs and some sugar are warmed over a water bath, then beaten to triple their volume, before being combined with some flour and usually a bit of melted butter, then baked.

The structure of cakes such as angel food cake rely on beaten egg whites, some flour and a flavouring. The amount of sugar will determine an egg white's or meringue's strength. Sugar is an egg white's insurance policy. Egg whites beaten with a proportionate amount of sugar (usually about 2 Tbsp/30 mL of sugar per 1 egg white) are the most stable, since the sugar adds moistness and flexibility to the foam. Always add the sugar gradually in a thin stream and start adding the sugar at the soft peak stage. If you wait much longer, the egg whites become tough and dry and well on their way to over-expansion, meaning they'll have no more room to expand in the oven. See whipping egg whites on page 47. Almost all egg white foam-based cakes call for ungreased pans, so that the foam has something to cling to as it rises in the oven.

Separated egg cakes, what the French call *biscuits*, rely on beaten egg yolks and beaten egg whites that are then folded together with a bit of flour and sometimes a touch of fat.

After all that, it's easy to understand how important your oven is. If your oven is too hot, the air bubbles expand too quickly, your cake will peak or dome and it may very well be ready sooner than you expected. If your oven is too cool, the cake will not be able to rise sufficiently, and it may sink in the middle or have a coarse texture.

PREPPING YOUR CAKE PANS FOR BAKING

In most of the recipes in the cake chapter (plus the quick breads), I have specified to grease your pans and then place a circle of parchment paper on the bottom. I almost always do the greasing with a cooking spray, notably Pam Baking Spray or regular Pam Spray. I find it easy, quick and reliable. There are exceptions to this rule, however. For example, in the Almond Crusted Cherry Pound Cake (see p. 376), butter is essential since the almonds have to cling to the side of the pan. When making angel food cake, on the other hand, the pans should never be greased.

If you are going to grease your pans with butter, spread some softened butter on a piece of plastic wrap or waxed paper. Thinly but evenly coat the bottom and inside edges of the pan and all of its nooks and crannies, then place about 1 Tbsp (15 mL) of flour into the pan. Lightly shake the pan around until it is lightly but entirely coated with the flour. Tap out any excess flour.

LAYER CAKES AND CUPCAKES

Layer cakes, more so than simple one-layer or carrying cakes, announce a special occasion. Whereas you may make the Crackle-Topped Peach Cake (p. 342) on a Wednesday in the middle of August when peaches are in season, making either the White Cake (p. 309) or the Chocolate Birthday Cake (p. 317), requires more advance planning, a little bit more of a time commitment and ultimately a great reason to celebrate. Which is not to say you have to do it all in one fell swoop. That's the great thing about layer cakes—you can compartmentalize the procedure to your liking. Most buttercreams can be made ahead and either be refrigerated for several days or tucked away in the freezer for a month. The cake layers too can be made ahead and frozen. Some fillings, such as the lemon curd on page 309 HAVE to be made ahead. Making layer cakes is a labour of love and a portal through which to unleash your creativity. Icings can be applied in a professional and utterly perfect way or they can be a cascade of swirls and peaks. Whether you choose to garnish your cake with candied lemon peel, store-bought lemon buttons or even fresh fruit is up to you. There are no hard and fast rules to decorating a cake **except** that you don't want to garnish with any ingredient that isn't immediately related to the cake. You wouldn't, for example, want to garnish the Lemon Cake with chocolate coffee espresso beans since those have absolutely nothing to do with what you're serving. Remember a garnish is a promise of what is about to be tasted, so keep it all in the family.

White Cake *with* Lemon Curd *and* White Chocolate Whipped Cream

THIS LOVELY, buttery cake pairs magnificently with the white chocolate–spiked whipped cream and the bright yellow, explode-in-your-mouth lemon curd. The cake layers are light textured and ethereal due to the use of cake and pastry flour. The risk of tunnelling is also minimal because of the chosen flour. Using only egg whites promises a wedding white colour. As with all delicate cakes, it's worth your while to add the dry ingredients by hand, thus certifying you will end with a fragrant and soft cake.

LEMON CURD The day before (or really, up to 2 days before) you want to serve the cake, make the lemon curd. Melt the butter in a heavy-bottomed saucepan set over medium heat. Remove the pot from the heat and stir in the sugar, lemon juice and egg yolks until very well blended. Cook the lemon mixture over low heat, without letting it boil, until thickened, 8–10 minutes. To check if the curd is sufficiently thickened, dip a wooden spoon in the mixture so that it coats the back of the spoon. Draw your finger across the back of the spoon. The mixture should be thick enough that a clean path is left on the back of the spoon, with no dripping. Place a fine mesh sieve over a clean stainless steel bowl. Pour the curd through the sieve, pressing it with a rubber spatula. Stir in the lemon zest. Place some plastic wrap directly on the surface of the curd and refrigerate until it's completely chilled and thickened, 1–2 days.

WHITE CHOCOLATE WHIPPED CREAM Again, the day before you want to ice and serve the cake, prepare the first part of this icing. Place the white chocolate in a bowl. Bring ⅔ cup (160 mL) of the whipping cream to a boil over medium-high heat. Store remaining whipping cream in the refrigerator until needed. Pour the hot cream over the white chocolate and let the mixture sit, without stirring, for 3 minutes. Whisk the mixture until the white chocolate is completely melted and the mixture is smooth. Refrigerate, without covering, overnight or for up to 2 days.

CAKE LAYERS Preheat the oven to 350°F (180°C). Lightly grease the bottom and sides of two 9-inch (23 cm) metal cake pans. Line the bottom of each with a circle of parchment paper cut to fit; set aside.

LEMON CURD

½ cup (125 mL) unsalted butter (4 oz/125 g)

¾ cup (180 mL) granulated sugar

½ cup (125 mL) freshly squeezed lemon juice (about 2 lemons)

6 large egg yolks, at room temperature

2 Tbsp (30 mL) finely grated lemon zest (about 2 lemons)

WHITE CHOCOLATE WHIPPED CREAM

6 oz (175 g) white chocolate, coarsely chopped

1¾ cups (430 mL) whipping cream, cold, divided

CAKE LAYERS

2⅓ cups (580 mL) cake and pastry flour, sifted (spooned into the measure and swept)

1 Tbsp (15 mL) baking powder

½ tsp (2 mL) salt

¼ tsp (1 mL) baking soda

1 cup (250 mL) unsalted butter, softened (8 oz/250 g)

1¾ cups (430 mL) granulated sugar

1 cup (250 mL) buttermilk, at room temperature

2 tsp (10 mL) vanilla

5 large egg whites, at room temperature

½ cup (125 mL) fresh blueberries (optional)

RECIPE CONTINUED . . .

Whisk together the flour, baking powder, salt and baking soda in a bowl until the dry ingredients are thoroughly combined; set aside.

In the bowl of a stand mixer fitted with the paddle attachment, or using a hand-held mixer, beat the butter for 1 minute. Add the sugar and beat until light and fluffy, about 3 minutes.

Remove the bowl from the stand. Using a wooden spoon, alternately stir in the flour mixture with the buttermilk and vanilla, making 3 additions of the flour and 2 of the buttermilk.

Using a clean bowl and a clean whisk attachment or beaters, beat the egg whites into stiff peaks. It's important that you not overbeat the whites at this stage. Remember that as you fold them into the batter, you are continuing to work them so they may become too stiff. Also, if they're too stiff, you might have difficulty folding them in—they may remain in globules and then you will have to work that much harder to incorporate them into the batter, potentially causing the batter to deflate.

Gently fold one-third of the egg whites into the cake batter. Fold in the remaining egg whites. Divide the batter between the 2 prepared pans.

Bake in the centre of the preheated oven until the tops of the cakes are golden and spring back when lightly pressed, 35–40 minutes. Cool the cakes in their pans on a wire rack for at least 30 minutes. Run a small knife around the edge of the pans to loosen the cakes. Remove the cakes from the pans and cool completely on the wire racks, parchment side down.

ASSEMBLY Remove the parchment paper from under one of the cake layers. Place on a cake plate or decorating turntable. Leaving ¼ inch (6 mm) of the edges uncovered, spread the lemon curd over the cake. Leaving some of the edge uncovered will prevent the curd from edging its way down the side of the cake, which can spell trouble when you go to ice the cake. If you are using them, sprinkle the blueberries over the lemon curd.

Remove the parchment from the second layer. Invert the cake and place on top of the lemon curd.

Stir the remaining whipping cream into the white chocolate mixture. Transfer to the bowl of a stand mixer (you can also use a hand-held mixer for this) fitted with the whisk attachment and beat until stiff peaks are formed. Using a palette knife, spread the whipping cream over the sides and then over the top of the cake. If you have any whipped cream left over, pipe rosettes on top of the cake. Refrigerate for at least 30 minutes before serving.

RECIPE CONTINUED . . .

BAKER'S TIP

MAKING A PAPER CONE   Writing personal notes on any cake is easily accomplished by making a paper cone and filling it with melted dark or white chocolate. To make a paper cone follow these instructions:

1. Cut out a large square of parchment paper.
2. Make a triangle by folding the square in half. Cut out the triangle. You should now have a three pointed triangle, with a long side and two shorter sides.
3. Take one of the points from the longer side and roll it over so that the long point meets the middle point. Tuck the larger point underneath slightly so that a cone is formed with the other half of the parchment paper left hanging.
4. Bring the hanging corner of paper over and wrap around the cone so that this point meets the first wrapped point.
5. Tuck all three points underneath to secure the cone.
6. Cut the tip of the cone into whatever sized opening you wish. The smaller the opening, the finer your words or decorations will be; the wider the hole, the thicker the script.
7. When the time comes, pour warm melted white or dark chocolate in the cone and use to write your message.

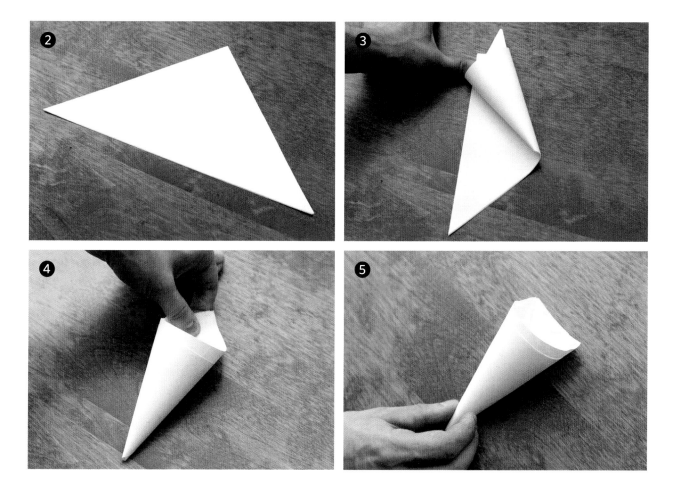

Golden Butter Cake *with* Mocha Buttercream

2½ cups (625 mL) cake and pastry
flour, sifted (spooned into the
measure and swept)
2 tsp (10 mL) baking powder
½ tsp (2 mL) salt
1 cup (250 mL) unsalted butter,
softened (8 oz/250 g)
1½ cups (375 mL) granulated
sugar
3 large eggs, at room temperature
2 tsp (10 mL) vanilla
1 cup (250 mL) milk, at room
temperature

MOCHA BUTTERCREAM

8 oz (250 g) milk chocolate,
coarsely chopped
¼ cup (60 mL) extra strong coffee
4 large egg whites, at room
temperature
¾ cup (180 mL) granulated sugar
Pinch of salt
1½ cups (375 mL) unsalted butter,
softened (12 oz/375 g)

I HAVE to admit, I get really excited about birthdays—not mine especially, but everybody else's because it means I can make a birthday cake (and shop for presents, but that's another story). This cake is especially popular because of its buttery flavour and its tender crumb. The butteriness pairs especially well with the coffee overtones in the buttercream.

Preheat the oven to 350°F (180°C). Lightly grease the bottoms and sides of two 8-inch (20 cm) metal cake pans. Line the bottom of each with a circle of parchment paper cut to fit; set aside.

Whisk together the flour, baking powder and salt in a bowl until the dry ingredients are thoroughly combined; set aside.

In the bowl of a stand mixer fitted with the paddle attachment, or using a hand-held mixer, beat the butter for 1 minute. Gradually add the sugar and beat until light and fluffy, at least 3 minutes. One at a time and beating well after each addition, add the eggs, waiting until the first one is fully incorporated before adding the next. Remember to scrape down the sides of the bowl between each egg. Beat in the vanilla.

Remove the bowl from the mixer. Switch to using a wooden spoon. Alternately, stir in the flour mixture with the milk, making 3 additions of the flour and 2 of the milk.

Divide the batter between the 2 prepared pans.

Bake in the centre of the preheated oven until the tops of the cakes are golden and spring back when lightly pressed in the centre, 30–35 minutes. Cool the cakes in their pans on a wire rack for at least 20 minutes. Run a small knife around the edge of the pans to loosen the cakes. Remove the cakes from the pans and cool completely on the wire racks, parchment side down.

MOCHA BUTTERCREAM Combine the chocolate and coffee in a heavy-bottomed saucepan set over medium-low heat. Cook, stirring often, until the chocolate is melted and the mixture is smooth. Remove from the heat and cool completely.

Whisk together the egg whites, sugar and salt in a large bowl. Place over a saucepan of simmering water. Cook, whisking frequently, until the mixture is very hot (about 110°F/43°C on a candy thermometer) or until your finger cannot remain in the mixture for longer than 10 seconds. Immediately transfer to a stand mixer fitted with the whisk attachment. Whisk on medium to medium-high speed until the mixture is completely cool and quite thick, about 10 minutes. Add in the butter about ¼ cup (60 mL) at a time, beating well in between each addition, and making sure that each addition is fully incorporated before adding the next, until all of the butter is used. It may start to look a bit curdled once about two-thirds of the butter has been added but keep going. Remove the bowl from the machine. Using a long wooden spoon, fold in the cooled chocolate-coffee mixture until it is entirely incorporated. The mixture will be a very light chocolate colour.

ASSEMBLY Remove the parchment paper from one of the cake layers. Using a serrated knife and making sure your eyes are just above the level of the cake, slice the cake in half horizontally. It helps if you keep the palm of your other hand on top of the cake and rotate the cake as you slice it in half.

Place one of the halved layers on a cake plate or a cake decorating turnstile. Place about ¾ cup (180 mL) of the buttercream on top of the cake and smooth it using a palette knife. Top with the second halved layer and repeat with another ¾ cup (180 mL) of the buttercream.

Remove the parchment and slice the second cake layer in half horizontally as you did for the first. Place another halved layer on top of the buttercream. Top with another ¾ cup (180 mL) of the buttercream and spread evenly. Invert the last cake layer and place on top of the buttercream, so that what was the bottom of the cake is now the top. This will ensure that you have a flat, even surface to ice. Spread the sides and top with the remaining icing. Refrigerate for at least 1 hour before serving. Remember, any butter-based icing will have the same properties as butter. It will harden upon refrigeration and then soften when brought to room temperature. So bring the cake to room temperature at least 30 minutes before serving.

RECIPE CONTINUED . . .

BAKER'S TIPS

Pulling a double shift, this cake can easily be transformed into perfect-for-any-occasion cupcakes. Fill 15 muffin cups with the batter and bake at 350°F (180°C) for 20 minutes. The buttercream makes about 4 cups (1 L), which is plenty for the cupcakes. If you like your buttercream a little darker, don't beat the mixture together too much and leave it out at room temperature for a while. The air will darken the colour.

See Icing Cakes page 187 for tips on icing.

HOW TO RECOVER SPLIT BUTTERCREAM Sometimes, despite your best efforts, your buttercream will split, which means that the egg whites will start to seep out of the mixture and the butter and egg whites separate. Often, though, not all is lost. If your buttercream splits, remove the mixture from the mixer. Add about ¼ cup (60 mL) of the split buttercream back to the bowl. With the paddle attachment (the whisk attachment will encourage further separation), beat for 1 minute. Beat in about 3 Tbsp (45 mL) of room temperature butter. Add another ¼ cup (60 mL) of the curdled buttercream. Add another 3 Tbsp (45 mL) of soft butter. Repeat this action until at least half of the split buttercream is used up. Your buttercream should be looking more silky and smooth by this point. Start adding more buttercream with some butter between each third or fourth addition. This buttercream, because of the extra butter added to it, should be flavoured with chocolate or some other strong flavour. The only buttercream that cannot be salvaged is soupy buttercream, usually a result of the butter being added before the meringue mixture is completely cool.

Always cool whatever flavouring is being added to buttercream. If the flavouring is too hot, as in melted chocolate, it will simply melt the buttercream into soup.

Chocolate Birthday Cake

THIS WONDERFUL cake is the little black dress of cakes: useful for just about any occasion. You can dress it up for nighttime by adding some interesting stenciled chocolate and lots of rosettes, or keep it simple by just dusting some cocoa powder on top. This is more of an old fashioned icing, with a touch of whipping cream to enrich it.

Preheat the oven to 350°F (180°C). Lightly grease the bottoms and sides of two 9-inch (23 cm) metal cake pans. Line the bottom of each with a circle of parchment paper cut to fit; set aside.

Whisk together the flour, granulated sugar, cocoa powder, baking soda and salt in a bowl until the dry ingredients are thoroughly combined. In a separate bowl, whisk together the water, oil, sour cream, eggs, butter and vanilla. Pour the oil mixture over the flour mixture; whisk gently until thoroughly combined. Divide the batter evenly between the 2 prepared pans.

Bake in the centre of the preheated oven until the top of the cake springs back when lightly pressed, 35–40 minutes. Cool the cakes in their pans on a wire rack for 30 minutes. Run a small knife around the edge of the pan to loosen the cakes from the pan. Remove the cakes from the pans and cool completely on the wire racks, parchment side down.

CHOCOLATE ICING In the top of a double boiler, set over hot, not boiling water, melt the chocolate. Remove from the heat and cool.

In the bowl of a stand mixer fitted with the paddle attachment, or using a hand-held mixer, beat the butter for 1 minute. Beat in 1 cup (250 mL) of the icing sugar until the icing sugar is thoroughly incorporated. Scrape the sides of the bowl with a rubber spatula. Beat in a third of the whipping cream. Scrape the sides of the bowl. Beat in another cup of the icing sugar, again beating until the sugar is thoroughly incorporated and scraping down the sides of the bowl once again. Beat in another third of the whipping cream. Beat in the remaining icing sugar and then the remaining whipping cream, Scrape down the sides of the bowl and then beat in the vanilla. Using a rubber spatula, stir in the chocolate.

2⅔ cups (660 mL) all-purpose flour
2⅓ cups (580 mL) granulated sugar
½ cup (125 mL) unsweetened Dutch-processed cocoa powder, sifted
1½ tsp (7 mL) baking soda
½ tsp (2 mL) salt
1½ cups (375 mL) warm water
¾ cup (180 mL) canola or vegetable oil
⅔ cup (160 mL) sour cream, at room temperature
3 large eggs, at room temperature
¼ cup (60 mL) unsalted butter, melted and cooled (2 oz/60 g)
1 Tbsp (15 mL) vanilla

CHOCOLATE ICING
4 oz (125 g) unsweetened chocolate, coarsely chopped
1 cup (250 mL) unsalted butter, softened (8 oz/250 g)
2½ cups (625 mL) icing sugar
½ cup (125 mL) whipping cream, at room temperature
2 tsp (10 mL) vanilla

RECIPE CONTINUED . . .

ASSEMBLY Remove the parchment from the bottom of one of the cake layers. Place on a cake plate or a decorating turntable. If the cake has domed significantly, use a serrated knife to even it off. Using a long metal palette knife, spread 1 heaping cup (250+ mL) of the icing over the top of this layer. Remove the parchment paper from the second layer. Again, if it has crowned significantly, even it off with a serrated knife. Invert the cake and place on top of the icing, so that what was previously the bottom of the cake is now the top. This will ensure that you have a flat, even surface to ice. Spread the sides and top with the remaining icing. Refrigerate for at least 1 hour before serving. Remember, any butter-based icing will have the same properties as butter. It will harden upon refrigeration and then soften when brought to room temperature. So bring the cake to room temperature for at least 30 minutes before serving.

BAKER'S TIPS
See Icing Cakes page 187 for tips on icing.

You get the most flavour when you blend cocoa powder with boiling or hot water: the hot water allows the cocoa to expand and release all of its flavour. Milk or cream, on the other hand, tends to dull its flavour.

This amount of cake batter will yield about 2 dozen cupcakes. Bake the cupcakes in two 12-cup cupcake tins at 350°F (180°C) for about 25 minutes.

DIVIDING BATTER EVENLY Most professional pastry chefs weigh the batter going into their cake pans to ensure their cake layers will be uniform in both size and height. It also means they will bake in the same amount of time. If you have a scale at home, I recommend you do the same. Place the empty cake pan on your scale, tare it to zero and divide the batter by weight. If you don't have a scale, you can eyeball the amount or use an ice cream scoop to ensure that each pan has the same number of scoops.

Spiced Layer Cake *with* Maple Cream Cheese Icing

I WAS tempted to dub this cake "My Stubborn Spice Cake," because it took me so many times to get it right. I know, it's a simple spice cake, but my first attempt was too gummy, my second, too dry. And on it went, until I deemed this one to be just right. It's a homey cake, not too tall or too rich, made special by the spices included and the maple in the icing.

Preheat the oven to 350°F (180°C). Lightly grease the bottoms and sides of two 8-inch (20 cm) metal cake pans. Line the bottom of each with a circle of parchment paper cut to fit; set aside.

Whisk together the flour, baking powder, baking soda, salt, cinnamon, cocoa powder, nutmeg, ginger, cloves, allspice and pepper in a bowl until the dry ingredients are thoroughly combined.

In the bowl of a stand mixer fitted with the paddle attachment, or using a hand-held mixer, beat the butter for 1 minute. In a thin stream, gradually add the sugar, beating until light and fluffy, about 3 minutes. One at a time, beat in the eggs, beating well after each addition before adding the second. Scrape down the bowl. Beat in the vanilla.

Remove the bowl from the stand. Using a wooden spoon, alternately stir in the flour mixture with the sour cream, making 3 additions of the flour and 2 of the sour cream.

Divide the cake batter between the 2 prepared cake pans, smoothing the top.

Bake in the centre of the preheated oven until the tops of the cake spring back when lightly pressed, 25–30 minutes. They will look pale. Cool the cakes in their pans on a wire rack for 30 minutes. Run a small knife around the edge of the cake pans to loosen the cakes. Remove the cakes from the pans and cool completely on the wire racks, parchment side down.

MAPLE CREAM CHEESE ICING In the bowl of a stand mixer fitted with the paddle attachment, or using a hand-held mixer, beat the cream cheese until very smooth, about 2 minutes. Add the butter. Beat on medium-high speed until very smooth, about 3 minutes. Remember to scrape down the bowl a few times or you will end up with some "globules" of cream cheese that have not been appropriately beaten. In a thin stream, beat in

2 cups (500 mL) sifted cake and pastry flour (spooned into the measure and then swept)

2 tsp (10 mL) baking powder

¼ tsp (1 mL) baking soda and salt

1½ tsp (7 mL) cinnamon

1 tsp (5 mL) unsweetened cocoa powder

½ tsp (2 mL) ground nutmeg

½ tsp (2 mL) ground ginger

¼ tsp (1 mL) ground cloves

¼ tsp (1 mL) ground allspice

¼ tsp (1 mL) ground black pepper

¾ cup (180 mL) unsalted butter, softened (6 oz/175 g)

1 cup (250 mL) granulated sugar

2 large eggs, at room temperature

1½ tsp (7 mL) vanilla

1 cup (250 mL) sour cream, at room temperature

MAPLE CREAM CHEESE ICING

12 oz (375 g) cream cheese, softened

½ cup (125 mL) unsalted butter, softened (4 oz/125 g)

¼ cup (60 mL) pure maple syrup

RECIPE CONTINUED . . .

the maple syrup. Scrape down the sides and bottom of the bowl. Beat until very smooth and creamy, about 2 minutes.

ASSEMBLY Remove the parchment from the bottom of one of the cake layers. Place on a cake plate or a decorating turntable. If the cake has domed significantly, use a serrated knife to even it off. Using a long metal palette knife, spread 1 heaping cup (250+ mL) of the icing over the top of this layer. Remove the parchment paper from the second layer. Again, if it has crowned significantly, even it off with a serrated knife. Invert the cake and place on top of the icing, so that what was previously the bottom of the cake is now the top. This will ensure that you have a flat, even surface to ice. Spread the top and sides with the remaining icing. Refrigerate for at least 1 hour before serving.

BAKER'S TIP

UNMOULDING CAKES Always make sure that the cake is entirely cool before trying to unmould it. Once it's cool, run a thin knife or palette knife between the cake and the side of the pan, pressing the knife against the pan, so that it doesn't tear the cake. Then place a large plate, tart pan bottom or piece of cardboard on top of the cake pan. Invert the cake pan and allow the cake to fall out. Invert the cake again, onto another plate, tart tin bottom or cardboard piece. If you're not going to use the cake or cake layer immediately, keep the parchment on the bottom of the cake and wrap it in plastic wrap. The only exception to this is when you are using shaped pans such as Bundt or Kugelhopf pans, which should be unmoulded gently while still a little warm, or they might stick to the pan.

Carrot Cake *with* Cream Cheese Icing

A CLASSIC if there ever was one. The popularity of this cake seemed to have peaked in the 1980s and 1990s but I think it's a keeper, regardless of the date. Wonderfully moist, with just a whisper of cinnamon, this cake contains carrots, walnuts and golden raisins. Much of its original oil has been replaced with orange juice. The moistness is abetted by the creaminess of the icing

Preheat the oven to 350°F (180°C). Lightly grease the bottoms and sides of two 9-inch (23 cm) metal cake pans. Line the bottom of each with a circle of parchment paper cut to fit; set aside.

Whisk together the flour, baking soda, cinnamon, baking powder and salt in a large bowl until the dry ingredients are thoroughly combined.

In a separate large bowl, whisk together the sugars, zest, juice, oil, eggs, vanilla and carrots. Pour the wet mixture over the dry mixture, whisking until almost smooth. Add the walnuts and raisins, whisking until completely smooth.

Evenly divide the batter between the 2 prepared pans.

Bake in the centre of the preheated oven until the tops of the cakes spring back when lightly pressed, 30–35 minutes. Cool the cakes in their pans on a wire rack for 20 minutes. Run a small knife around the edge of the cake pans to loosen the cakes. Remove the cakes from the pans and cool completely on the wire racks, parchment side down.

CREAM CHEESE ICING In the bowl of a stand mixer fitted with the paddle attachment, or using a hand-held mixer, beat the cream cheese for 1 minute. Scrape down the sides of the bowl. Add the butter; beat for 3–5 minutes, scraping down the sides of the bowl frequently to make sure that there are no unabsorbed lumps. Beat in the orange zest. Beat in the icing sugar ½ cup (125 mL) at a time beating well after each addition before adding the next.

ASSEMBLY Remove the parchment paper from the bottom of one of the cake layers. Place on a cake plate or a decorating turntable. Using a long metal palette knife, spread 1 heaping cup (250+ mL) of the icing over

2⅓ cups (580 mL) all-purpose flour

2 tsp (10 mL) baking soda

1½ tsp (7 mL) cinnamon

½ tsp (2 mL) baking powder

Pinch of salt

1½ cups (375 mL) granulated sugar

⅓ cup (80 mL) packed light brown sugar

1 Tbsp (15 mL) finely grated orange zest

⅔ cup (160 mL) orange juice or orange mango juice

⅔ cup (160 mL) canola or vegetable oil

3 large eggs, at room temperature

2 tsp (10 mL) vanilla

2 cups (500 mL) grated carrots

½ cup (125 mL) walnut pieces

½ cup (125 mL) golden raisins

CREAM CHEESE ICING

12 oz (375 mL) cream cheese, softened

½ cup (125 mL) unsalted butter, softened (4 oz/125 g)

1 Tbsp (15 mL) finely grated orange zest (about 1 orange)

1½ cups (375 mL) icing sugar

RECIPE CONTINUED . . .

the top of this layer. Remove the parchment paper from the second layer. Invert the cake and place on top of the icing, so that what was previously the bottom of the cake is now actually the top. This will ensure that you have a flat, even surface to ice. Spread the top and sides with the remaining icing. Refrigerate for at least 1 hour before serving. Remember, any butter-based icing will have the same properties as butter. It will harden upon refrigeration and then soften when brought to room temperature. So bring the cake to room temperature for at least 30 minutes before serving.

BAKER'S TIPS

CAKE PAN SIZING For optimal results, use the pan size identified in the recipe. Baking cakes in smaller pans than is called for means the cake will have to bake longer because there's more batter in a pan with a smaller circumference and the longer baking time may dry it out. Smaller pans also run the risk of the batter spilling over and burning on the oven floor. Too large and your cake will bake much quicker, but the texture will suffer. If you have to choose a different size pan, try to get one as close to the volume capacity as the original pan. For example, you may not have the 8- × 2-inch (20 × 5 cm) cake pan requested but a 9- × 1½-inch (23 × 4 cm) cake pan actually has the same 6 cup (1.2 L) capacity, so the two can be interchanged. You can measure the volume of your pans by filling them to the top with water, and measuring the amount of water they contain.

For this cake, use carrots grated in the food processor and not on the shred side of a box grater.

Mom's Napoleon Cake

YOU KNOW the expression, "A rose by any other name would smell as sweet"? The same is true of this fabulous old-world cake. I have heard it called many things, chief among them Neapolitan cake, but my family has always called it Napoleon Cake. That's when we weren't calling it Elana's birthday cake. Elana is my younger sister and my mom made this cake every year for her birthday. That's actually the only time she made it, so perhaps that's what made it so special. That is, aside from the wonderfully crisp biscuit-like pastry layers that are sandwiched between layers of rich dark chocolate custard. This cake has to sit before you serve it so that the custard softens the pastry.

CHOCOLATE CUSTARD FILLING Whisk the egg yolks in a medium-sized bowl to break them up. Gradually, whisk in the sugar until a thick paste is formed. Meanwhile, heat the milk in a saucepan set over medium heat until small bubbles form around the edges of the milk. Whisking constantly, pour about ¼ cup (60 mL) of the hot milk into the eggs. Pour in another ¼ cup (60 mL), again whisking constantly. Continue adding the hot milk to the eggs, whisking constantly, until all of the hot milk has been slowly mixed into the egg mixture. Return the mixture to the saucepan. Whisk in the chocolate and the cocoa powder until the chocolate is melted and the mixture is smooth.

Return the saucepan to a medium-low heat. Cook, stirring often with a wooden spoon, until the mixture is thick enough to leave a trail on the back of a wooden spoon when you run your finger across it, about 10 minutes. Transfer the mixture to a clean bowl, cover the surface directly with plastic wrap to prevent a skin from forming and refrigerate until completely chilled, at least 3–24 hours.

PASTRY Combine the flour, baking soda and salt in a bowl; set aside.

In the bowl of a stand mixer fitted with the paddle attachment, or using hand-held beaters, cream the butter for 1 minute. Add the sugar and beat together until lightly coloured, about 3 minutes. Beat in the egg yolks, one at a time. On low speed, add one-third of the flour mixture. Beat in half of the sour cream. Beat in another third of the flour mixture and then

CHOCOLATE CUSTARD FILLING

5 large egg yolks, at room temperature

1⅔ cups (410 mL) granulated sugar

3 cups (725 mL) milk, at room temperature

6 oz (175 g) unsweetened chocolate, coarsely chopped

3 Tbsp (45 mL) unsweetened cocoa powder, sifted

PASTRY

4¼ cups (1.075 L) all-purpose flour

½ tsp (2 mL) baking soda

¼ tsp (1 mL) salt

1 cup (250 mL) unsalted butter, softened (8 oz/250 g)

1 cup (250 mL) granulated sugar

3 large egg yolks, at room temperature

1 cup (250 mL) sour cream, at room temperature

RECIPE CONTINUED . . .

the remaining sour cream. Beat in the remaining flour mixture. Dump the mixture onto a clean work surface. Working quickly, knead into a large ball. It may still be a bit sticky, but don't worry about this because you will need a bit of flour when you roll it out anyway. At this point, you can proceed with the recipe or wrap the dough in plastic wrap and refrigerate it for up to 24 hours.

Preheat the oven to 350°F (180°C).

Divide the dough into 7 equal pieces. Working with one piece at a time, liberally flour both your work surface and the surface of the piece of dough. Moving the dough around to make sure it's not sticking to the work surface, and sprinkling with flour as necessary, roll out the dough to an 11- × 14-inch (28 × 35 cm) rectangle. The dough will be quite thin. Starting at a short edge of the pastry, roll the dough around the rolling pin. Unroll the dough onto a parchment paper–lined unrimmed cookie sheet. Repeat with the remaining 6 pieces of dough. Of course, I realize that most people do not have 7 unrimmed cookie sheets, and quite frankly, neither do I. What I do when I make this recipe is I unroll the dough onto a large piece of parchment paper and then transfer the piece of parchment to an upside-down rimmed baking sheet. I try to refrigerate them, mercilessly moving things around in my fridge to accommodate the pans while a layer is baking. Then, I transfer the whole piece of parchment paper onto one of 3 unrimmed baking sheets that I own and bake them.

One layer at a time, bake the biscuit in the centre of the preheated oven until the edges are just starting to turn golden, about 10 minutes. You don't want the biscuit to get too golden or it will become brittle and hard to work with during the assembly of the Napoleon. Let the biscuit cool on the pan on a wire rack until cool. Repeat with the remaining 6 layers.

It's okay if your layers are not uniform in size. Look at them all and visually decide which ones are a bit smaller (these will be used in the middle), which one is slightly larger (this can be the base) and which one is the best looking (save for the top).

ASSEMBLY Place one of the biscuits on a large rectangular or square serving platter. Spread with one-seventh of the chocolate custard, spreading the custard almost but not quite to the edge of the biscuit. Top with another biscuit and then another seventh of the custard. Repeat layering—the last layer should be custard. Trim the cake by breaking off any jagged edges or very large edges with your hands. The edges are not meant to be perfectly aligned. Crumble the broken edges on top of the last layer of the custard. Wrap the entire cake loosely with plastic wrap and refrigerate for 12–36 hours.

Bring the cake to room temperature for 30 minutes before serving. Serve in squares or large triangles.

Passover Chocolate Cake

LEAVENED ONLY by eggs and using vanilla powder instead of vanilla extract (which is made with alcohol and fermented), this cake is the last word on flourless chocolate cakes. It is as deeply chocolatey as they come and sports the signature crater-like middle. Try to use the best chocolate you can for this cake, it makes all the difference. I like to use a bittersweet Cacao Barry or Callebaut chocolate, although if I have it, I adore the resonance of Scharffen Berger.

Preheat the oven to 350°F (180°C). Lightly grease the sides and bottom of a 10-inch (25 cm) springform pan. Line the bottom with a circle of parchment paper cut to fit; set aside.

Melt the chocolate and butter in the top of a double boiler set over hot, not boiling water. Once the chocolate is melted and smooth, transfer the mixture to a large bowl.

In the bowl of stand mixer fitted with the whisk attachment, or using a hand-held mixer, beat the egg yolks until broken up. In a thin stream, gradually add half of the sugar. Beat until the mixture is very pale and thick and has reached the ribbon stage (see baker's tip), about 5 minutes; set aside.

Using a clean bowl and a clean whisk attachment or beaters, whisk the egg whites with the salt until soft peaks appear. In a thin stream, gradually add the remaining sugar and beat until stiff glossy peaks form.

Using a plastic spatula, stir one-third of the yolk mixture into the chocolate mixture in order to lighten it. Fold in the second third and then the remaining third.

Fold one-third of the egg whites into the chocolate mixture in order to lighten it. In 2 additions, fold in the remaining egg whites, adding the vanilla powder with the last third.

Transfer the batter to the prepared pan. Place the springform pan on a rimmed baking sheet.

Bake in the centre of the preheated oven until puffy and golden, 30–35 minutes. The cake should still be moist in the centre although not runny. Let the cake cool completely in the pan on a wire rack. Run a small knife around the edge of the pan to loosen the cake. Unmould the cake and cover in plastic wrap. Refrigerate for at least 8 hours or up to 2 days. Bring to room temperature before serving.

1 lb (500 g) bittersweet chocolate, finely chopped

1 cup (250 mL) unsalted butter or margarine, softened (8 oz/250 g)

8 large eggs, at room temperature, separated

1 cup (250 mL) granulated sugar, divided

¼ tsp (1 mL) salt

1 tsp (5 mL) vanilla powder (or vanilla)

TOPPING

1 cup (250 mL) cold whipping cream or liquid whip topping

1 Tbsp (15 mL) unsweetened Dutch-processed cocoa powder

2 tsp (10 mL) granulated sugar

RECIPE CONTINUED . . .

TOPPING In the bowl of a stand mixer fitted with the whisk attachment, or using a hand-held mixer, whip the cream with the cocoa powder and sugar to soft peaks.

Remove the parchment paper from the cake. Transfer to a cake plate. Spread the whipped cream just on top of the cake. Serve slightly chilled

---

BAKER'S TIP

THE RIBBON STAGE When beating egg yolks, cookbooks will inevitably tell you to take it to the ribbon stage. This will only happen when whole eggs are beaten with sugar. On their own, they'll never reach this stage. To test accurately, lift the whisk attachment from the egg mixture. Hold it an inch or two (2.5–5 cm) above the bowl. It should fall slowly back into the bowl, as if in a thick ribbon. If you can hold the beaters over the bowl and write your initials with it so that they are visible against the foam in the bowl, then you've reached the ribbon stage. If what you're trying to write simply falls back into the foam without the letters being identifiable, then you haven't reached the ribbon stage yet.

Buttery Cupcakes

Perhaps I should call this the "8 Cake." With just eight ingredients, all of which you're likely to have on hand, these cupcakes are a breeze. With eight different icings from which to choose, your birthdays will be brighter, the guests happier and your pocketbook lighter since you didn't have to rush out to the local bakery to pick up cupcakes. What makes these especially great is getting the kids in on the action.

1¼ cups (310 mL) all-purpose flour
1½ tsp (7 mL) baking powder
Pinch of salt
½ cup (125 mL) unsalted butter, softened (4 oz/125 g)
¾ cup (180 mL) granulated sugar
1 large egg, at room temperature
1 tsp (5 mL) vanilla
⅔ cup (160 mL) milk, at room temperature
Icing (see next page)

Preheat the oven to 350°F (180°C). Line a 12-cup muffin tin with paper liners; set aside.

Whisk together the flour, baking powder and salt in a bowl until the dry ingredients are thoroughly combined; set aside.

In the bowl of a stand mixer fitted with the paddle attachment, or using a hand-held mixer, beat the butter for 1 minute. Gradually add the sugar and beat until light and fluffy, about 3 minutes. Scrape down the sides of the bowl. Add the egg and beat just until incorporated. Beat in the vanilla.

Remove the bowl from the stand. Using a wooden spoon, alternately stir in the flour mixture with the milk, making 3 additions of the flour and 2 of the milk.

Divide the batter evenly among the prepared muffin tins, filling them about three-quarters full.

Bake in the centre of the preheated oven until the tops spring back when lightly pressed, 25–30 minutes. Cool the cupcakes in the pan set on a wire rack for 15 minutes. Remove the cupcakes from the pan and cool completely on the wire rack.

The cupcakes can be frozen successfully for up to 3 months before icing. Ice with the icing of your choice (see next page).

VARIATION

SOUR CREAM GOLDEN CUPCAKES Follow the method above, but replace the baking powder with ½ tsp (2 mL) baking soda and ½ tsp (2 mL) baking powder. Increase the sugar to 1 cup (250 mL) and the eggs from 1 to 2. Replace the ⅔ cup (160 mL) milk with ½ cup (125 mL) sour cream, at room temperature.

A Palette's Worth *of* Icings

WHEN IT comes to icings, I don't think I've ever really grown up. The more icing there is, the more I will enjoy a slice of cake or a cupcake. Chocolate icing is my personal favourite, but here are a number of variations for when a different flavour is required. They're all easy and scrumptious and ready in no time at all.

¾ cup (180 mL) unsalted butter, softened (6 oz/175 g)

2½ cups (625 mL) icing sugar

2 tsp (10 mL) vanilla

¼ cup (60 mL) whipping cream, at room temperature

Basic Icing

In the bowl of a stand mixer fitted with the paddle attachment, or using a hand-held mixer, beat the butter for 1 minute. Add ½ cup (125 mL) of the sugar at a time, beating well between each addition before adding the next ½ cup (125 mL). Beat in the vanilla. Adding 1 Tbsp (15 mL) at a time, beat in the whipping cream until a creamy and fluffy icing is formed. Makes about 2½ cups (625 mL).

VARIATIONS

ORANGE ICING Add 1 Tbsp (15 mL) finely grated orange zest and replace the vanilla with 1 tsp (5 mL) orange extract. And 1 Tbsp (15 mL) orange juice concentrate.

LEMON ICING Add 2 tsp (10 mL) finely grated lemon zest and 2 Tbsp (30 mL) lemon juice. Omit the vanilla.

WHITE CHOCOLATE ICING Melt 1 oz (30 g) coarsely chopped white chocolate in the top of a double boiler set over hot, boiling water. Let cool and add to icing.

COFFEE ICING Add 1 Tbsp (15 mL) coffee liqueur.

RASPBERRY ICING Add 3 Tbsp (45 mL) raspberry purée.

½ cup (125 mL) unsalted butter,
   softened (4 oz/125 g)
⅔ cup (160 mL) smooth peanut
   butter
2 cups (500 mL) icing sugar
¼ cup (60 mL) whipping cream, at
   room temperature

Peanut Butter Icing

In the bowl of a stand mixer fitted with the paddle attachment, or using a hand-held mixer, beat the butter and peanut butter together for 1 minute. Add ½ cup (125 mL) of the sugar at a time, beating well before adding the next ½ cup (125 mL). Adding 1 Tbsp (15 mL) at a time, beat in the whipping cream until a creamy and fluffy icing is formed. Makes about 3 cups (750 mL).

8 oz (250 g) bittersweet or
   semisweet chocolate, coarsely
   chopped
1 cup (250 mL) sour cream, at
   room temperature
1 tsp (5 mL) vanilla

Sour Cream Chocolate Icing

Melt the chocolate in the top of a double boiler set over hot, not boiling water. Let cool. Stir together the cooled chocolate with the sour cream until well combined. Stir in the vanilla. Makes about 2½ cups (625 mL).

Pavlova Cupcakes *with* Honey Roasted Strawberries

CUPCAKES

6 large egg whites, at room
   temperature

¼ tsp (1 mL) cream of tartar

¼ tsp (1 mL) salt

1½ cups (375 mL) granulated
   sugar

2 tsp (10 mL) white vinegar

1 tsp (5 mL) vanilla

HONEY ROASTED STRAWBERRIES

8 cups (2 L) stemmed and halved
   fresh strawberries, divided

¼ cup (60 mL) honey

2 Tbsp (30 mL) granulated sugar

2 Tbsp (30 mL) orange juice

BRILLIANT TOGETHER, these cupcakes and strawberries are also scrumptious on their own. I like to change up the colour of the cupcake liners I use for the cupcakes (a must). I have served them in ultra-pink cupcake liners for a baby shower, in gold for an elegant outside dinner party and in multicoloured cups for another party. They're always a hit.

Preheat the oven to 300°F (150°C). Line a 12-cup muffin tin with large paper cups; set aside.

In the bowl of a stand mixer fitted with the whisk attachment, or using a hand-held mixer, beat together the egg whites, cream of tartar and salt until soft peaks form. In a thin stream, gradually add the sugar, beating until stiff shiny peaks are formed. Whisk in the vinegar and vanilla. Transfer the mixture to a piping bag and pipe evenly into the prepared muffin cups (or use a large spoon to dollop mixture evenly into prepared muffin cups).

Bake in the centre of the preheated oven until the tops are very light golden and dry, about 75 minutes.

Turn off the oven and let the cupcakes sit inside for 30 minutes. Remove the cupcakes and let them cool in the pan on a wire rack. (Cupcakes can be kept in an airtight container for up to 2 days.)

HONEY ROASTED STRAWBERRIES Preheat the oven to 400°F (200°C). Place 6 cups (1.5 L) of the strawberries into a 13 × 9 inch (33 × 23 cm) baking dish. Gently stir in the honey, sugar and orange juice. Bake in the centre of the preheated oven until juicy and the strawberries have wilted, 15–20 minutes. Set aside to cool. Stir in the remaining 2 cups (500 mL) fresh strawberries. (Strawberry mixture can be cooled and refrigerated for up to 24 hours. Bring to room temperature before serving.)

ASSEMBLY Gently pry off or cut off the top of the meringue cupcake. Place the bottom part on a dessert plate. Spoon some of the roasted strawberries into the cupcake. Replace the cupcake top on top of the strawberries. Serve with remaining roasted strawberries.

ANGEL FOOD CAKES

A FEW THINGS TO GET YOU STARTED

The success of an angel food cake depends entirely on the egg whites being whipped properly. There is no other leavening in an angel food cake so the onus is on the whites. When the cake is baked, some volume builds from the air cells that have been whipped into the whites. Most of the volume is in fact produced by the steam that evaporates from the liquid in those egg whites and passes through their air cells, effectively expanding them.

See page 47 for details about beating egg whites. The whites should really be beaten until JUST before they're stiff. The visual clue is always the best here. When you stop the machine and raise the beater, the whites should hold their shape but the very tip should just fall over. As my cooking school teacher made us do, you can (should you want to) hold the bowl upside-down over your head: if the whites stay where they are, they're good to go.

Sugar is the other main ingredient in angel food cakes and where it is added is a crucial step. Whip the whites with just under half of the sugar called for. The remainder of the sugar should be added with the dry ingredients. This technique produces a more tender cake than one in which all of the sugar is added to the egg whites. Use superfine sugar if you can, as it disperses quickly.

Cake and pastry flour is used due to its low protein content. Its fine particles also help it disperse better in the foamy batter.

Cream of tartar helps to produce a lily-white angel food cake. Its stabilizing action is also essential because it enables the air cells to hold up longer without collapsing before they coagulate.

A dry and ungreased tube pan allows the batter to cling to its sides and rise to its full height. The tube pan's even distribution of heat, coming from both the sides and the centre, allows an angel food cake batter to bake more quickly, helping to avoid problems such as loss of volume or weeping of the egg whites. Get the cake right into the oven as soon as you've folded in the last bit of flour. Angel food cakes that sit around won't expand as high as you would hope for.

There's one big last caveat: **Unlike when I measure all-purpose flour where I scoop and sweep, when working with cake and pastry flour I always spoon my flour into the cup and then sweep.**

Classic Angel Food Cake

SWEET, GOSSAMER textured and cloud-white, angel food cakes are the ideal light dessert. You can serve them with whipped cream, fresh fruit compote or all on their own. Try to be as deft as possible when making angel food cakes, fold gently but efficiently and get the cake directly into the oven.

Preheat the oven to 325°F (160°C).

Sift together ¾ cup (180 mL) of the granulated sugar and the cake and pastry flour; set aside.

In the bowl of a stand mixer fitted with the whisk attachment, or using hand-held beaters, whisk the egg whites until frothy. Add the cream of tartar and the salt. Beat on medium-high speed until soft peaks form. Gradually, add the remaining sugar, about 2 Tbsp (30 mL) at a time. Beat until soft peaks form. They should be shiny and stiff but not dry.

Remove the bowl from the mixer. One-quarter at a time, sift the flour-sugar mixture over the egg whites, folding gently into the egg whites before the next addition. Some people prefer to do this with a plastic spatula, some prefer a balloon whisk. It's up to you. Both will do a fine job—the spatula may end up deflating the mixture a bit while the balloon whisk may cause you to end up with slightly overbeaten egg whites. The point is to be careful!

Fold in the vanilla. Scrape the mixture into an ungreased (for why see previous page) 10-inch (25 cm) tube pan.

Bake in the centre of the preheated oven until the top of the cake springs back when lightly pressed, 40–45 minutes. Remove the tube pan from the oven and immediately turn the pan upside-down so that it rests on the legs attached to the pan. If your pan doesn't have legs (some of the older ones don't), invert the pan onto a large funnel or bottle. The important thing is that it stays inverted until it cools since it lacks the structure to remain intact on its own. Once cooled, run a long thin knife around the centre and the sides of the pan to loosen the cake. Remove the cake from the pan and serve, bottom side up.

1½ cups (325 mL) superfine granulated sugar, divided

1½ cups (325 mL) sifted cake and pastry flour (spooned into the measure and then swept)

1½ cups (375 mL) egg whites, at room temperature (about 11 or 12)

1 tsp (5 mL) cream of tartar

¼ tsp (1 mL) salt

1½ tsp (7 mL) vanilla

EVERYDAY AND FRUIT-BASED CAKES

The cakes that follow are what I consider to be homey cakes, the sort of cake you might whip up just because the urge hits, or because your kids had a rough day, or even for no reason at all. They're simple and seasonal. With the exception of the Dacquoise, they are all one layer, baked in an 8- or 9-inch (20 or 23 cm) cake pan or in a Bundt pan. Unlike cake pans, Bundt pans are sold by volume, most commonly in a 10- or 12-cup (2.5 or 3 L) capacity. Like cake pans, they are increasingly only available with a dark non-stick coating. Since a lighter material, such as aluminum, is actually optimal for baking (it reflects the heat, creating a tender crumb), carefully watch cakes baked in a darker coloured pan. It may shave a couple of minutes off your baking time.

French Toast Cake

This cake is two cakes rolled into one: a wonderfully light crumbed cake made tender by sour cream, and a swirl reminiscent of both French and cinnamon toast. It is just as good as waking up to French toast on a blistery winter morning or indulging in cinnamon toast after an afternoon spent skating. It's great served warm or at room temperature.

Preheat the oven to 350°F (180°C). Lightly grease an 8½- or 9-inch (22 or 23 cm) springform pan. Line the bottom with a circle of parchment paper cut to fit; set aside.

FRENCH TOAST FILLING In a small bowl, combine the brown sugar, butter and cinnamon, working them together until crumbly; set aside.

CAKE In a small bowl or wet measure, whisk together the eggs, 1 Tbsp (15 mL) of the sour cream and the vanilla; set aside.

In the bowl of a stand mixer or a regular stainless steel bowl, combine the flour, sugar, baking powder, baking soda and salt. Add the butter and the remaining sour cream. Using the paddle attachment or a hand-held mixer, beat the ingredients together until they start to clump together. Increase the speed to medium-high and beat, scraping down the sides of the bowl once, for 1½ minutes or until satiny smooth. Beat in half of the egg mixture. Scrape down the sides of the bowl. Beat in the remaining egg mixture.

Remove 1 heaping cup (250+ mL) of the batter; stir in the French toast filling. Scrape the remaining batter into the prepared springform pan. Dollop the French toast batter over the top of the cake. Swirl it briefly into the main batter but not so much that it disappears. Place the springform pan on a rimmed baking sheet.

Bake in the centre of the preheated oven until a cake tester inserted in the centre comes out dry, about 55 minutes. The cake will look quite brown on the outside, just as the surface of French toast does, but it will not be over-baked. Cool the cake in the pan on a wire rack for at least 30 minutes. Run a small knife around the edge of the pan to loosen the cake. Remove the cake from the pan and cool completely on the wire rack, parchment side down. Serve warm or at room temperature.

FRENCH TOAST FILLING

½ cup (125 mL) packed light brown sugar

2 Tbsp (30 mL) unsalted butter, softened (1 oz/30 g)

1 Tbsp (15 mL) cinnamon

CAKE

2 large eggs, at room temperature

⅔ cup (160 mL) sour cream, at room temperature, divided

1 tsp (5 mL) vanilla

1¾ cups (430 mL) all-purpose flour

1 cup (250 mL) granulated sugar

1 tsp (5 mL) baking powder

½ tsp (2 mL) baking soda

Pinch of salt

¾ cup (180 mL) unsalted butter, softened (6 oz/175 g)

Plum Kuchen

2 cups (500 mL) all-purpose flour

¼ cup (60 mL) ground almonds

1½ tsp (7 mL) baking powder

½ tsp (2 mL) baking soda

¼ tsp (1 mL) salt

½ cup (125 mL) unsalted butter, softened (4 oz/125 g)

1½ cups (375 mL) granulated sugar

3 large eggs, at room temperature

⅛–¼ tsp (0.5–1 mL) almond extract

1½ cups (375 mL) sour cream, at room temperature

¼ cup (60 mL) canola or vegetable oil

TOPPING

4 red plums, pitted and sliced into ¼-inch (6 mm) thick slices

1 Tbsp (15 mL) unsalted butter, melted and cooled (0.5 oz/15 g)

2 Tbsp (30 mL) granulated sugar

THE GERMAN word for cake, "kuchen," is often associated with a cake meant to be eaten with coffee or made with yeast. This cake has no yeast and can be enjoyed any time of the day, but it still seems right to call it a kuchen. It has no pretensions except to be the best it can be. And that it does, in spades. Be sure to make this at the height of plum season and to use deeply red, large plums.

Preheat the oven to 350°F (180°C). Lightly grease the bottoms and sides of a 10-inch (25 cm) springform pan. Line the bottom with a circle of parchment paper cut to fit; set aside.

Whisk together the flour, almonds, baking powder, baking soda and salt in a bowl until the dry ingredients are thoroughly combined; set aside.

In the bowl of a stand mixer fitted with the paddle attachment, or using a hand-held mixer, beat the butter for 1 minute. Add the sugar and beat for 3 minutes or until light and fluffy. One at a time, beat in the eggs, beating well after each egg before adding the next. Beat in the almond extract, how much you use depends on how much you like this flavour. The smaller amount will give you just a hint of almond, whereas the larger amount will result in a stronger flavour.

Stir the sour cream and oil together.

Remove the bowl from the stand. Using a wooden spoon, alternately stir in the flour mixture with the sour cream mixture, making 3 additions of the flour and 2 of the sour cream. Scrape the batter into the prepared pan, smoothing the top.

TOPPING Arrange the plums over the batter in 2 concentric circles, facing the plums one way in the first circle and the other way in the second smaller circle. They should fit snugly together. Brush the melted butter over the plums and then sprinkle with the sugar. Place the springform on a rimmed baking sheet.

RECIPE CONTINUED . . .

Bake in the centre of the preheated oven until a cake tester inserted in the centre comes out clean, 70–85 minutes. Let the cake cool in the pan on a wire rack for 20 minutes. Run a small knife around the edge of the pan to loosen the cake. Remove the cake from the pan and cool completely on the wire rack, parchment side down.

Serve warm or at room temperature.

BAKER'S TIP

Later in the season, when Italian plums are for sale, use these instead, quartering them instead of slicing them.

Banana Bundt Cake

REALLY BANANA-Y, this cake is moist and fine crumbed, dense but not as dense as my banana bread. It looks lovely dusted with some icing sugar or left alone. The older I get, the more I tend toward simplicity, and this cake positively shines in its down-to-earth, simple and straight-forward flavour.

Preheat the oven to 350°F (180°C). Grease a 10-cup (2.5 L) Bundt pan; set aside.

Whisk together the flour, baking soda, baking powder and salt in a bowl until the dry ingredients are thoroughly moistened; set aside.

In the bowl of a stand mixer fitted with the paddle attachment, or using a hand-held mixer, beat the butter for 1 minute. Add the sugars and beat until light and fluffy, about 3 minutes. One at a time, beat in the eggs, beating well after each egg and scraping the sides of the bowl before adding the next one. Beat in the vanilla.

Remove the bowl from the stand. Using a wooden spoon, stir in the bananas. Alternately stir in the flour mixture and the yogurt, making 3 additions of the flour and 2 of the yogurt. Transfer the mixture to the prepared Bundt pan.

Bake in the centre of the preheated oven until the top of the cake springs back when lightly pressed, 50–60 minutes. Cool the cake in the pan on a wire rack for 30 minutes. Invert the cake onto the wire rack, remove the Bundt pan and let cool completely on the wire rack. Serve at room temperature.

3 cups (725 mL) all-purpose flour

1½ tsp (7 mL) baking soda

½ tsp (2 mL) baking powder

¼ tsp (1 mL) salt

1 cup (250 mL) unsalted butter, softened (8 oz/250 g)

1¼ cups (310 mL) granulated sugar

½ cup (125 mL) packed light brown sugar

3 large eggs, at room temperature

2 tsp (10 mL) vanilla

1½ cups (375 mL) mashed very ripe bananas (about 4 bananas)

1 cup (250 mL) yogurt, at room temperature

Crackle-Topped Peach Cake

1¾ cups (430 mL) all-purpose flour

3 Tbsp (45 mL) finely chopped crystallized ginger

1½ tsp (7 mL) baking powder

½ tsp (2 mL) ground ginger

½ tsp (2 mL) baking soda

¼ tsp (1 mL) salt

¾ cup (180 mL) light sour cream or yogurt, at room temperature

¼ cup (60 mL) peach or mango or mixed juice, at room temperature

1 tsp (5 mL) vanilla

¼ cup (60 mL) unsalted butter, softened (2 oz/60 g)

½ cup (125 mL) granulated sugar

⅓ cup (80 mL) packed light brown sugar

2 large eggs, at room temperature

PEACH CRACKLE TOPPING

¾ cup (180 mL) packed light brown sugar (2 oz/60 g)

¼ cup (60 mL) unsalted butter (2 oz/60 g)

2 large fresh peaches, pitted and sliced

¼ cup (60 mL) sliced hazelnuts

Oₙₑ ₒғ the great things about living in Southern Ontario is fresh peaches from the Niagara region. I can hardly wait 'til peach season arrives every year. There's nothing more wonderful than biting into a fresh, juicy peach, its vibrant juices running down your chin. I remember one summer being in Niagara-on-the-Lake, walking around until a matinee started. As luck would have it, in the main park, just down the street from the theatre, there was a peach festival going on. Vendors and local farmers were selling peach jam, peach pies and peach scones. The afternoon inspired me to go home and make my own peach cake, with a wonderful, homey crackle topping made of butter, brown sugar and hazelnuts.

This is the only place in this book that I have called for light sour cream. When I was developing this recipe, I tried full-fat sour cream, light sour cream and yogurt. As weird as it was, the full-fat sour cream was too heavy for this cake. Light sour cream (and not no-fat sour cream, which has far too much water) or yogurt are the best choices.

Preheat the oven to 375°F (190°C). Lightly grease an 8½- or 9-inch (22 or 23 cm) springform pan. Line the bottom with a circle of parchment paper cut to fit; set aside.

Whisk together the flour, crystallized ginger, baking powder, ground ginger, baking soda and salt in a bowl until the dry ingredients are thoroughly combined; set aside. In a separate bowl, whisk together the sour cream, juice and vanilla.

In the bowl of a stand mixer fitted with the paddle attachment, or using a hand-held mixer, beat the butter with the sugars. It will not get fluffy due to the small amount of butter but will definitely combine. One at a time, beat in the eggs, beating well after the first egg before adding the second.

Remove the bowl from the stand. Using a wooden spoon, alternately stir in the flour mixture with the sour cream mixture, making 3 additions of the flour and 2 of the sour cream. Scrape the batter into the prepared pan, smoothing the top.

PEACH CRACKLE TOPPING Combine the brown sugar and butter in a small saucepan set over medium heat. Cook, stirring, until the sugar has dissolved and the mixture is bubbling.

Arrange the peach slices in a tight concentric ring on top of the cake batter, placing the few remaining slices in the centre. Sprinkle the hazelnuts over the peaches. Drizzle the brown sugar mixture over the peaches and nuts. Place the cake pan on a baking sheet (so if the caramel boils over it won't burn on the bottom of your oven).

Bake in the centre of the preheated oven until a cake tester inserted in the centre of the cake comes out clean, about 45 minutes. Let the cake cool in the pan on a wire rack for 20 minutes. Run a small knife around the edge of the pan to loosen the cake. Remove the cake from the pan and cool completely on the wire rack, parchment side down. Serve at room temperature.

BAKER'S TIP
If you absolutely have to make these with frozen peaches, thaw the peach slices completely and dry them using a paper towel.

Individual Plum Cornmeal Cakes *with* Rosemary

4–5 red plums
¼ cup (60 mL) unsalted butter,
 melted and cooled (2 oz/60 g)
½ cup (125 mL) granulated sugar

CAKE
1¼ cups (310 mL) all-purpose flour
¾ cup (180 mL) fine yellow
 cornmeal
1½ tsp (7 mL) baking powder
1 tsp (5 mL) dried rosemary,
 crumbled
¼ tsp (1 mL) baking soda
¼ tsp (1 mL) salt
½ cup (125 mL) unsalted butter,
 softened (4 oz/125 g)
¾ cup (180 mL) granulated sugar
2 large eggs, at room temperature
1 tsp (5 mL) vanilla
¾ cup (180 mL) buttermilk, at
 room temperature

THESE INDIVIDUAL cakes are such a pleasure to eat. First of all, you get your own ramekin full of cake and you don't even have to share it. You might be surprised by the combination of rosemary and plums, but they know how to send each other up and are the better for it. The cornmeal adds a touch of crunch, which contrasts beautifully with the silken smoothness of the baked plums.

I know, I know, it seems like an awful lot of butter and an awful lot of sugar. But trust me. The butter and the sugar create a lovely syrup once the plums start to release their juices during baking and this is what creates the lovely sauce that will run down the sides of the cake once you unmould it.

Preheat the oven to 350°F (180°C).

Cut each plum in half and remove the pit. Score each half with a small paring knife—without going all the way through. Divide the butter among either eight 5-oz (150 mL) or ten 4-oz (125 mL) ovenproof ramekins. Swirl the butter around or brush it so that it coats the insides of each ramekin. Evenly distribute the sugar into each ramekin. Place a plum half, cut side down, in each ramekin. Place the ramekins on a baking sheet.

CAKE Whisk together the flour, cornmeal, baking powder, rosemary, baking soda and salt in a bowl until the dry ingredients are thoroughly combined; set aside.

In a stand mixer fitted with the paddle attachment, or using a handheld mixer, beat the butter for 1 minute. Beat in the sugar and beat together for 3 minutes or until well combined. One at a time, beat in the eggs, beating well after the first egg and scraping down the sides of the bowl before adding the second. Beat in the vanilla.

Remove the bowl from the stand. Using a wooden spoon, alternately stir in the flour mixture with the buttermilk, making 3 additions of the flour and 2 of the buttermilk. Evenly divide the batter between the prepared ramekins, on top of the plums. Each ramekin will be very full.

Bake in the centre of the preheated oven until the top is golden and springs back when lightly pressed, 25–30 minutes. Let the ramekins cool, still on the baking sheet, on a wire rack for 15–20 minutes. Run a small knife around the inside edge of each ramekin and invert the cakes onto dessert-sized plates. Serve warm.

VARIATION

PLUM CORNMEAL CAKES WITH ORANGE Replace the dried rosemary with 2 tsp (10 mL) finely grated orange zest.

Tarte Tatin Cake

CARAMEL TOPPING

1 cup (250 mL) granulated sugar

¼ cup (60 mL) water

¼ cup (60 mL) unsalted butter, softened (2 oz/60 g)

2 large apples

CAKE

1½ cups (375 mL) all-purpose flour

1½ tsp (7 mL) baking powder

½ tsp (2 mL) cinnamon

¼ tsp (1 mL) baking soda

¼ tsp (1 mL) salt

½ cup (125 mL) unsalted butter, softened (4 oz/125 g)

1 cup (250 mL) granulated sugar

2 large eggs, at room temperature

2 tsp (10 mL) vanilla

½ cup (125 mL) buttermilk, at room temperature

SINCE TARTE Tatin is so fabulous, wouldn't a cake topped with the same unctuous apples be remarkable? You bet. The sultry caramel seeps into the cake, making every bite memorable.

This cake is stunning with other fruits as well. You can substitute pears, mango and even peaches or apricots for the apples.

Preheat the oven to 350°F (180°C). Grease the bottom and sides of a 9-inch (23 cm) cake pan (you need to use a cake pan here and not a springform to prevent the caramel from leaking out during baking). Line the bottom of the pan with a round of parchment paper cut to fit; set aside.

CARAMEL TOPPING Combine the sugar and water in a saucepan set over medium-heat. Cook without stirring, but brush down the sides of the pan occasionally with a brush dipped in cool water, until the mixture turns a deep golden colour, 5–7 minutes. Remove the pan from the heat and start to whisk in the butter, about 1 Tbsp (15 mL) at a time. Be careful, the caramel will bubble and spit, but keep going. Pour the hot caramel into the bottom of the prepared pan.

Peel and core the apples. Cut into thin slices and arrange in concentric circles on top of the caramel, fitting the slices snugly together.

CAKE Whisk together the flour, baking powder, cinnamon, baking soda and salt in a bowl until the dry ingredients are thoroughly combined; set aside.

In the bowl of a stand mixer fitted with the paddle attachment, or using a hand-held mixer, beat the butter for 1 minute. Add the sugar and beat together until light and fluffy, about 3 minutes. One at a time, beat in the eggs, beating well after the first egg before adding the second. Beat in the vanilla.

Remove the bowl from the stand. Using a wooden spoon, alternately stir in the flour mixture with the buttermilk, making 3 additions of the flour and 2 of the buttermilk. Scrape the batter on top of the apples, smoothing the top with an offset spatula knife. Place the cake pan on a rimmed baking sheet.

Bake in the centre of the preheated oven until the cake springs back when lightly pressed in the centre, 35–40 minutes. Let the cake cool in the pan on a wire rack for 3 minutes. Run a small sharp knife around the edge of the pan. Place a large serving platter on top of the cake pan. Carefully invert the pan and cake onto the platter. Remove the pan and the parchment paper and scrape any remaining caramel from the pan onto the apples. Serve the cake warm or at room temperature.

BAKER'S TIP

Be sure to choose an apple that is firm and will hold its shape when making this cake. Look for Gala, Golden Delicious or Spy apples.

Apple Cake *with* Pecan Glaze

1½ cups (375 mL) all-purpose flour

1½ tsp (7 mL) cinnamon

1 tsp (5 mL) baking soda

Pinch of salt

1 cup (250 mL) unsalted butter, softened (8 oz/250 g)

1 cup (250 mL) granulated sugar

2 large eggs, at room temperature

1 tsp (5 mL) vanilla

3 tart apples, peeled, cored and finely chopped

½ cup (125 mL) pecan pieces

TOPPING

1 Tbsp (15 mL) unsalted butter, softened (0.5 oz/15 g)

⅔ cup (160 mL) pecan halves

½ cup (125 mL) whipping cream, at room temperature

⅓ cup (80 mL) packed light brown sugar

I HAVE made this cake ever since I was a pastry chef. It's a great apple cake to have in your repertoire as an everyday dessert or to grace a more sophisticated dessert buffet. It's chock-a-bloc full of chopped apples and pecans, with just enough batter to classify it as a cake. Be sure to test the cake with a cake tester or wooden skewer; from the outside it will look done, but the batter may not be fully baked inside.

Preheat the oven to 350°F (180°C). Lightly grease the bottom and sides of an 8½- or 9-inch (22 or 23 cm) springform pan. Line the bottom of the pan with a round of parchment paper cut to fit; set aside.

Whisk together the flour, cinnamon, baking soda and salt in a bowl until the dry ingredients are thoroughly combined; set aside.

In the bowl of a stand mixer fitted with the paddle attachment, or using a hand-held mixer, beat the butter for 1 minute. Add the sugar and beat until light and fluffy, about 3 minutes. One at a time, beat in the eggs, beating well after the first egg before adding the second. Beat in the vanilla.

Remove the bowl from the stand. Switch to using a wooden spoon. In 3 separate additions, stir in the flour mixture. Fold in the apples and pecans. Scrape the batter into the prepared pan. Don't worry—it will look like an awful lot of apples but the cake will come out beautifully. Place the cake pan on a rimmed baking sheet.

Bake in the centre of the preheated oven until a cake tester inserted in the centre of the cake comes out clean, 50–60 minutes. Cool the cake in the pan on a wire rack for 30 minutes. Run a small knife around the edge of the pan to loosen the cake. Remove the cake from the pan and cool on the wire rack, parchment side down.

TOPPING In a saucepan set over medium heat, melt the butter. Add the nuts and cook, stirring occasionally until the nuts are lightly toasted, about 3 minutes. Stir in the cream and brown sugar; bring to a boil. Reduce heat slightly and boil gently until the mixture has thickened, about 5 minutes.

Remove the parchment paper from underneath the cake. Transfer the cake to a serving platter or cake plate. Pour the pecan glaze over the cake, letting the excess run down the sides of the cake. Let the glaze set; serve at room temperature.

Apple Honey Cardamom Cake

A LOT of people return to baking once the fall appears and perhaps that's why I have an abundance of apple recipes. It also may be that I live in Southern Ontario (and come from Quebec), where the apples are plentiful. This cake is just another excuse to buy apples from September to the spring months. Perfumed with exquisitely aromatic cardamom, this golden-hued cake is the meaning behind the saying, "The whole is greater than the sum of its parts." I like to eat raw apples all the time, but they really do shine in this cake, supported by the tender batter and nudged by the accompaniment of honey and spice.

Preheat the oven to 350°F (180°C). Lightly grease the bottom and sides of an 8½- or 9-inch (22 or 23 cm) springform pan. Line the bottom of the pan with a round of parchment paper cut to fit; set aside.

TOPPING In a bowl, combine the almonds, sugar and flour. Add the butter and rub it into the mixture with your fingertips, until crumbly.

CAKE Whisk together the flour, baking powder, cardamom, baking soda and salt in a bowl until the dry ingredients are thoroughly combined; set aside.

In the bowl of a stand mixer fitted with the paddle attachment, or using a hand-held mixer, beat together the honey and butter, scraping down the sides of the bowl occasionally, until smooth and no lumps of butter remain, about 3 minutes. One at a time, beat in the eggs, beating well after the first egg before adding the second. Beat in the vanilla.

Remove the bowl from the stand. Using a wooden spoon, alternately stir in the flour mixture with the sour cream, making 3 additions of the flour and 2 of the sour cream. Gently fold in the apples. Scrape the batter into the prepared pan, smoothing the top. Sprinkle the topping evenly over the batter. Place the cake pan on a rimmed baking sheet.

Bake in the centre of the preheated oven until a cake tester inserted in the centre comes out clean, 55–60 minutes. Cool the cake in the pan on a wire rack for 20 minutes. Run a small knife around the edge of the pan to loosen the cake. Remove the cake from the pan and cool on the wire rack, parchment side down.

Serve warm or at room temperature.

RECIPE CONTINUED . . .

TOPPING

½ cup (125 mL) sliced almonds
½ cup (125 mL) packed light brown sugar
¼ cup (60 mL) all-purpose flour
3 Tbsp (45 mL) unsalted butter, softened (1.5 oz/45 g)

CAKE

2 cups (500 mL) all-purpose flour
1 tsp (5 mL) baking powder
1 tsp (5 mL) ground cardamom
½ tsp (2 mL) baking soda
¼ tsp (1 mL) salt
1 cup (250 mL) honey
½ cup (125 mL) unsalted butter, softened (4 oz/125 g)
2 large eggs, at room temperature
1 tsp (5 mL) vanilla
¾ cup (180 mL) sour cream or yogurt, at room temperature
1 cup (250 mL) peeled chopped apples (about 1 apple)

VARIATIONS

PEAR HONEY CARDAMOM CAKE Replace the apples with the same amount of chopped pears.

APPLE HONEY GINGER CAKE Replace the cardamom with 3 Tbsp (45 mL) grated fresh ginger and 1 tsp (5 mL) dried ginger. Omit the apples, if desired.

BAKER'S TIP

Cardamom pods, now widely available, have long been used in Indian dishes as well as Asian, Germanic and Scandinavian cuisines. Sweetly spicy, with lemony overtones, cardamom is available both in pods and already ground. I heartily recommend you buy the pods and grind them yourself since pre-ground cardamom quickly loses its flavour.

Blueberry Coffee Cream Cheese Cake

CRUMB TOPPING

1 cup (250 mL) all-purpose flour

¼ cup (60 mL) packed light brown sugar

¼ cup (60 mL) granulated sugar

½ tsp (2 mL) cinnamon

⅓ cup (80 mL) unsalted butter, melted (3 oz/90 g)

CREAM CHEESE FILLING

8 oz (250 g) cream cheese, softened

¼ cup (60 mL) granulated sugar

1 large egg, at room temperature

2 tsp (10 mL) finely grated lemon zest

CAKE BATTER

1½ cups (375 mL) all-purpose flour

1 tsp (5 mL) baking powder

½ tsp (2 mL) baking soda

¼ tsp (1 mL) salt

⅓ cup (80 mL) unsalted butter, softened (3 oz/90 g)

⅔ cup (160 mL) granulated sugar

2 large eggs, at room temperature

2 tsp (10 mL) vanilla

½ cup (125 mL) sour cream, at room temperature

1½ cups (375 mL) fresh or frozen wild blueberries

I HAVE to come clean; this cake has been around the block a few times. I didn't think I should include it because it had been published before, first in *Canadian Living Magazine* and then in the cookbook *Canadian Living Cooks*, but it's just that it's so darn good and no matter how I tried to change it or morph it into something else, there was just no point. I could not improve on the original.

Preheat the oven to 350°F (180°C). Lightly grease the bottom and sides of a 9-inch (23 cm) springform pan. Line the bottom of the pan with a round of parchment paper cut to fit; set aside.

CRUMB TOPPING In a small bowl, combine the flour, sugars and cinnamon. Drizzle the melted butter over the mixture, tossing with a fork until it is thoroughly moistened; set aside.

CREAM CHEESE FILLING In a stand mixer fitted with the paddle attachment, or using a hand-held mixer, beat the cream cheese with the sugar until light and fluffy, scraping down the sides of the bowl occasionally. Beat in the egg and the lemon zest; set aside.

CAKE BATTER Whisk together the flour, baking powder, baking soda and salt in a bowl until the dry ingredients are thoroughly combined. In a stand mixer fitted with the paddle attachment and a clean bowl, or using a hand-held mixer, beat the butter for 1 minute. Add the sugar and beat thoroughly. One at a time, beat in the eggs, beating well after the first egg before adding the second. Beat in the vanilla.

Remove the bowl from the stand. Using a wooden spoon, alternately stir in the flour mixture with the sour cream, making 3 additions of the flour and 2 of the sour cream.

Spread the cake batter in the prepared pan, mounding it slightly higher in the centre. Sprinkle 1 cup (250 mL) of the blueberries over top of the cake batter. Gently spread the cream cheese filling over the blueberries. Sprinkle the remaining blueberries over the cheese filling. Sprinkle the entire surface with the crumb topping. Place the cake pan on a rimmed baking sheet.

Bake in the centre of the preheated oven until the edges of the cake are set and just beginning to pull away from the sides of the pan, about 75 minutes. Let the cake cool in the pan on a wire rack for 30 minutes. Run a small knife around the edge of the pan to loosen the cake. Remove the cake from the pan and cool on the wire rack, parchment side down.

Serve warm or at room temperature.

Blueberry Lime Bundt Cake

Bursting with blueberries, this cake is heart wrenchingly moist, and is lovely with the glaze or unadorned. It's not too sweet even though it has almost 2 cups (500 mL) of sugar in it. The cream cheese and the lime see to that.

Preheat the oven to 350°F (180°C). Grease a 10-cup (2.5 L) Bundt pan; set aside.

Whisk together the cake and pastry flour, baking powder and salt in a bowl, making sure the 3 ingredients are well mixed. In a separate bowl, stir together the sugar and the lime zest until the zest is well distributed; set aside.

In the bowl of a stand mixer fitted with the paddle attachment, or using a hand-held mixer, beat the butter with the cream cheese for 1 minute or until well combined. In a thin stream, gradually add the lime-infused sugar. Beat until light and fluffy, about 3 minutes. One at a time, beat in the eggs, beating well after each egg before adding the next. Beat in the egg yolk.

Remove the bowl from the stand. Switch to using a wooden spoon. In 3 additions, stir in the flour mixture. Gently stir in the blueberries. Transfer the mixture to the prepared pan. With the back of the spoon, smooth the surface.

Bake in the centre of the preheated oven until the top of the cake springs back when lightly pressed, 55–60 minutes. Cool the cake in the pan on a wire rack for 20 minutes. Unmould and cool completely on the wire rack.

GLAZE In the bowl of a stand mixer fitted with the paddle attachment, or using a hand-held mixer, beat together the cream cheese and the sugar, scraping down the sides of the bowl often. Pour in the lime juice and beat just until it is of a drizzle-able consistency.

Drizzle the icing over the cake, allowing the excess to drip down the sides. Serve at room temperature.

2½ cups (625 mL) sifted cake and pastry flour (spooned into the measure, then swept)

1½ tsp (7 mL) baking powder

½ tsp (2 mL) salt

1¾ cups (430 mL) granulated sugar

1 Tbsp (15 mL) finely grated lime zest

1 cup (250 mL) unsalted butter, softened (8 oz/250 g)

6 oz (175 g) cream cheese, softened

4 large eggs, at room temperature

1 large egg yolk, at room temperature

2¼ cups (560 mL) fresh blueberries

GLAZE

2 oz (60 g) cream cheese, softened

1 cup (250 mL) icing sugar

1 Tbsp (15 mL) freshly squeezed lime juice

HISTORY NOTE

Bundt cakes were introduced in the 1950s by the company NordicWare. The Bundt cake was based on the traditional Kugehopf moulds of Eastern Europe. These were typically cast iron, used for shaping yeast-based breads. I still prefer the heavier gauged Bundt pans to the newer thinner models.

Roasted Pineapple Cake

PINEAPPLE

1 small ripe pineapple, peeled,
   quartered lengthwise and cored
3 Tbsp (45 mL) unsalted butter,
   melted and cooled (1.5 oz/45 g)
⅔ cup (160 mL) packed light
   brown sugar

TOPPING

1¼ cups (310 mL) all-purpose flour
½ cup (125 mL) packed light
   brown sugar
¼ cup (60 mL) granulated sugar
1 tsp (5 mL) cinnamon
½ cup (125 mL) unsalted butter,
   melted (4 oz/125 g)

CAKE

1¼ cups (310 mL) all-purpose flour
¾ tsp (4 mL) baking powder
½ tsp (2 mL) baking soda
¼ tsp (1 mL) salt
⅓ cup (80 mL) unsalted butter,
   softened (3 oz/90 g)
¾ cup (180 mL) granulated sugar
1 large egg, at room temperature
1 tsp (5 mL) vanilla
⅔ cup (160 mL) sour cream, at
   room temperature

THIS CAKE came about because I am drawn to crumb cakes and because I love roasted pineapple. I have been making both for years, enjoying roasted pineapple over scones and ice cream. Then I finally had a eureka moment—why not introduce the two to each other and see how they get along. Well, I'm happy to report, they have incredible chemistry, evident in this yummy cake.

PINEAPPLE Preheat the oven to 400°F (200°C). Line a rimmed baking sheet with parchment paper.

Slice each pineapple quarter vertically into 5 long pieces. Place on the prepared baking sheet. Brush the pineapple pieces with half of the melted butter. Sprinkle half of the sugar over the pineapple.

Roast in the centre of the preheated oven for 15 minutes. Turn the pineapple over. Brush with the remaining butter and sprinkle with the remaining sugar. Roast for 10 minutes. Let cool in the pan.

Meanwhile, reduce the oven temperature to 350°F (180°C). Lightly grease the bottom and sides of a 9-inch (23 cm) square metal baking pan.

TOPPING In a bowl, combine the flour, sugars and cinnamon. Pour the melted butter over, stirring until the butter is well blended and the mixture has formed clumps; set aside.

Cut about 8 of the roasted pineapples slices into chunks—you should have about 1 cup (250 mL); set aside. Reserve the remaining pineapple to serve over the cake, over ice cream or with yogurt for breakfast!

CAKE Whisk together the flour, baking powder, baking soda and salt in a bowl until the dry ingredients are thoroughly combined.

In the bowl of a stand mixer fitted with the paddle attachment, or using a hand-held mixer, beat the butter for 1 minute. Gradually add the sugar in a thin stream and beat until light, about 3 minutes. Beat in the egg. Scrape down the sides of the bowl. Beat in the vanilla.

Remove the bowl from the stand. Using a wooden spoon, alternately stir in the flour mixture with the sour cream, making 3 additions of the flour and 2 of the sour cream. Gently stir in the reserved pineapple chunks.

Scrape the mixture into the prepared pan, smoothing the top. Sprinkle the crumble topping over, so that it covers the entire surface. Place the cake pan on a rimmed baking sheet.

Bake in the centre of the preheated oven until a cake tester inserted in the centre of the cake comes out clean, 50–60 minutes. Let the cake cool in the pan on a wire rack.

Serve warm with the remaining roasted pineapple and with ice cream.

BAKER'S TIP

Most fruits take well to roasting but need some protection so that they don't dry out. They need to be coated with a bit of sugar, some butter or a combination of the two. You can do this easily right on the barbecue as well. Brush or toss the fruit as required, then wrap tightly in aluminum foil. Place on a medium or low grill and barbecue, checking 5–10 minutes earlier than if you were roasting in a conventional oven.

HISTORY NOTE

Crumb cakes hail from Germany and Austria, where they were very common in coffee houses. Brought over to North America by immigrants, they grew in popularity in New York State, where they still hold a place of honour.

Gingerbread-Style Sticky Date Pudding Cake

1⅓ cups (330 mL) warm water

1⅓ cups (330 mL) chopped pitted dates

2 tsp (10 mL) baking soda

2½ cups (625 mL) all-purpose flour

2 tsp (10 mL) baking powder

2 tsp (10 mL) ground ginger

½ tsp (2 mL) cinnamon

½ tsp (2 mL) freshly ground black pepper

½ tsp (2 mL) salt

¼ tsp (1 mL) ground cloves

1 cup (250 mL) unsalted butter, softened (8 oz/250 g)

⅔ cup (160 mL) packed light brown sugar

¼ cup (60 mL) fancy molasses

4 large eggs, at room temperature

1 tsp (5 mL) vanilla

TOFFEE SAUCE

¾ cup (180 mL) unsalted butter (6 oz/175 g)

1 cup (250 mL) packed light brown sugar

½ cup (125 mL) whipping cream

1 tsp (5 mL) vanilla

2 Tbsp (30 mL) rum (optional)

JUST AS is true of the Roasted Pineapple Cake, this dessert is a hybrid. I knew I wanted to include a gingerbread cake in this collection but figured I should also include some type of sticky pudding cake as well. Serendipity struck and after a few attempts, I came up with this comforting cross breed. It's amazing with a splash of rum added to the sauce.

Preheat the oven to 350°F (180°C). Lightly grease a metal 13- × 9-inch (33 × 23 cm) metal baking pan; set aside.

Combine the water, dates and baking soda in a saucepan set over medium heat. Bring to a boil, then remove from the heat. Let the mixture cool to room temperature.

Whisk together the flour, baking powder, ginger, cinnamon, pepper, salt and cloves in a bowl until the dry ingredients are thoroughly combined; set aside.

In the bowl of a stand mixer fitted with the paddle attachment, or using a hand-held mixer, beat the butter for 1 minute. Add the brown sugar and beat until light and fluffy. Scrape down the sides of the bowl. Beat in the molasses until well blended. Scrape down the sides of the bowl again. One at a time, beat in the eggs, beating well after each egg before adding the next one. Beat in the vanilla.

Remove the bowl from the stand. Using a wooden spoon, alternately stir in the flour mixture and the cooled date mixture, making 3 additions of the flour and 2 of the date mixture. Transfer the mixture to the prepared pan.

Bake in the centre of the preheated oven until the top of the cake springs back when lightly pressed, about 30 minutes.

TOFFEE SAUCE While the cake is baking, make the toffee sauce. Combine the butter, sugar and whipping cream in a saucepan set over medium heat. Cook, stirring, until the butter and the sugar are melted. Increase the heat to medium-high and cook, stirring often, until the mixture is smooth and slightly thickened, 5–8 minutes. Remove from the heat and stir in the vanilla and rum, if using; let cool.

Cool the cake in the pan on a wire rack for 5 minutes. With the sharp end of a small paring knife, poke holes all over the surface of the cake. Pour about ½ cup (125 mL) of the sauce over the cake. Let the cake cool completely on the wire rack.

Cut the cake into squares and serve topped with additional sauce.

BAKER'S TIP

Try to buy Medjool dates, they're plumper and tastier. Deglet Noor dates are a nice amber colour but tend to be drier. Thoory dates are lighter in colour, drier and have a distinctive nutty flavour. Other kinds, such as Halawi and Barhi, are soft and sticky, and sweeter than the Medjool. Fancy molasses is lighter tasting than blackstrap molasses, so be sure to use this in the cake. Blackstrap molasses will overwhelm the subtler spices and take your cake hostage.

Honey Cake

3 cups (725 mL) all-purpose flour

2½ tsp (12 mL) baking powder

2 tsp (10 mL) cinnamon

1 tsp (5 mL) baking soda

½ tsp (2 mL) grated nutmeg

¼ tsp (1 mL) ground cloves

¼ tsp (1 mL) ground allspice

¼ tsp (1 mL) salt

1 cup (250 mL) honey

1 cup (250 mL) strong brewed
coffee

1 cup (250 mL) canola or vegetable oil

3 large eggs, at room temperature

1 Tbsp (15 mL) finely grated
orange zest (about 1 orange)

½ cup (125 mL) freshly squeezed
orange juice (about 2 oranges)

¾ cup (180 mL) granulated sugar

¾ cup (180 mL) packed light
brown sugar

1 tsp (5 mL) vanilla

IT WASN'T until I moved from Montreal to Toronto that my career as a honey cake baker started. The honey cakes I had tried before always tasted flat and dry, if not outright sandy, so I simply never bothered trying my hand at one. I didn't really like them so didn't really want to make them. Then I tasted a cake that was like an epiphany. Moist, laden with honey tones, just sweet enough and bearing absolutely no resemblance to the stuffy cake I had known previously. Now *this* I could and would make. I tried several iterations before I felt satisfied that this honey cake could carry the banner.

Preheat the oven to 325°F (160°C). Grease a 12-cup (3 L) Bundt pan; set aside.

Whisk together the flour, baking powder, cinnamon, baking soda, nutmeg, cloves, allspice and salt in a large bowl until the dry ingredients are thoroughly combined.

In a separate bowl, whisk together the honey, coffee, oil, eggs, orange zest and juice, granulated and brown sugars and the vanilla. Make sure that there are no lumps. Pour the wet mixture over the flour mixture and whisk together until all of the flour has been absorbed—the mixture will be runny.

Pour the batter into the prepared Bundt pan.

Bake in the centre of the preheated oven until the top of the cake springs back when lightly pressed, 55–60 minutes. Cool the cake in the pan for at least 20 minutes. Unmould the cake and let cool completely on a wire rack. Serve at room temperature.

BAKER'S TIP

Lore has it that honey cake calls for coffee since the strong bitter flavour counterbalances the inherent sweetness of the cake. However, if you're not a coffee lover, you can replace the coffee with an equal amount of brewed tea or even just lightly flavoured water.

Meyer Lemon Pudding Cake

EVERY BAKER needs a cake that they can pull out of their hat at a moment's notice and that they know practically off by heart. Half pudding and half cake, this is one of those desserts that is incredibly easy to put together, and it is ready in just over 30 minutes. Meyer lemons are sweeter than regular lemons, but the latter will do as well, just expect a bit more of a pucker.

¾ cup (180 mL) granulated sugar, divided

¼ cup (60 mL) all-purpose flour

¼ tsp (1 mL) salt

1 cup (250 mL) milk, at room temperature

3 Tbsp (45 mL) unsalted butter, melted and cooled (1.5 oz/45 g)

3 large eggs, at room temperature, separated

2 Tbsp (30 mL) finely grated Meyer lemon zest (about 2 lemons)

¼ cup (60 mL) freshly squeezed Meyer lemon juice (about 1 lemon)

Preheat the oven to 350°F (180°C).

Whisk together ½ cup (125 mL) of the sugar, the flour and salt in a large bowl. Whisk in the milk, butter and egg yolks. Whisk in the lemon zest and the lemon juice.

In the bowl of a stand mixer fitted with the whisk attachment, or using a hand-held mixer, beat the egg whites until soft peaks form. In a thin stream, gradually add the remaining ¼ cup (60 mL) of sugar, beating until stiff and glossy peaks form.

Using a rubber spatula, fold one-third of the beaten egg whites into the lemon mixture. Fold in the remaining egg whites.

Transfer the mixture to an 8-inch (20 cm) square glass cake pan. Set the pan in a larger roasting pan. Without disturbing the batter at all, pour enough hot water into the larger roasting pan to come halfway up the sides of the 8-inch (20 cm) dish.

Bake in the centre of the preheated oven until the top of the cake is golden and springs back when lightly pressed, 30–40 minutes. Remove the roasting pan from the oven. Remove the 8-inch (20 cm) dish from the water bath and let it cool on a wire rack.

Pudding cakes should be eaten warm or at room temperature.

Pistachio Lemon Dacquoise

LEMON CURD

⅓ cup (80 mL) unsalted butter, in
pieces (3 oz/90 g)

1¼ cups (310 mL) granulated
sugar

⅔ cup (160 mL) freshly squeezed
lemon juice (about 3 lemons)

¼ tsp (1 mL) salt

3 large eggs, at room temperature

3 large egg yolks, at room
temperature

2 Tbsp (30 mL) finely grated
lemon zest (about 2 lemons)

MERINGUES

1½ cups (375 mL) shelled
pistachios

¼ cup (60 mL) icing sugar

6 large egg whites, at room
temperature

¼ tsp (1 mL) salt

1¼ cups (310 mL) granulated
sugar

1 tsp (5 mL) vanilla

1 cup (250 mL) cold whipping
cream

GARNISH

½ cup (125 mL) shelled pistachios,
coarsely chopped

WHEN I was developing the recipes for this book, my main point of view was that the book would represent home baking at its best— no fancy, multi-tiered concoctions that would take hours to understand and more hours to make. All in all, I think I've kept my word, but I so desperately wanted to include this recipe that I snuck it in hoping that my editor wouldn't notice. Yes, it's a tad more complicated and perhaps has one more step than my other cakes. Yes, you have to make lemon curd, and yes, you have to make meringues, and even whip some cream (a must in a dacquoise cake). But the end result is so show stopping, impressive and grand that I urge you to try your hand at it.

LEMON CURD The day before you make the dacquoise, make the lemon curd. Combine the butter, sugar, lemon juice and salt in a stainless steel bowl large enough to sit on top of a medium-sized saucepan. Place the bowl over a saucepan of simmering, not boiling water. Cook gently until the butter is melted and the sugar is dissolved. Whisk together the eggs and egg yolks in a separate bowl. Whisking constantly, pour about 3 Tbsp (45 mL) of the hot lemon mixture into the eggs. Pour in another 3 Tbsp (45 mL), again whisking constantly. Continue adding the hot mixture to the eggs, whisking constantly, until about three-quarters of the hot lemon mixture has been mixed into the egg mixture. Slowly whisk the remaining hot lemon mixture into the eggs. Return the mixture to the larger bowl and put it back on top of the saucepan filled with the simmering water.

Cook, whisking often, until the mixture is thick and a deep yellow, about 8 minutes. Transfer to a clean bowl. Stir in the lemon zest. Place some plastic wrap directly on top of the curd to prevent a skin from forming. Refrigerate until completely chilled, at least 3 hours or up to 2 days.

MERINGUES Combine the pistachios and icing sugar in the bowl of a food processor fitted with the metal "S" blade. Pulse a few times until the pistachios are coarsely chopped; set aside.

Preheat the oven to 325°F (160°C). Line 2 large, rimmed baking sheets with parchment paper. Using a pencil, draw two 10- × 4-inch (25 × 10 cm) rectangles on each baking sheet. Turn the parchment over so that the pencil marks are on the underside.

RECIPE CONTINUED . . .

In the bowl of a stand mixer fitted with the whisk attachment, or using a hand-held mixer, beat the whites with the salt until soft peaks form. In a thin stream, gradually add the sugar, beating until stiff and shiny peaks form. In 2 additions, fold in the pistachio mixture. Fold in the vanilla.

Transfer the mixture to a piping bag with a ¾- to 1-inch (2–2.5 cm) tip or opening. Starting at the outer edge, pipe the meringue onto the traced rectangles. If you don't have a piping bag, you can simply use a plastic spatula or spoon to heap the mixture into the rectangles and then spread until the entire rectangle is filled.

Bake one tray in the centre of the oven and the other tray on the top third of the oven for 50 minutes. Switch the positions of the trays. Bake for another 15 minutes. Turn the oven off and let the meringues cool and bake a little longer in the turned-off oven, until dry, about 1 hour. Remove both trays to wire racks to cool completely. If your kitchen is cool and dry, you can keep them at room temperature for up to 24 hours.

Whip the cream to soft peaks. Fold half of the lemon curd into the whipped cream.

ASSEMBLY Remove 1 meringue rectangle from the parchment. Transfer to a square serving plate. Spread the top of the meringue with a quarter of the remaining curd. Spread a quarter of the whipped cream over the curd. Place another layer of meringue on top. Spread with another quarter of the lemon curd and then another quarter of the whipped cream. Repeat 2 more times. Sprinkle the chopped pistachios in a line down the centre on top of the cake. Refrigerate for at least 2 hours before serving.

Gâteau Breton

THIS IS one of my favourite cakes and one of the simplest to make. It comes from France, and in every way exemplifies the simple yet buttery cakes for which the French are known. Originally, I made it the way the French make it, much the same method you use when you make biscotti: the flour is placed on a work counter, a well is shaped in the middle of the flour and the butter is cut into very small pieces and added to the well along with the egg yolks and sugar; after the butter, egg yolks and sugar are stirred together, the flour is gradually worked into the wet mixture until a sticky dough is formed. You can use this method if you want, although I have included a more modern one below that takes advantage of modern mixers; it cuts the time in half and results in a somewhat lighter texture.

1 cup (250 mL) unsalted butter, softened (8 oz/250 g)
1 cup (250 mL) granulated sugar
⅓ cup (80 mL) ground almonds
2 tsp (10 mL) rose water or vanilla
6 large egg yolks, at room temperature
1¾ cups (430 mL) all-purpose flour

Preheat the oven to 325°F (160°C).

In the bowl of a stand mixer fitted with the paddle attachment, or using a hand-held mixer, beat the butter for 1 minute. In a thin stream, gradually add the sugar. Beat for 1 minute, scraping down the sides of the bowl. Beat in the almonds and rose water (or vanilla). Using one egg yolk at a time, with the machine on low, beat in the egg yolks, leaving about 1 tsp (5 mL) behind.

In 4 separate additions, with the machine still on low, beat in the flour, just until the flour is combined. Scrape the batter into a 9-inch (23 cm) French tart tin or a lightly greased 9-inch (23 cm) springform pan. It will be quite low and that is as it should be. Brush the top with the remaining 1 tsp (5 mL) of egg yolk. Place the tart tin on a rimmed baking sheet.

Bake in the centre of the preheated oven until the top is cracked and golden and the cake is firm to the touch, 35–45 minutes. Let the cake cool in the pan on a wire rack for 20 minutes. Remove the cake from the tart tin or springform pan and let cool completely on the wire rack. Serve at room temperature.

BAKER'S TIP

Rose water is available in specialty or Middle Eastern stores. It's the flavoured water resulting from rose petals being steeped in hot water. It makes a huge difference to this cake, but of course, vanilla will do as well.

COFFEE CAKES AND POUND CAKES

Coffee cakes and pound cakes bring to mind good old fashioned baking. They've been around a long time—the pound cake is said to have been around since the 1700s. Some historians say its popularity was due to the fact that even the illiterate could remember a pound of butter, a pound of sugar, a pound of eggs and a pound of flour. With a pound of each, the loaves were large and sturdy, enough to feed the larger families of the time. Originally, pound cakes had no chemical leaveners. They relied on beating the batter for their texture. Nowadays, of course, the proportions have changed to accommodate more modern palates, and baking powder or baking soda has been added to lighten the texture of the cake. Yet, there's still a whiff of nostalgia when a pound cake is made. They're relatively simple and straightforward, both in the technique they require and the types of flavourings they attract. The best pound cakes are redolent with butter and sometimes buttermilk, cream cheese or sour cream. They take well to simple additions, be it in the form of fresh or dried fruit, citrus flavours, nuts or spices. There's really no need to be lavish with a pound cake—they simply shine in their simplicity.

Much the same can be said of coffee cakes. Brought to North America by Hungarians, Germans and Scandinavians, the coffee cake was originally a yeasted sweet bread, and not a cake at all. Over time, it evolved into a cake leavened by yeast but also by baking powder and baking soda. It was still quite plain then, often sweetened by dried fruit and other naturally sweet inclusions. It was only after the concept of leisure time became a part of modern life that coffee cakes became much sweeter and a delicacy to be enjoyed with a cup of coffee. By the 1880s, the term "coffee cake" was part of the broad lexicon.

Coffee cakes today run the gamut, although they are not typically fancy, layered or iced. I am more than partial to sour cream–based ones, with a sweet ripple of sugar, cinnamon, coffee and nuts or raisins coursing through the cake. Like quick breads, coffee cakes are almost always made by using the creaming method. Whether you make them in a Bundt pan, an angel food cake pan or a regular cake pan, the design should be the same: a tender crumbed cake, with a sweet filling (either in a ribbon through the cake or sandwiched between two layers of batter), often accompanied by a streusel topping. Many bakers include crumb cakes and kuchen in the coffee cake category but given my Eastern European heritage, I'm sticking to my roots and only calling the aforementioned cakes true coffee cakes.

Ye Olde Fashioned Sour Cream Coffee Cake

A s THE name suggests, this cake calls for sour cream, which is ubiquitous in good coffee cakes because of the tender crumb it provides. When you combine the baking soda with the sour cream, it automatically dives into action, aerating the sour cream by starting to bubble. This makes for a particularly moist and delightful cake, its delicacy pronounced by the buttery pecans in the swirl.

Preheat the oven to 350°F (180°C). Lightly grease a 10-inch (25 cm) angel food cake pan; set aside.

Combine the pecans, sugars and cinnamon in a bowl; set aside.

CAKE BATTER Stir together the sour cream and baking soda.

Whisk together the flour, baking powder and salt in a bowl.

In the bowl of a stand mixer fitted with the paddle attachment, or using a hand-held mixer, beat the butter for 1 minute. Gradually add the sugar in a thin stream and beat until light, about 3 minutes. One at a time, beat in the eggs, scraping down the sides of the bowl between additions and making sure that each egg is incorporated before adding the next. Beat in the vanilla.

Remove the bowl from the stand. Using a wooden spoon, alternately stir in the flour mixture with the sour cream mixture, making 3 additions of the flour and 2 of the sour cream.

Spoon one-third of the batter into the bottom of the prepared pan. Sprinkle with one-third of the pecan mixture. Gently spread another third of the cake batter on top of the pecan mixture. Sprinkle another third of the pecan mixture over the second layer of batter. Scrape the remaining cake batter on top, spreading it carefully so that it covers the pecans. Sprinkle the remaining pecans over the batter.

Bake in the centre of the preheated oven until a cake tester inserted in the centre comes out clean, 60–70 minutes. Cool the cake in the pan on a wire rack for 30 minutes. Run a small knife around the edge of the pan to loosen the cake. Remove the cake from the pan and cool completely on the wire rack. Serve at room temperature.

1½ cups (375 mL) toasted pecans, finely chopped

¼ cup (60 mL) packed light brown sugar

¼ cup (60 mL) granulated sugar

2 tsp (10 mL) cinnamon

CAKE BATTER

1½ cups (375 mL) sour cream, at room temperature

1 tsp (5 mL) baking soda

3 cups (750 mL) all-purpose flour

2 tsp (10 mL) baking powder

¾ tsp (4 mL) salt

1 cup (250 mL) unsalted butter, softened (8 oz/250 g)

1½ cups (375 mL) granulated sugar

3 large eggs, at room temperature

1½ tsp (7 mL) vanilla

BAKER'S TIP Keep in mind the baker's motto, if it starts off wrong, it's going to end up wrong. So it's especially important to make sure that your butter, eggs and sour cream are at room temperature.

Chocolate Ribbon Coffee Cake

STREUSEL TOPPING

⅔ cup (160 mL) all-purpose flour

2 Tbsp (30 mL) granulated sugar

2 Tbsp (30 mL) light brown sugar

1 tsp (5 mL) cinnamon

¼ tsp (1 mL) baking powder

¼ tsp (1 mL) salt

¼ cup (60 mL) unsalted butter,
melted and cooled (2 oz/60 g)

FILLING

½ cup (125 mL) pecans or walnuts,
chopped

4 oz (125 g) semisweet chocolate,
finely chopped

¼ cup (60 mL) packed light brown
sugar

3 Tbsp (45 mL) granulated sugar

2 Tbsp (30 mL) unsweetened
cocoa powder

CAKE

2¾ cups (680 mL) all-purpose
flour

1½ tsp (7 mL) baking powder

1 tsp (5 mL) baking soda

½ tsp (2 mL) salt

1 cup (250 mL) unsalted butter,
softened (8 oz/250 g)

1⅔ cups (410 mL) granulated
sugar

4 large eggs, at room temperature

2 tsp (10 mL) vanilla

2 cups (500 mL) sour cream, at
room temperature

COFFEE CAKES that include chocolate in their filling often contain cocoa powder, both to help allay the sweetness and to provide a contrasting colour. I've opted to combine cocoa with some chopped semisweet chocolate to punch up the flavour. This cake stands tall and sprightly and is an irresistible dessert table confection, perfect for brunch or late night snacking.

Preheat the oven to 350°F (180°C). Lightly grease a 10-inch (25 cm) angel food cake pan; set aside.

STREUSEL TOPPING Combine the flour, sugars, cinnamon, baking powder and salt in a small bowl. Pour the melted butter over and stir with a fork (or your fingertips!) until the mixture is thoroughly moistened and starting to turn crumbly; set aside.

FILLING Combine the nuts, chocolate, sugars and cocoa in a bowl, stirring until well mixed; set aside.

CAKE Whisk together the flour, baking powder, baking soda and salt in a bowl until the dry ingredients are thoroughly combined; set aside.

In the bowl of a stand mixer fitted with the paddle attachment, or using a hand-held mixer, beat the butter for 1 minute. In a thin stream, gradually add the sugar. Beat until light and fluffy, about 3 minutes. One at a time, beat in the eggs, scraping down the sides of the bowl between additions and making sure that each egg is incorporated before adding the next. Beat in the vanilla.

Remove the bowl from the stand. Using a wooden spoon, alternately stir in the flour mixture with the sour cream, making 4 additions of the flour and 3 of the sour cream.

Spoon about 2 cups (500 mL) of the batter into the bottom of the prepared pan, smoothing the batter so that there are no gaps between the batter and the pan. Sprinkle ½ cup (125 mL) of the filling over the batter. Repeat with another 2 cups (500 mL) of the batter and ½ cup (125 mL) of the filling. Repeat one more time. Smooth remaining batter over the last sprinkling of filling. You should have 4 layers of batter and 3 of filling. Using a small knife, draw gently through the batter to make a ribbon effect. Sprinkle the streusel topping over the batter and any remaining filling.

Bake in the centre of the preheated oven until the top of the cake springs back when lightly pressed, 60–70 minutes. Cool the cake in the pan on a wire rack for at least 30 minutes. This is a very fragile cake so please be sure to resist unmoulding it before then. Run a small paring knife around the edge of the cake to loosen it from the pan. Remove from the angel food cake pan and let cool completely on the wire rack. Serve at room temperature.

Individual Yeasted Coffee Cakes *with* Cherries *and* Almonds

COFFEE CAKE DOUGH

½ cup (125 mL) milk, warm

1½ tsp (7 mL) active dry yeast

⅓ cup (80 mL) granulated sugar, divided

2 cups (500 mL) all-purpose flour

½ tsp (2 mL) salt

½ tsp (2 mL) cinnamon

2 large eggs, at room temperature

⅔ cup (160 mL) unsalted butter, very soft (5 oz/150 g)

1 tsp (5 mL) vanilla

FILLING

¾ cup (180 mL) dried cherries

¾ cup (180 mL) sliced almonds, toasted

½ cup (125 mL) mini chocolate chips

⅓ cup (80 mL) packed light brown sugar

½ tsp (2 mL) cinnamon

2 Tbsp (30 mL) unsalted butter, melted and cooled (1 oz/30 g)

1 large egg yolk, lightly beaten, at room temperature

THESE ARE like small kuchens, each one the perfect size just for you. Some of my friends who tasted them thought they tasted like really really good muffins, whereas others thought of them as sweet bread rolls. Whatever the moniker, you will marvel at this Old World flavour combination.

COFFEE CAKE DOUGH Pour the warm milk into a 1-cup (250 mL) wet measure. Sprinkle the yeast over the milk. Sprinkle 2 tsp (10 mL) of the sugar over the yeast and stir gently to combine. Let the milk-yeast mixture stand until frothy, 8–10 minutes.

Meanwhile, combine the flour, remaining sugar, salt and cinnamon in the bowl of a stand mixer fitted with the paddle attachment.

Once the yeast has proofed, add it along with the eggs, butter and vanilla to the flour mixture. Beat on medium-low speed until the mixture comes together. Increase the speed to medium and beat for 6 minutes. The dough will resemble a sticky mass—it will not come away from the sides of the bowl as other yeast-based breads do. Scrape the dough into a greased bowl. Cover with plastic wrap and refrigerate overnight or for up to 24 hours.

FILLING Combine the cherries, almonds, chocolate chips, sugar and cinnamon in a bowl; set aside.

Lightly grease a 12-cup muffin tin.

Transfer the dough to a well-floured work surface. It won't be puffy and light like a regular yeast-based dough, rather somewhat dense and sticky. Using a rolling pin, roll out the dough to a 12- × 10-inch (30 ×25 cm) rectangle, working quickly so that the dough doesn't become too elastic. Brush the melted butter over the surface of the dough. Sprinkle the filling over the dough, leaving a 1-inch (2.5 cm) border on all sides. Starting with the long side, roll the dough up jelly roll–style, pinching the ends of the seam to close it firmly.

Using a sharp chef's knife, cut the log in half. Cut each half into 6 separate pieces. Place each slice, cut side up, into the prepared muffin tin. Press the top of each gently. Cover the muffin tin with plastic wrap and let rise in a warm, draft-free area, for 1½–2 hours or until doubled in bulk.

Meanwhile, preheat the oven to 350°F (180°C). Brush the tops of the dough with the beaten egg yolk.

Bake in the centre of the preheated oven until puffed and golden, 20–25 minutes. Let the coffee cakes cool in the pan on a wire rack for 15 minutes. Remove from the muffin tins and let cool or serve warm.

BAKER'S TIP

This recipe calls for plain old active dry yeast, not quick acting, instant or otherwise. This typically comes in ½ oz (15 g) packages, sold in the baking aisle. Once home, store the yeast in the refrigerator where it will last longer. All yeast packages come with a best before date which I urge you to heed. Always proof yeast in warm water that's about 110–118°F (43–48°C). Too hot and the water will kill the yeast, too cool and it won't sufficiently proof.

Orange Cardamom Coffee Cake *with* Almond Swirl

ALMOND SWIRL

1 cup (250 mL) coarsely chopped
 unblanched almonds

½ cup (125 mL) granulated sugar

⅓ cup (80 mL) packed light brown
 sugar

¼ tsp (1 mL) cinnamon

CAKE

2 cups (500 mL) all-purpose flour

½ cup (125 mL) cake and pastry
 flour (sifted, spooned into the
 measure and then swept)

1 Tbsp (15 mL) finely grated orange
 zest (1 large orange)

1 tsp (5 mL) baking powder

¾ tsp (4 mL) ground cardamom

½ tsp (2 mL) baking soda

½ tsp (2 mL) salt

1 cup (250 mL) unsalted butter,
 softened (8 oz/250 g)

2 cups (500 mL) granulated sugar

3 large eggs, at room temperature

2 tsp (10 mL) vanilla

1 cup (250 mL) buttermilk, at room
 temperature

¼ cup (60 mL) sour cream, at
 room temperature

THERE'S NO question that I am partial to certain spices, one of them being cardamom. Its sweet spicy perfume has captured my heart. Cardamom marries well with most fruits and especially oranges, which is why I combined the two in this recipe. As I have suggested before, buy whole cardamom seeds and grind them yourself for a truly top notch flavour. I use both all-purpose and cake and pastry flour, as well as both buttermilk and sour cream, so that you will be the joyous recipient of a moist and fragrant coffee cake.

Preheat the oven to 325°F (160°C). Grease a 10-cup (2.5 L) Bundt pan; set aside.

ALMOND SWIRL In a small bowl, stir together the almonds, sugars and cinnamon; set aside.

CAKE Whisk together the flours, orange zest, baking powder, cardamom, baking soda and salt in a bowl until the dry ingredients are thoroughly combined; set aside.

In the bowl of a stand mixer fitted with the paddle attachment, or using a hand-held mixer, beat the butter for 1 minute. Gradually add the sugar in a thin stream, beating until light and fluffy, about 3 minutes. One at a time, beat in the eggs, beating well after each egg before adding the next. Beat in the vanilla.

Remove the bowl from the stand. Using a wooden spoon, alternately stir in the flour, buttermilk and sour cream, making 3 additions of the flour mixture, 2 of buttermilk and 1 of the sour cream.

Using a rubber spatula, spread half of the batter into the prepared Bundt pan. Sprinkle with the almond filling. Using the handle of a spoon or a thin knife, swirl the filling lightly through the batter. Top with the remaining cake batter. Smooth the surface with a small offset spatula knife or the back of a spoon.

Bake in the centre of the preheated oven until the top of the cake springs back when lightly pressed, 65–70 minutes. Cool the cake in the pan on a wire rack for 30 minutes.

Unmould the cake and cool completely on the wire rack. Serve at room temperature.

Sour Cream Pound Cake

2 cups (500 mL) all-purpose flour

1½ tsp (7 mL) baking powder

½ tsp (2 mL) salt

1 cup (250 mL) unsalted butter, softened (8 oz/250 g)

1 cup (250 mL) granulated sugar

4 large eggs, at room temperature, lightly beaten

1½ tsp (7 mL) vanilla

½ cup (125 mL) sour cream, at room temperature

As MENTIONED pound cakes used to be made with a pound each of flour, eggs, sugar and butter. In France, this was called *quatre quarts* (literally "four fourths"), also reflecting the fact that all four ingredients were used in equal amounts. The cake is still very popular in the Brittany region of France. Over here in North America, sour cream is most often added to pound cake to provide a moist fluffy crumb and that distinctive tangy flavour, embellished here only by a dash of vanilla.

Preheat the oven to 325°F (160°C). Grease a 9- × 5-inch (23 × 13 cm) loaf pan; set aside.

Whisk together the flour, baking powder and salt in a bowl until the dry ingredients are thoroughly combined; set aside.

In the bowl of a stand mixer fitted with the paddle attachment, or using a hand-held mixer, beat the butter for 1 minute. With the machine running, gradually add the sugar in a thin stream. Beat until very light and fluffy, 2–3 minutes. About 2 Tbsp (30 mL) at a time, beat in the eggs, beating well after each addition before adding more. Beat in the vanilla.

Remove the bowl from the stand. Using a wooden spoon, stir in half of the flour mixture. Stir in the sour cream. Stir in the remaining flour mixture. Turn the mixture into the prepared pan, smoothing the top. Place on 2 baking sheets stacked together.

Bake in the centre of the preheated oven until the top springs back when lightly pressed, 65–75 minutes. Cool the cake in the pan on a wire rack for 30 minutes. Run a small knife around the edge of the loaf pan to loosen the cake. Remove the loaf from the pan and cool completely on the wire rack. Serve at room temperature.

CHOCOLATE MARBLE POUND CAKE Just before making the batter, melt 4 oz (120 g) of chopped bittersweet chocolate in the top of a double boiler set over hot, not boiling water. Let cool. Remove about one-third of the entire batter. Stir the melted and cooled chocolate into this batter. Build the cake by layering the plain batter and the chocolate batter into the loaf pan then using a metal spatula to softly meld them together.

BAKER'S TIPS

You can substitute ½ cup (125 mL) whipping cream, whipped, for the sour cream. It makes a luscious, somewhat lighter, pound cake.

Double stacking the baking sheets under a pound cake protects it from baking too quickly and overbrowning. If the top of the cake is getting too brown, tent aluminum foil over the cake.

Almond Crusted Cherry Pound Cake

NUT CRUST
1¼ cups (310 mL) whole
    unblanched almonds
2 Tbsp (30 mL) granulated sugar

CAKE
2 cups (500 mL) all-purpose flour
½ tsp (2 mL) baking powder
¼ tsp (1 mL) baking soda
¼ tsp (1 mL) salt
1 cup (250 mL) unsalted butter,
    softened (8 oz/250 g)
1¼ cups (310 mL) granulated
    sugar
4 large eggs, at room temperature,
    lightly beaten
1 tsp (5 mL) vanilla
¼ tsp (1 mL) almond extract
½ cup (125 mL) sour cream, at
    room temperature
1 cup (250 mL) dried cherries

THIS POUND cake is visually striking as well as an interesting study in contrasts. The sides are coated with chopped almonds and sugar, lending an irresistible crunch while the cake itself is velvety and close grained. For extra oomph, try plumping the cherries in some brandy for 5 minutes before starting to beat the butter.

Preheat the oven to 325°F (160°C). Grease a 9- × 5-inch (23 × 13 cm) loaf pan generously with butter. In this particular case, using a spray will not work as the nuts will not adhere to the side or bottom of the pan. Trust me. The butter will be worth it.

NUT CRUST Combine the almonds and the sugar in the bowl of a food processor fitted with the metal "S" blade. Pulse until the nuts are finely chopped with a few coarse ones. Pour about ½ cup (125 mL) of the nuts into the prepared loaf pan. Tilt the pan so that the nuts coat all of the sides. Pour in remaining almond mixture and tilt pan again. Don't worry if most of them fall to the bottom—you're looking for a thin coating on the sides and a heavier one on the bottom.

CAKE Whisk together the flour, baking powder, baking soda and salt in a bowl until the dry ingredients are thoroughly combined; set aside.

In the bowl of a stand mixer fitted with the paddle attachment, or using a hand-held mixer, beat the butter for 1 minute. With the machine running, gradually add the sugar in a thin stream. Beat until very light and fluffy, about 3 minutes. Adding 2 Tbsp (30 mL) at a time, beat in the eggs, beating well after each addition before adding more. Beat in the vanilla and almond extract.

Remove the bowl from the stand. Using a wooden spoon, stir in half of the flour mixture. Stir in the sour cream. Stir in the remaining flour mixture. Stir in the cherries. Turn the mixture into the prepared pan, smoothing the top. Place on 2 baking sheets.

Bake in the centre of the preheated oven until the top springs back when lightly pressed, 70–80 minutes. Cool the cake in the pan on a wire rack for 30 minutes. Remove the loaf from the pan and cool completely on the wire rack. Serve at room temperature.

Substituting some of the all-purpose flour (about 10%) with potato starch creates a pound cake with a softer crumb.

Many pound cakes come out of the oven with a cracked top. Sometimes the crack forms straight down the middle, sometimes it's a bit more haphazard. If it's precision you're looking for, draw a greased spatula lengthwise through the batter after it's baked for 10 minutes. The crack will follow the line created by the spatula.

Lemon Pound Cake *with* Ginger Speckles

3 cups (725 mL) all-purpose flour

2½ tsp (12 mL) baking powder

¼ tsp (1 mL) baking soda

¼ tsp (1 mL) salt

3 Tbsp (45 mL) finely grated
lemon zest (about 3 lemons)

1 cup (250 mL) unsalted butter,
softened (8 oz/250 g)

1½ cups (375 mL) granulated
sugar

6 large eggs, at room temperature,
beaten

¼ cup (60 mL) freshly squeezed
lemon juice (from 1 lemon)

1 tsp (5 mL) vanilla

1 cup (250 mL) sour cream, at
room temperature

⅔ cup (160 mL) finely chopped
crystallized ginger

LEMON GLAZE

⅓ cup (80 mL) granulated sugar

¼ cup (60 mL) freshly squeezed
lemon juice (from 1 lemon)

ALTHOUGH A pound cake, this cake is baked in a Bundt pan, all the better to show it off. Though it is best the day it's made, the cake will keep reasonably well for up to 4 days.

Preheat the oven to 325°F (160°C). Grease a 10-cup (2.5 L) Bundt pan; set aside.

Whisk together the flour, baking powder, baking soda and salt in a bowl until the dry ingredients are thoroughly combined. Stir in the lemon zest.

In the bowl of a stand mixer fitted with the paddle attachment, or using a hand-held mixer, beat the butter for 1 minute. Gradually add the sugar in a thin stream, beating until light and fluffy, about 3 minutes. Adding ¼ cup (60 mL) at a time, beat in the eggs, beating well after each addition before adding more. Beat in the lemon juice and vanilla. The mixture may seem a bit curdled at this point, but it will come together as soon as you start to add the flour.

Remove the bowl from the stand. Using a wooden spoon, alternately stir in the flour and sour cream, making 3 additions of the flour mixture and 2 of the sour cream. Gently fold in the crystallized ginger. Turn the batter into the prepared Bundt pan, smoothing the surface.

Bake in the centre of the preheated oven until the top of the cake springs back when lightly pressed, about 50 minutes. Cool the cake in the pan on a wire rack for 15 minutes.

LEMON GLAZE Heat together the sugar and lemon juice in a small saucepan over medium-high heat just until the sugar has dissolved. Remove from the heat.

Remove the cake from the Bundt pan. Place a wire rack on top of a rimmed baking sheet. Place the cake on top of the wire rack. With the tines of a fork, poke holes all over the top of the cake. Pour half of the glaze over the cake. Return whatever glaze has fallen onto the baking sheet to the saucepan. Wait 20 minutes. Pour the remaining glaze over the cake. If some still falls onto the baking sheet, repeat the process once more. Serve at room temperature.

BAKER'S TIP

SUGAR SYRUPS The technique of adding extra moistness and flavour to a pound cake through a sugar syrup is a time-proven technique. Usually, holes are poked into the top surface of the cake immediately after it's removed from the oven and then a flavoured syrup is drizzled over, the holes allowing it to penetrate to the crumb of the cake. This should always be done when the cake is still warm, so that it can fully absorb the flavoured syrup. You can try this technique with almost any pound cake. Make a simple syrup by combining ½ cup (125 mL) granulated sugar and ½ cup (125 mL) water in a saucepan. Cook it over a moderate heat until the sugar has melted. You can add freshly squeezed lemon juice at this point, or strained tea or a splash of brewed coffee to flavour the simple syrup. You can also infuse the syrup with a cinnamon stick, cardamom pods, star anise or cloves while the sugar is melting. Just be sure to remove the solids by straining or plucking them from the syrup before pouring it over the cake. You can either pour the syrup from the pan onto the cake or, if you prefer a defter touch, brush it on with a pastry brush.

Orange Cream Cheese Pound Cake

1¼ cups (310 mL) all-purpose flour

3 Tbsp (45 mL) finely grated orange zest (about 3 oranges)

¾ tsp (4 mL) baking powder

Pinch of salt

¾ cup (180 mL) unsalted butter, softened (6 oz/175 g)

4 oz (125 g) cream cheese, softened

1 cup (250 mL) granulated sugar

3 large eggs, at room temperature

1 large egg yolk, at room temperature

1½ tsp (7 mL) vanilla

REPLACING WHIPPING cream or sour cream with cream cheese creates a denser—but no less delicious—spin on pound cake. Many master bakers also add an extra yolk, as I have done here, to increase the richness of the cake.

Preheat the oven to 325°F (160°C). Grease an 8- × 4-inch (20 ×10 cm) loaf pan; set aside.

Whisk together the flour, zest, baking powder and salt in a bowl until the dry ingredients are thoroughly combined; set aside.

In the bowl of a stand mixer fitted with the paddle attachment, or using a hand-held mixer, beat the butter with the cream cheese for 1 minute. With the machine running, gradually add the sugar in a thin stream. Beat, scraping down the sides of the bowl twice, until very light and fluffy, about 3 minutes. One at a time, beat in the eggs, beating well after each egg before adding the next. Beat in the egg yolk and then the vanilla.

Remove the bowl from the stand. Using a wooden spoon, stir in the flour mixture in 2 additions. Turn the mixture into the prepared pan, smoothing the top. Place on 2 baking sheets.

Bake in the centre of the preheated oven until the top springs back when lightly pressed, 55–65 minutes. Cool the cake in the pan on a wire rack for 30 minutes. Remove the loaf from the pan and cool completely on the wire rack. Serve at room temperature.

FROZEN CAKES

For those of us who are kids at heart, nothing beats an ice cream cake. Ice cream cakes take us back to another time when life was simpler, responsibilities fewer and play, not work, was the activity of choice. They're exceptionally easy to make, especially if you buy store-bought ice cream, which, of course, you can. Homemade ice cream, as you'll see in this chapter, is not only wonderful but quite easy to make, even if you don't own an ice cream machine. The latter will definitely result in a smooth, aerated frozen treat, but you can also enjoy almost the same results by pouring the custard into a metal square cake pan and placing it in the freezer. You just have to stir the mixture about every 10 minutes to keep it aerated and malleable.

Reine de Saba Ice Cream Cake

CAKE

½ cup (125 mL) blanched slivered almonds

½ cup (125 mL) granulated sugar, divided

¼ cup (60 mL) all-purpose flour

3 Tbsp (45 mL) unsweetened cocoa powder

½ tsp (2 mL) baking powder

3 large eggs, at room temperature, separated

Pinch of salt

¼ cup (60 mL) unsalted butter, melted and cooled (2 oz/60 g)

CHOCOLATE MOUSSE PARFAIT

6 oz (175 g) semisweet chocolate, coarsely chopped

½ cup (125 mL) milk, at room temperature

4 large egg yolks, at room temperature

⅔ cup (160 mL) granulated sugar

1 cup (250 mL) whipping cream, cold

⅓ cup (80 mL) strawberry jam

2 Tbsp (30 mL) brandy or water

TOPPING

10–12 strawberries, depending on their size

4 oz (125 g) semisweet chocolate, melted

THIS EXTRAVAGANT ice cream cake is a bit of a riff on the classic Reine de Saba cake, a dense chocolate cake made with ground almonds and usually topped with a glossy chocolate ganache. I've made a chocolate almond cake, layered it with an airy chocolate mousse and frozen the whole kit and kaboodle. Remarkably, after just a few minutes at room temperature, this cake slices sharply and cleanly and you have a riot of flavours and textures in your mouth.

Preheat the oven to 350°F (180°C). Lightly grease the bottom and sides of a 9-inch (23 cm) springform pan. Line the bottom with a circle of parchment paper cut to fit; set aside.

CAKE Place the almonds and 2 Tbsp (30 mL) of the sugar in the bowl of a food processor fitted with the metal "S" blade. Pulse until the nuts are finely ground. Transfer the nuts to a bowl; stir in the flour, cocoa powder, baking powder and salt.

In the bowl of a stand mixer fitted with the whisk attachment, or using a hand-held mixer, beat the egg yolks with ¼ cup (60 mL) of the remaining sugar until pale and thickened, about 5 minutes.

Using a clean bowl and a clean whisk attachment or beaters, beat the egg whites until soft peaks form. In a thin stream, gradually beat in the remaining 2 Tbsp (30 mL) of sugar and beat until stiff shiny peaks form.

Using a plastic spatula, fold one-third of the almond mixture into the yolk mixture, then one-third of the whites. Repeat twice more, folding in the melted butter just before the final addition of the egg whites. Scrape the mixture into the prepared pan.

Bake in the centre of the preheated oven until the top of the cake springs back when lightly pressed, 20–25 minutes. Cool the cake in the pan on a wire rack for 20 minutes. Run a small knife around the edge of the pan to loosen the cake. Remove the cake from the pan and cool completely on a wire rack, parchment side down.

CHOCOLATE MOUSSE PARFAIT Meanwhile, make the mousse parfait. Melt the chocolate in a bowl set over a saucepan of hot, not boiling water. Remove and let cool slightly.

Bring the milk just to a boil in a saucepan set over medium heat. Whisk together the egg yolks and sugar in a bowl until well combined. Pour one-third of the milk into the yolk mixture, whisking constantly. This is called tempering the eggs—or getting the eggs gradually used to the heat without curdling or overcooking them. Still whisking constantly, pour the remaining milk mixture into the yolk mixture. Pour the entire mixture back into the saucepan. Cook, stirring with a wooden spoon over low heat, until the mixture thickens enough to coat the back of the spoon and leave a trail when you draw your finger through it, 5–8 minutes. Do not let the mixture boil or you will end up with little pieces of cooked egg in your custard as opposed to a smooth texture.

Remove the custard from the heat. Gradually whisk the custard into the melted chocolate. Let cool completely to room temperature.

In the bowl of a stand mixer fitted with the whisk attachment, or using a hand-held mixer, whip the cream to soft peaks. Fold one-third of the cream into the chocolate mixture. In 2 additions, fold in the remaining whipped cream.

ASSEMBLY Using a serrated knife, cut the cake in half horizontally. Remove the parchment paper from the bottom half and fit into a clean 9-inch (23 cm) springform pan. Heat the strawberry jam with the brandy or water just until liquefied, about 2 minutes. Brush half of the strawberry jam on top of the cake. Scrape in half of the mousse, smoothing the top. Place the second layer of cake directly on top of the mousse. Brush with the remaining strawberry jam. Scrape in the remaining mousse, smoothing the top. Wrap the springform in plastic wrap and freeze until it is firm, about 4–24 hours.

Just before serving, dip the strawberries into the melted chocolate, so that the bottom third of the berry is coated. Place on a piece of parchment paper to let them dry at room temperature. Run a small knife around the edge of the cake to loosen it from the springform. Remove the sides of the springform and then the bottom. Transfer the cake to a cake plate. Decorate the top with the chocolate dipped strawberries. Serve immediately.

BAKER'S TIPS

For easier unmoulding, line the bottom and sides of the springform with plastic wrap before assembling the cake layers and mousse in it, with at least a 3-inch (8 cm) overhang. This will make removing the cake from the pan easier and, if your springform is a bit older, avoid any discolouration on your cake.

To cut as clean a slice as possible, dip a thin chef's knife in some hot water before slicing.

Caffe Latte Chocolate Bar Explosion Ice Cream Cake

BROWNIE BASE

6 oz (175 g) semisweet chocolate, coarsely chopped

¼ cup (60 mL) strong brewed coffee

½ cup (125 mL) unsalted butter, softened (4 oz/125 g)

¾ cup (180 mL) granulated sugar

4 large eggs, at room temperature

3 Tbsp (45 mL) all-purpose flour

ICE CREAM FILLING

6 cups (1.5 L) Coffee Ice Cream (see p. 386)

4 cups (1 L) vanilla ice cream or Rich Chocolate Ice Cream (see p. 387)

9 chocolate bars, coarsely chopped

2 oz (60 g) semisweet chocolate, melted

IF YOU want a cake that is fun to assemble and even more fun to eat, then this is the cake for you. Pretty well perfect any time of the year, layers of vanilla and coffee ice cream are sandwiched between layers of chopped candy bars, conveniently situated on top of a brownie base. I like to use Twix, Skor and Caramilk bars but the choice is entirely up to you. This irresistible cake will keep for up to 1 week in the freezer, well wrapped, so you can enjoy it with or without your family. I've included recipes for coffee and chocolate ice cream if you choose to make your own. If not, purchase really high quality ice cream.

Preheat the oven to 350°F (180°C). Lightly grease the bottom and sides of a 10-inch (25 cm) springform pan. Line the bottom with a circle of parchment paper cut to fit; set aside.

BROWNIE BASE Melt the chocolate, coffee and butter together in a saucepan set over medium-low heat, stirring frequently, until smooth. Remove from the heat. Whisk in the sugar. One at a time, whisk in the eggs. Whisk in the flour. Transfer the batter to the prepared pan.

Bake in the centre of the preheated oven until the centre feels just set, it will still look a little wet, 25–30 minutes. Cool the cake in the pan on a wire rack for 20 minutes. Run a small knife around the edges of the pan to loosen the cake. Remove the cake from the pan and cool completely on the wire rack, parchment side down.

ICE CREAM FILLING Bring the ice cream to room temperature for 30 minutes. Combine all of the chopped chocolate bars in a bowl, stirring well to combine. Remove 3 Tbsp (45 mL) chocolate bars to another bowl.

Remove the parchment paper from the bottom of the brownie. Place in a clean 10-inch (25 cm) springform pan. Spread half of the coffee ice cream on top of the brownie. Sprinkle with half of the mixed chocolate bars, covering the surface entirely. Spread all of the vanilla ice cream over the chocolate bars. Sprinkle the remaining chocolate bars over the vanilla layer. Spread the remaining coffee ice cream over. Sprinkle the reserved 3 Tbsp (45 mL) of chopped chocolate bars around the edge of the cake. Cover the springform pan with plastic wrap and freeze for at least 4 hours or for up to 2 weeks.

Remove the cake from the freezer. Let the cake stand at room temperature for 15 minutes. Remove the plastic wrap. Dip a long thin knife in hot water. Run the knife around the edge of the pan to help release the sides of the pan. Remove the base of the springform and transfer the cake to a cake plate. Drizzle the top with the melted chocolate and serve immediately.

Coffee Ice Cream

1 cup (250 mL) half and half
  cream, at room temperature

⅓ cup (80 mL) whole coffee beans

¾ cup (180 mL) granulated sugar

6 egg yolks, at room temperature

2 cups (500 mL) whipping cream,
  cold

⅓ cup (80 mL) brewed extra-
  strength coffee, at room
  temperature

I AM almost fanatical about ice cream. It has to be made with real cream and I am outraged at what has happened to store-bought ice cream. Now they call it a frozen food product since most of the ice creams you buy don't even contain real cream but loads of gums and stabilizers. However, I'll stash my soapbox away to rant another time and just say that homemade ice cream is incomparably good—creamy, soft, full flavoured and unctuous. This coffee ice cream is one of my favourites and rarely lasts more than one sitting.

Pour the cream into a medium-sized saucepan. Stir in the coffee beans. Heat over very low heat. Simmer for 30 minutes.

Whisk together the sugar and egg yolks in a stainless steel bowl until well combined. Place a fine mesh sieve over a separate bowl and pour the cream-coffee mixture through the sieve to separate the coffee beans from the cream mixture. Return the cream mixture to the saucepan and rewarm gently.

Whisking constantly, add about 3 Tbsp (45 mL) of the warm cream mixture to the yolk-sugar mixture. This slowly tempers the yolks, getting them used to some heat without cooking them. Very slowly, in a thin stream, pour the remaining cream mixture into the yolk mixture, whisking constantly. Pour the whole mixture back into the saucepan. Cook, stirring constantly, until the mixture thickens enough to coat the back of a spoon, about 5 minutes. Do not allow the mixture to come to a boil

Remove the custard from the heat. Pour in the cream and the brewed coffee. Transfer the mixture to a bowl and stir until well combined. Place a piece of plastic wrap directly on the surface of the custard. Refrigerate until completely chilled. Freeze in an ice cream machine according to the manufacturer's directions.

BAKER'S TIP

To tell if a custard has sufficiently thickened, stir a wooden spoon around the custard. Remove the spoon from the saucepan and, holding perpendicular to your chest or chin, draw your finger across the back of the custard-coated spoon. If the line stays as it is, with no custard dripping down into the line you made, then your custard is fully thickened. If the line fills in quickly, it needs more cooking.

Rich Chocolate Ice Cream

ICE CREAM, per se, does not really file under the heading of baked goods. But ice cream looms large in the realm of family favourites. There's rarely a time when I don't have ice cream in my freezer. It also looms large in the highlights of my career. When I was a pastry chef at David Wood Food Shop in Toronto, we used to rent out or borrow the restaurant beside the main shop (a restaurant at that time called Lakes) to host dinner parties. One of my favourite parts of this, other than concocting up a fanciful and decadent dessert, was planning the sorbets that would delineate each course. I could be as whimsical as I wanted or as serious as I deemed fit, within the confines of making sure that they properly distinguished each course and acted as an entremets or intermezzo (a light sorbet served in between courses to cleanse the palate).

The second part ice cream plays in my professional past is when, as Director of the test kitchen at *Canadian Living Magazine,* the food team was lucky enough to host Julia Child for lunch. While other well-known Canadian chefs (Jamie Kennedy, Anne Desjardins, John Bishop) concentrated furiously on feeding her the main course, I was given the privilege of ending the meal. I served poached pears ensconced in a buttery puff pastry served with a fresh pear ice cream. And I will NEVER forget the "AHH" that Julia breathed out when she tasted that ice cream. So...

2 cups (500 mL) whipping cream, at room temperature

1 cup (250 mL) half and half cream, at room temperature

6 egg yolks, at room temperature

¾ cup (180 mL) granulated sugar

5 oz (150 g) bittersweet chocolate, coarsely chopped

3 Tbsp (45 mL) unsweetened Dutch-processed cocoa powder

1½ tsp (7 mL) vanilla

In a heavy saucepan, heat the whipping cream and half and half until tiny bubbles form around the edge.

In a bowl, whisk together the yolks and sugar. Whisking constantly, add about 3 Tbsp (45 mL) of the warm cream mixture to the yolk-sugar mixture. This slowly tempers the yolks, getting them used to some heat without cooking them. Whisking constantly, gradually pour the remaining warm cream mixture into the yolk mixture. Return the mixture to the saucepan; cook, stirring constantly with a wooden spoon, over medium-low heat until the mixture thickens enough to coat the back of the spoon, about 5 minutes. Do not allow the mixture to come to a boil.

Pour the custard through a fine mesh sieve into a clean bowl. This is simply a precaution in case some of the egg has slightly curdled. Add the chopped chocolate, cocoa and vanilla, stirring until the chocolate is completely melted and smooth. Place a piece of plastic wrap directly on the surface of the custard. Refrigerate until completely chilled. Freeze in an ice cream machine according to the manufacturer's directions.

CHEESECAKES

I have an absurdly large amount to say about cheesecakes and the proper way to make them. My pet peeve is cheesecake recipes that start to bake cheesecakes in a really hot oven, say 400°F (200°C) or 450°F (230°C). I think it's a misguided notion to help set the cheesecake, but nothing could be farther from the truth. Cheesecakes are fragile creations and you don't want to shock them in any way. They need tender loving, steady care. Read on to find out why.

Cheesecakes are essentially really, really large custards. They just happen to be made with cream cheese. And much like custards, cheesecakes fall into one of two categories (this is putting aside no-bake cheesecakes for the moment), those made with starch and those made without. Adding starch to a cheesecake, be it in the form of flour or cornstarch, affects both the cooking method and the texture.

A cheesecake made without starch, as the ones in my book are, tends to come out incredibly smooth. And if it has sour cream in it, as mine do, then it will be incredibly creamy, sensuous and luxurious.

In the absence of a starch, cheesecakes rely on eggs for their thickening power. Without getting too scientific about it, thickening happens when the proteins in the eggs unwind and start to link together. Egg yolks also contain natural emulsifiers, which help provide a smooth texture.

Cheesecakes made without starch are in even more need of a gentle, even heat to bake properly. A gentle approach at the right temperature cooks the proteins just enough to make them loosely link together to form a thick but smooth texture. If the heat nudges up even a bit, the proteins tighten up and curds result. Hence, the need for a water bath. It provides a calm, soothing, steady environment in which the cheesecake can do its thing—that is to say, set, and not poof too much or expand too much. The water allows the heat to stay constant, another important element for baking cheesecakes. Wild fluctuations in temperature can wreak havoc with cheesecakes. That's why I don't suggest you start it off in a hot oven and reduce the temperature, That's also why I leave the cheesecake in a turned-off oven for 1 hour before exposing it to the colder room temperature air.

The same reasoning applies to whipping your eggs. Just beat them until they are mixed in. Too much beating will encourage the custard batter to expand too much in the oven. Without any flour, the cake has no foundation and the only place for the batter to go is down, resulting in unwanted cracks.

Bake your cheesecakes until they are still quite jiggly in the centre. Remember, they will continue to bake, albeit at a much lower temperature, in the turned-off oven. They will also firm up once they have chilled.

Cracks are due to overbeating, over-baking, exposure to sudden changes in temperature and too high of a heat.

Cheesecakes made with a starch can withstand a slightly higher oven temperature and are not as reliant on a water bath, although I would still use one for insurance purposes. These cheesecakes tend to be firmer but still creamy.

When making a cheesecake, opt for a high-sided springform pan, since it's rather impossible to get a cheesecake out of a regular cake pan in one piece. If a water bath is called for, wrap the cheesecake in an extra large piece of aluminum foil, bracing the extra foil around the exterior sides of the pan. I like to bring some water to a boil before I start beating the cream cheese and then let it cool before I pour the hot water into the roasting pan for a bain-marie. Ideally, the pan in which you place the cheesecake should be just a few inches wider than the springform and about the same height. A higher-sided pan will slow down the baking time.

Vanilla Cheesecake

CRUST

1¾ cups (430 mL) graham cracker crumbs

1 Tbsp (15 mL) granulated sugar

¼ cup (60 mL) unsalted butter, melted and cooled (2 oz/60 g)

FILLING

1 lb (500 g) cream cheese, softened (two 250 g pkgs)

¾ cup (180 mL) granulated sugar

2 tsp (10 mL) vanilla

3 large eggs, at room temperature

2 cups (500 mL) sour cream, at room temperature

A WONDERFUL blank canvas on which to build your repertoire. This cheesecake is lovely on its own, and it's even more impressive served with a fresh peach sauce or a raspberry purée. However, it's also a great base for a marble chocolate cheesecake, a raspberry cheesecake, a mocha or coffee cheesecake. See the variations at the bottom of the recipe for more ideas.

CRUST Preheat the oven to 325°F (160°C). Lightly grease the bottom of an 8½- or 9-inch (22 or 23 cm) springform pan. Line the bottom with a circle of parchment paper cut to fit. Centre the pan on a very large piece of aluminum foil; press the foil against the sides of the pan.

Stir together the crumbs, sugar and butter in a small bowl until the crumbs are thoroughly moistened. Press onto the bottom of the prepared springform, using the back of a spoon to pat it down evenly. Bake in the centre of the preheated oven for 10 minutes. Let cool slightly.

FILLING Meanwhile, in the bowl of a stand mixer fitted with the paddle attachment, or using hand-held beaters, beat the cream cheese until fluffy. Scrape down the sides of the bowl. In a thin stream, gradually add the sugar, pausing halfway through to scrape down the side of the bowl. It's really important to scrape down the sides of the bowl so that when you add the eggs, there aren't any clumps in the mixture but rather a smooth homogenous batter. One at a time, beat in the eggs on low speed, making sure that each one is completely incorporated before adding the next. It's important to do this step on low speed because you don't want to introduce too much air at this juncture. Too much air will actually encourage the cheesecake to leaven in the oven. Since there's no foundation to support any height, the cake has to fall, resulting in cracks.

Blend in the vanilla. Remove the bowl from the mixer and using a plastic spatula, fold in the sour cream. Pour the batter on top of the cooled crust in the springform.

Place the springform pan in a larger roasting pan. Pour enough hot water into the roasting pan, avoiding the springform altogether, to come halfway up the sides of the springform.

Bake in the centre of the preheated oven until the cake is just set around the edges but still somewhat jiggly in the centre, 60–70 minutes. Turn the oven off. Let the cake cool down in the turned-off oven for 60 minutes. Remove the cake and the roasting pan from the oven. Remove the springform from the water bath. Remove the foil and let the cheesecake cool on a wire rack until it is at room temperature. Cover with plastic wrap and refrigerate for at least 12 hours or up to 2 days.

To serve, run a thin knife around the edge of the cake. Remove the sides. Wedge a small knife between the cake and the bottom of the springform to loosen the cake. Remove the bottom of the springform, remove the parchment paper and transfer the cake to a cake plate. Serve slightly chilled or at room temperature.

VARIATIONS

BLUEBERRY-TOPPED CHEESECAKE Make the cake as above and serve with a blueberry sauce. Combine 4 cups (1 L) of fresh or frozen blueberries, 3 Tbsp (45 mL) granulated sugar, 3 Tbsp (45 mL) water, 2 Tbsp (30 mL) freshly squeezed lemon juice and a pinch of cinnamon in a saucepan. Bring to a boil. Dissolve 4 tsp (20 mL) of cornstarch in 1 Tbsp (15 mL) water. Stir into the boiling mixture and bring it back to a boil. Cook, stirring, until thickened, 3–5 minutes. Let cool. Makes 2 cups (500 ml) of sauce.

GINGER CHEESECAKE Crush about 30 regular-sized gingersnap cookies to make 1¾ cups (430 mL) of crumbs, replacing the graham cracker crumbs. Combine with the sugar and butter as a base. Stir 2 Tbsp (30 mL) of finely chopped crystallized ginger and 2 Tbsp (30 mL) of finely chopped fresh ginger into the batter along with the sour cream.

DULCE DE LECHE CHEESECAKE Substitute 1¾ cups (430 mL) of crushed vanilla wafer crumbs for the graham cracker crumbs. After transferring the cheesecake batter to the prepared pan, swirl ¾ cup (180 mL) of Dulce de Leche sauce (see p. 118) into the batter.

RECIPE CONTINUED . . .

CHOCOLATE PEANUT BUTTER CHEESECAKE Substitute 1¾ cups (430 mL) of chocolate wafer crumbs for the graham cracker crumbs. Beat ½ cup (125 mL) of smooth peanut butter into the cream cheese before adding the granulated sugar. Bake and cool as directed. Once the cheesecake has been removed from the springform, bring ¾ cup (180 mL) of whipping cream to a boil. Pour over 6 oz (175 g) of finely chopped semisweet chocolate and whisk together until smooth. Let the ganache mixture cool slightly and then pour over the cheesecake, allowing any excess to drip down the sides.

CAPPUCCINO CHEESECAKE Substitute 1½ cups (375 mL) of chocolate wafer crumbs for the graham cracker crumbs. After the sour cream has been folded in, fold in 2 Tbsp (30 mL) of instant espresso powder and ¼ tsp (1 mL) cinnamon. Bake as directed.

Pumpkin Cheesecake

I**F YOU'RE** making pumpkin cheesecake, the main point of the matter is pumpkin. Even though you're combining it with cream cheese, eggs and sugar, the overwhelming flavour should be pumpkin, not cheese, not eggs and certainly not an overabundance of spices. I've kept the spices to a minimum here to allow the unadulterated pumpkin flavour full self-determination. I've also added 1 Tbsp (15 mL) of flour to help absorb some of the pumpkin's moisture.

Preheat the oven to 325°F (160°C). Lightly grease the bottom of a 10-inch (25 cm) springform pan. Line the bottom with a circle of parchment paper cut to fit. Centre the pan on a very large piece of aluminum foil; press the foil against the sides of the pan.

CRUST Stir together the crumbs, sugar and butter in a small bowl until the crumbs are thoroughly moistened. Press onto the bottom of the prepared springform, using the back of a spoon to pat it down evenly. Bake in the centre of the preheated oven for 10 minutes. Let cool slightly.

FILLING Meanwhile, in the bowl of a stand mixer fitted with the paddle attachment, or using a hand-held mixer, beat the cream cheese until fluffy. Scrape down the sides of the bowl. Beat in the sugar. Beat until thoroughly incorporated, scraping down the sides of the bowl twice, about 5 minutes. It's really important so scrape down the sides of the bowl so that when you add the pumpkin, there aren't any clumps in the mixture but rather a smooth homogenous batter. Add the pumpkin and the cream. Beat for 1 minute or until smooth. Scrape down the sides of the bowl. Beat in the flour, cinnamon and nutmeg. One at a time, beat in the eggs on low speed, beating well after each egg before adding the next. It's important to do this step on low speed because you don't want to introduce too much air at this juncture. Pour the batter on top of the cooled crust in the springform.

Place the springform pan in a larger roasting pan. Pour enough hot water into the roasting pan, avoiding the springform altogether, to come halfway up the sides of the springform.

RECIPE CONTINUED . . .

CRUST

1¾ cups (430 mL) gingersnap cookie crumbs (about 30 regular-sized gingersnaps)

1 Tbsp (15 mL) granulated sugar

¼ cup (60 mL) unsalted butter, melted and cooled (2 oz/60 g)

FILLING

1 lb (500 g) cream cheese, softened (two 250 g pkgs)

¾ cup (180 mL) packed light brown sugar

1 cup (250 mL) canned pumpkin

½ cup (125 mL) whipping cream, at room temperature

1 Tbsp (15 mL) all-purpose flour

½ tsp (2 mL) cinnamon

¼ tsp (1 mL) nutmeg

3 large eggs, at room temperature

GARNISH

½ cup (125 mL) granulated sugar

¼ cup (60 mL) water

18 pecan halves

Bake in the centre of the preheated oven until the cake is just set around the edges but still somewhat jiggly in the centre, 45–55 minutes. Turn the oven off. Let the cake cool down in the turned-off oven for 60 minutes. Remove the cake and the roasting pan from the oven. Remove the springform from the water bath. Remove the foil and let the cheesecake cool on a wire rack until it is at room temperature. Cover with plastic wrap and refrigerate for at least 12 hours or up to 2 days.

GARNISH Place the sugar in a small saucepan. Stir in ¼ cup (60 mL) water and set the saucepan over medium-high heat. Cook, without stirring, until the sugar is dissolved. Cook, brushing down the sides of the pan with a brush dipped in cold water, for 5–8 minutes until the mixture turns a deep golden colour. Immediately remove from the heat. Using tongs or tweezers, submerge half of each pecan into the sugar until coated. Place on a piece of parchment. Working quickly, repeat with remaining pecan halves. If the sugar begins to harden too much, simply return the saucepan to a low heat for a few minutes to reliquefy the sugar.

To serve, run a thin knife around the edge of the cake. Remove the sides. Wedge a small knife between the cake and the bottom of the springform to loosen the cake. Remove the bottom of the springform, remove the parchment paper and transfer the cake to a cake plate. Line the edge with the sugar-kissed pecan halves. Serve slightly chilled or at room temperature.

BAKER'S TIP
Springform bottoms come with a flat side and a ridged side. For best results and easier removal, make sure that the flat side is on the inside of the cake pan. The ridge makes it more difficult to remove the cake or cheesecake from the pan.

Light-as-a-Feather Lemon Mousse Cheesecake

THERE'S A FULL ⅔ cup (160 mL) of freshly squeezed lemon juice in this cheesecake—so much lemon juice that you have to add it gradually lest you break the cream cheese and sugar emulsion. To add more pizzaz, there's also 2 Tbsp (30 mL) of lemon zest, bringing the lemon quotient way up. This is, without a doubt, a lemony cheesecake. It's also light as a feather, and rich, due to the addition of an extra egg yolk. You can enjoy it on its own but if you're having company, take the time to make the candied lemon garnish, it polishes the cake up smartly.

Preheat the oven to 325°F (160°C). Lightly grease the bottom of a 9-inch (23 cm) springform pan. Line the bottom with a circle of parchment paper cut to fit. Centre the pan on a very large piece of aluminum foil; press the foil against the sides of the pan.

CRUST Stir together the crumbs, sugar and butter in a small bowl until the crumbs are thoroughly moistened. Press onto the bottom of the prepared springform, using the back of a spoon to pat it down evenly. Bake in the centre of the preheated oven for 10 minutes. Let cool slightly.

FILLING Meanwhile, in the bowl of a stand mixer fitted with the paddle attachment, or using a hand-held mixer, beat the cream cheese until fluffy. Scrape down the sides of the bowl. In a thin stream, gradually add the sugar, pausing halfway through to scrape down the side of the bowl. It's really important to scrape down the sides of the bowl so that when you add the lemon juice there aren't any clumps in the mixture but rather a smooth homogenous batter. Beat in the lemon zest. Pour in one-third of the lemon juice. Beat until the juice is well incorporated. Scrape down the sides of the bowl. Beat in another third of the juice. Scrape down the sides of the bowl. Beat in the remaining juice. One at a time, beat in the eggs on low speed, making sure that each egg is completely incorporated before adding the next. It's important to do this step on low speed because you don't want to introduce too much air at this juncture. Too much air will actually encourage the cheesecake to leaven in the oven and will inevitably encourage cracks, since once leavened it has no foundation to support

CRUST

1½ cups (375 mL) crushed vanilla wafer cookies

2 Tbsp (30 mL) granulated sugar

¼ cup (60 mL) unsalted butter, melted and cooled (2 oz/60 g)

FILLING

1 lb (500 g) cream cheese, softened (two 250 g pkgs)

¾ cup (180 mL) granulated sugar

2 Tbsp (30 mL) finely grated lemon zest

⅔ cup (160 mL) freshly squeezed lemon juice

3 large eggs, at room temperature

1 egg yolk, at room temperature

1 cup (250 mL) sour cream, at room temperature

CANDIED LEMON PEEL GARNISH

1 lemon, washed and scrubbed well

2¼ cups (560 mL) granulated sugar, divided

1 cup (250 mL) water

RECIPE CONTINUED . . .

it and will automatically fall. Beat in the egg yolk. Remove the bowl from the mixer and, using a plastic spatula, fold in the sour cream. Pour the batter on top of the cooled crust in the springform.

Place the springform pan in a larger roasting pan. Pour enough hot water into the roasting pan, avoiding the springform altogether, to come halfway up the sides of the springform.

Bake in the centre of the preheated oven until the cake is just set around the edges but still somewhat jiggly in the centre, about 70 minutes. Turn the oven off. Let the cake cool down in the turned-off oven for 60 minutes. Remove the cake and the roasting pan from the oven. Remove the springform from the water bath. Remove the foil and let the cheesecake cool on a wire rack until it is at room temperature. Cover with plastic wrap and refrigerate for at least 12 hours or up to 2 days.

CANDIED LEMON PEEL GARNISH Using a vegetable peeler, peel off the lemon peel from the lemon, being careful to not include any of the white bitter pith. Slice each piece into thin strips, about ⅛ inch (3 mm) wide.

Bring a small pot of water to a boil. Add the lemon peel strips and cook gently until tender, about 5 minutes. Drain and cool the lemon peel for a few minutes. Meanwhile, combine 1½ cups (375 mL) of the sugar with 1 cup (250 mL) water in a saucepan. Bring to a boil. Add the lemon peel and cook over medium heat until the lemon is translucent and the liquid has thickened slightly, about 8 minutes. Drain the lemon and let cool on a wire rack for about 1 hour.

Place the remaining ¾ cup (180 mL) of sugar in a small bowl. Toss the cooled lemon pieces in the sugar until well coated.

To serve, run a thin knife around the edge of the cake. Remove the sides. Wedge a small knife between the cake and the bottom of the springform pan to loosen the cake. Remove the bottom of the springform pan, remove the parchment paper and transfer the cake to a cake plate. Garnish with the candied lemon peel.

This is a very delicate cheesecake so it should be served right out of the fridge and should not be brought to room temperature.

PIES, TARTS AND FRUIT DESSERTS

401   PASTRY PRIMER

407   Fresh Fruit Tart with Shortcrust Pastry

409   Double Blueberry Tart with Almond
         Shortbread Pastry

411   Bluberry Pie with Sour Cream Pastry

414   Blueberry Tart with Lemon Curd and Oat
         Pastry

417   Apple Pie

420   Country Apple Cranberry Galette

422   French Apple Tart

424   Tarte Tatin with Quick Puff Pastry

426   Just Peachy Peach Pie

428   Peach Blueberry Gingersnap Galette

431   Beurre Noisette Tart with Strawberries

433   Hand-Held Tarts with Rhubarb
         Strawberry Filling

435   Anise-Scented Rhubarb Tart

437   Plum Raspberry Crostata

440   Fresh Fig and Raspberry Tart with
         Mascarpone and Honey

442   Fresh Apricot Custard Tarts

444   Blackberry Buttermilk Pie

446   Pear Frangipane Tart

448   Tarte au Citron

451   Lemon Meringue Pie Cups

453   Pumpkin Pie

455   Banana Cream Pie

458   Pecan Pie

460   As-Canadian-As-They-Come Butter Tarts

462   Chocolate Caramel Nut Tart

465   Apple Berry Crisp

466   Nectarine Cobbler with
         Spiced Biscuits

Pastry is one area of baking where you can be both a technician as well as an artisan. In fact, both are required. A technician, because there is a lot of theory required to understand how to make good pastry, though the information is easy to process and easy to follow. An artisan, not only because you will be the author of the pies and tarts you make, and the sole arbiter of what fruits and flavours are going to be combined, but mostly because it will be your hands that get to know the essence of good pastry and that will produce great pastry.

There's no real substitute for your hands and what they know and feel instinctively when making pastry. It does take some practice, but I assure you, you will get there. I distinctly remember when my hands became their own pastry master. I was making pastry for the first time upon my arrival in Italy. At that point I didn't know that the flour in Italy was much softer than the flour in North America. I started off making my usual shortcrust pastry and before it registered in my brain, my hands could tell that something was dreadfully off. The pastry was simply not coming together as it should. I tried again, adding the liquid by feeling the dough, by listening to my hands and lo and behold, I ended up making great pastry with unfamiliar flour.

It's your hands that will tell you, after kneading the dough lightly together (see the section on fraisage, p. 402), whether your dough stretches easily and therefore will be amenable to rolling. It's your hands that will tell you if your dough is too cold to roll or whether it's just right.

PASTRY PRIMER

THE TECHNIQUE BEHIND FINE PASTRY

Much like when you make biscuits, making pastry involves cutting very cold butter into a mixture of flour, salt and sometimes a bit of sugar. The cold butter is cut into the pastry until it resembles the size of peas that should be visually distinct from the flour mixture. Then just enough liquid—be it in the form of water, cream, eggs or milk—is added to the mixture until a dough is formed, surrounding and enveloping the butter pieces, which again you should be able to see as distinct pieces. The rolling of the dough itself helps to flatten these pieces of butter into flakes, in between the layers of dough. As the dough bakes, the flakes melt, pushing apart the layers of dough around them and creating a flaky pastry.

Sounds easy and straightforward, yet so many people I know are totally intimidated by the spectre of making pies or tarts. Let's break it down a little and banish the fear altogether.

Use regular or unbleached all-purpose flour. Cake and pastry flour, in spite of its name, has too little gluten to keep the pastry strong and bread flour has too much protein.

Always use unsalted butter. Too much salt can toughen your pastry and can make it absorb too much water. In addition, make sure your butter is very cold. Some people prefer to use frozen butter. Butter has a very low melting point, about 94°F (34°C), which means that your hands can easily soften or even melt the butter, allowing it to blend with the flour as opposed to remaining separate. No flakes and separation, no flaky pastry.

CUTTING IN THE BUTTER

You can cut in the butter using a pastry cutter, your hands or a food processor. If you opt to use a food processor, get used to the sounds your food processor makes. After a few spins, you will hear when the fat is broken down enough. Whether using your hands or the food processor, do not cut the pieces of butter too small or they won't be able to do their job.

The usual ratio of flour to butter in good pastry is three parts flour to one part butter or fat.

I think the trickiest part for a novice baker is knowing how much liquid to add. This can vary depending on where you live, on the season and even on what type of flour you're using. The best course of action is to add the minimum amount of very cold water or liquid called for in the recipe and to check the dough after that. If a clump of dough holds together in your palm, without seeming too sticky or wet, then the dough is ready to be gently kneaded and formed into a ball. If the handful of dough does not clump together, then a bit more liquid is required. I am not an advocate of adding the water a bit at a time, especially if you are using a food processor. It causes gluten to develop unevenly in the dough, with more gluten bonds forming in some areas of the dough and less in others, leaving a dough that may become tough. The key is to add just enough liquid to form a cohesive dough, but not so much that the dough is sticky or wet.

If you are using a food processor, never add the liquid while the machine is running. The liquid will be unevenly distributed, causing gluten bonds to develop in some areas and not in others. Always take off the top of the food processor and drizzle your liquid all around the bowl, distributing it evenly among the flour mixture. Never process the dough so much that it comes together in a ball. There's virtually no chance of this happening if you're making pastry with your hands. The speed of the processor, however, makes this an identifiable risk. Pulse only, and pulse just until a shaggy mass is created. With beginning bakers, I often advise them to remove the flour mixture from the food processor to a bowl after the butter has been cut in. The liquid can then be added to the bowl and fluffed with a fork, giving you more control of the procedure.

Using very cold liquid helps keep the butter firm.

WORKING THE DOUGH—HOW MUCH IS ENOUGH?

After I remove the shaggy mass from the food processor or my bowl, I use a French technique called *fraisage*, to bring it together. This is slightly different than kneading, although you can gently and lightly knead the mass into a ball as well. When you use the *fraisage* technique, you are actually assisting in the formation of long strands of butter within the dough. To accomplish this, you use the palm of your hand to smear the barely mixed dough together, moving the dough a quarter turn in between each smear, until the mass comes together in a cohesive ball of dough. You have to work quite quickly so that you don't melt the butter. Overworking the dough will also result in a tough dough and a couple of tears.

Flatten the dough into a disc to facilitate rolling, wrap well in plastic wrap and refrigerate.

WHY CHILL THE DOUGH?

Chilling the dough allows the gluten strands to relax (less toughness, less shrinkage in the oven) and gives the flour the necessary time to hydrate

by absorbing some of the liquid. Chilling ensures that the butter remains cold. Relaxing the gluten not only makes for a more tender crust but it also makes rolling the dough that much easier. Avoid chilling the just made pastry in the freezer because it will set too quickly.

WHAT IS THE DIFFERENCE BETWEEN FLAKY AND TENDER DOUGH?

The ideal pastry crust is often termed "tender flaky." Yet, this is really a contradiction in baking terms. They are separate qualities, achieved by different ingredients.

Flaky pastry is characterized by thin, crisp layers of pastry and is achieved by flattening cold butter between layers of dough or flour. The fat has to be cold to allow the dough to start to cook in the oven before the butter starts to melt. Then, as the butter melts, steam from the dough pushes the layers apart. The more layers of fat, the flakier the crust. In flaky pastry, the pieces of butter must be large enough that they won't melt instantly in the hot oven, but not so large that they leave holes in the dough as they melt.

Tender pastry, on the other hand, is pastry that crumbles easily, like shortbread cookies. This is achieved by using a soft fat such as shortening which coats the flour, preventing it from bonding together into gluten.

Flaky tender pastry results when both fats, cold butter and shortening are used. The softer shortening coats the proteins in the flour and the harder fat produces the flakiness.

If truth be told, lard is the fat that provides the most flakiness, not butter, but it has mostly gone out of favour. Still, you can certainly use it if you like.

ROLLING: WHAT IT CONTRIBUTES

If you refrigerate your dough for longer than 1 hour, it may be too firm to roll directly from the refrigerator. Place it on your work surface, still covered in plastic wrap, and let it rest for about 20 minutes, until it is still cold but pliable.

Rolling your dough actually promotes flakiness. As pieces of fat are rolled and flattened, they actually grease the flour around them, coating the proteins yet remaining intact enough to form layers as the crust bakes.

Remember to flour your work surface lightly with flour and to also flour the top of your pastry with flour. As long as your pastry is cold, it will not absorb too much flour. Some pastry chefs steadfastly believe that a pastry cloth is the only way to go. This is a sleeve that slips over the rolling pin and is lightly dusted with flour. Pastry sleeves, they contend, prevent the dough from picking up any excess flour. Personally, I keep a pastry brush reserved for brushing off excess flour.

Most pastries take about 40 minutes to bake fully. The exception to this is some shortcrust pastries that need to be blind baked and can take as little as 30 minutes. Fully-baked pastry crust is flaky, golden brown and should be delicious eaten out of hand.

Fresh Fruit Tart *with* Shortcrust Pastry

I HAVE been making this wonderfully buttery pastry ever since I was a pastry chef. It's easy, tender and sweet. One of the members of my team at the time was a lovely woman named Tsu Yung, who spoke almost no English but was devoted to the pastry department. I remember sending her home with this recipe, as well as others, so that her son could translate them, on cue cards, into Chinese. Every day, Tsu Yung would come into work, make this pastry in a large Hobart mixing machine and then press the pastry, perfectly, into 100 tart tins. It's best made with plain old white vinegar, but in a pinch, you can use cider vinegar.

The pastry cream in this recipe, unlike other pastry creams that call for egg yolks, calls for whole eggs. The whole egg makes for a lighter pastry cream with barely a loss of richness. Using both all-purpose flour and cornstarch contributes to the lightness as well.

SHORTBREAD PASTRY In the bowl of a food processor fitted with the metal "S" blade, or in a large bowl, pulse or whisk together the flour, sugar and salt until well mixed and slightly aerated. Cut the butter into cubes and add to the food processor or the bowl. Pulse in food processor or cut in with a pastry cutter (or 2 knives) until the flour resembles coarse meal with the butter the size of peas. Drizzle the vinegar over and pulse or fluff the mixture until it is lightly but evenly moistened. The mixture will NOT come into a ball but should remain crumbly. Using handfuls of the mixture at a time, lightly hand knead the dough until it comes together in a clump. I know this flies in the face of good pastry making since you're essentially using the heat of your hands to help the dough come together, but because this pastry is more like a shortbread with a high proportion of fat (in this case, butter), it won't toughen. Press the clumps of shortbread evenly onto the bottom and sides of a 9-inch (23 cm) round French tart tin with a removable bottom. Chill for at least 40 minutes or for up to 2 days.

PASTRY CREAM Meanwhile, make the pastry cream: Bring the milk to a simmer in a saucepan set over medium heat. In a bowl, whisk together the egg, sugar, flour and cornstarch. Very gradually and whisking constantly, pour the hot milk into the egg mixture. Return the mixture to

SHORTBREAD PASTRY

1½ cups (375 mL) all-purpose flour

¼ cup (60 mL) granulated sugar

Pinch of salt

¾ cup (180 mL) cold unsalted butter (6 oz/175 mL)

2 tsp (10 mL) white vinegar

PASTRY CREAM

1 cup (250 mL) milk, at room temperature

1 large egg

¼ cup (60 mL) granulated sugar

1 Tbsp (15 mL) all-purpose flour

2 tsp (10 mL) cornstarch

2 Tbsp (30 mL) unsalted butter, in pieces (1 oz/30 g)

½ tsp (2 mL) vanilla

FRUIT TOPPING

2–3 cups (500–750 mL) fruit of your choice

RECIPE CONTINUED . . .

the saucepan. Cook over medium heat, whisking constantly, for about 5 minutes or until the mixture is thickened. Remove the saucepan from the heat. Whisk in the butter until it is melted and the mixture is smooth. Stir in the vanilla. Transfer the custard to a clean bowl. Place plastic wrap directly on the surface and refrigerate for at least 2 hours or for up to 2 days.

Preheat the oven to 375°F (190°C). Place the tart shell on a baking sheet. Place a piece of parchment paper in the tart tin. Fill it with pie weights. Bake the tart in the centre of the preheated oven for 20 minutes. Carefully remove the parchment paper and the pie weights. Prick the bottom of the tart shell all over with the tines of a fork. Bake for an additional 10 minutes or until the pastry is golden. Cool the pastry completely in the tart tin on a wire rack.

ASSEMBLY Remove the sides of the tart tin. Run a small knife between the bottom and the pastry and gently slide the tart shell onto a flat serving plate. The plate should not be rimmed or even curved upwards as this may encourage the tart shell to break.

Scrape the chilled pastry cream into the baked tart shell, spreading it so that it is even and smooth. Top with fresh fruit. Refrigerate for at least 30 minutes or for up to 6 hours. Bring to room temperature for 10 minutes before serving.

BAKER'S TIP

SHORTCRUST Any pastry that is titled short means that it has a higher proportion of fat to flour than is common in a flaky dough. Called *pâte sablée* in French, it's crunchier, more tender and more cookie-like than a typical pie dough. In shortcrust pastry, the added amount of fat—almost always butter—actually coats the gluten strands, preventing them from combining with other strands so that they form long, tight bonds. In this manner, it's the butter that "shortens" the gluten strands, ensuring a dough that is tender and crumbly.

Double Blueberry Tart *with* Almond Shortbread Pastry

DOUBLE BECAUSE it has both a cooked blueberry filling as well as fresh blueberries stirred into the cooked mixture. It's also extraordinary because of the way the crisp and crumbly shortbread contrasts with the soft, sweet blueberry filling, and it's easy because it's a pat-in shortcrust pastry flavoured by the addition of almonds.

ALMOND SHORTBREAD PASTRY In the bowl of a food processor fitted with the metal "S" blade, pulse together the flour, almonds, sugar and salt until the almonds are completely ground. Cut the butter into cubes and add to the food processor, or transfer the mixture to a bowl and add the butter cubes to the bowl. Pulse in the food processor or cut in with a pastry cutter (or 2 knives) until the flour resembles coarse meal with butter the size of peas. Drizzle the vinegar over and pulse or fluff the mixture until it is evenly but lightly moistened. The mixture will NOT come into a ball but should remain crumbly. Using handfuls of the mixture at a time, lightly hand knead the dough until it comes together in a clump. I know this flies in the face of good pastry making since you're essentially using the heat of your hands to help the dough come together, but because this pastry is more like a shortbread with a high proportion of fat (in this case, butter), it won't toughen. Press the clumps of shortbread evenly onto the bottom and sides of a 9-inch (23 cm) round French tart tin with a removable bottom. Chill for at least 40 minutes or for up to 2 days.

Preheat the oven to 375°F (190°C). Place the tart shell on a baking sheet. Place a piece of parchment paper in the tart pan. Fill it with pie weights. Bake the tart in the centre of the preheated oven for 20 minutes. Carefully remove the parchment paper and the pie weights. Prick the bottom of the tart shell all over with the tines of a fork. Bake for an additional 10 minutes or until the pastry is golden. Cool the pastry completely in the tart tin on a wire rack.

BLUEBERRY FILLING Stir together the lemon zest, sugar and cornstarch in a bowl; set aside.

Place 1½ cups (375 mL) of the blueberries, the water and lemon juice in a saucepan set over medium-high heat. Bring to a boil. Reduce the heat

ALMOND SHORTBREAD PASTRY

1⅓ cups (330 mL) all-purpose flour

⅓ cup (80 mL) slivered almonds

¼ cup (60 mL) granulated sugar

Pinch of salt

¾ cup (180 mL) cold unsalted butter (6 oz/175 g)

2 tsp (10 mL) white vinegar

BLUEBERRY FILLING

2 tsp (10 mL) grated lemon zest

½ cup (125 mL) granulated sugar

2 Tbsp (30 mL) cornstarch

4 cups (1 L) fresh blueberries, divided

½ cup (125 mL) water

2 Tbsp (30 mL) freshly squeezed lemon juice

RECIPE CONTINUED . . .

to low and simmer, stirring occasionally, until the juices have turned a bluish-purple and the blueberries have softened, 3–4 minutes. Stir in the sugar-cornstarch mixture. Stirring constantly, return the mixture to a boil. Cook, stirring, until the mixture is thickened and translucent, 1–2 minutes. Remove the saucepan from the heat. Gently stir in the remaining 2½ cups (625 mL) of the blueberries. Transfer the mixture to a clean bowl, cover the surface directly with a piece of plastic wrap and refrigerate for at least 2 hours or until completely cool.

ASSEMBLY Remove the sides of the tart tin. Run a small knife between the bottom and the pastry and gently slide the tart shell onto a flat serving plate. The plate should not be rimmed or even curved upwards as this may encourage the tart shell to break.

Scrape the blueberry mixture into the prepared pastry shell, smoothing the surface. Serve immediately or refrigerate for up to 24 hours, bringing the tart to room temperature for 30 minutes before serving.

BAKER'S TIP

THE SKINNY ON TARTS Tarts, like pies, can be double crusted, but they primarily have a single bottom crust. Since the sides of a tart tin are usually low, only about 1 inch (2.5 cm) high, the amount of filling in a tart is usually more or less commensurate with the height of the pastry. A pie, in contrast, has much more filling, due to the depth of the pie plate. As a result, eating a tart is very different than eating a pie. Both the filling AND the pastry have to be great, because you're eating as much pastry as you are filling.

Blueberry Pie *with* Sour Cream Pastry

Throughout this chapter I have tried to introduce the reader to as many different pastries as possible (though by no means is this all there are). Sour cream pastry is especially luscious and pairs beautifully with blueberries. That's not to say, however, that you couldn't use the all-butter flaky pastry from the Apple Pie (see p. 411) or the yolk-based pastry used in the Just Peachy Peach Pie (see p. 426) and have excellent results. The crusts can be used interchangeably, depending on what you feel like making, what ingredients you have on hand and your level of confidence. This pie is not overly sweet; you hear the song of the lemon juice behind the blueberries in every bite. Increase the sugar if you prefer your pies sweeter.

SOUR CREAM PASTRY In the bowl of a food processor fitted with the metal "S" blade, or in a large bowl, pulse or whisk together the flour and salt until well mixed and aerated. Cut the butter and shortening into cubes and add to the food processor or the bowl. Pulse in the food processor or cut in with a pastry cutter (or 2 knives) until the flour resembles coarse meal with butter the size of peas. In a small bowl, whisk together the water and sour cream. Pour the sour cream mixture over the flour-butter mixture. Pulse or fluff the mixture until thoroughly moistened and shaggy or clumpy, but not yet formed into a ball. Dump the entire mixture onto a lightly floured work surface. Using the palm of your hand, smear together the dough along the work surface, until it comes together in a cohesive whole or ball. Flatten the dough into a disc. Wrap the dough in plastic wrap and refrigerate it for at least 45 minutes or for up to 2 days.

On a lightly floured work surface, roll out two-thirds of the dough to an 11-inch (28 cm) circle, sprinkling the surface and underside with flour as needed to prevent the dough from sticking to the work surface and to prevent the rolling pin from sticking to the surface of the dough. Roll the dough up around the rolling pin and gently unroll on top of a 9-inch (23 cm) Pyrex or glass pie plate. Gently press the dough into the pie plate. Trim away any ragged edges of the dough and trim the edges so that there is about a ¾-inch (2 cm) overhang. Refrigerate the pie shell while you roll out the top pastry and prepare the blueberry filling.

SOUR CREAM PASTRY

2½ cups (625 mL) all-purpose flour

½ tsp (2 mL) salt

¾ cup (180 mL) cold unsalted butter (6 oz/175 g)

¼ cup (60 mL) cold vegetable shortening

¼ cup (60 mL) cold water

¼ cup (60 mL) cold sour cream

BLUEBERRY FILLING

6 cups (1.5 L) fresh blueberries

1 cup (250 mL) granulated sugar

⅓ cup (80 mL) cornstarch

1 tsp (5 mL) grated lemon zest

3 Tbsp (45 mL) lemon juice

1 tsp (5 mL) cinnamon

1 Tbsp (15 mL) cold unsalted butter, in pieces (0.5 oz/15 g)

TOPPING

1 large egg, beaten, at room temperature

1 Tbsp (15 mL) coarse or Turbinado sugar (optional)

RECIPE CONTINUED . . .

Still working on a lightly floured work surface, roll out the remaining piece of pastry to an 11-inch (28 cm) circle. This will be the top so it will be much thinner than the bottom crust. Gently transfer the circle to a parchment paper–lined baking sheet. Place the baking sheet in the refrigerator.

Preheat the oven to 400°F (200°C).

BLUEBERRY FILLING In a large bowl, using a wooden spoon, stir together the blueberries, sugar, cornstarch, lemon zest, lemon juice and cinnamon until the fruit is well coated with the sugar and the cornstarch.

Remove the pastry-lined pie plate from the refrigerator. Scrape the blueberry filling into the pie shell. Scatter the butter over the filling. Remove the 11-inch (28 cm) pastry circle from the refrigerator. Brush some of the beaten egg over the rim of the bottom crust. Place the top crust on top of the bottom crust, centreing it evenly. Trim the top crust so that it aligns with the edge of the bottom crust's overhang. Gently press the top crust against the bottom crust so that it seals well. Tuck the overhanging pastry together and then roll up to form a thick crust or edge. Crimp the border decoratively with your fingers or the tines of a fork. Using a small sharp knife, cut 3 air vents into the top crust. Transfer the pie to a baking sheet.

Brush the entire surface of the pie with some of the beaten egg. Sprinkle the pie with the coarse sugar, if using.

Bake the pie in the centre of the preheated oven for 20 minutes. Reduce the heat to 350°F (180°C) and bake until the pastry is golden and the fruit filling is thick and bubbling, about an additional 60–70 minutes. Cool the pie on a wire rack until cool. Serve slightly chilled or at room temperature.

BAKER'S TIP

ROLLING Always allow the dough to warm a little at room temperature before rolling it out. If the dough is too cold, you'll end up overworking it and it will probably crack at the edges. Try to roll the dough in the coolest part of your kitchen. After you've lightly floured your work surface with some flour, start to roll the dough from the centre out, using a firm steady pressure, without rolling the pin back and forth too much. It's easier on the pastry if you roll with one fell motion from the centre to the outside, lifting your rolling pin just a touch when it comes to the edge, so that your edges don't become too thin. Turn the dough just a fraction, lifting it to ensure that it's not sticking to your work surface. Then again, roll from the centre to the edge. Repeat this motion until the pastry is rolled out to the size you want. Do not turn the pastry over. The best way to tell if a pastry is evenly rolled out is to lightly glide your hand all over the pastry, using your fingers to check for any inconsistencies. Rolling between two sheets of waxed or parchment paper is also helpful.

If your pastry tears as you're rolling it out, just wet your fingers with a little water, moisten the area around the tear and patch with a piece of dough from the outer circle.

HISTORY NOTE

Etchings depicting pies date as far back as the reign of Ramses II in Egypt. It is known that rudimentary pies made from ground meal and filled with dried fruit and nuts were made during that time. Sweet pies were evidently popular during the Persian Empire. As this form of cookery made its way west, to what is now known as Europe, pies were increasingly filled with meat, game or fish. In 1270, the first pastry guild was formed in France. Even Chaucer made reference to pies in his Prologue to *The Canterbury Tales*, published in 1306.

Blueberry Tart *with* Lemon Curd *and* Oat Pastry

OAT PASTRY

¾ cup (180 mL) large flake rolled oats

¾ cup (180 mL) all-purpose flour

⅓ cup (80 mL) whole-wheat flour

¼ cup (60 mL) packed light brown sugar

½ tsp (2 mL) salt

½ cup (125 mL) cold unsalted butter (4 oz/125 g)

1 cold large egg

2 Tbsp (30 mL) cold whipping cream

LEMON CURD

2 large egg yolks, at room temperature

⅔ cup (160 mL) granulated sugar

⅓ cup (80 mL) lemon juice

¼ cup (60 mL) unsalted butter, cubed (2 oz/60 g)

Pinch of salt

1 Tbsp (15 mL) finely grated lemon zest

TOPPING

2¼ cups (560 mL) fresh blueberries

Icing sugar, to taste

BLUEBERRIES AND lemons are a classic pairing but I've thrown some oats into the mix for this refreshing tart. I've made this pastry for a long time and it has converted many a student. I had one student who had stubbornly refused to make pies for years because of a disaster when she was a young adult. When she heard the class was about pies and tarts, she almost bolted. But she stayed and through the ease of this pastry, became comfortable enough to make it on her own at home. With some encouragement, she lost her fear and is now happy making pies any time of the year.

This is first and foremost a blueberry pie; the layer of lemon curd is thin but enough to provide just the right amount of zing.

———

OAT PASTRY In the bowl of a food processor fitted with the metal "S" blade, or in a large bowl, whisk or pulse together the oats, flours, sugar and salt until well mixed. Cut the butter into cubes and add to the food processor or the bowl. Pulse in the food processor or cut in with a pastry cutter (or 2 knives) until the flour resembles coarse meal, with butter the size of peas amidst a few larger pieces. In a small bowl, whisk together the egg and whipping cream. Pour the egg-cream mixture over the flour-butter mixture. Pulse or fluff the mixture until thoroughly moistened and shaggy or clumpy, but not yet formed into a ball. Dump the entire mixture onto a lightly floured work surface. Using the palm of your hand, smear together the dough along the work surface, until it comes together in a cohesive whole or ball. Flatten the dough into a disc. Wrap the dough in plastic wrap and refrigerate for at least 1 hour or for up to 3 days.

LEMON CURD In a bowl large enough to sit on top of a medium-sized saucepan, gently whisk together the egg yolks, sugar, lemon juice, butter and salt. Place the bowl over a saucepan of barely simmering water. Cook, whisking occasionally, until the butter has melted and the mixture has thickened enough to coat the back of a wooden spoon. Strain through a fine mesh sieve into a clean bowl to remove any minute cooked bits. Stir in the lemon zest. Place a piece of plastic wrap directly on the surface of the lemon curd and refrigerate for at least 2 hours or for up to 2 days.

Preheat the oven to 375°F (190°C).

On a lightly floured work surface, roll out the dough to an 11-inch (28 cm) circle, sprinkling the surface and underside with flour as needed to prevent the dough from sticking to the work surface and to prevent the rolling pin from sticking to the surface of the dough. Roll the dough up around the rolling pin and gently unroll on top of a 9-inch (23 cm) French tart tin with a removable bottom. Gently press the dough into the pan, into the edges and up the sides. Roll the rolling pin over the pan rim to trim away any excess dough. Place the tart shell on a baking sheet and then place a piece of parchment paper directly onto the tart shell. Fill with pie weights. Bake for 10 minutes.

Remove the tart shell from the oven. Remove the parchment paper and the pie weights. Prick the bottom of the tart shell with the tines of a fork. Return to the oven and bake until golden, about 15 minutes. Cool the pastry completely in the tart tin on a wire rack.

Remove the sides of the tart tin. Run a small knife between the bottom and the pastry and gently slide the tart shell onto a flat serving plate. The plate should not be rimmed or even curved upwards as this may encourage the tart shell to break.

TOPPING Spread the cooled and thickened lemon curd evenly into the pastry shell. Scatter the blueberries over top. The tart can be refrigerated for up to 8 hours.

Bring the tart to room temperature for at least 20 minutes before serving. Sprinkle with icing sugar just before serving.

RECIPE CONTINUED . . .

BAKER'S TIPS

TRANSFERRING THE DOUGH There are two different methods of transferring rolled-out dough to a pie plate or a tart tin. My preferred method is to gently and slowly roll the dough up onto my rolling pin, brushing the underside of the dough to remove any excess flour as I roll it up and over the rolling pin. Then I gently unroll the pastry onto the pie plate or tart tin. Another method that is extremely helpful is to fold the dough into quarters, again brushing off any excess flour from the top and underside. Then place the point of the folded dough right in the centre of the pie plate or tart tin that you will be using, and unfold it gently, lifting it so that it can fit snugly into the bottom and edges of the pan.

TART PANS I always tell people NOT to wash their tart tins with soap and water. Much like a well seasoned cast iron skillet, an oft used tart tin develops a natural patina on it so that pastries, once baked, slip out easily and evenly. Washing them in soap would destroy this patina requiring the baker then to grease the pan. So go ahead and wash it in hot water to remove any residue, but omit the soap if you please.

Apple Pie

〈》》》〉

Apple pie is as old fashioned as they come. And as good as they come. Some authors create apple pie recipes that have you cook the apple filling first so that the bottom crust of your pie doesn't get soggy. Others suggest that you brush the bottom crust with an egg white as protection against the fruit's juices. I have done both with great success but prefer the latter method of using an egg wash if you're going to go the extra step. I personally love the way the juices of the pie seep into the crust so, for this recipe, I have kept things simple. The crust in this pie still gets fully baked and is flaky and toothsome. This is a pie to sit down with, savour and let your mind wander.

ALL-BUTTER FLAKY PASTRY In the bowl of a food processor fitted with the metal "S" blade, or in a large bowl, pulse or whisk together the flour, sugar and salt until well mixed and aerated. Cut the butter into cubes and add to the food processor or the bowl. Pulse in food processor or cut in with a pastry cutter (or 2 knives) until the flour resembles coarse meal, with butter the size of peas amidst a few larger pieces. In a 1-cup (250 mL) wet measure, whisk together the egg and vinegar. Add in enough cold water to measure ⅔ cup (160 mL). Pour about ½ cup (125 mL) of the water mixture over the flour mixture and pulse or toss briefly. If the mixture looks too dry and is not starting to get thoroughly moistened, add the remaining water mixture. Pulse or toss again briefly until the mixture is thoroughly moistened and shaggy or clumpy, but not yet formed into a ball. Dump the entire mixture onto a lightly floured work surface. Using the palm of your hand, smear together the dough along the work surface, until it comes together in a cohesive whole or ball. Flatten the dough into a disc. Wrap the dough in plastic wrap and refrigerate for at least 45 minutes or for up to 2 days.

On a lightly floured work surface, roll out two-thirds of the dough to an 11-inch (28 cm) circle, sprinkling the surface and underside with flour as needed to prevent the dough from sticking to the work surface and to prevent the rolling pin from sticking to the surface of the dough. Roll the dough up around the rolling pin and gently unroll on top of a 9-inch (23 cm) Pyrex or glass pie plate. Gently press the dough into the pie plate. Trim away any ragged edges of the dough and trim the edges so that there is about a ¾-inch (2 cm) overhang. Refrigerate the pie shell while you roll out the top pastry and prepare the apple filling.

RECIPE CONTINUED . . .

ALL-BUTTER FLAKY PASTRY

3 cups (725 mL) all-purpose flour

3 Tbsp (45 mL) granulated sugar

¾ tsp (4 mL) salt

1 cup (250 mL) cold unsalted butter (8 oz/250 g)

1 cold large egg

2 tsp (10 mL) white vinegar

APPLE FILLING

6 large tart apples, peeled, cored and cut into large pieces or wedges

½ cup (125 mL) packed light brown sugar

¼ cup (60 mL) granulated sugar

1 Tbsp (15 mL) grated lemon zest

1 Tbsp (15 mL) freshly squeezed lemon juice

2 Tbsp (30 mL) all-purpose flour

1 tsp (5 mL) cinnamon

¼ tsp (1 mL) ground nutmeg

2 Tbsp (30 mL) cold unsalted butter, in pieces (1 oz/30 g)

TOPPING

1 large egg, beaten, at room temperature

1 Tbsp (15 mL) coarse or Turbinado sugar

Still working on a lightly floured work surface, roll out the remaining piece of pastry to an 11-inch (28 cm) circle. This will be the top so it will be much thinner than the bottom crust. Gently transfer the circle to a parchment paper–lined baking sheet. Place the baking sheet in the refrigerator.

APPLE FILLING Preheat the oven to 400°F (200°C).

In a large bowl, using a wooden spoon, stir together the apples, sugars, lemon zest, lemon juice, flour, cinnamon and nutmeg until the apple slices are well coated with the sugars and the flour.

Remove the pastry-lined pie plate from the refrigerator. Scrape the apple filling into the pie shell. Scatter the butter over the filling. Remove the 11-inch (28 cm) pastry circle from the refrigerator. Brush some of the beaten egg over the rim of the bottom crust. Place the top crust on top of the bottom crust, centreing it evenly. Trim the top crust so that it aligns with the edge of the bottom crust's overhang. Gently press the top crust against the bottom crust so that it seals well. Tuck the overhanging pastry together and then roll up to form a thick crust or edge. Crimp the border decoratively with your fingers or the tines of a fork. Using a small sharp knife, cut 3 air vents into the top crust. Transfer the pie to a baking sheet.

TOPPING Brush the entire surface of the pie with some of the beaten egg. Sprinkle the pie with the coarse sugar.

Bake the pie in the centre of the preheated oven for 20 minutes. Reduce the heat to 350°F (180°C) and bake until the pastry is golden and the fruit filling is thick and bubbling, about an additional 45–50 minutes. Place the pie on a wire rack until cool. Serve warm or at room temperature.

BAKER'S TIP

SHAPING PIE CRUST How large you should roll out your pastry is determined by what shape of pie plate or tart tin you're using as well as what sort of edge or border you want. If you're using a 9-inch (23 cm) pie plate and are making a single-crust pie, then you should be rolling out the pastry to roughly an 11-inch (28 cm) circle, which will allow you to fit the pastry snugly into the pie plate. The extra dough allows you to trim it so that it's even and then to roll the pastry under itself to create a thick edge. The same goes for a two-crust pie, although you will trim a bit more since you are folding together two crusts with which to make your edge. Tarts are much the same. Roll your pastry to a circle that is 1½ inches (4 cm) larger than the circumference of the tart tin.

Country Apple Cranberry Galette

GALETTE PASTRY

2¼ cups (560 mL) all-purpose flour

2 Tbsp (30 mL) granulated sugar

½ tsp (2 mL) salt

¾ cup (180 mL) cold unsalted butter (6 oz/175 g)

⅔ cup (160 mL) cold sour cream

STREUSEL TOPPING

¼ cup (60 mL) all-purpose flour

2 Tbsp (30 mL) granulated sugar

2 Tbsp (30 mL) packed light brown sugar

2 Tbsp (30 mL) cold unsalted butter (1 oz/30 g)

1 large egg, lightly beaten, at room temperature

FILLING

6 tart apples, peeled, cored and thinly sliced

1 cup (250 mL) fresh or frozen whole cranberries

½ cup (125 mL) granulated sugar

2 Tbsp (30 mL) all-purpose flour

½ tsp (2 mL) cinnamon

1 Tbsp (15 mL) freshly squeezed lemon juice

I N FRENCH, *galette* means "free form," so just throw away any well intentioned specificity or intimidation. There's a lot of room for error here. Not when you make the pastry, but when you roll and shape it. It should look a bit haphazard and folksy, not pastry-case perfect. Galette pastries run the gamut, from ones that resemble flaky pastry, to ones that contain sour cream, buttermilk, almonds or cornmeal as part of their ingredients. I love them all but am particularly fond of the tenderness that sour cream provides to the pastry. Galettes can be both sweet and savoury but what I love about this galette is how the pastry hugs the not-too-sweet filling, giving you a taste of both the pastry and the bubbling fruit filling in one bite.

GALETTE PASTRY In the bowl of a food processor fitted with the metal "S" blade, or in a large bowl, pulse or whisk together the flour, sugar and salt until well mixed and aerated. Cut the butter into cubes and add to the food processor or the bowl. Pulse in the food processor or cut in with a pastry cutter (or 2 knives) until the flour resembles coarse meal, with butter the size of peas amidst a few larger pieces. Pour the sour cream over the flour-butter mixture. Pulse or fluff the mixture until thoroughly moistened and shaggy or clumpy, but not yet formed into a ball. Dump the entire mixture onto a lightly floured work surface. Using the palm of your hand, smear together the dough along the work surface, until it comes together in a cohesive whole or ball. Flatten the dough into a disc. Wrap the dough in plastic wrap and refrigerate for at least 45 minutes or for up to 3 days.

STREUSEL TOPPING In a small bowl, combine the flour and sugars. Cut in the butter until the mixture is crumbly; set aside.

Bring the galette dough to room temperature for 20 minutes if refrigerated for longer than 3 hours. Preheat the oven to 400°F (200°C).

FILLING In a large bowl, toss together the apples, cranberries, sugar, flour, cinnamon and lemon juice until the apples are well coated and the cranberries are evenly distributed; set aside.

On a lightly floured surface, roll out the dough to a 15- or 16-inch (38–40 cm) circle, making sure the underside does not stick to your work surface. Roll up the dough onto your rolling pin and then gently unroll it onto a parchment paper–lined baking sheet. Leaving a 3-inch (8 cm) border of the dough uncovered, arrange the apple mixture on the dough. Bring the pastry up and over the fruit filling, gluing the pleats together with the beaten egg and making sure that there is an opening in the middle of the galette where the fruit is exposed. Sprinkle the streusel topping over the exposed fruit.

Brush the beaten egg all over the top of the pastry.

Bake in the centre of the preheated oven until the fruit is cooked through and the pastry is crisp and golden, 40–45 minutes. Let the galette cool on the pan on a wire rack for at least 30 minutes. Slide onto a flat serving plate and serve either warm or at room temperature.

French Apple Tart

SWEET PASTRY

1¼ cups (310 mL) all-purpose flour

¼ cup (60 mL) granulated sugar

Pinch of salt

½ cup (125 mL) cold unsalted
   butter (4 oz/125 g)

1 cold large egg yolk

1 tsp (5 mL) vanilla

3 Tbsp (45 mL) cold water

FILLING

6 tart apples, peeled, cored and
   cut into chunks

¼ cup (60 mL) water

⅓ cup (80 mL) granulated sugar

Pinch of cinnamon

1 tsp (5 mL) lemon juice

TOPPING

3 medium-sized tart apples

1 Tbsp (15 mL) unsalted butter,
   melted and cooled (0.5 oz/15 g)

1 Tbsp (15 mL) granulated sugar

½ cup (125 mL) apricot jam

1 Tbsp (15 mL) water

THIS, TO me, is the quintessential French tart: simple, elegant, understated and absolutely sensational. The recipe takes me back to the first time I visited France. I was lucky enough to stay in a relative's apartment in Paris situated in the St. Germain des Pres area in the 6th arrondissement. During my week long stay, I visited countless markets and museums, ate my way through many a café and even made one or two meals at the apartment. Despite repeated visits to France since then, it is the memory of this tart, which I ate at a small café near the Jeu De Paume gallery in the Place de la Concorde, that will forever have a special place in my heart.

Arrange the paper-thin slices of apple in a rosette pattern for a polished look.

SWEET PASTRY In the bowl of a food processor fitted with the metal "S" blade, or in a large bowl, pulse or whisk together the flour, sugar and salt until well mixed and aerated. Cut the butter into cubes and add to the food processor or the bowl. Pulse in food processor or cut in with a pastry cutter (or 2 knives) until the flour resembles coarse meal, with butter the size of peas amidst a few larger pieces. In a 1-cup (250 mL) wet measure, stir together the egg yolk, vanilla and water. Pour the yolk-water mixture over the flour-butter mixture. Pulse or fluff the mixture until thoroughly moistened and shaggy or clumpy, but not yet formed into a ball. Dump the entire mixture onto a lightly floured work surface. Using the palm of your hand, smear together the dough along the work surface, until it comes together in a cohesive whole or ball. Flatten the dough into a disc. Wrap the dough in plastic wrap and refrigerate for at least 45 minutes or for up to 3 days.

Preheat the oven to 375°F (190°C).

On a lightly floured work surface, roll out the dough to an 11-inch (28 cm) circle, sprinkling the surface and underside with flour as needed to prevent the dough from sticking to the work surface and to prevent the rolling pin from sticking to the surface of the dough. Roll the dough up around the rolling pin and gently unroll on top of a 9-inch (23 cm) French tart tin with a removable bottom. Gently press the dough into the pan, into the edges and up the sides. Roll the rolling pin over the pan rim to trim away any excess dough. Place the tart shell on a baking sheet and then place a piece of parchment paper directly onto the tart shell. Fill with pie weights. Bake for 20 minutes.

Remove the tart shell from the oven. Remove the parchment paper and the pie weights. Prick the bottom of the tart shell with the tines of a fork. Return to the oven and bake until golden, about 10 minutes. Let the tart shell cool on the baking sheet on a wire rack.

FILLING Place the apples in a saucepan along with the water, sugar, cinnamon and lemon juice. Cook over medium heat, stirring often, until the apples are very soft and most of the liquid has been absorbed, 15–18 minutes. Using a potato masher or large fork, mash the apple mixture to the texture of a rough applesauce; let cool.

TOPPING   Peel the apples; cut each one in half. Remove the core from each apple half and then slice each half thinly. Spread the cooled apple filling into the cooled tart shell. Arrange the apples in tight, slightly overlapping concentric circles on top of the applesauce, starting at the outer edge and working your way into the centre. Brush the melted butter over the apples. Sprinkle the sugar over the apples.

Place the tart shell on a baking sheet and bake in the centre of the oven (still at 375°F/190°C) until the apples are very tender and the pastry is golden brown, about 30 minutes. Cool the tart on the baking sheet on the wire rack. Remove the sides of the tart tin. Run a small knife between the bottom and the pastry and gently slide the tart shell onto a flat serving plate.

Combine the apricot jam with water in a small saucepan. Heat gently until the jam is liquefied. Let the mixture cool slightly. Brush the apricot jam over the apples slices. Serve the tart warm or at room temperature.

BAKER'S TIP

BLIND BAKING This is an essential step when you need a partially or wholly baked crust, into which you're going to put an already or partially baked filling. Whichever scenario applies, blind baking means lining a chilled unbaked pie or tart crust with parchment paper (or aluminum foil) and then filling it with pie weights, either in the form of uncooked rice or commercially sold round pie weights. The pie or tart is then baked for 15–20 minutes until the crust has sufficiently set so that the bottom crust won't puff up and the sides won't cave in. What you do after that depends on how long the crust needs to be baked. After the pie weights are removed, the crust can be baked until it is lightly golden and dry across the bottom of the pan for partially baked crusts, or baked until a golden brown for fully baked crusts.

Tarte Tatin *with* Quick Puff Pastry

QUICK PUFF PASTRY

1⅔ cups (410 mL) all-purpose
   flour

2 Tbsp (30 mL) granulated sugar

¾ tsp (4 mL) salt

1 cup (250 mL) cold unsalted
   butter (8 oz/250 g)

⅓ cup (80 mL) cold water

APPLE TOPPING

¼ cup (60 mL) unsalted butter
   (2 oz/60 g)

¾ cup (180 mL) granulated sugar

1 Tbsp (15 mL) lemon juice

7 large tart apples, peeled, cored
   and cut into quarters

THE STORY of Tarte Tatin is the story of the Tatin sisters—French inn-keepers, who were baking a pie when they realized that they had forgotten to line the pan with crust. Ever frugal, they quickly decided to top their apples with some pastry instead of starting again from scratch. Out of such mishaps, legends are born. If you peruse cookbooks, you will see that the pastry for Tarte Tatin ranges from flaky pastry to sweet pastry to puff pastry. Making puff pastry from scratch is a time consuming, albeit rewarding task. I want everyone to know the glory of Tarte Tatin, so I exchanged the classic puff pastry with a quick puff pastry, which can be made in one fell swoop instead of the hours-long process the classic usually entails. You'll love the results.

QUICK PUFF PASTRY Combine the flour, sugar and salt in the bowl of a food processor fitted with the metal "S" blade. Cut in ¼ cup (60 mL) of the cold butter (keeping the remaining ¾ cup/180 mL refrigerated). Pulse until the butter is thoroughly incorporated into the flour mixture and is indistinguishable from the flour. This will tenderize the flour.

Cut the remaining cold ¾ cup (180 mL) butter into cubes and add to the food processor. Pulse 5 or 6 times, just until the butter has been reduced to smaller but still visible pieces.

Pour the water over the butter-flour mixture. Pulse briefly, about 6 times, just until a rough mass takes shape. Again, like other pastry, it should NOT be formed into a ball or you will have taken it too far. Transfer the mixture to a very lightly floured work surface. Knead very gently until the dough comes together. Press the dough into a rectangle.

Place the dough, now shaped into a rectangle, on a piece of waxed paper. Top with another piece of waxed paper. Roll the dough out into a 15- × 12-inch (38 × 30 cm) rectangle.

Pry away the top piece of waxed paper. Starting at the long edge of the pastry, fold one-third of the pastry to the centre of the rectangle. Fold the opposite long edge right over top, so that the long edge is flush with the other newly created long edge. You should now have a 15- × 4-inch (38 × 10 cm) rectangle. Starting from a short end, roll the dough up firmly and flatten into a book-like disc. Wrap the dough in plastic wrap. Refrigerate the dough for at least 2 hours, until firm, or for up to 2 days.

Bring the pastry to room temperature for 20 minutes. On a lightly floured work surface, roll out the pastry to a rough 11-inch (28 cm) circle. Roll the circle around the rolling pin and unroll it onto a parchment paper–lined baking sheet. Refrigerate the baking sheet while you prepare the apples.

APPLE TOPPING Preheat the oven to 400°F (200°C).

Melt the butter in a large, 9- to 10-inch (22–25 cm), preferably cast iron, ovenproof skillet, tilting the pan so that the butter coats the sides of the skillet. Stir in the sugar and the lemon juice. Cook for 1 minute. Remove the skillet from the heat.

Arrange the apple quarters, rounded side down, in tight concentric circles in the pan. If you have any leftover pieces, simply cut them in half and tuck them into any unused space. Return the skillet to the burner and cook over medium heat until the sugar turns a deep caramel colour, 8–12 minutes. Immediately remove the skillet from the stove. Remove the pastry from the refrigerator and gently transfer it on top of the apples, tucking any extra pastry in between the pan and the apples.

Bake in the centre of the preheated oven until the sugar is bubbling and the pastry is golden brown, 25–30 minutes. Remove the skillet from the oven. Let the skillet sit on a wire rack or the top of the stove for 3 minutes. Carefully run a knife around the edge of the pan, loosening the pastry from the skillet. Place a large serving plate directly on top of the skillet. Carefully, invert the skillet so that the tart falls onto the plate. Scrape any remaining caramel from the pan onto the top of the tart. Serve warm.

Just Peachy Peach Pie

PASTRY

3 cups (725 mL) all-purpose flour

3 Tbsp (45 mL) granulated sugar

¾ tsp (4 mL) salt

1 cup (250 mL) cold unsalted
butter (8 oz/250 g)

2 cold large egg yolks

⅓ cup (80 mL) cold water

FILLING

6½ cups (1.6 L) sliced peaches

⅔ cup (160 mL) granulated sugar

3 Tbsp (45 mL) cornstarch

2 Tbsp (30 mL) peach schnapps
(optional)

1 Tbsp (15 mL) freshly squeezed
lemon juice

1 tsp (5 mL) cinnamon

TOPPING

1 large egg, lightly beaten, at room
temperature

2 Tbsp (30 mL) sliced almonds

MOST CANADIANS, fed up with the winters we have to endure, can't wait for spring and summer to start. Being an avid skier, I don't mind the winter, but I do eagerly anticipate the bounty that Southern Ontario offers—fresh tree fruit that lasts throughout the summer and early autumn months. Peaches are one of the treasures of the earth. I love coming home with a basket full of peaches, not only to eat as part of my meals and for snacks, but also because I can then indulge in all sorts of wonderful baking—cobblers, pandowdies, muffins and of course, pies. Peaches take especially well to being enveloped in a golden, crispy, just-verging-on-sweet butter pastry.

PASTRY In the bowl of a food processor fitted with the metal "S" blade, or in a large bowl, pulse or whisk together the flour, sugar and salt until well mixed and aerated. Cut the butter into cubes and add to the food processor or the bowl. Pulse in the food processor or cut in with a pastry cutter (or 2 knives) until the flour resembles coarse meal, with butter the size of peas amidst a few larger pieces. In a 1-cup (250 mL) wet measure, whisk together the egg yolks and water. Pour the yolk-water mixture over the flour-butter mixture and pulse or toss briefly. If the mixture looks too dry and is not starting to get thoroughly moistened, add 1–2 Tbsp (15–30 mL) more water to the mixture. Pulse or toss again briefly until the mixture is thoroughly moistened and shaggy or clumpy, but not yet formed into a ball. Dump the entire mixture onto a lightly floured work surface. Using the palm of your hand, smear together the dough along the work surface, until it comes together in a cohesive whole or ball. Flatten the dough into a disc. Wrap the dough in plastic wrap and refrigerate for at least 45 minutes or for up to 2 days.

On a lightly floured work surface, roll out two-thirds of the dough to an 11-inch (28 cm) circle, sprinkling the surface and underside with flour as needed to prevent the dough from sticking to the work surface and to prevent the rolling pin from sticking to the surface of the dough. Roll the dough up around the rolling pin and gently unroll on top of a 9-inch (23 cm) Pyrex glass pie plate. Gently press the dough into the pie plate. Trim away any ragged edges of the dough and trim the edges so that there is about a ¾-inch (2 cm) overhang.

Refrigerate the pie shell while you roll out the top pastry and prepare the peach filling.

Still working on a lightly floured work surface, roll out the remaining piece of pastry to an 11-inch (28 cm) circle. This will be the top so it will be much thinner than the bottom crust. Gently transfer the circle to a parchment paper–lined baking sheet. Place the baking sheet in the refrigerator.

Preheat the oven to 400°F (200°C).

FILLING Preheat the oven to 400°F (200°C).

In a large bowl, using a wooden spoon, stir together the peaches, sugar, cornstarch, peach schnapps (if using), lemon juice and cinnamon until the peach slices are well coated with the sugar and the cornstarch.

Remove the pastry-lined pie plate from the refrigerator. Scrape the peach filling into the pie shell. Remove the 11-inch (28 cm) pastry circle from the refrigerator. Brush some of the beaten egg over the rim of the bottom crust. Place the top crust on top of the bottom crust, centreing it evenly. Trim the top crust so that it aligns with the edge of the bottom crust's overhang. Gently press the top crust against the bottom crust so that it seals well. Tuck the overhanging pastry together and then roll up to form a thick crust or edge. Crimp the border decoratively with your fingers or the tines of a fork. Using a small sharp knife, cut 3 air vents into the top crust. Transfer the pie to a baking sheet.

TOPPING Brush the entire surface of the pie with some of the beaten egg. Sprinkle the almonds over the surface of the pie.

Bake the pie in the centre of the preheated oven for 20 minutes. Reduce the heat to 375°F (190°C) and bake until the pastry is golden and the fruit filling is thick and bubbling, about an additional 50–55 minutes. Cool the pie on a wire rack until cool. Serve warm or at room temperature.

BAKER'S TIPS

THICKENERS There are basically three choices of thickener that bakers will use to help thicken fruit pies. Flour is often used but can give a cloudy look to the thickened juices. Cornstarch is also very popular and will result in a shiny filling. Tapioca flour provides a shiny, clear look much the same way cornstarch does. If you have run out of one or the other and want to substitute, remember that flour has only about half the thickening power as cornstarch or tapioca flour so you will need to double up.

If at any time during the baking process your pie looks like the pastry surface is browning too quickly, simply cover it with some aluminum foil to shield it from the heat of the oven.

Peach Blueberry Gingersnap Galette

PASTRY

2 cups (500 mL) all-purpose flour

¼ cup (60 mL) granulated sugar

¼ tsp (1 mL) salt

¼ tsp (1 mL) baking powder

¾ cup (180 mL) cold unsalted
butter (6 oz/175 g)

½ cup (125 mL) cold cream cheese
(4 oz/125 g)

¼ cup (60 mL) cold water

2 tsp (10 mL) white vinegar

FILLING

4 cups (1 L) sliced fresh peaches

1 cup (250 mL) fresh blueberries

¼ cup (60 mL) granulated sugar

1 tsp (5 mL) all-purpose flour

3 Tbsp (45 mL) crushed gingersnap cookies

1 large egg, lightly beaten, at room
temperature

THE MECHANICS of the galette are pastry, fruit filling and a topping. This is where the creativity of baking comes in. Choose whatever fruits you like, or you can let the seasons be your muse. This galette is slightly different due to the inclusion of cream cheese and baking powder. The cream cheese makes it ultra tender and the added fat makes it easier to roll. The baking powder makes the pastry light and airy. With a negligible amount of thickener, the filling is juicy without being runny.

PASTRY In the bowl of a food processor fitted with the metal "S" blade, or in a large bowl, pulse or whisk together the flour, sugar, salt and baking powder until well mixed and aerated. Cut the butter and cream cheese into cubes and add to the food processor or the bowl. Pulse in the food processor or cut in with a pastry cutter (or 2 knives) until the flour resembles coarse meal, with butter the size of peas amidst a few larger pieces. In a 1-cup (250 mL) wet measure, stir together the water and vinegar. Pour the water mixture over the flour-butter mixture. Pulse or fluff the mixture until thoroughly moistened and shaggy or clumpy, but not yet formed into a ball. Dump the entire mixture onto a lightly floured work surface. Using the palm of your hand, smear together the dough along the work surface, until it comes together in a cohesive whole or ball. Flatten the dough into a disc. Wrap the dough in plastic wrap and refrigerate for at least 45 minutes or for up to 3 days.

Bring the galette dough to room temperature for 20 minutes if refrigerated for longer than 3 hours.

FILLING Preheat the oven to 400°F (200°C).

In a large bowl, toss together the peaches, blueberries, sugar and flour until the fruit is well coated with sugar and the flour; set aside.

On a lightly floured surface, roll out the dough, making sure the underside does not stick to your work surface, to roughly a 15- to 16-inch (38–40 cm) circle. Roll up the dough onto your rolling pin and then gently unroll it onto a parchment paper–lined baking sheet. Sprinkle the gingersnap cookies into the centre of the dough. Leaving a 3-inch (8 cm) border of the dough uncovered, arrange the peach mixture over the cookie

RECIPE CONTINUED . . .

crumbs. Bring the pastry up and over the fruit filling, gluing the pleats together with the beaten egg and making sure that there is an opening in the middle of the galette where the fruit is exposed.

Brush the beaten egg all over the top of the pastry.

Bake in the centre of the preheated oven until the fruit is cooked through and the pastry is crisp and golden, about 40 minutes. Let the galette cool on the pan on a wire rack for at least 30 minutes. Slide onto a flat serving plate and serve either warm or at room temperature.

Beurre Noisette Tart *with* Strawberries

B**EURRE NOISETTE** is literally translated as "hazelnut butter," but is also known simply as browned butter. The French term refers to butter that has been cooked until it has turned a golden brown and acquired a nutty flavour. *Beurre noisette* is great with savoury dishes and sauces but it also lends an unmistakable depth to sweet items. Be careful melting the butter, you want it brown, not black or burned. When accompanied by some sugar, eggs and just a bit of flour, it makes an irresistible tart, brilliantly showing off the ripe fruit that covers it. This tart is also great with blackberries, raspberries, peaches, nectarines or poached pears. On occasion, I have made it with red wine poached pears, the ruby of the pear surface contrasting beautifully with the creamy ivory of its interior.

PASTRY In the bowl of a food processor fitted with the metal "S" blade, or in a large bowl, whisk or pulse together the flour, sugar and salt until well mixed and aerated. Cut the butter into cubes and add to the food processor or the bowl. Pulse in the food processor or cut in with a pastry cutter (or 2 knives) until the flour resembles coarse meal, with butter the size of peas amidst a few larger pieces. Stir together the egg yolks and cold water. Pour the yolk mixture over the flour-butter mixture. Pulse or fluff the mixture until thoroughly moistened and shaggy or clumpy, but not yet formed into a ball. Dump the entire mixture onto a lightly floured work surface. Using the palm of your hand, smear together the dough along the work surface, until it comes together in a cohesive whole or ball. Flatten the dough into a disc. Wrap the dough in plastic wrap and refrigerate for at least 45 minutes or for up to 3 days.

On a lightly floured work surface, roll out the dough to a 16- × 6-inch rectangle (40 × 15 cm), sprinkling the surface and underside with flour as needed to prevent the dough from sticking to the work surface and to prevent the rolling pin from sticking to the surface of the dough. Roll the dough up around the rolling pin and gently unroll on top of a 14- × 4-inch (35 × 10 cm) French tart tin with a removable bottom. Gently press the dough into the pan, into the edges and up the sides. Roll the rolling pin over the pan rim to trim away any excess dough. Refrigerate the tart while you prepare the filling.

PASTRY

1⅓ cups (330 mL) all-purpose flour

¼ cup (60 mL) granulated sugar

Pinch of salt

⅔ cup (160 mL) cold unsalted butter (5 oz/150 g)

2 cold large egg yolks

3 Tbsp (45 mL) cold water

FILLING

¼ cup (60 mL) cold unsalted butter (2 oz/60 g)

2 large eggs, at room temperature

¾ cup (180 mL) granulated sugar

¼ cup (60 mL) all-purpose flour

1 tsp (5 mL) vanilla

TOPPING

2 cups (500 mL) hulled, halved strawberries

RECIPE CONTINUED . . .

FILLING Preheat the oven to 375°F (190°C).

In a small saucepan set over medium heat, melt the butter until it starts to turn brown and little browned bits form. Remove the saucepan from the stovetop and let the butter cool slightly. In a bowl, whisk together the eggs, sugar, flour and vanilla. Slowly whisk in the browned butter until it is thoroughly incorporated. Remove the pastry shell from the refrigerator and place on a rimmed baking sheet. Pour the browned butter mixture into the unbaked pastry shell.

Bake in the centre of the preheated oven until the filling is golden and baked through, 30–35 minutes. Let the pastry cool completely on a wire rack.

Remove the sides of the tart tin. Run a small knife between the bottom and the pastry and gently slide the tart shell onto a flat rectangular serving plate. The plate should not be rimmed or even curved upwards as this may encourage the tart shell to break. Arrange the strawberries on top of the tart. Serve at room temperature.

BAKER'S TIP

Don't discard the dough that's left over once you've cut the pastry to size. Use it as decorations for the top or side of your pie, in the shape of leaves, small circles or triangles.

Hand-Held Tarts *with* Rhubarb Strawberry Filling

RHUBARB AND strawberries fall into one of those perfect relationships that never falters or goes out of fashion. The two just seem to go happily on their way through life together, in blissful matrimony, defying all the odds that trends and fads throw their way. I can hardly wait for rhubarb season every year. I adore stewed rhubarb, love folding it into my muffin batter and finding new ways to flaunt its exemplary flavour. These hand-held tarts seem to do the trick nicely.

PASTRY In the bowl of a food processor fitted with the metal "S" blade, or in a large bowl, whisk or pulse together the flour, sugar and salt until well mixed and aerated. Cut the butter into cubes and add to the food processor or the bowl. Pulse in the food processor or cut in with a pastry cutter (or 2 knives) until the flour resembles coarse meal, with butter the size of peas amidst a few larger pieces. Pour the buttermilk over the flour-butter mixture. Pulse or fluff the mixture until thoroughly moistened and shaggy or clumpy, but not yet formed into a ball. Dump the entire mixture onto a lightly floured work surface. Using the palm of your hand, smear together the dough along the work surface, until it comes together in a cohesive whole or ball. Divide the dough in half and press each into a disc. Wrap each piece of dough in plastic wrap and refrigerate for at least 45 minutes or for up to 3 days.

FILLING Combine the rhubarb, sugar, water and cornstarch in a saucepan set over medium-high heat. Bring to a boil, stirring. Reduce the heat to low and simmer, stirring often, for 5–10 minutes or until the rhubarb has broken down and the mixture has thickened. Remove the saucepan from the heat. Transfer the mixture to a bowl. Stir in the strawberries. Place plastic wrap directly on the surface of the fruit mixture and refrigerate for at least 2 hours, until completely chilled, or for up to 3 days.

ASSEMBLY Preheat the oven to 400°F (200°C).

Roll 1 disc of pastry to a ⅛-inch (3 mm) thickness. With a cookie cutter or the bottom of a bowl, cut out 5-inch (12 cm) circles. Repeat with remaining disc. You should have about 14 or 15 circles in total. Place

PASTRY

3¾ cups (930 mL) all-purpose flour

2 Tbsp (30 mL) granulated sugar

1 tsp (5 mL) salt

1½ cups (375 mL) cold unsalted butter (12 oz/375 g)

1 cup (250 mL) cold buttermilk

FILLING

½ lb (250 g) chopped rhubarb, fresh or frozen

⅔ cup (160 mL) granulated sugar

¼ cup (60 mL) water

1½ Tbsp (22 mL) cornstarch

1 cup (250 mL) chopped stemmed strawberries

1 large egg, lightly beaten, at room temperature

RECIPE CONTINUED . . .

1 heaping Tbsp (15+ mL) of the rhubarb mixture in the centre of each circle. Brush the bottom edge of the circle with the beaten egg. Fold the upper half over the filling to form a crescent. Make a small hole in the centre. Repeat with all of the circles. Transfer the circles to 2 parchment paper–lined baking sheets. Refrigerate one sheet while you bake the other. Brush the surface of the crescents with the beaten egg.

Bake the first sheet in the centre of the preheated oven until the crescents are puffed and golden, about 20 minutes. Let the crescents cool on the baking sheet on a wire rack. Repeat with the remaining baking sheet of crescents. Serve warm or at room temperature.

Anise-Scented Rhubarb Tart

Aʜ, ᴛʜᴇ glories of fresh rhubarb. Due to the proliferation of hot houses, rhubarb is now available almost year round. The difference between locally harvested and hot house rhubarb is the colour and the taste. The former is slightly more bitter and the stalks are greener and paler. Hot house rhubarb, on the other hand, is sweeter and has a bright pink hue. You can use either for this alluring tart. Be sure to use brown sugar in the streusel since it harmonizes so well with the rhubarb and accentuates the anise.

PASTRY In the bowl of a food processor fitted with the metal "S" blade, or in a large bowl, whisk or pulse together the flour, sugar and salt until well mixed and aerated. Cut the butter into cubes and add to the food processor or the bowl. Pulse in the food processor or cut in with a pastry cutter (or 2 knives) until the flour resembles coarse meal, with butter the size of peas amidst a few larger pieces. In a 1-cup (250 mL) wet measure, whisk the yolk with enough very cold water to make ⅓ cup (80 mL). Pour the yolk mixture over the flour-butter mixture. Pulse or fluff the mixture until thoroughly moistened and shaggy or clumpy, but not yet formed into a ball. Dump the entire mixture onto a lightly floured work surface. Using the palm of your hand, smear together the dough along the work surface, until it comes together in a cohesive whole or ball. Flatten the dough into a disc. Wrap the dough in plastic wrap and refrigerate for at least 1 hour or for up to 2 days.

FILLING Preheat the oven to 400°F (200°C).

Stir together the rhubarb and sugar in an 8-inch (20 cm) square glass dish. Let the fruit stand at room temperature for 20 minutes. Cover the dish with a piece of aluminum foil. Bake in the centre of the preheated oven for 10 minutes. Remove the aluminum foil, stir the mixture gently and then bake until the rhubarb has broken down and the mixture has thickened somewhat but still looks quite juicy, about 15 minutes. Remove from the oven.

RECIPE CONTINUED . . .

PASTRY

1½ cups (375 mL) all-purpose flour

¼ cup (60 mL) packed light brown sugar

Pinch of salt

½ cup (125 mL) cold unsalted butter, cubed (4 oz/125 g)

1 cold large egg yolk

FILLING

1½ lb (750 g) chopped rhubarb (4½ heaping cups/1.1 L)

¾ cup (180 mL) granulated sugar

STREUSEL

⅓ cup (80 mL) large flake rolled oats

⅓ cup (80 mL) all-purpose flour

3 Tbsp (45 mL) packed light brown sugar

¼ tsp (1 mL) anise seeds, crushed

¼ cup (60 mL) unsalted butter, melted and cooled (2 oz/60 g)

STREUSEL While the rhubarb is baking, make the streusel. In a bowl, whisk together the oats, flour, brown sugar and anise seeds until well mixed. Pour the melted butter over the mixture and fluff with a fork or your hands until the mixture is thoroughly moistened; set aside.

ASSEMBLY On a lightly floured work surface, roll out the dough to an 11-inch (28 cm) circle, sprinkling the surface and underside with flour as needed to prevent the dough from sticking to the work surface and to prevent the rolling pin from sticking to the surface of the dough. Roll the dough up around the rolling pin and gently unroll on top of a 9-inch (23 cm) French tart tin with a removable bottom. Gently press the dough into the pan, into the edges and up the sides. Roll the rolling pin over the pan rim to trim away any excess dough. Place the tart shell on a baking sheet and then place a piece of parchment paper directly onto the tart shell. Fill with pie weights. Bake for 10 minutes. Remove the tart shell from the oven. Remove the parchment paper and the pie weights from the tart shell.

Reduce the oven heat to 350°F (180°C).

Spread the rhubarb filling into the partially baked shell. Sprinkle the streusel evenly over the rhubarb. Bake the tart in the oven until the rhubarb filling is thickened and both the pastry and the streusel are golden brown, 25–30 minutes. Remove the baking sheet from the oven and transfer the tart to a wire rack to cool.

Remove the sides of the tart tin. Run a small knife between the bottom and the pastry and gently slide the tart shell onto a flat serving plate. The plate should not be rimmed or even curved upwards as this may encourage the tart shell to break. Serve warm or at room temperature.

BAKER'S TIP

Related to fennel, dill, tarragon and caraway, anise has a sweet, licorice flavour. Anise seeds should be purchased whole and then crushed in a mortar and pestle, or ground in a spice or coffee mill. Because the amount called for in this recipe is rather small, I use my mortar and pestle which is way easier to clean than my spice mill. In a pinch, you can use the back of a spoon against a wooden cutting board.

Plum Raspberry Crostata

Tᴴɪꜱ ᴛᴀʀᴛ is a gorgeous deep ruby red colour, full of vibrant fruit, with a buttery, tender crust on the bottom and the top. The juiciness of the plums (only fresh, in season plums will do) accompanied by the tartness of the raspberries and the lemon rind and juice gracefully meld together, making each bite a symphony.

PASTRY In the bowl of a food processor fitted with the metal "S" blade, or in a large bowl, pulse or whisk together the flour, sugar, lemon zest, baking powder and salt until well mixed and aerated. Cut the butter into cubes and add to the food processor or the bowl. Pulse in the food processor or cut in with a pastry cutter (or 2 knives) until the flour resembles coarse meal, with butter the size of peas amidst a few larger pieces. In a small bowl, gently whisk together the eggs until they are broken up. Pour the eggs over the flour-butter mixture. Pulse or fluff the mixture until thoroughly moistened and shaggy or clumpy, but not yet formed into a ball. Dump the entire mixture onto a lightly floured work surface. Using the palm of your hand, smear together the dough along the work surface, until it comes together in a cohesive whole or ball. Flatten the dough into a disc. Wrap in plastic wrap and refrigerate for at least 1 hour or for up to 3 days.

On a lightly floured work surface, roll out two-thirds of the dough to an 11-inch (28 cm) circle, sprinkling the surface and underside with flour as needed to prevent the dough from sticking to the work surface and to prevent the rolling pin from sticking to the surface of the dough. Roll the dough up around the rolling pin and gently unroll on top of a 9-inch (23 cm) French tart tin with a removable bottom. Gently press the dough into the pan, into the edges and up the sides. Roll the rolling pin over the pan rim to trim away any excess dough. Refrigerate the tart shell for 20 minutes.

Roll out the smaller piece of dough, again flouring the top and underside of the dough to prevent it from sticking, to roughly a 10-inch (25 cm) circle. Using a sharp chef's knife, cut twelve ½-inch (1 cm) wide strips (you may only need 10, but I've given you 2 extra just in case). Transfer the strips to a parchment paper–lined cookie sheet and refrigerate while you make the filling.

PASTRY

2 cups (500 mL) all-purpose flour

¼ cup (60 mL) granulated sugar

1 Tbsp (15 mL) finely grated lemon zest

½ tsp (2 mL) baking powder

¼ tsp (1 mL) salt

⅔ cup (160 mL) cold unsalted butter (5 oz/150 g)

2 cold large eggs

FILLING

4 red plums (about ¾ lb/375 g)

3 cups (725 mL) fresh raspberries

¾ cup (180 mL) granulated sugar

1 tsp (5 mL) finely grated lemon zest

3 Tbsp (45 mL) all-purpose flour

1 Tbsp (15 mL) freshly squeezed lemon juice

TOPPING

1 large egg, beaten lightly, at room temperature

RECIPE CONTINUED . . .

FILLING Preheat the oven to 375°F (190°C).

Cut the plums in half, remove the pits and slice into ¼-inch (6 mm) slices. Place in a bowl along with the raspberries. Transfer half of the fruit mixture into a wide shallow saucepan. Stir in the sugar, lemon zest, flour and lemon juice. Bring to a boil. Reduce the heat, and simmer, stirring often with a wooden spoon, until the fruit has released its juices and the mixture has thickened. Stir into the reserved fruit, scraping all of the juices into the bowl. Let cool for 5 minutes.

ASSEMBLY Remove the tart shell from the refrigerator. Scrape the fruit filling into the tart shell, smoothing the surface of the fruit. Brush the beaten egg over the pastry edges. Remove the pastry strips from the refrigerator.

Arrange 5 strips of the dough evenly over the fruit filling, starting with a long strip for the centre. Gently fold back every other strip (the second and fourth) to a little past the centre of the pie.

Place another strip of dough in the centre, this time perpendicular to the other strips.

Unfold or unroll the two folded strips so they lie flat on top of the perpendicular strip. Now fold back the strips that weren't folded back last time (the first, third and fifth ones). Place another strip of dough about ¾ inch (2 cm) away from the one you placed horizontally in the centre. Unfold the 3 folded strips so that they are now lying on top of the second strip of dough. Fold back the original two strips, set a strip of dough ¾ inch (2 cm) from the last one, and unfold the two strips.

Repeat on the other side with the two remaining strips: fold back alternating strips, lay a strip of dough on top, and unfold. Remember to alternate the strips that are folded back to create a woven effect. Trim the strips to a ½-inch (1 cm) overhang. Press the edges of the strips onto the egg moistened edge of the tart. Brush the lattice with some more of the beaten egg. Place the tart on a baking sheet.

Bake in the centre of the preheated oven until the pastry is golden and the fruit filling is bubbling, 40–45 minutes. Cool the tart on the baking sheet on a wire rack. Remove the sides of the tart tin. Run a small paring knife between the bottom and the pastry and gently slide the tart shell onto a flat serving plate. The plate should not be rimmed or even curved upwards as this may encourage the tart shell to break.

Serve warm or at room temperature.

Fresh Fig *and* Raspberry Tart *with* Mascarpone *and* Honey

PASTRY

1 cup (250 mL) all-purpose flour

¼ cup (60 mL) granulated sugar

¼ cup (60 mL) ground blanched almonds

¼ cup (60 mL) crushed amaretti cookies

¾ cup (180 mL) cold unsalted butter (6 oz/175 g)

1 cold large egg

1 Tbsp (15 mL) whipping cream, cold

FILLING

8 oz (250 g) mascarpone cheese, softened (or a 9 oz/275 g container)

¼ cup (60 mL) icing sugar

⅓ cup (80 mL) whipping cream, at room temperature

2 Tbsp (30 mL) brandy

8 ripe figs

1 heaping cup (250+ mL) fresh raspberries

2 Tbsp (30 mL) honey

THIS TART is a bit of a romantic culinary adventure. I use the word romantic carefully here, both to allude to the voluptuousness of the mascarpone cream but also because anything that includes figs has got to be romantic. I distinctly remember the first time I ate a fresh fig. It was dusk, which is a magical time of day in Italy. The sky acquires this shimmery blue quality, almost incandescent. There I was on Lake Albano, which surrounds the Pope's summer residence at Castel Gandolfo, having a late picnic. My host offered me a ripe fig and I was lost forever. This tart may not transport you to an idyllic meal just outside of Rome, but it will entice you with its lusciousness and sweet bite. Try to use the ripest figs you can for this dessert.

PASTRY In the bowl of a food processor fitted with the metal "S" blade, or in a large bowl, pulse or whisk together the flour, sugar, almonds and amaretti cookies until well mixed and aerated. Cut the butter into cubes and add to the food processor or the bowl. Pulse in the food processor or cut in with a pastry cutter (or 2 knives) until the flour resembles coarse meal, with butter the size of peas amidst a few larger pieces.

In a small bowl, gently whisk together the egg and the whipping cream. Pour the egg mixture over the flour-butter mixture. Pulse or fluff the mixture until thoroughly moistened and starting to clump together. Using handfuls of the mixture at a time, lightly hand knead the dough until it comes together in a clump. Press the clumps of shortbread evenly onto the bottom and sides of a 9- or 10-inch (23 or 25 cm) round French tart tin with a removable bottom. Chill for at least 40 minutes or for up to 2 days.

Preheat the oven to 375°F (190°C).

Place the tart shell on a baking sheet and then place a piece of parchment paper directly into the tart shell. Fill with pie weights. Bake for 10 minutes. Remove the pie weights and parchment paper from the tart shell. Prick the bottom with the tines of a fork. Return to the oven and bake until the crust is golden, 10–12 minutes. Remove the baking sheet from the oven and transfer the tart shell to a wire rack to cool completely.

FILLING In a stand mixer fitted with the paddle attachment or using a hand-held mixer, beat the mascarpone cheese with the icing sugar until well combined and fluffy, about 3 minutes. Pour in the whipping cream and brandy. Beat the mixture together until well mixed and very creamy looking.

Scrape the mascarpone filling into the baked tart shell, using an offset spatula to smooth it out evenly. Trim and quarter the figs. Arrange the fig quarters on top of the filling around the border of the tart shell with the tapered end facing the centre of the tart. Arrange the raspberries in 2 circles next to the figs and then fill in the centre with a few more figs. Refrigerate the tart for 1–4 hours before serving.

Remove the sides of the tart tin. Run a small knife between the bottom and the pastry and gently slide the tart shell onto a flat serving plate. The plate should not be rimmed or even curved upwards as this may encourage the tart shell to break. Drizzle the honey over the fruit and serve slightly chilled.

Fresh Apricot Custard Tarts

PASTRY

2½ cups (625 mL) all-purpose
  flour

1 Tbsp (15 mL) granulated sugar

½ tsp (2 mL) salt

1 cup (250 mL) cold unsalted
  butter (8 oz/250 g)

½ cup (125 mL) cold water

½ tsp (2 mL) vinegar

FILLING

6 fresh medium-sized apricots

¾ cup (180 mL) whipping cream,
  at room temperature

1 large egg, at room temperature

⅓ cup (80 mL) granulated sugar

¼ cup (60 mL) all-purpose flour

2 tsp (10 mL) vanilla

IF YOU crave fresh apricots—and though I find it hard to believe, I've been informed that there are people who don't even like apricots or know what a fresh one tastes like—then you'll adore these individual tarts. Fresh, ripe apricots have a short and thrifty season, roughly mid-July to mid-August, and they don't store well at room temperature. Their level of sweetness and flavour always remain the same as when they were picked, although they will ripen in colour, texture and juiciness with time. Their sweetness and juicy texture are exquisitely revealed by the vanilla-laced custard that surrounds them. And the best thing? These custard tarts are made in a 4-inch (10 cm) tart shell, so you can have one all to yourself.

PASTRY In the bowl of a food processor fitted with the metal "S" blade, or in a large bowl, pulse or whisk together the flour, sugar and salt until well mixed and aerated. Cut the butter into cubes and add to the food processor or the bowl. Pulse in the food processor or cut in with a pastry cutter (or 2 knives) until the flour resembles coarse meal, with butter the size of peas amidst a few larger pieces. In a small bowl, whisk together the water and vinegar. Pour the water over the flour-butter mixture. Pulse or fluff the mixture until thoroughly moistened and shaggy or clumpy, but not yet formed into a ball. Dump the entire mixture onto a lightly floured work surface. Using the palm of your hand, smear together the dough along the work surface, until it comes together in a cohesive whole or ball. Then divide the dough into 8 equal-sized pieces. Wrap each piece of dough in plastic wrap and refrigerate for at least 1 hour or for up to 3 days.

Preheat the oven to 375°F (190°C).

Working with one piece of dough at a time, roll out the dough on a lightly floured work surface to a 6-inch (15 cm) circle, sprinkling the surface and underside with flour as needed to prevent the dough from sticking to the work surface and to prevent the rolling pin from sticking to the surface of the dough. Roll the dough up around the rolling pin and gently unroll on top of a 4-inch (10 cm) French tart tin with a removable bottom.

Gently press the dough into the bottom, edges and sides of the pan. Roll the rolling pin over the pan rim to trim away any excess dough. Refrigerate the tart shell while you roll out the remaining 7 pieces of dough.

Place the tart shells on a baking sheet and then place a small piece of parchment paper directly into each tart shell. Fill with pie weights. Bake for 15 minutes. Remove the pie weights and parchment paper from each tart shell. Prick the bottom of each with the tines of a fork.

Return the tray of tart shells to the oven and bake for 10 minutes. Remove the tray of tart shells from the oven and let cool for 5 minutes.

FILLING Meanwhile, cut each apricot in half and then in half again to make quarters. Place 3 apricot quarters in each tart shell.

In a bowl, whisk together the whipping cream, egg, sugar, flour and vanilla. Dividing the custard evenly, pour the custard into the tart shells. Return the baking tray to the oven and bake until the custard is puffed and golden, 20–25 minutes. Cool the tarts on the baking sheet on a wire rack for 20 minutes. Unmould from the tart tins and serve warm or at room temperature.

Blackberry Buttermilk Pie

PASTRY

1½ cups (375 mL) all-purpose flour

2 Tbsp (30 mL) granulated sugar

Pinch of salt

½ cup (125 mL) cold unsalted butter (4 oz/125 g)

¼ cup (60 mL) cold buttermilk

FILLING

1 cup (250 mL) granulated sugar

½ cup (125 mL) unsalted butter, melted and cooled (4 oz/125 g)

3 Tbsp (45 mL) all-purpose flour

3 large eggs, lightly beaten, at room temperature

1 cup (250 mL) buttermilk, at room temperature

2 tsp (10 mL) finely grated lemon zest

2 tsp (10 mL) vanilla

1¾ cups (430 mL) fresh blackberries

A SOUTHERN—as in the southern States—specialty, buttermilk pie is often confused with chess pie. Although the two share much in common, chess pie almost always includes cornmeal and buttermilk pie, which does not include cornmeal, has a more custardy texture. They're both quite sweet. I've taken the liberty of updating the pie with the addition of blackberries, not only to give it a spot of colour but so that the tartness of the berries balances the sweet rich filling.

PASTRY In the bowl of a food processor fitted with the metal "S" blade, or in a large bowl, pulse or whisk together the flour, sugar and salt until well mixed and aerated. Cut the butter into cubes and add to the food processor or the bowl. Pulse in the food processor or cut in with a pastry cutter (or 2 knives) until the flour resembles coarse meal, with butter the size of peas amidst a few larger pieces. Pour the buttermilk over the flour mixture and pulse or toss briefly until the mixture is thoroughly moistened and shaggy or clumpy, but not yet formed into a ball.

Dump the entire mixture onto a lightly floured work surface. Using the palm of your hand, smear together the dough along the work surface, until it comes together in a cohesive whole or ball. Flatten the dough into a disc. Wrap the dough in plastic wrap and refrigerate for at least 45 minutes or for up to 2 days.

On a lightly floured work surface, roll out the dough to an 11-inch (28 cm) circle, sprinkling the surface and underside with flour as needed to prevent the dough from sticking to the work surface and to prevent the rolling pin from sticking to the surface of the dough. Roll the dough up around the rolling pin and gently unroll on top of a 9-inch (23 cm) Pyrex or glass pie plate. Gently press the dough into the pie plate. Trim away any ragged edges of the dough and trim the edges so that there is about a ¾-inch (2 cm) overhang. Roll up the overhang to the edge to make a thick crust. With your fingers or the tines of a fork, crimp the edge of the pie decoratively. Refrigerate the pie shell while you prepare the filling.

FILLING Preheat the oven to 350°F (180°C).

In the bowl of a food processor fitted with the metal "S" blade, pulse together the sugar, butter and flour. With the machine running, add the eggs in a thin steady stream through the feed tube. Scrape the mixture down with a rubber spatula. Start the machine again and in a thin steady stream, add the buttermilk through the feed tube, mixing just until it is fully blended in. Quickly pulse in the lemon zest and vanilla.

Remove the pie shell from the refrigerator and place on a rimmed baking sheet. Scatter the blackberries over the bottom of the pie shell. Pour the buttermilk mixture over the berries.

Bake in the centre of the preheated oven until the pie is just set and is very slightly golden on top, 40–45 minutes. Let the pie cool on the baking sheet on a wire rack. Serve the pie at room temperature.

BAKER'S TIP

Although the filling is best made in a food processor, you can definitely make it by hand with care. It's important to remember that you're trying to create an emulsification here (much like you do when you're making a vinaigrette) so that the butter doesn't create a hard layer on top while the pie is baking. In a large bowl and using a very sturdy whisk, whisk together the cooled butter and the sugar. Whisk in the flour and then about a third of the beaten eggs. Blend the mixture well. Add another third of the eggs and blend well. You do not want to add the ingredients too quickly or else the mixture will separate. A few tablespoons at a time, whisk in the buttermilk. Gently fold in the lemon zest and the vanilla. Proceed with the recipe.

Pear Frangipane Tart

PASTRY

2½ cups (625 mL) all-purpose
   flour

2 Tbsp (30 mL) granulated sugar

¾ tsp (4 mL) salt

1 cup (250 mL) cold unsalted
   butter (8 oz/250 g)

⅓ cup (80 mL) cold water
   (approx.)

POACHED PEARS

2 cups (500 mL) dry white wine

2 slices lemon zest

1 Tbsp (15 mL) freshly squeezed
   lemon juice

¾ cup (180 mL) granulated sugar

½ vanilla bean

5 ripe Bartlett pears

FRANGIPANE FILLING

½ cup (125 mL) unsalted butter,
   softened (4 oz/125 g)

½ cup (125 mL) granulated sugar

1 large egg, at room temperature

1 cup (250 mL) finely ground
   blanched almonds

3 Tbsp (45 mL) pear nectar

½ tsp (2 mL) almond extract

1 Tbsp (15 mL) all-purpose flour

ANOTHER CLASSIC, by way of France. Frangipane, a delicious almond filling, is a terrific filling for croissants, Danish and turnovers. Almonds are traditionally the nut of choice, but you can use other nuts such as pecans, hazelnuts, macadamia nuts or pistachios. Once poached, the pears are velvety soft, with a little give. The frangipane is creamy and smooth. Together, they form a seductive duet. You'll need no other embellishment when you serve this stunner for dessert.

PASTRY In the bowl of a food processor fitted with the metal "S" blade, or in a large bowl, pulse or whisk together the flour, sugar and salt until well mixed and aerated. Cut the butter into cubes and add to the food processor or the bowl. Pulse in the food processor or cut in with a pastry cutter (or 2 knives) until the flour resembles coarse meal, with butter the size of peas amidst a few larger pieces. Pour the water over the flour-butter mixture. Pulse or fluff the mixture until thoroughly moistened and shaggy or clumpy, but not yet formed into a ball. Dump the entire mixture onto a lightly floured work surface. Using the palm of your hand, smear together the dough along the work surface, until it comes together in a cohesive whole or ball. Flatten into a disc. Wrap the dough in plastic wrap and refrigerate for at least 1 hour or for up to 3 days.

POACHED PEARS Stir together the white wine, lemon zest, lemon juice, sugar and vanilla bean in a large shallow saucepan. Bring the mixture to a boil. Boil for 3 minutes. Peel, halve and core the pears. Add the pears to the poaching liquid so that they fit in a single layer. Reduce the heat and simmer, turning the pears once, until the pears are very tender, 15–20 minutes. Let the pears cool in the poaching liquid. (If your pears aren't ripe, poaching can take as long as 35 minutes.)

On a lightly floured work surface, roll out the dough to an 11-inch (28 cm) circle, sprinkling the surface and underside with flour as needed to prevent the dough from sticking to the work surface and to prevent the rolling pin from sticking to the surface of the dough. Roll the dough up around the rolling pin and gently unroll on top of a 9-inch (23 cm) French tart tin with a removable bottom. Gently press the dough into the pan, into the edges and up the sides. Roll the rolling pin over the pan rim to trim away any excess dough. Refrigerate the tart while you prepare the filling.

FRANGIPANE FILLING Preheat the oven to 350°F (180°C).

In the bowl of a stand mixer fitted with the paddle attachment, or using hand-held beaters, beat together the butter and the sugar until light and fluffy, about 3 minutes. Beat in the egg, almonds, pear nectar, almond extract and flour.

ASSEMBLY Remove the tart shell from the refrigerator. Spread the frangipane filling evenly over the base of the tart shell. Remove the pears from the poaching liquid. Set the poaching liquid aside. Without cutting all the way through, cut each pear half crosswise into thin slices. Arrange the pear halves around the edge of the tart, with about ½-inch (1 cm) in between each half. Arrange 1 pear half in the centre of the tart. Place the tart shell on a baking sheet and bake in the centre of the preheated oven until the filling is puffed and golden, about 45 minutes.

Meanwhile, boil down the reserved poaching liquid until reduced by half. Remove the baking sheet from the oven; place on a wire rack. Immediately brush the poaching syrup over the pears. Let the tart cool on the baking sheet on the wire rack.

Remove the sides of the tart tin. Run a small knife between the bottom and the pastry and gently slide the tart shell onto a flat serving plate. The plate should not be rimmed or even curved upwards as this may encourage the tart shell to break. Serve warm or at room temperature.

BAKER'S TIP

Poached pears can be a wonderful dessert all by themselves. Serve with some whipped mascarpone or a chocolate sauce. Or mix up the spices in the poaching liquid by adding some Chinese star anise or even cardamom.

Tarte au Citron

PASTRY

1¼ cups (310 mL) all-purpose flour

3 Tbsp (45 mL) icing sugar

Pinch of salt

⅓ cup (80 mL) cold butter
(3 oz/90 g)

1 cold large egg yolk

2 Tbsp (30 mL) cold water

FILLING

3 large eggs, at room temperature

1 large egg yolk, at room
temperature

¾ cup (180 mL) granulated sugar

1 Tbsp (15 mL) finely grated lemon
zest

½ cup (125 mL) freshly squeezed
lemon juice

2 Tbsp (30 mL) whipping cream,
at room temperature

1 Tbsp (15 mL) all-purpose flour

BY NOW, you're probably aware that I have an abiding adoration of French desserts. This tart is one that is available throughout France and is easily reproduced in the comfort of your own kitchen. As I was developing this recipe I took it with me to a meeting, and although there were only five people at the meeting, the tart was finished by the end. Sometimes you will see a *tarte au citron* that calls for lemon curd, but I much prefer this melt-in-your-mouth baked rendition. There's no need to serve it with any other garnish. Its tart personality is all it needs.

PASTRY In a bowl or the bowl of a food processor fitted with the metal "S" blade, or in a large bowl, whisk or pulse together the flour, sugar and salt until well mixed and aerated. Cut the butter into cubes and add to the food processor or the bowl. Pulse in the food processor or cut in with a pastry cutter (or 2 knives) until the flour resembles coarse meal, with butter the size of peas amidst a few larger pieces. In a small bowl, whisk together the egg yolk and water. Pour the yolk-water mixture over the flour-butter mixture. Pulse or fluff the mixture until thoroughly moistened and shaggy or clumpy, but not yet formed into a ball. Dump the entire mixture onto a lightly floured work surface. Using the palm of your hand, smear together the dough along the work surface, until it comes together in a cohesive whole or ball. Flatten into a disc. Wrap the dough in plastic wrap and refrigerate for at least 1 hour or for up to 3 days.

Preheat the oven to 375°F (190°C).

On a lightly floured work surface, roll out the dough to an 11-inch (28 cm) circle, sprinkling the surface and underside with flour as needed to prevent the dough from sticking to the work surface and to prevent the rolling pin from sticking to the surface of the dough. Roll the dough up around the rolling pin and gently unroll on top of a 9-inch (23 cm) French tart tin with a removable bottom. Gently press the dough into the pan, into the edges and up the sides. Roll the rolling pin over the pan rim to trim away any excess dough. Refrigerate the tart shell for 20 minutes.

Place the tart shell on a baking sheet and then place a piece of parchment paper directly onto the tart shell. Fill with pie weights. Bake for 10 minutes.

Remove the tart shell from the oven. Remove the parchment paper and the pie weights. Prick the bottom of the tart shell with the tines of a fork. Return to the oven and bake until just golden, 10–15 minutes. Remove the tart shell from the oven and reduce the oven temperature to 325°F (160°C).

FILLING In a bowl, gently whisk together the eggs, egg yolk and sugar. Whisk in the lemon zest, lemon juice, whipping cream and flour. Do not over-whisk or the mixture will become foamy. Gently pour the mixture into the baked pie shell.

Bake in the centre of the oven until just set, about 30 minutes. Let the tart cool on the baking sheet set on a wire rack. Remove the sides of the tart tin. Run a small knife between the bottom and the pastry and gently slide the tart shell onto a flat serving plate. The plate should not be rimmed or even curved upwards as this may encourage the tart shell to break. Serve at room temperature.

BAKER'S TIPS

Even if you're in a rush, refrain from letting eggs and sugar sit together in the same bowl without first mixing them well together. If left on their own, the sugar can actually "cook" the eggs, resulting in little, hard clumps. Always whisk your eggs together to break them up and then whisk in the sugar. Once this step is completed, you don't need to worry about letting the mixture sit at room temperature.

TO BRULEE THE TART Sprinkle the tart with 2 Tbsp (30 mL) of granulated sugar. Broil at least 6 inches (15 cm) away from the heat (you don't want to burn the crust) for 1–2 minutes or use a blow torch to caramelize the sugar.

Lemon Meringue Pie Cups

THERE IS no official handbook for making lemon meringue pie but here are a few guidelines you can follow to ensure success. The ideal meringue pie has a rich lemony filling that should be firm enough to cut into, but not overly stiff or gummy, so be cautious with the cornstarch. In general it takes about 1 Tbsp (15 mL) of cornstarch to thicken 1 cup (250 mL) of liquid into a sauce. Since the filling here has to be firmer than a sauce, the ratio is closer to 2 Tbsp (30 mL) to 1 cup (250 mL) of liquid (counting the water, lemon juice AND egg yolks as liquid). The meringue should be airy but not so sweet that it detracts from the lemon flavour of the filling. Water should always be used in the filling rather than milk, as the latter tames the lemon flavour. Lastly, the meringue should be warm and be placed on a warm or hot filling (see baker's tip). There you go, an official Lemon Meringue Pie Playbook. These cups make lemon meringue pie that much easier by making individual portions.

GRAHAM CRACKER BASE Preheat the oven to 375°F (190°C).

Place the graham cracker crumbs into a bowl. Pour the melted butter over the crumbs and toss gently with a fork until the crumbs are thoroughly moistened. Divide the moistened crumbs evenly among eight 4-ounce (125 mL) ramekins. Using the back of a spoon, pack the crumbs firmly into a base. Place the ramekins on a rimmed baking sheet. Bake in the centre of the preheated oven for 10 minutes. Remove from the oven and let cool slightly.

LEMON FILLING Increase the oven heat to 400°F (200°C).

In a saucepan, whisk together the sugar, cornstarch, salt and water. Set over medium heat and cook, whisking constantly, until thickened. Still whisking, add about 3 Tbsp (45 mL) of the sugar–corn starch mixture to the yolks. This slowly tempers the yolks, getting them used to some heat without cooking them. Very slowly, in a thin stream, pour the remaining water mixture into the egg yolks, whisking constantly. Pour the whole mixture back into the saucepan. Add the lemon zest and juice and cook over medium-low heat until very thick, 3–5 minutes, stirring occasionally with a wooden spoon. Remove the saucepan from the heat. Stir in the butter until it is fully melted. Place a kitchen towel over the saucepan to keep the mixture warm while you prepare the meringue.

RECIPE CONTINUED . . .

GRAHAM CRACKER BASE

¾ cup (180 mL) graham cracker crumbs

¼ cup (60 mL) unsalted butter, melted and cooled (2 oz/60 g)

LEMON FILLING

1 cup (250 mL) granulated sugar

⅓ cup (80 mL) cornstarch

¼ tsp (1 mL) salt

2 cups (500 mL) water

6 large egg yolks, at room temperature

1 Tbsp (15 mL) finely grated lemon zest

½ cup (125 mL) freshly squeezed lemon juice

2 Tbsp (30 mL) unsalted butter, softened (1 oz/30 g)

MERINGUE TOPPING

½ cup (125 mL) granulated sugar

3 Tbsp (45 mL) water

4 large egg whites, at room temperature

¼ tsp (1 mL) cream of tartar

MERINGUE TOPPING In a separate saucepan, whisk together the sugar and water. Set the saucepan over medium-high heat and cook, without stirring and brushing down the sides of the pan with a wet brush, until a candy thermometer registers 236°F (113°C).

Simultaneously, in a stand mixer fitted with the whisk attachment, beat the egg whites with the cream of tartar until they reach soft peaks. Once the sugar mixture has reached the appropriate temperature, immediately remove the saucepan from the heat. With the stand mixer running on medium speed, slowly pour the hot sugar syrup down the side of the bowl. Continue beating until stiff shiny peaks form.

ASSEMBLY Spoon the still-hot lemon mixture into the ramekins, dividing it evenly. Scrape the meringue mixture into a piping bag fitted with a rosette tip. Starting at the edge of one of the ramekins, continuously pipe a circle on top of the lemon mixture, working toward the centre. Alternatively, you can spoon the meringue on top of the lemon mixture, spooning the meringue into large cloud-like billows.

Bake in the centre of the preheated oven until the meringue is browned, about 5 minutes. Let the ramekins cool completely on the baking sheet on a wire rack. Serve at room temperature or slightly chilled.

BAKER'S TIPS

WEEPING OR BEADING MERINGUES Weeping is a term used in pastry for when some liquid appears between a meringue and a filling. Beading refers to the little brown syrup droplets you often see on the surface of the meringue. There are two solutions to these common problems, often seen when making lemon meringue pie. Weeping is caused by undercooking—when the meringue does not get sufficiently hot to cook all the way through. Using an Italian or Swiss meringue solves this problem by heating the mixture first. Placing the meringue on a hot filling also solves the problem. Beading, meanwhile, is most often caused by cooking for too long or at too high a heat.

Cornstarch can break down or turn watery if it is cooked at too high a heat, whisked too vigorously or cooked for too long. Cook only over medium-low to medium heat and stop cooking as soon as your mixture has thickened.

Pumpkin Pie

W HAT'S FALL and Thanksgiving without pumpkin pie? "Lifeless and boring," I would say. I would also say, however, "Why wait for that special weekend to make this pie?" I have taken no liberties with this heirloom recipe, because it is hassle free, true to its origins and really pumpkin-y.

PASTRY In the bowl of a food processor fitted with the metal "S" blade, or in a large bowl, whisk or pulse together the flour, sugar and salt until well mixed and aerated. Cut the butter into cubes and add to the food processor or the bowl. Pulse in the food processor or cut in with a pastry cutter (or 2 knives) until the flour resembles coarse meal, with butter the size of peas amidst a few larger pieces. Pour the water over the flour-butter mixture. Pulse or fluff the mixture until thoroughly moistened and shaggy or clumpy, but not yet formed into a ball. Dump the entire mixture onto a lightly floured work surface. Using the palm of your hand, smear together the dough along the work surface, until it comes together in a cohesive whole or ball. Flatten the dough into a disc. Wrap the dough in plastic wrap and refrigerate for at least 45 minutes or for up to 3 days.

On a lightly floured work surface, roll out the dough to an 11-inch (28 cm) circle, sprinkling the surface and underside with flour as needed to prevent the dough from sticking to the work surface and to prevent the rolling pin from sticking to the surface of the dough. Roll the dough up around the rolling pin and gently unroll on top of a 9-inch (23 cm) Pyrex or glass pie plate. Gently press the dough into the pie plate. Trim away any ragged edges of the dough and trim the edges so that there is about a ¾-inch (2 cm) overhang. Roll up the overhang to the edge to make a thick crust. With your fingers or the tines of a fork, crimp the edge of the pie decoratively. Refrigerate the pie shell for 20 minutes.

FILLING Preheat the oven to 375°F (190°C).

Place the pie shell on a baking sheet and then place a piece of parchment paper directly into the pie shell. Fill with pie weights. Bake in the centre of the preheated oven for 20 minutes. Remove to a wire rack. Reduce the oven heat to 350°F (180°C).

PASTRY

1½ cups (375 mL) all-purpose flour
1 Tbsp (15 mL) granulated sugar
¼ tsp (1 mL) salt
½ cup (125 mL) cold unsalted butter (4 oz/125 g)
5-6 Tbsp (75–90 mL) cold water

FILLING

2 cups (500 mL) canned pumpkin purée
1 cup (250 mL) packed light brown sugar
3 large eggs, at room temperature
1 cup (250 mL) whipping cream, at room temperature
½ cup (125 mL) sour cream, at room temperature
2 tsp (10 mL) ground ginger
¾ tsp (4 mL) cinnamon
Pinch of nutmeg
Pinch of salt
2 tsp (10 mL) vanilla

TOPPING

¾ cup (180 mL) cold whipping cream

RECIPE CONTINUED . . .

Meanwhile, prepare the filling. In a large bowl, gently whisk together the pumpkin purée, brown sugar and eggs until well blended. If there are any lumps of brown sugar, break them up with a fork or with your fingers. Pour in the whipping cream and then add the sour cream, ginger, cinnamon, nutmeg, salt and vanilla. Gently whisk everything together until the mixture is very well combined with no streak of whipping cream or sour cream.

ASSEMBLY Pour the pumpkin filling into the partially baked pie shell. Bake in the centre of the oven until the edges of the pie have set and the centre retains an ever so slight jiggle, about 50 minutes. Let the pie cool on the baking sheet on a wire rack and then refrigerate.

Just before serving, whip the cream. Spoon the whipped cream into a piping bag fitted with a rosette tip. Pipe rosettes around the perimeter of the pie. Serve slightly chilled or at room temperature.

VARIATION

CHOCOLATE BOTTOM PUMPKIN PIE Brush 4 oz (125 g) of melted semisweet chocolate over the bottom of the partially baked pie shell. Allow the chocolate to cool and set completely before pouring in the filling and proceeding with the recipe.

Banana Cream Pie

GENERALLY SPEAKING I am not a huge fan of cream pies, unless it is a chocolate cream pie (see p. 210). When I grew up they tended to be made with boxed pudding mixes (feh) and not at all memorable. So it wasn't nostalgia that prompted me to develop this recipe, but rather the belief that a really good banana cream pie was something attainable and altogether desirable. Adding the vanilla bean significantly increased the appeal of the custard. I purposely kept the cornstarch at a moderate amount to avoid rigidity. It's a diner specialty made by a modern bistro.

PASTRY In the bowl of a food processor fitted with the metal "S" blade, or in a large bowl, whisk or pulse together the flour and salt until well mixed and aerated. Cut the butter into cubes and add to the food processor or the bowl. Pulse in the food processor or cut in with a pastry cutter (or 2 knives) until the flour resembles coarse meal, with butter the size of peas amidst a few larger pieces. In a 1-cup (250 mL) wet measure, stir together the egg yolk and white vinegar. Add enough cold water to make ⅓ cup (80 mL). Pour the yolk mixture over the flour-butter mixture. Pulse or fluff the mixture until thoroughly moistened and shaggy or clumpy, but not yet formed into a ball. Dump the entire mixture onto a lightly floured work surface. Using the palm of your hand, smear together the dough along the work surface, until it comes together in a cohesive whole or ball. Flatten the dough into a disc. Wrap the dough in plastic wrap and refrigerate for at least 45 minutes or for up to 3 days.

On a lightly floured work surface, roll out the dough to an 11-inch (28 cm) circle, sprinkling the surface and underside with flour as needed to prevent the dough from sticking to the work surface and to prevent the rolling pin from sticking to the surface of the dough. Roll the dough up around the rolling pin and gently unroll on top of a 9-inch (23 cm) Pyrex or glass pie plate. Gently press the dough into the pie plate. Trim away any ragged edges of the dough and trim the edges so that there is about a ¾-inch (2 cm) overhang. Roll up the overhang to the edge to make a thick crust. With your fingers or the tines of a fork, crimp the edge of the pie decoratively. Refrigerate the pie shell while you prepare the filling.

RECIPE CONTINUED . . .

PASTRY

1½ cups (375 mL) all-purpose flour
Pinch of salt
½ cup (125 mL) cold unsalted butter (4 oz/125 g)
1 cold large egg yolk
1 tsp (5 mL) white vinegar

FILLING

2½ cups (625 mL) 2% milk, at room temperature
1 vanilla bean, split open
4 large egg yolks, at room temperature
½ cup (125 mL) granulated sugar
⅓ cup (80 mL) cornstarch
Pinch of salt
2 Tbsp (30 mL) unsalted butter, softened (1 oz/30 g)
2 large ripe bananas

TOPPING

1½ cups (375 mL) cold whipping cream
2 Tbsp (30 mL) icing sugar

FILLING Preheat the oven to 375°F (190°C).

Combine the milk and the vanilla bean in a saucepan. Simmer the milk over medium-low heat for 10 minutes. Meanwhile, in a bowl, whisk together the yolks, sugar, cornstarch and salt. Remove the vanilla pod from the hot milk. Whisking constantly, add about 3 Tbsp (45 mL) of the warm milk to the yolks. This slowly tempers the yolks, getting them used to some heat without cooking them. Very slowly, in a thin stream, pour the remaining milk into the egg yolks, whisking constantly. Pour the whole mixture back into the saucepan and return it to the stovetop. Whisking constantly, cook the milk-yolk mixture over medium-high heat until it starts to boil. Reduce the heat to medium-low and cook, whisking, until very thick, about 5 minutes. Remove the saucepan from the heat. Whisk in the butter until it is completely melted. Transfer the custard to a bowl. Place a piece of plastic wrap directly on the surface of the custard. Refrigerate for 2–24 hours.

Place the pie shell on a baking sheet and then place a piece of parchment paper directly into the pie shell. Fill with pie weights. Bake in the centre of the preheated oven for 20 minutes. Remove the pie weights and parchment paper from the pie shell. Prick the bottom with the tines of a fork. Return to the oven and bake until the crust is golden, 15 minutes. Remove the baking sheet from the oven and transfer the pie shell to a wire rack to cool completely.

To assemble, remove the custard from the refrigerator. Whisk the custard gently to loosen it up a bit. Spoon half of the custard into the cooled pie shell. Peel the bananas and cut into thin slices. Arrange the banana slices over the custard. Top with the remaining custard, smoothing the top with an offset spatula. Refrigerate.

TOPPING In a stand mixer fitted with the whisk attachment or using a hand-held mixer, beat the whipping cream with the sugar until soft peaks form. Spread the cream over the custard in large billowy movements. Serve slightly chilled.

VARIATION

COCONUT CREAM PIE Omit bananas. Instead of using milk, use 1¾ cups (430 mL) 18% cream and ¾ cup (180 mL) coconut milk. Along with the butter, stir in 1 Tbsp (15 mL) rum. Stir 1 cup (250 mL) toasted sweetened shredded coconut into the custard. Proceed as above with recipe, topping it before serving with 1 cup (250 mL) whipping cream, whipped, and 2 Tbsp (30 mL) toasted sweetened shredded coconut.

Pecan Pie

PASTRY

1⅓ cups (330 mL) all-purpose
flour

1 Tbsp (15 mL) granulated sugar

¼ tsp (1 mL) salt

½ cup (125 mL) cold unsalted
butter (4 oz/125 g)

6 Tbsp (90 mL) cold water

FILLING

¾ cup (180 mL) golden corn syrup

¾ cup (180 mL) packed light
brown sugar

3 large eggs, at room temperature

¼ cup (60 mL) unsalted butter,
melted and cooled (2 oz/60 g)

1 tsp (5 mL) vanilla

1⅔ cups (410 mL) pecan halves

YOU KNOW how recipes usually start or end with a reference to how many people they serve? I've always fretted about that. What if you're really hungry? Then this pie might only feed eight. What if all the people eating the cake are ravenous teenagers? Then this pie might only feed four! I was once invited to spend a week at Canyon Ranch Spa located just outside Tucson, Arizona. The first night there, I ordered spaghetti for dinner and was so taken aback when the (really teensy) portion arrived that I blubbered, "Who is this for, Barbie?!?" I ended up eating two portions. Know your audience before you put too much stock in the allotted number of servings.

This is a pie with gumption. Tons of pecans and a warm toasty flavour, this pie is sensational topped with some lightly whipped cream (about 1 cup/250 mL), perhaps even spiked with some bourbon (2 Tbsp/30 mL).

PASTRY In the bowl of a food processor fitted with the metal "S" blade, or in a large bowl, pulse or whisk together the flour, sugar and salt until well mixed and aerated. Cut the butter into cubes and add to the food processor or the bowl. Pulse in the food processor or cut with a pastry cutter (or 2 knives) until the flour resembles coarse meal, with butter the size of peas amidst a few larger pieces. Pour the water over the flour mixture and pulse or toss briefly. If the mixture looks too dry and is not starting to get thoroughly moistened, add 1–2 Tbsp (15 mL) more water. Pulse or toss again briefly until the mixture is thoroughly moistened and shaggy or clumpy, but not yet formed into a ball. Dump the entire mixture onto a lightly floured work surface. Using the palm of your hand, smear together the dough along the work surface, until it comes together in a cohesive whole or ball. Flatten the dough into a disc. Wrap the dough in plastic wrap and refrigerate for at least 45 minutes or for up to 2 days.

On a lightly floured work surface, roll out the dough to an 11-inch (28 cm) circle, sprinkling the surface and underside with flour as needed to prevent the dough from sticking to the work surface and to prevent the rolling pin from sticking to the surface of the dough. Roll the dough up around the rolling pin and gently unroll on top of a 9-inch (23 cm) Pyrex or glass pie plate. Gently press the dough into the pie plate. Trim away any ragged edges of the dough and trim the edges so that there is about a ¾-inch (2 cm) overhang. Roll up the overhang to the edge to make a thick crust. With your fingers or the tines of a fork, crimp the edge of the pie decoratively. Refrigerate the pie shell while you prepare the filling.

FILLING Preheat the oven to 350°F (180°C).

In a large bowl, whisk together the corn syrup, brown sugar, eggs, butter and vanilla until smooth and well combined. If there are any clumps of brown sugar, break them up with your fingertips or a fork.

Remove the pie shell from the refrigerator. Place it on a rimmed baking sheet. Scatter the pecan halves over the bottom of the pie shell. Pour the brown sugar filling over the pecans.

Bake in the centre of the preheated oven until the crust is golden brown and the filling is set, 45–50 minutes. Transfer the pie from the baking sheet to a wire rack to cool completely. Serve the pie at room temperature.

VARIATION

CHOCOLATE PECAN PIE Stir ¾ cup (180 mL) chopped semisweet or bittersweet chocolate into the filling along with the corn syrup, sugar, eggs, butter and vanilla.

BAKER'S TIP

Incredibly popular in Southern baking, pecans are one of the sweetest, meatiest nuts available. Unlike hazelnuts, you don't need to skin them, but toasting them will go a long way in diffusing some of the skin's mild but inherent bitterness. As you would with most nuts, try to buy pecans from a store with a high turnover for the freshest possible selection. Older pecans tend to get a bit bitter.

As-Canadian-As-They-Come Butter Tarts

PASTRY

1½ cups (375 mL) all-purpose flour

Pinch of salt

½ cup (125 mL) cold unsalted butter (4 oz/125 g)

1 cold large egg yolk

1 tsp (5 mL) white vinegar

FILLING

¼ cup (60 mL) packed light brown sugar

¾ cup (180 mL) corn syrup

1 large egg, at room temperature

2 Tbsp (30 mL) unsalted butter, softened (1 oz/30 g)

Pinch of salt

¼ cup (60 mL) currants

WELL, THE title really sums it all up.

PASTRY In the bowl of a food processor fitted with the metal "S" blade, or in a large bowl, whisk or pulse together the flour and salt until well mixed and aerated. Cut the butter into cubes and add to the food processor or the bowl. Pulse in the food processor or cut in with a pastry cutter (or 2 knives) until the flour resembles coarse meal, with butter the size of peas amidst a few larger pieces. In a 1-cup (250 mL) wet measure, stir together the egg yolk and white vinegar. Add enough cold water to make ⅓ cup (80 mL). Pour the yolk mixture over the flour-butter mixture. Pulse or fluff the mixture until thoroughly moistened and shaggy or clumpy, but not yet formed into a ball. Dump the entire mixture onto a lightly floured work surface. Using the palm of your hand, smear together the dough along the work surface, until it comes together in a cohesive whole or ball. Flatten the dough into a disc. Wrap the dough in plastic wrap and refrigerate for at least 45 minutes or for up to 3 days.

On a lightly floured work surface, roll out the dough to ⅛-inch (3 mm) thickness, sprinkling the surface and underside with flour as needed to prevent the dough from sticking to the work surface and to prevent the rolling pin from sticking to the surface of the dough. Using a cookie cutter or the edge of a small bowl, cut out twelve 4-inch (10 cm) circles. If you don't have enough pastry for 12 circles, cut out as many as you can and then gently re-knead the remaining scraps. Let the pastry rest for 10 minutes and then re-roll the pastry out and cut out as many more circles as you need.

Fit each 4-inch (10 cm) circle into the cups of a muffin tin. Refrigerate while you prepare the filling.

FILLING Preheat the oven to 425°F (220°C).

In a large bowl, whisk together the brown sugar, corn syrup, egg, butter and salt. You will still see some very small pieces of butter—don't worry about this.

Remove the muffin tin from the refrigerator and place on a rimmed baking sheet. Evenly distribute the currants among the shells. Dividing it equally, pour the filling into the pastry shells.

Bake in the centre of the preheated oven until the pastry is golden and the filling has JUST set, 15–20 minutes. Immediately place the baking sheet on a wire rack to cool for 3 minutes. Run a small knife around the edge of one of the tarts. Ease the tart out of the pan, using the knife to help remove the gooey tart from the cupcake tin. Transfer the tart to a wire rack to cool completely. Repeat with the remaining tarts. Serve at room temperature.

VARIATIONS

CHOCOLATE BUTTER TARTS Omit currants—add ¼ cup (60 mL) mini chocolate chips.

CRANBERRY BUTTER TARTS Omit currants—add ¼ cup (60 mL) dried cranberries.

STIFFER BUTTER TARTS Increase the brown sugar to ¾ cup (180 mL) and decrease the corn syrup to ¼ cup (60 mL).

Chocolate Caramel Nut Tart

PASTRY

1 cup (250 mL) all-purpose flour

¼ cup (60 mL) ground hazelnuts

3 Tbsp (45 mL) granulated sugar

Pinch of salt

⅓ cup (80 mL) cold unsalted
butter (3 oz/90 g)

2 Tbsp (30 mL) cold water

CARAMEL FILLING

½ cup (125 mL) blanched whole
almonds

½ cup (125 mL) hazelnuts

1 cup (250 mL) granulated sugar

¼ cup (60 mL) water

½ cup (125 mL) whipping cream,
at room temperature

2 Tbsp (30 mL) unsalted butter,
softened (1 oz/30 g)

1 tsp (5 mL) vanilla

TOPPING

8 oz (250 g) semisweet chocolate,
coarsely chopped

2 Tbsp (30 mL) unsalted butter,
softened (1 oz/30 g)

1 cup (250 mL) whipping cream, at
room temperature

WHEN THIS recipe was being tested by Heather Trim (an excellent cook and baker), her daughters Nicole and Katie (both brilliant bakers in their own right, with amazing palattes) gave this tart their most rigorous thumbs up. And these are two discerning young women. Heather, Nicole and Katie have travelled to many exotic locales, eating their way through the local cuisine. Their endorsement is good enough for me. It's rather a swanky tart, posh in its presentation but authentically rich and exquisite.

PASTRY In the bowl of a food processor fitted with the metal "S" blade, or in a large bowl, pulse or whisk together the flour, hazelnuts, sugar and salt until well mixed and aerated. Cut the butter into cubes and add to the food processor or the bowl. Pulse in the food processor or cut in with a pastry cutter (or 2 knives) until the flour resembles coarse meal, with butter the size of peas amidst a few larger pieces. Pour the water over the flour-butter mixture. Pulse or fluff the mixture until thoroughly moistened and shaggy or clumpy, but not yet formed into a ball. Dump the entire mixture onto a lightly floured work surface. Using the palm of your hand, smear together the dough along the work surface, until it comes together in a cohesive whole or ball. Flatten the dough into a disc. Wrap in plastic wrap and refrigerate for at least 1 hour or for up to 3 days.

On a lightly floured work surface, roll out dough to an 11-inch (28 cm) circle, sprinkling the surface and underside with flour as needed to prevent the dough from sticking to the work surface and to prevent the rolling pin from sticking to the surface of the dough. Roll the dough up around the rolling pin and gently unroll on top of a 10-inch (25 cm) French tart tin with a removable bottom. Gently press the dough into the pan, into the edges and up the sides. Roll the rolling pin over the pan rim to trim away any excess dough. Refrigerate the tart shell for 20 minutes.

Preheat the oven to 350°F (180°C).

Place the tart shell on a baking sheet and then place a piece of parchment paper directly into the tart shell. Fill with pie weights. Bake in the centre of the preheated oven for 20 minutes.

Remove the tart shell from the oven. Remove the parchment paper and the pie weights. Prick the bottom of the tart shell with the tines of a fork. Return to the oven and bake until golden, 8–10 minutes. Let the tart shell cool on the baking sheet on a wire rack.

CARAMEL FILLING Place the almonds and hazelnuts on a separate rimmed baking sheet. Bake in the oven until golden, 5–8 minutes. Immediately scrape the nuts off the baking sheet into a clean kitchen towel. Rub the nut vigorously to remove as much of the skin off the hazelnuts as possible. Let the nuts cool.

In a heavy-bottomed saucepan set over low heat, stir together the sugar and water. Cook gently until the sugar dissolves. Increase the heat to medium-high and bring to a boil. Boil, without stirring but brushing down the sides of the pan with a brush dipped in cold water, until the mixture turns a deep amber colour, 5–8 minutes. Averting your face (to avoid any sputtering caramel), pour the cream into the saucepan. Add in the butter. Cook, stirring constantly, until the mixture stops boiling and the caramel is smooth. Remove from the heat; stir in the vanilla. Stir in the almond and hazelnuts. Scrape the caramel into the fully baked pie shell, making sure it is evenly distributed. Let the tart stand at room temperature.

TOPPING Place the chopped chocolate in a bowl along with the butter. Pour the cream into a saucepan and bring just to a boil. Immediately remove the cream from the heat and pour over the chocolate and butter. Let the mixture stand for 2–3 minutes and then whisk it together until all of the chocolate is melted and the mixture is smooth.

Pour the chocolate ganache over the caramel nut filling, tilting the pan from one side to the other to make sure that the chocolate is smooth and evenly distributed. Refrigerate the tart for 2–24 hours.

Remove the sides of the tart tin. Run a small knife between the bottom and the pastry and gently slide the tart shell onto a flat serving plate. The plate should not be rimmed or even curved upwards as this may encourage the tart shell to break. Serve chilled or at room temperature.

Apple Berry Crisp

THERE'S REALLY only two things to keep in mind when making fruit-based homey crisps, cobblers and the like. Keep it simple and keep it seasonal. In season fruit will take care of the flavour and a simple topping will let the fruit shine through.

Preheat the oven to 350°F (180°C).

In a large bowl, combine the apples, blueberries, raspberries, sugar and flour. Using a wooden spoon, toss very gently, so as not to break up the fruit, until the fruit is well coated with the sugar and flour. Transfer to a lightly greased 8-inch (20 cm) square glass baking dish.

TOPPING In another bowl, mix together the oats, flour, sugar and cinnamon. Add the butter, and with your fingertips, work it into the oat mixture until the butter is in small pieces and is evenly distributed throughout the mixture. Pour the melted butter over the mixture. Toss gently with a fork until the mixture is thoroughly moistened. The topping should be clumpy and starting to hold together.

Evenly distribute the topping over the fruit. Place the baking dish on a rimmed baking sheet and bake in the middle of the preheated oven until the topping is golden and the fruit is bubbling and tender when poked with a long thin knife, about 50 minutes.

Remove the baking sheet to a wire rack for the crisp to cool slightly. Serve warm or at room temperature.

5 cups (1.25 L) sliced, cored and peeled apples (4 large apples, about 2 lb/1 kg)
1½ cups (375 mL) fresh blueberries
1 cup (250 mL) fresh raspberries
2 Tbsp (30 mL) packed light brown sugar
1 Tbsp (15 mL) all-purpose flour

TOPPING
¾ cup (180 mL) large flake rolled oats
¾ cup (180 mL) all-purpose flour
¾ cup (180 mL) packed light brown sugar
1 tsp (5 mL) cinnamon
⅓ cup (80 mL) cold unsalted butter, in pieces (3 oz/90 g)
¼ cup (60 mL) unsalted butter, melted and cooled (2 oz/60 g)

BAKER'S TIP
This can also be made in individual 4-oz (125 g) ramekins. Evenly divide the fruit among 8–10 ramekins. Top with the oat mixture. Set the ramekins on a rimmed baking sheet and bake for about 30 minutes.

Nectarine Cobbler *with* Spiced Biscuits

10 nectarines (about 2½ lb/1.25 kg), halved, pitted and cut into wedges
1 cup (250 mL) blackberries
⅔ cup (160 mL) granulated sugar
4 tsp (20 mL) cornstarch

SPICED BISCUITS
1⅓ cups (330 mL) all-purpose flour
3 Tbsp (45 mL) granulated sugar
2 tsp (10 mL) baking powder
¼ tsp (1 mL) salt
¼ tsp (1 mL) cinnamon
¼ tsp (1 mL) five-spice powder
¼ tsp (1 mL) nutmeg
⅓ cup (80 mL) cold unsalted butter (3 oz/90 g)
½ cup (125 mL) cold whipping cream
1 cold large egg

TOPPING
2 Tbsp (30 mL) granulated sugar
¼ tsp (1 mL) cinnamon

WHEN CHOOSING fresh nectarines, always go for heft. Ripe stone fruit should always feel heavy for its size, a sign that the fruit is juicy and ripe. Colour by itself is not a good indicator. If unsure, gently feel the fruit; it should yield a bit to the touch without feeling mushy.

Preheat the oven to 400°F (200°C).

In a large bowl, gently toss together the nectarine wedges, blackberries, sugar and cornstarch until the nectarines are well coated with the sugar. Transfer the mixture to an 8-inch (20 cm) square glass baking dish. Place the baking dish on a rimmed baking sheet.

Bake the nectarine mixture in the centre of the preheated oven for 30 minutes.

SPICED BISCUITS In a bowl, whisk together the flour, sugar, baking powder, salt, cinnamon, five-spice powder and nutmeg until it is well combined and slightly aerated.

Cut the butter into cubes and add to the flour mixture. Using a pastry cutter or 2 knives, cut the butter in until the mixture resembles coarse meal. In a 1-cup (250 mL) liquid measure, whisk the cream and the egg together until well combined. Pour the whipping cream mixture evenly over the flour-butter mixture. Fluff with a fork until the mixture is thoroughly moistened. With your hands, gently knead until the dough almost holds together—it will be quite sticky.

Remove the baking dish on the rimmed baking sheet from the oven. Break off large pieces from the dough and plop them on top of the hot fruit, spacing them evenly. Sprinkle the dough with the sugar and cinnamon. Bake for an additional 20–25 minutes until the fruit is bubbling and the biscuits are lightly golden. Remove the baking sheet to a wire rack for the cobbler to cool slightly. Serve warm or at room temperature.

ACKNOWLEDGEMENTS

Much like it takes a village to raise a child, I am indebted to a veritable collegiate of individuals, some of whom I know and some of whom I know only through their cookbooks, but without whom this cookbook would not have sprung to life.

Thank you to Nick Rundall, who believed in the concept of this book and loved its title from the get go. Likewise, the team at Whitecap, Jordie Yow, Jesse Marchand, Michelle Furbacher, Andrew Bagatella and Patrick Geraghty thank you for your tireless work, your dedication and your vision.

Much thanks is due to Elizabeth Baird, not only for her mentorship and patience over the years but also because by suggesting that Nick call me, she finally got me off of my duff (I mean fence) to commit to a book.

I am wholly indebted to master photographer David Scott and food stylist extraordinaire, Olga Truchan, whose generosity knows no bounds. It was an honour and a privilege to work with two such creative and talented individuals. In their gentle and inspired hands, my recipes came to life on the page, made all the more beautiful by Olga's keen eye for detail and nuance and David's unerring sense of lighting and colour. Their sense of humour and friendship helped make this book what it is. Additionally, Olga worked tirelessly to assemble mounds and mounds of props so that each photograph would be unique and mouth-watering. (Thank you too Pat and Wendy for all your lovely bakeware. Our baby is finally here!)

I consider myself extraordinarily lucky to count Heather Trim as a good friend. She was my cookbook fairy godmother, advising me through the whole process, admonishing me to think of photographs when I didn't want to, testing whole chapters, jotting down invaluable tips and notes and holding my nervous hand throughout the year when I was writing the book.

Joanne Leese, a wisp of a woman with an oversized talent for baking, was an invaluable and unflappable recipe tester. I'm incredibly grateful for her friendship, her unerring sense of taste and style and for her contributions to my life.

I was also incredibly fortunate to have Risa Worth test the entire chocolate chapter. Risa is a marvellous baker and an outstanding caterer, although she did grumble a bit about the weight she gained during those weeks! Risa, you're wonderful.

Abby Kalan, my beautiful niece, friend and honourary goddaughter, also helped me test many of the muffins and cookies for the book. We share a love of baking and the time we spent together in my kitchen will always be a special time for me.

Without David Wood, to whom I am grateful, I would not have started my career as a pastry chef. He gave me my first job, taught me how to be a good manager, how to understand what people want and how to always take that extra step.

I am especially grateful to Huzur Altay who helped me find my voice.

And finally to my family, both the one I was born into and the immediate and extended ones I have created as an adult, thank you for making my life so very sweet and fulfilling.

INDEX

Add-In All-Purpose Cookies, 76–77
agave, 23
Alfajores, 116
all-purpose flour
    about, 24–26
    in pastry, 401
    substitutes for, 27, 107
    in yeast breads, 283
almonds
    Almond Crusted Cherry Pound Cake, 376–77
    Almond Peanut Butter Chip Cookies, 76
    Almond Tuiles, 120–21
    Baci di Dama, 115
    Biscotti di Prato, 113–14
    Caramel Almond Cherry Shortbread Bars, 159
    Chocolate Caramel Nut Tart, 462–63
    Coconut Oatmeal Cookies with Chocolate-
        Covered Raisins and Almonds, 84
    Double Blueberry Tart with Almond
        Shortbread Pastry, 409–10
    Fresh Fig and Raspberry Tart with
        Mascarpone and Honey, 440–41
    Individual Yeasted Coffee Cakes with
        Cherries and Almonds, 370–71
    Marmalade and Almond Filling in My
        Favourite Rugelach, 111
    Orange Cardamom Coffee Cake with Almond
        Swirl, 372
    Passover Chocolate Clouds, 80–81
    Pear Cranberry Muffins with Crunchy
        Almond Topping, 229
    Pear Frangipane Tart, 446–47
    Reine de Saba Ice Cream Cake, 382–83
    Strawberry Almond Scones, 263
    Triple Chocolate Almond Biscotti, 216
angel food cake
    about, 20, 25, 334
    Classic Angel Food Cake, 335
    pans, 56, 307, 334
    texture, 25, 334
anise
    about, 436
    Anise-Flavoured Challah, 289
    Anise-Scented Rhubarb Tart, 435–36
apples
    Apple Berry Crisp, 465
    Apple Cake with Pecan Glaze, 348
    Apple Cheesecake Bars, 165
    Apple Honey Cardamom Cake, 349, 351
    Apple Honey Ginger Cake, 351
    Apple Pie, 417, 419
    Country Apple Cranberry Galette, 420–21
    Double Apple Muffins, 236
    French Apple Tart, 422–23
    Morning Glory Hallelujah Muffins, 224
    Morning Oatmeal Scones with Dried Fruit
        Pear Compote, 257–58

Tarte Tatin Cake, 346–47
Tarte Tatin with Quick Puff Pastry, 424–25
apricots
    Apricot Walnut Filling in My Favourite
        Rugelach, 109
    Fresh Apricot Custard Tarts, 442–43
    Fruit and Nut Brownies, 132
    Morning Oatmeal Scones with Dried Fruit
        Pear Compote, 257–58
    storage, 442
As-Canadian-As-They-Come Butter Tarts,
    460–61
asiago
    Sun-Dried Tomato Scones with Asiago and
        Basil, 269

babka
    Special Occasion Chocolate Coffee Babka,
        294–95
Baci di Dama, 115
bain-marie. See water bath
baking powder
    about, 29–30
    cocoa powder and, 37
    during Passover, 81
    storage, 30
baking sheets, 54, 375
baking soda
    about, 30
    buttermilk and, 42
    cocoa powder and, 37
    storage, 30
bananas
    Banana Bundt Cake, 341
    Banana Cream Pie, 455, 457
    Banana Wheat Muffins, 226
    Bubbie's Banana Bread, 274
    My Very Favourite Banana Bread, 276
    storage, 226
bars and squares. See also blondies, brownies
    about, 126
    Apple Cheesecake Bars, 165
    Caffe Latte Chocolate Chip Squares, 153
    Caramel Almond Cherry Shortbread Bars, 159
    Caramel Shortbread Bars, 170
    Caramelita Bars, 147, 149
    Chocolate Chip Cookie Bars, 152
    Chocolate-Filled Nanaimo Bars, 169
    choosing chocolate for, 34, 177
    Crumble Bumble Bars, 164
    Extra Thick Date Squares, 166
    Nanaimo Bars, 167–68
    Peanutty Peanut Butter Bars, 146
    Pecan Pie Bars, 157
    Pecan Toffee Bars, 158
    Pucker Up Bars, 162
    Seven-Layer Bars with Marshmallows and
        Dried Cranberries, 161

Three Nut Brittle Squares, 154, 156
Truffle Hazelnut Petits Four Bars, 212
Basic Icing, 330
basil
    Lime Basil Meltaways, 103
    Sun-Dried Tomato Scones with Asiago and
        Basil, 269
beating. See also creaming
    for cakes, 305, 306, 307, 334, 388–89
    chocolate buttercreams, 203
    for cookies, 93
    egg whites, 17, 29, 47–48, 306, 334
    egg yolks, 31, 328
berries. See specific types of berries
Beurre Noisette Tart with Strawberries, 431–32
biscotti
    about, 217
    Biscotti di Prato, 113–14
    Triple Chocolate Almond Biscotti, 216
biscuits
    about, 220, 241, 243, 250
    Buttermilk Biscuits, 246
    Citrus Sunshine Biscuits, 250
    Everyday Buttery Biscuits, 244–45
    Nectarine Cobbler with Spiced Biscuits, 466
    Parmesan Thyme Biscuits, 251
    Sour Cream Biscuits with Cinnamon, 248
    storage, 245, 248
    Tender Flaky Biscuits, 249
Bittersweet Brownies, 133
bittersweet chocolate, 35
blackberries
    Blackberry Buttermilk Pie, 444–45
    Nectarine Cobbler with Spiced Biscuits, 466
Black Forest Scones, 259–60
blind baking, 44, 423
blondies
    Coconut and Toffee Blondies, 145
    Just for the Fun of It Blondies, 143
blueberries
    Apple Berry Crisp, 465
    Blueberry and White Chocolate Shortbread,
        106
    Blueberry Coffee Cream Cheese Cake, 352–53
    Blueberry Lime Bundt Cake, 355
    Blueberry Pie with Sour Cream Pastry, 411–13
    Blueberry Raspberry Loaf, 279
    Blueberry Tart with Lemon Curd and Oat
        Pastry, 414–16
    Blueberry-Topped Cheesecake, 391
    Crumble Bumble Bars, 164
    Double Blueberry Scones, 264
    Double Blueberry Tart with Almond
        Shortbread Pastry, 409–10
    Peach Blueberry Gingersnap Galette, 428,
        430
    Sour Cream Bluebaby Muffins, 230, 232
    using frozen, 230

bowls, stainless steel, 51
bran
 Incredibly Moist Bran Muffins, 222
bread flour
 about, 27
 in yeast breads, 283
breads. *See* quick breads, yeast
 breads
Brownie Cookies, 77
brownies. *See also* blondies
 about, 127–29
 Bittersweet Brownies, 133
 cakey vs. fudgey, 127–28
 Cocoa Brownies, 134
 Double Chocolate Ganache Brownies with
 Fleur de Sel, 141–42
 Dulce de Leche Cream Cheese Brownies,
 137, 139
 Espresso Brownies, 135
 My Fudgey Brownies, 130, 132
 Orange Cranberry Brownies, 136
 S'more Brownies, 140
 storage, 142
 texture, 127–28, 177
brown rice syrup, 23
brown sugar
 about, 19, 20
 measuring, 9
 substitutes involving, 23–24
 storage, 20
Bubbie's Banana Bread, 274
Bundt cakes
 Banana Bundt Cake, 341
 Blueberry Lime Bundt Cake, 355
 Chocolate Bundt Cake, 190
 Honey Cake, 360
 Lemon Pound Cake with Ginger Speckles,
 378–79
 Orange Cardamom Coffee Cake with Almond
 Swirl, 372
Bundt pans, 56, 320, 336
buns
 Sticky Cinnamon Buns, 296, 299
butter
 about, 13–15
 Buttery Cupcakes, 329
 creaming, 45–46, 64, 93
 Everyday Buttery Biscuits, 244–45
 Five-Spice Butter Cookies, 112
 Golden Butter Cake with Mocha Buttercream,
 314–16
 measuring, 8, 10
 storage, 15
 substitutes for, 15, 221
 temperature, 15, 64, 93, 176–77, 226, 241,
 243, 246, 305, 401, 404
buttercreams
 about, 181, 316
 All-Occasion Chocolate Cupcakes with
 French Buttercream, 202–3
 beating chocolate, 203
 Chocolate Devil's Food Cake with Chocolate
 Buttercream, 179–81
 Golden Butter Cake with Mocha Buttercream,
 314–16
 storage, 181, 308

buttermilk
 about, 42
 Blackberry Buttermilk Pie, 444–45
 Buttermilk Biscuits, 246
 Oversized Buttermilk Blueberry Muffins, 232
 in yeast breads, 283
butter tarts
 As-Canadian-As-They-Come Butter Tarts,
 460–61

caffe latte
 Caffe Latte Chocolate Bar Explosion Ice
 Cream Cake, 384–85
 Caffe Latte Chocolate Chip Squares, 153
Cajeta Caramel, 116, 119
cake and pastry flour
 about, 26
 in angel food cakes, 334
 measuring, 8, 9
cake flour, 26
cake pans
 for frozen cakes, 381
 preparing for baking, 307
 sizing, 54, 322
cakes. *See also* angel food cakes, cheesecakes,
 coffee cakes, cupcakes, everyday and fruit-
 based cakes, frozen cakes, layer cakes,
 pound cakes
 about, 7, 11, 304–7
 Chocolate Blackout Cake, 185–86
 Chocolate Bundt Cake, 190
 Chocolate Crater Cake, 192
 Chocolate Devil's Food Cake with Chocolate
 Buttercream, 176, 179–81
 Chocolate Gâteau with White Chocolate
 Cream Cheese Swirl, 195–96
 Dairy-Free Chocolate Coconut Milk Cake,
 182–83
 dividing batter evenly, 318
 spreading icing on, 183, 187, 189
 texture, 29, 42, 307, 377, 388–89
 Tiramisu, 123
 unmoulding, 320, 383
cake testers, 11
cake turntables, 60
Cappuccino Cheesecake, 392
caramel. *See also* Dulce de Leche, Skor bars and
 bits, toffee
 Caramel Almond Cherry Shortbread Bars, 159
 Caramelita Bars, 147, 149
 Caramel Shortbread Bars, 170
 Chocolate Caramel Nut Tart, 462–63
 Chocolate Truffle Pecan Tart with Spun Sugar
 Dome, 207–8
 Pecan Toffee Bars, 158
 Tarte Tatin Cake, 346–47
caramelizing sugar, 44–45, 149–51
cardamom
 about, 41, 351
 Apple Honey Cardamom Cake, 349, 351
 Cardamom-Cinnamon Butter Cookies, 112
 Orange Cardamom Coffee Cake with Almond
 Swirl, 372

carrots
 Carrot Cake with Cream Cheese Icing, 321–22
 Carrot Loaf with Mascarpone Frosting, 277
 Morning Glory Hallelujah Muffins, 224
 storage of grated, 224
cashews
 Three Nut Brittle Squares, 154, 156
caster sugar. *See* superfine sugar
Chai Shortbread, 104
Challah, 287–89
cheddar
 Cheddar Cheese Biscuits, 245
cheese. *See specific types of cheese*
cheesecakes
 about, 388–89
 Chocolate Cheesecake, 197–98
 Light-as-a-Feather Lemon Mousse
 Cheesecake, 395–96
 Pumpkin Cheesecake, 393–94
 Vanilla Cheesecake, 390–92
Cheese Danish, 300–1
chemical leaveners, 28–30. *See also* baking
 powder, baking soda
cherries
 Almond Crusted Cherry Pound Cake, 376–77
 Black Forest Scones, 259–60
 Caramel Almond Cherry Shortbread Bars, 159
 Cherry Sauce, 259–60
 Cherry White Chocolate Filling in My
 Favourite Rugelach, 111
 Cherry White Chocolate Scones, 253
 Individual Yeasted Coffee Cakes with
 Cherries and Almonds, 370–71
 White Chocolate Cherry Cookies, 77
chocolate. *See also* brownies, chocolate chip
 cookies and bars, white chocolate
 about, 33–39, 174, 176–77
 All-Occasion Chocolate Cupcakes with
 French Buttercream, 202–3
 Baci di Dama, 115
 Black Forest Scones, 259–60
 in brownies, 127–28, 135
 Caffe Latte Chocolate Bar Explosion Ice
 Cream Cake, 384–85
 Cappuccino Cheesecake, 392
 Caramelita Bars, 147, 149
 Chocolate Bar Cookies, 77
 Chocolate Birthday Cake, 308, 317–18
 Chocolate Blackout Cake, 185–86
 Chocolate Bottom Pumpkin Pie, 454
 Chocolate Bundt Cake, 190
 Chocolate Butter Tarts, 461
 Chocolate Caramel Nut Tart, 462–63
 Chocolate Cheesecake, 197–98
 Chocolate Crater Cake, 192
 Chocolate Custard Filling in Mom's Napoleon
 Cake, 323–25
 Chocolate Devil's Food Cake with Chocolate
 Buttercream, 176, 179–81
 Chocolate-Filled Nanaimo Bars, 169
 Chocolate Gâteau with White Chocolate
 Cream Cheese Swirl, 195–96
 Chocolate Icing, 317–18
 Chocolate Marble Pound Cake, 375
 Chocolate Peanut Butter Cheesecake, 392

Chocolate Pecan Pie, 459
Chocolate Pots de Crème, 209
Chocolate Pound Cake with Chocolate Tres
    Leches, 193–94
Chocolate Ribbon Coffee Cake, 368–69
Chocolate Truffle Pecan Tart with Spun Sugar
    Dome, 207–8
Coconut and Toffee Blondies, 145
Dairy-Free Chocolate Coconut Milk Cake,
    182–83
decorating with, 211
Double Chocolate Shortbread with Pumpkin
    Seeds and Flax, 108
Fruit and Chocolate Fun Blondies, 143
Fudge Truffle Tart, 204–5
in ganache, 35, 213
Golden Butter Cake with Mocha Buttercream,
    314–16
Just for the Fun of It Blondies, 143
My Head's in the Clouds Chocolate Cream
    Pie, 210–11
Nanaimo Bars, 167–68
Oh So Chocolatey Chip Muffins, 223
Passover Chocolate Cake, 34, 327–28
Passover Chocolate Clouds, 80–81
Peek-A-Boo Chocolate Cupcakes, 200
Raspberry Chocolate Filling in My Favourite
    Rugelach, 111
Reine de Saba Ice Cream Cake, 382–83
Rich Chocolate Ice Cream, 384–85, 387
S'more Cookies, 77
Sour Cream Chocolate Icing, 331
Special Occasion Chocolate Coffee Babka,
    294–95
storage, 36, 39
Three Chocolate Fun Blondies, 143
Triple Chocolate Almond Biscotti, 216
Truffle Hazelnut Petits Four Bars, 212
Tweed Scones, 261
chocolate chip cookies and bars
    about, 69
    Caffe Latte Chocolate Chip Squares, 153
    Chocolate Chip Cookie Bars, 152
    Chocolate Chip Crispies, 74
    Chocolate Chip Meringue Kisses, 199
    Chocolate Intensities, 79
    Double Trouble Chocolatey Chip Cookies, 78
    My Go-To Chocolate Chip Cookie, 71
    One Damn Good Cookie, 69, 72–73
    Oversized Peanut Butter and Oat Cookies, 87
    Passover Chocolate Chip Cookies, 75
    Seven-Layer Bars with Marshmallows and
        Dried Cranberries, 161
cinnamon
    Cardamom-Cinnamon Butter Cookies, 112
    Cinnamon Raisin Whole-Wheat Bread,
        292–93
    Cocoa Cinnamon Meringue, 214
    Sour Cream Biscuits with Cinnamon, 248
    Sticky Cinnamon Buns, 296, 299
citrus fruits. See also lemons, limes, oranges
    Citrus Scones, 253
    Citrus Sunshine Biscuits, 250

cobbler
    Nectarine Cobbler with Spiced Biscuits, 466
cocoa powder
    about, 36–37, 318
    in brownies, 127
    Cocoa Brownies, 134
    Cocoa Cinnamon Meringue, 214
    vs. chocolate, 174, 176–77
coconut
    Chocolate-Filled Nanaimo Bars, 169
    Coconut and Toffee Blondies, 145
    Coconut Cream Pie, 457
    Coconut Oatmeal Cookies with Chocolate-
        Covered Raisins and Almonds, 84
    Nanaimo Bars, 167–68
    Seven-Layer Bars with Marshmallows and
        Dried Cranberries, 161
coconut milk
    Chocolate Pound Cake with Chocolate Tres
        Leches, 193–94
    Coconut Cream Pie, 457
    Dairy-Free Chocolate Coconut Milk Cake,
        182–83
coffee and coffee liqueur
    Caffe Latte Chocolate Bar Explosion Ice
        Cream Cake, 384–85
    Caffe Latte Chocolate Chip Squares, 153
    Cappuccino Cheesecake, 392
    Chocolate Devil's Food Cake with Chocolate
        Buttercream, 179–80
    Coffee Cake Muffins, 227
    Coffee Ice Cream, 384–86
    Coffee Icing, 330
    Espresso Brownies, 135
    Espresso Shortbread, 96
    Golden Butter Cake with Mocha Buttercream,
        314–16
    Honey Cake, 360
    One Damn Good Cookie, 72–73
    Special Occasion Chocolate Coffee Babka,
        294–95
    Tiramisu, 123
Coffee Cake Muffins, 227
coffee cakes
    about, 366
    Chocolate Ribbon Coffee Cake, 368–69
    Individual Yeasted Coffee Cakes with
        Cherries and Almonds, 370–71
    Orange Cardamom Coffee Cake with Almond
        Swirl, 372
    Ye Olde Fashioned Sour Cream Coffee Cake,
        367
coffee grinders, 60, 436
colanders, 60
compote
    Morning Oatmeal Scones with Dried Fruit
        Pear Compote, 257–58
convection ovens, 7
cookie cutters, 58
Cookie-Filled Cookies, 77
cookies. See also biscotti, chocolate chip cookies
        and bars, shortbread cookies
    about, 64–67
    Add-In All-Purpose Cookies, 76–77

Alfajores, 116
Almond Tuiles, 120–21
Baci di Dama, 115
chewy vs. crispy, 67, 77
Coconut Oatmeal Cookies with Chocolate-
    Covered Raisins and Almonds, 84
cooling, 66
Five-Spice Butter Cookies, 112
Ginger Cookies, 88
Ladyfingers, 122
Lemon Cornmeal and Currant Cookies, 90
My Favourite Rugelach, 109, 111
Oatmeal Raisin Cookies, 82–83
Passover Chocolate Clouds, 80–81
Peanut Butter Cookies, 85
Snickerdoodles, 89
storage, 66
Sugar Cookies, 91–92
texture, 9, 20, 67, 77
cookie sheets, 54, 64–66
cornmeal
    about, 28
    Cornmeal Pear Loaf, 280
    Golden Corn Muffins, 235
    Individual Plum Cornmeal Cakes with
        Rosemary, 344–45
    Lemon Cornmeal and Currant Cookies, 90
cornstarch
    about, 28, 452
    in cheesecakes, 388
    in pastry, 427
corn syrup
    about, 19, 21
    in caramelizing sugar, 149
    in cookies, 67
Crackle-Topped Peach Cake, 308, 342–43
cranberries
    Citrus Scones, 253
    Country Apple Cranberry Galette, 420–21
    Cranberry Butter Tarts, 461
    Cranberry Lemon Biscuits, 245
    Cranberry Shortbread, 107
    Fruit and Chocolate Fun Blondies, 143
    Morning Oatmeal Scones with Dried Fruit
        Pear Compote, 257–58
    Orange Cranberry Brownies, 136
    Pear Cranberry Muffins with Crunchy
        Almond Topping, 229
    Seven-Layer Bars with Marshmallows and
        Dried Cranberries, 161
cream
    about, 42–43
    Banana Cream Pie, 455, 457
    Classic Cream Scones, 253
    Coconut Cream Pie, 457
cream cheese
    about, 43
    Blueberry Coffee Cream Cheese Cake, 352–53
    Carrot Cake with Cream Cheese Icing, 321–22
    Chocolate Gâteau with White Chocolate
        Cream Cheese Swirl, 195–96
    Cream Cheese Frosting for Carrot Loaf, 277
    Orange Cream Cheese Pound Cake, 380

Spiced Layer Cake with Maple Cream Cheese Icing, 319–20
creaming. *See also* beating, leavening
    about, 16–17, 19, 45–46
    for cakes, 305–6
    for cookies, 64, 93
    sugar substitutes, 24
cream of tartar
    about, 29
    in angel food cakes, 334
crisps
    Apple Berry Crisp, 465
crostata
    Plum Raspberry Crostata, 437, 439
Crumble Bumble Bars, 164
Crunchy Fun Blondies, 143
cupcake pans, 56
cupcakes
    about, 308
    All-Occasion Chocolate Cupcakes with French Buttercream, 202–3
    Buttery Cupcakes, 329
    Chocolate Birthday Cake, 318
    Golden Butter Cake with Mocha Buttercream, 316
    Pavlova Cupcakes with Honey Roasted Strawberries, 332
    Peek-A-Boo Chocolate Cupcakes, 200
    Sour Cream Golden Cupcakes, 329
currants
    Lemon Cornmeal and Currant Cookies, 90
custard powder
    Nanaimo Bars, 167–68
custards
    about, 386, 388
    Chocolate Custard Filling, 323–25
    Chocolate Pots de Crème, 209
    Fresh Apricot Custard Tarts, 442–43
    tempering, 46
cutting boards, 54

dacquoise
    Pistachio Lemon Dacquoise, 362, 364
Dairy-Free Chocolate Coconut Milk Cake, 182–83
dairy products
    about, 42–43
    storage, 42
Danish, Cheese, 300–1
dates
    about, 359
    Extra Thick Date Squares, 166
    Gingerbread-Style Sticky Date Pudding Cake, 358–59
    Incredibly Moist Bran Muffins, 222
decorating
    cakes, 308, 312
    cookies, 91–92
    equipment, 58, 60
    pies, 211, 432
demerara sugar, 20
devil's food cakes
    Chocolate Devil's Food Cake with Chocolate Buttercream, 176, 179–81

doneness, testing for, 10–11, 128, 386
Double Trouble Chocolatey Chip Cookies, 78
dough
    about, 7
    biscuit, 241, 243
    bread, 283, 284–85
    cookie, 66–67, 92
    pastry, 400–2, 404–5, 413, 416, 419, 432
dough scrapers, 58
dried fruit
    Morning Oatmeal Scones with Pear Compote, 257–58
Dulce de Leche
    Dulce de Leche Cheesecake, 391
    Dulce de Leche Cream Cheese Brownies, 137, 139
    Dulce de Leche sauce, 116, 118, 137, 139, 391

eggs
    about, 31–32
    adding sugar to, 16–17, 449
    beating yolks, 31, 328
    tempering, 46
    whipping whites, 17, 29, 47–48, 306, 334
equipment, 50–61. *See also specific types of equipment*
espresso powder. *See* coffee and coffee liqueur
everyday and fruit-based cakes
    about, 336
    Apple Cake with Pecan Glaze, 348
    Apple Honey Cardamom Cake, 349, 351
    Banana Bundt Cake, 341
    Blueberry Coffee Cream Cheese Cake, 352–53
    Blueberry Lime Bundt Cake, 355
    Crackle-Topped Peach Cake, 308, 342–43
    French Toast Cake, 337
    Gâteau Breton, 365
    Gingerbread-Style Sticky Date Pudding Cake, 358–59
    Honey Cake, 360
    Individual Plum Cornmeal Cakes with Rosemary, 344–45
    Meyer Lemon Pudding Cake, 361
    Pistachio Lemon Dacquoise, 362, 364
    Plum Kuchen, 338, 340
    Roasted Pineapple Cake, 356–57
    Tarte Tatin Cake, 346–47

feta
    Feta, Olive and Rosemary Scones, 268
    Red Pepper and Feta Muffins, 237–38
Fig and Raspberry Tart with Mascarpone and Honey, Fresh, 440–41
filberts. *See* hazelnuts
Five-Spice Butter Cookies, 112
flax seeds
    Double Chocolate Shortbread with Pumpkin Seeds and Flax, 108
    Morning Glory Hallelujah Muffins, 224
    Multi-Seed Bread, 290
fleur de sel
    about, 142
    Double Chocolate Ganache Brownies with Fleur de Sel, 141–42

flour, 24–28. *See also specific types of flour*
    bleached vs. unbleached, 25, 26, 27
    measuring, 8
    storage, 11, 28
flourless desserts
    Chocolate Chip Meringue Kisses, 199
    Chocolate Crater Cake, 192
    Chocolate Pots de Crème, 209
    Chocolate Truffle Pecan Tart with Spun Sugar Dome, 207–8
    Coffee Ice Cream, 386
    Passover Chocolate Cake, 34, 327–28
    Passover Chocolate Chip Cookies, 75
    Passover Chocolate Clouds, 80–81
    Pavlova Cupcakes with Honey Roasted Strawberries, 332
    Pistachio Lemon Dacquoise, 362, 364
    Rich Chocolate Ice Cream, 387
    testing for doneness, 11
folding, 46, 48, 205
Fontina
    Zucchini Cheese Muffins with Sun-Dried Tomatoes, 237–38
food processors
    about, 53
    for biscuits, 243
    for pastry, 401, 402
fraisage, 402
French Apple Tart, 422–23
French Toast Cake, 337
frozen cakes
    about, 381
    Caffe Latte Chocolate Bar Explosion Ice Cream Cake, 384–85
    Reine de Saba Ice Cream Cake, 382–83
frozen storage
    bananas, 226
    biscuits, 245
    brownies, 142
    butter, 15
    buttercreams, 181, 308
    cakes, 183
    cookie dough, 67
    muffins and scones, 220
    nuts, 42
    whole-wheat flour, 27
fruit. *See also specific types of fruit*
    barbecuing fruit, 357
    buying stone, 466
    Cocoa Cinnamon Meringue, 214
    Dried Fruit Biscuits, 245
    Fresh Fruit Tart with Shortcrust Pastry, 407–8
    Fruit and Chocolate Fun Blondies, 143
    Fruit and Nut Brownies, 132
    plumping dried, 224
    in quick breads vs. muffins, 273
    roasting, 357
    in scones, 265
fruit-based cakes. *See* everyday and fruit-based cakes
Fudge Truffle Tart, 35, 204–5

galettes
    Country Apple Cranberry Galette, 420–21
    Peach Blueberry Gingersnap Galette, 428, 430
ganache, 35, 213
garnish
    Candied Lemon Peel, 395–96
    Spun Sugar Dome, Chocolate Truffle Pecan Tart with, 207–8
Gâteau Breton, 365
ginger
    Apple Honey Ginger Cake, 351
    Chai Shortbread, 104
    Crackle-Topped Peach Cake, 342–43
    Gingerbread Scones, 256
    Gingerbread-Style Sticky Date Pudding Cake, 358–59
    Ginger Cheesecake, 391
    Ginger Cookies, 88
    Ginger Shortbread, 95
    Lemon Pound Cake with Ginger Speckles, 378–79
    Morning Oatmeal Scones with Dried Fruit Pear Compote, 257–58
    Peach of a Scone, A, 265
    Triple Ginger Muffins, 240
gingersnap cookies and crumbs
    Ginger Cheesecake, 391
    Peach Blueberry Gingersnap Galette, 428, 430
    Pumpkin Cheesecake, 393–94
glazes, 285
gluten
    in bread dough, 283, 284, 285
    in cake batter, 306
    in flour, 24, 25, 26
    in pastry, 401, 402, 404, 408
Golden Butter Cake with Mocha Buttercream, 314–16
Golden Corn Muffins, 235
graham crackers and crumbs
    Chocolate-Filled Nanaimo Bars, 169
    Lemon Meringue Pie Cups, 451–52
    Nanaimo Bars, 167–68
    Seven-Layer Bars with Marshmallows and Dried Cranberries, 161
    S'more Brownies, 140
    S'more Cookies, 77
    storage, 168
    Vanilla Cheesecake, 390–92
granulated sugar
    about, 16–17, 19, 20
    beating with egg whites, 47–48
    in cookies, 67, 69
    creaming, 45–46
    measuring, 8
    substitutes for, 20, 21, 22, 23
grating vs. shredding carrots, 224
greasing equipment
    cake pans, 307
    cookie sheets, 65
    muffin tins, 223
    pans for bars and squares, 132
Green Tea Shortbread, 96

Gruyère
    Cheese Biscuits, 245
    Gruyère, Prosciutto and Chive Scones, 266
    Zucchini Cheese Muffins with Sun-Dried Tomatoes, 237–38

Hand-Held Tarts with Rhubarb Strawberry Filling, 433–34
hand mixers, 53, 64
hazelnuts
    about, 213
    Cherry White Chocolate Filling in My Favourite Rugelach, 111
    Chocolate Caramel Nut Tart, 462–63
    Hazelnut Shortbread Batons, 98
    Truffle Hazelnut Petits Four Bars, 212
honey
    about, 19, 21–22
    Apple Honey Cardamom Cake, 349, 351
    in cookies, 67
    Fresh Fig and Raspberry Tart with Mascarpone and Honey, 440–41
    Honey Cake, 360
    Pavlova Cupcakes with Honey Roasted Strawberries, 332
    storage, 21
    substitutes for, 23

ice cream
    Coffee Ice Cream, 384–86
    Rich Chocolate Ice Cream, 384–85, 387
ice cream cakes. See frozen cakes
ice cream scoops, 60, 318
icing cakes, 183, 187, 189
icings
    Basic Icing, 330
    Carrot Cake with Cream Cheese Icing, 321–22
    Chocolate Icing, 317–18
    Peanut Butter Icing, 331
    Sour Cream Chocolate Icing, 331
    Spiced Layer Cake with Maple Cream Cheese Icing, 319–20
icing sugar, 20
Individual Plum Cornmeal Cakes with Rosemary, 344–45
Individual Yeasted Coffee Cakes with Cherries and Almonds, 370–71

jam
    My Favourite Rugelach fillings, 109, 111
    Raspberry Jam Cream Cheese Brownies, 139
juicers, 60
Just for the Fun of It Blondies, 143
Just Peachy Peach Pie, 426–27

kneading bread dough, 284
knives
    bench, 58
    chef's, 53, 383
    palette, 58, 187, 189, 320
    paring knives, 53
    serrated, 53, 217
kosher desserts
    Challah, 287–89

Chocolate Truffle Pecan Tart with Spun Sugar Dome, 207–8
    Dairy-Free Chocolate Coconut Milk Cake, 182–83
    Passover Chocolate Cake, 34, 327–28
    Passover Chocolate Chip Cookies, 75
    Passover Chocolate Clouds, 80–81
kosher salt, 31
kuchen
    Plum Kuchen, 338, 340

ladles, 61
Ladyfingers, 122
Lavender Shortbread, 104
layer cake pans, 56
layer cakes
    about, 308
    Carrot Cake with Cream Cheese Icing, 321–22
    Chocolate Birthday Cake, 308, 317–18
    Golden Butter Cake with Mocha Buttercream, 314–16
    Mom's Napoleon Cake, 54, 323–25
    Passover Chocolate Cake, 34, 327–28
    Spiced Layer Cake with Maple Cream Cheese Icing, 319–20
    White Cake with Lemon Curd and White Chocolate Whipped Cream, 308, 309, 311–12
leavening. See also baking powder, baking soda, creaming
    role of eggs in, 16–17, 29, 31, 47, 306
    types of, 28–29
lecithin, 32
lemon curd
    Blueberry Tart with Lemon Curd and Oat Pastry, 414–16
    Lemon Curd, 308
    Pistachio Lemon Dacquoise, 362, 364
    White Cake with Lemon Curd and White Chocolate Whipped Cream, 309, 311–12
lemons
    Blueberry Pie with Sour Cream Pastry, 411–13
    Candied Lemon Peel, 396
    in caramelizing sugar, 149
    Citrus Scones, 253
    Citrus Sunshine Biscuits, 250
    Cranberry Lemon Biscuits, 245
    Double Blueberry Tart with Almond Shortbread Pastry, 409–10
    Lemon Cornmeal and Currant Cookies, 90
    Lemon Icing, 330
    Lemon Meringue Pie Cups, 451–52
    Lemon Pound Cake with Ginger Speckles, 378–79
    Light-as-a-Feather Lemon Mousse Cheesecake, 395–96
    Meyer Lemon Pudding Cake, 361
    Morning Oatmeal Scones with Dried Fruit Pear Compote, 257–58
    Pistachio Lemon Dacquoise, 362, 364
    Plum Raspberry Crostata, 437, 439
    Pucker Up Bars, 162
    Rosemary Lemon Shortbread, 96
    Tarte au Citron, 448–49

Light-as-a-Feather Lemon Mousse Cheesecake, 395–96
limes
  Blueberry Lime Bundt Cake, 355
  Crumble Bumble Bars, 164
  Lime Basil Meltaways, 103
  Lime Shortbread, 103
  Pucker Up Bars, 162
loaf pans, 56, 273
loaves. See quick breads

macadamia nuts
  Peach Macadamia Nut Filling in My Favourite Rugelach, 109, 111
  Truffle Hazelnut Petits Four Bars, 212
maple syrup
  about, 22, 282
  grades of, 282
  Spiced Layer Cake with Maple Cream Cheese Icing, 319–20
  Spiced Pumpkin Loaf with Maple Drizzle, 281–82
  substitutes for, 23
marmalade
  Marmalade and Almond Filling in My Favourite Rugelach, 111
  Orange Vanilla Muffins with Marmalade Glaze, 239
marshmallows, mini
  Seven-Layer Bars with Marshmallows and Dried Cranberries, 161
  S'more Brownies, 140
  S'more Cookies, 77
mascarpone
  about, 43
  Carrot Loaf with Mascarpone Frosting, 277
  Fresh Fig and Raspberry Tart with Mascarpone and Honey, 440–41
  storage, 43
  Tiramisu, 123
matcha (green tea powder)
  Green Tea Shortbread, 96
matzah cake meal
  Passover Chocolate Chip Cookies, 75
Mayan Chocolate Crisps, 97
measuring, 7–10, 12, 26, 50, 318, 322
measuring cups, 8–10, 50
measuring spoons, 9–10, 50
meringues
  in buttercreams, 181
  Chocolate Chip Meringue Kisses, 199
  Cocoa Cinnamon Meringue, 214
  Lemon Meringue Pie Cups, 451–52
  Pistachio Lemon Dacquoise, 362, 364
  weeping or beading, 452
  whipping, 17, 47–48, 306, 334
Meyer Lemon Pudding Cake, 361
microplanes, 61
milk
  about, 42
  in yeast breads, 283
milk chocolate, 36
mise en place, 11–12, 43
M&M's Shortbread, 96

Mocha Buttercream, Golden Butter Cake with, 314–16
molasses
  about, 22–23
  substitute for brown sugar, 20
Mom's Napoleon Cake, 54, 323–25
Monster Cookies, 87
Morning Glory Hallelujah Muffins, 224
Morning Oatmeal Scones with Dried Fruit Pear Compote, 257–58
mortars and pestles, 60–61, 436
mousse
  Light-as-a-Feather Lemon Mousse Cheesecake, 395–96
  Reine de Saba Ice Cream Cake, 382–83
muffin pans, 56
muffins
  about, 220–21
  Banana Wheat Muffins, 226
  Coffee Cake Muffins, 227
  Double Apple Muffins, 236
  Golden Corn Muffins, 235
  Incredibly Moist Bran Muffins, 222
  Morning Glory Hallelujah Muffins, 224
  Nutella Swirl Muffins, 233
  Oh So Chocolatey Chip Muffins, 223
  Orange Vanilla Muffins with Marmalade Glaze, 239
  Pear Cranberry Muffins with Crunchy Almond Topping, 229
  Sour Cream Bluebaby Muffins, 230, 232
  storage, 220, 229, 273
  Triple Ginger Muffins, 240
  Zucchini Cheese Muffins with Sun-Dried Tomatoes, 237–38
Multi-Seed Bread, 290
muscavado sugar, 21

Nanaimo bars, 167–68
  Nanaimo Bars, 167–68
  Chocolate-Filled Nanaimo Bars, 169
Napoleon cake
  Mom's Napoleon Cake, 54, 323–25
Nectarine Cobbler with Spiced Biscuits, 466
Nutella Swirl Muffins, 233
nutmeg graters, 61
nuts. See also specific types of nuts
  in quick breads vs. muffins, 273
  storage, 42

oats
  about, 83
  Anise-Scented Rhubarb Tart, 435–36
  Apple Berry Crisp, 465
  Blueberry Tart with Lemon Curd and Oat Pastry, 414–16
  Caramelita Bars, 147, 149
  Chocolate Chip Crispies, 74
  Coconut Oatmeal Cookies with Chocolate-Covered Raisins and Almonds, 84
  Crumble Bumble Bars, 164
  Extra Thick Date Squares, 166
  Morning Oatmeal Scones with Dried Fruit Pear Compote, 257–58

Oatmeal Raisin Cookies, 82–83
Oversized Peanut Butter and Oat Cookies, 87
Oh So Chocolatey Chip Muffins, 223
oils
  in muffins, 222
  substitute for butter, 15, 221
  vegetable, 33, 176
olives
  Feta, Olive and Rosemary Scones, 268
One Damn Good Cookie, 69, 72–73
oranges
  adding zest of, 90
  Carrot Cake with Cream Cheese Icing, 321–22
  Citrus Scones, 253
  Citrus Sunshine Biscuits, 250
  Extra Thick Date Squares, 166
  Honey Cake, 360
  Marmalade and Almond Filling in My Favourite Rugelach, 111
  Morning Oatmeal Scones with Dried Fruit Pear Compote, 257–58
  Orange Cardamom Coffee Cake with Almond Swirl, 372
  Orange Chocolate Shortbread, 95
  Orange Cranberry Brownies, 136
  Orange Cream Cheese Pound Cake, 380
  Orange Icing, 330
  Orange Kissed Scones with Vanilla Roasted Plums, 254–55
  Orange Vanilla Muffins with Marmalade Glaze, 239
  Pecan Orange Sandies, 101
  Plum Cornmeal Cakes with Orange, 345
organization, suggestions for, 11–12, 43
ovens, radiant vs. convection, 7
oven temperature
  about, 6–7
  biscuits and scones, 241, 249
  brownies, 129
  cakes, 307
  cheesecakes, 388, 389
  quick breads vs. muffins, 273
  when substituting ingredients, 21–22, 23
Oversized Buttermilk Blueberry Muffins, 232
Oversized Peanut Butter and Oat Cookies, 87

palm sugar, 21
pans
  angel food cake, 56, 307, 334
  for brownies, 129
  Bundt, 56, 320, 336
  cake and cupcake, 56
  choosing, 11
  lining, 132
  loaf, 56, 273
  saucepans, 60, 208
  springform, 56, 383, 389, 394
  tube, 334
paper cones, making, 312
parchment paper
  about, 54
  for bars and squares, 132
  blind baking with, 44, 423
  for cookies, 65

for icing cakes, 183
for rolling pastry dough, 413
Parmesan
  buying, 238
  Parmesan, Rosemary and Pine Nut
    Shortbread, 105
  Parmesan Thyme Biscuits, 251
  Zucchini Cheese Muffins with Sun-Dried
    Tomatoes, 237–38
Passover Chocolate Cake, 34, 327–28
Passover Chocolate Chip Cookies, 75
Passover Chocolate Clouds, 80–81
pastry. *See specific types of pastry*
  about, 400–2, 404–5, 413, 416, 432
  butter in, 14–15, 401, 402, 404, 408
  flaky vs. tender, 404
  texture, 401, 404
pastry flour, 26
pastry tools, 58, 405
Pavlova Cupcakes with Honey Roasted
    Strawberries, 332
peaches
  Crackle-Topped Peach Cake, 308, 342–43
  Just Peachy Peach Pie, 426–27
  Peach Blueberry Gingersnap Galette, 428,
    430
  Peach Macadamia Nut Filling in My Favourite
    Rugelach, 109, 111
  Peach of a Scone, A, 265
peanut butter
  Almond Peanut Butter Chip Cookies, 76
  Chocolate Peanut Butter Cheesecake, 392
  Oversized Peanut Butter and Oat Cookies, 87
  Peanut Butter, Chocolate and Caramel Filling
    in My Favourite Rugelach, 111
  Peanut Butter Cookies, 85
  Peanut Butter Icing, 331
  Peanutty Peanut Butter Bars, 146
peanuts
  Peanut Butter, Chocolate and Caramel Filling
    in My Favourite Rugelach, 111
  Peanut Butter Cookies, 85
  Peanutty Peanut Butter Bars, 146
  Three Nut Brittle Squares, 154, 156
pears
  Cornmeal Pear Loaf, 280
  Morning Oatmeal Scones with Dried Fruit
    Pear Compote, 257–58
  Pear Cranberry Muffins with Crunchy
    Almond Topping, 229
  Pear Frangipane Tart, 446–47
  Pear Honey Cardamom Cake, 351
pecans
  about, 459
  Apple Cake with Pecan Glaze, 348
  Chocolate Chip Crispies, 74
  Chocolate Pecan Pie, 459
  Chocolate Truffle Pecan Tart with Spun Sugar
    Dome, 207–8
  Morning Oatmeal Scones with Dried Fruit
    Pear Compote, 257–58
  Pecan Orange Sandies, 101
  Pecan Pie, 458–59
  Pecan Pie Bars, 157

  Pecan Toffee Bars, 158
  Raspberry Chocolate Filling in My Favourite
    Rugelach, 109, 111
  Seven-Layer Bars with Marshmallows and
    Dried Cranberries, 161
  Sticky Cinnamon Buns, 296, 299
  Ye Olde Fashioned Sour Cream Coffee Cake,
    367
Peek-A-Boo Chocolate Cupcakes, 200
pie crusts
  blind baking, 44, 423
  rolling and shaping, 404–5, 413, 416, 419
pie plates, 57, 419
pies. *See also* galettes, pastry, tarts
  Apple Pie, 417, 419
  Banana Cream Pie, 455, 457
  Blackberry Buttermilk Pie, 444–45
  Blueberry Pie with Sour Cream Pastry, 411–13
  Just Peachy Peach Pie, 426–27
  Lemon Meringue Pie Cups, 451–52
  My Head's in the Clouds Chocolate Cream
    Pie, 210–11
  Pecan Pie, 458–59
  Pumpkin Pie, 453–54
pie weights, 44, 57, 423
pineapple
  Carrot Loaf with Mascarpone Frosting, 277
  Roasted Pineapple Cake, 356–57
pine nuts
  Parmesan, Rosemary and Pine Nut
    Shortbread, 105
pistachios
  Pistachio Lemon Dacquoise, 362, 364
  Three Nut Brittle Squares, 154, 156
plums
  Individual Plum Cornmeal Cakes with
    Rosemary, 344–45
  Orange Kissed Scones with Vanilla Roasted
    Plums, 254–55
  Plum Cornmeal Cakes with Orange, 345
  Plum Kuchen, 338, 340
  Plum Raspberry Crostata, 437, 439
poppy seeds
  Multi-Seed Bread, 290
potato starch
  Passover Chocolate Chip Cookies, 75
  in pound cakes, 377
Pots de Crème
  Chocolate Pots de Creme, 209
pound cakes
  about, 366, 377, 379
  Almond Crusted Cherry Pound Cake, 376–77
  Chocolate Pound Cake with Chocolate Tres
    Leches, 193–94
  Lemon Pound Cake with Ginger Speckles,
    378–79
  Orange Cream Cheese Pound Cake, 380
  Sour Cream Pound Cake, 374–75
prosciutto
  Gruyère, Prosciutto and Chive Scones, 266
Pucker Up Bars, 162
pudding
  filling in Chocolate Blackout Cake, 185–86
  Gingerbread-Style Sticky Date Pudding Cake,
    358–59

  Meyer Lemon Pudding Cake, 361
puff pastry
  Tarte Tatin with Quick Puff Pastry, 60,
    424–25
pumpkins
  Pumpkin Cheesecake, 393–94
  Pumpkin Pie, 453–54
  Spiced Pumpkin Loaf with Maple Drizzle,
    281–82
pumpkin seeds
  Double Chocolate Shortbread with Pumpkin
    Seeds and Flax, 108
  Morning Glory Hallelujah Muffins, 224
  Multi-Seed Bread, 290

quick breads. *See also* biscuits, muffins, scones
  about, 272–73
  Blueberry Raspberry Loaf, 279
  Bubbie's Banana Bread, 274
  Carrot Loaf with Mascarpone Frosting, 277
  Cornmeal Pear Loaf, 280
  My Very Favourite Banana Bread, 276
  Spiced Pumpkin Loaf with Maple Drizzle,
    281–82
  storage, 273

radiant ovens, 7
raisins
  about, 83
  Cinnamon Raisin Whole-Wheat Bread,
    292–93
  Coconut Oatmeal Cookies with Chocolate-
    Covered Raisins and Almonds, 84
  Fruit and Nut Brownies, 132
  Incredibly Moist Bran Muffins, 222
  Morning Glory Hallelujah Muffins, 224
  Morning Oatmeal Scones with Dried Fruit
    Pear Compote, 257–58
  My Favourite Rugelach, 109, 111
  Oatmeal Raisin Cookies, 82–83
  Raisin Scones, 253
  Round Loaf for Rosh Hashanah, 289
  Special Occasion Chocolate Coffee Babka,
    294–95
  Sticky Cinnamon Buns, 296, 299
ramekins, 61
raspberries
  Apple Berry Crisp, 465
  Blueberry Raspberry Loaf, 279
  Chocolate Crater Cake, 192
  Crumble Bumble Bars, 164
  Fresh Fig and Raspberry Tart with
    Mascarpone and Honey, 440–41
  Plum Raspberry Crostata, 437, 439
  Raspberry Chocolate Filling in My Favourite
    Rugelach, 109, 111
Raspberry Jam Cream Cheese Brownies, 139
reamers, 60
Red Pepper and Feta Muffins, 237–38
Reine de Saba Ice Cream Cake, 382–83
rhubarb
  about, 435
  Anise-Scented Rhubarb Tart, 435–36
  Hand-Held Tarts with Rhubarb Strawberry
    Filling, 433–34

rice cereal
    Chocolate Chip Crispies, 74
rice flour, 107
rice syrup, brown, 23
Rich Chocolate Ice Cream, 384–85, 387
rising. *See* leavening
Roasted Pineapple Cake, 356–57
rolling pastry dough, 404–5, 413, 416, 419
rolling pins, 57
Romano Sage Biscuits, 251
Round Loaf for Rash Hashanah, 289
rosemary
    Feta, Olive and Rosemary Scones, 268
    Individual Plum Cornmeal Cakes with
        Rosemary, 344–45
    Parmesan, Rosemary and Pine Nut
        Shortbread, 105
    Rosemary Lemon Shortbread, 96
rose water
    Gâteau Breton, 365
rugelach
    My Favourite Rugelach, 109, 111

sage
    Romano Sage Biscuits, 251
    Sage Shortbread, 96
salt
    about, 31
    measuring, 9
    in yeast breads, 283, 284, 285
sauce ladles, 61
saucepans, 60, 208
sauces
    Cajeta Caramel, 116, 119
    Cherry Sauce, 259–60
    Dulce de Leche, 116, 118, 137, 139, 391
sauce whisks, 51
scales, 10, 51, 318
scones
    about, 220, 241, 243, 249, 252, 265
    Black Forest Scones, 259–60
    Classic Cream Scones, 253
    Double Blueberry Scones, 264
    Feta, Olive and Rosemary Scones, 268
    Gingerbread Scones, 256
    Gruyère, Prosciutto and Chive Scones, 266
    Morning Oatmeal Scones with Dried Fruit
        Pear Compote, 257–58
    Orange Kissed Scones with Vanilla Roasted
        Plums, 254–55
    Peach of a Scone, A, 265
    Strawberry Almond Scones, 263
    Sun-Dried Tomato Scones with Asiago and
        Basil, 269
    Tweed Scones, 261
seeds. *See specific types of seeds*
semisweet chocolate, 35–36

sesame seeds
    Multi-Seed Bread, 290
Seven-Layer Bars with Marshmallows and Dried
    Cranberries, 161
shaped pans, 56, 320, 336
shaping pie crusts, 416, 419
shelf life. *See* storage

shells. *See* pie crusts, tart crusts
shortbread cookies and bars
    about, 20, 93
    Blueberry and White Chocolate Shortbread,
        106–7
    Caramel Almond Cherry Shortbread Bars, 159
    Caramel Shortbread Bars, 170
    Chai Shortbread, 104
    Classic Shortbread, 95–96
    Double Chocolate Shortbread with Pumpkin
        Seeds and Flax, 108
    Hazelnut Shortbread Batons, 98
    Lime Basil Meltaways, 103
    Mayan Chocolate Crisps, 97
    Parmesan, Rosemary and Pine Nut
        Shortbread, 105
    Pecan Orange Sandies, 101
    Toffee Meltaways, 102
shortcrust pastry
    about, 408
    Double Blueberry Tart with Almond
        Shortbread Pastry, 409–10
    Fresh Fig and Raspberry Tart with
        Mascarpone and Honey, 440–41
    Fresh Fruit Tart with Shortcrust Pastry,
        407–8
shortening
    in chocolate, 33, 34, 36
    in pastry, 404
shredding vs. grating carrots, 224
sieves, 61
sifting, 9, 25, 26
silicone mats, 54, 65
skewers, 196
skillets, 60
Skor bars and bits
    Caffe Latte Chocolate Bar Explosion Ice
        Cream Cake, 384–85
    Coconut and Toffee Blondies, 145
    One Damn Good Cookie, 72–73
    Peanut Butter, Chocolate and Caramel Filling
        in My Favourite Rugelach, 111
    Toffee Meltaways, 102
    Tweed Scones, 261
S'more Brownies, 140
S'more Cookies, 77
Snickerdoodles, 89
sour cream
    about, 42
    Blueberry Pie with Sour Cream Pastry, 411–13
    Sour Cream Biscuits with Cinnamon, 248
    Sour Cream Bluebaby Muffins, 230, 232
    Sour Cream Chocolate Bundt Cake, 190
    Sour Cream Chocolate Icing, 331
    Sour Cream Golden Cupcakes, 329
    Sour Cream Pound Cake, 374–75
    Ye Olde Fashioned Sour Cream Coffee Cake,
        367
spatulas
    for folding, 46
    for icing cakes, 187
    metal, 58
    for pound cakes, 377
    rubber, 51
Spiced Layer Cake with Maple Cream Cheese
    Icing, 319–20

Spiced Pumpkin Loaf with Maple Drizzle,
    281–82
spice grinders, 60, 436
spices, 41. *See also specific spices*
spoons
    slotted, 61
    wooden, 51, 69, 93
springform pans
    about, 56
    for cheesecakes, 389
    unmoulding cakes from, 383, 394
square cake pans, 56
squares. *See* bars and squares
stand mixers, 51, 53, 64
starch in cheesecakes, 388, 389. *See also*
    cornstarch, flour
Sticky Cinnamon Buns, 296, 299
Stiffer Butter Tarts, 461
storage. *See specific items*
strawberries
    Beurre Noisette Tart with Strawberries,
        431–32
    Hand-Held Tarts with Rhubarb Strawberry
        Filling, 433–34
    Pavlova Cupcakes with Honey Roasted
        Strawberries, 332
    Strawberry Almond Scones, 263
streusel
    Anise-Scented Rhubarb Tart, 435–36
    Chocolate Ribbon Coffee Cake, 368–69
    Country Apple Cranberry Galette, 420–21
sugar. *See also specific types of sugar,* creaming
    about, 16–17, 19–24, 449
    in brownies, 128
    in cakes, 305, 306, 334
    caramelizing, 44–45, 149–51
    in muffins, 222
    storage, 11, 19
    Sugar Cookies, 91–92
    syrups made with, 379
    in yeast breads, 283
sugar substitutes, 23–24
sun-dried tomatoes
    about, 269
    Sun-Dried Tomato Scones with Asiago and
        Basil, 269
    Zucchini Cheese Muffins with Sun-Dried
        Tomatoes, 237–38
sunflower seeds
    Double Chocolate Shortbread with Pumpkin
        Seeds and Flax, 108
    Morning Glory Hallelujah Muffins, 224
    Multi-Seed Bread, 290
superfine sugar, 17, 20, 48, 334
syrups made with sugar, 379

tapioca flour, 427
tart crusts
    blind baking, 44, 423
    rolling and shaping, 404–5, 413, 416, 419
Tarte Tatin Cake, 346–47
tarts. *See also* galettes, pastry, pies
    about, 7, 410
    Anise-Scented Rhubarb Tart, 435–36
    As-Canadian-As-They-Come Butter Tarts,
        460–61

Beurre Noisette Tart with Strawberries, 431–32
Blueberry Tart with Lemon Curd and Oat Pastry, 414–16
Chocolate Caramel Nut Tart, 462–63
Chocolate Truffle Pecan Tart with Spun Sugar Dome, 207–8
Double Blueberry Tart with Almond Shortbread Pastry, 409–10
French Apple Tart, 422–23
Fresh Apricot Custard Tarts, 442–43
Fresh Fig and Raspberry Tart with Mascarpone and Honey, 440–41
Fresh Fruit Tart with Shortcrust Pastry, 407–8
Fudge Truffle Tart, 204–5
Hand-Held Tarts with Rhubarb Strawberry Filling, 433–34
Pear Frangipane Tart, 446–47
Tarte au Citron, 448–49
Tarte Tatin with Quick Puff Pastry, 60, 424–25
tart tins, 56–57, 208, 416, 419
techniques, 43–48. See specific techniques
temperature. See also oven temperature
    butter, 15, 64, 93, 176–77, 226, 241, 243, 246, 305, 401, 404
    chocolate, 39
    chocolate cakes, 176
    cookie ingredients, 67
    cooking sheets, 65
    eggs, 7, 10, 31, 46, 47, 128, 226, 306
    yeast bread ingredients, 283
tempering, 46–47
Tender Flaky Biscuits, 249
testing for doneness, 10–11, 128, 386
texture, 21, 22, 23, 27, 28, 30, 32. See also specific baked goods
    biscuits and scones, 42, 241, 243, 249, 250
    cake pans' influence on, 54, 322, 336
    chocolate desserts, 176–77
    quick breads vs. muffins, 273
thermometers
    candy and deep fry, 60
    oven, 6
thickeners for fruit pies, 427
thyme
    Parmesan Thyme Biscuits, 251
timers, 53
Tiramisu, 123
toffee. See also caramel, Skor bars and bits
    Coconut and Toffee Blondies, 145
    Gingerbread-Style Sticky Date Pudding Cake, 358–59
    Pecan Toffee Bars, 158
    Toffee Meltaways, 102
tongs, 61
tools. See specific types of tools, equipment
transferring pastry dough, 416
tres leches
    Chocolate Pound Cake with Chocolate Tres Leches, 193–94
Truffle Hazelnut Petits Four Bars, 212
Truffle Pecan Tart with Spun Sugar Dome, Chocolate, 207–8

Truffle Tart, Fudge, 204–5
tube pans, 334
turbinado sugar, 21
Tweed Scones, 261

unsweetened chocolate, 34

vanilla, 40–41
vanilla beans
    about, 40–41
    Banana Cream Pie, 455, 457
    Orange Kissed Scones with Vanilla Roasted Plums, 254–55
    Orange Vanilla Muffins with Marmalade Glaze, 239
    Pear Frangipane Tart, 446–47
    storage, 41
    Sugar Cookies, 91–92
Vanilla Cheesecake, 390–92
vanilla powder
    Passover Chocolate Cake, 327–28
    Passover Chocolate Chip Cookies, 75
vanilla wafer crumbs
    Dulce de Leche Cheesecake, 391
    Light-as-a-Feather Lemon Mousse Cheesecake, 395–96
vegetable oil and chocolate, 33, 176
volume measurements, 7–10, 322

walnuts
    Apricot Walnut Filling in My Favourite Rugelach, 109, 111
    Caramelita Bars, 147, 149
    Carrot Cake with Cream Cheese Icing, 321–22
    Carrot Loaf with Mascarpone Frosting, 277
    Fruit and Nut Brownies, 132
    My Go-To Chocolate Chip Cookie, 71
water bath
    about, 38
    for cakes, 306, 388, 389
weight measurements, 7–8, 10, 318
wheat, 283
wheat, cracked
    Multi-Seed Bread, 290
wheat bran, 27–28
wheat flour, 24–28
wheat germ
    about, 27–28
    Banana Wheat Muffins, 226
    Chocolate Chip Crispies, 74
whipping cream
    about, 42–43
    in ganache, 35, 213
whipping egg whites, 17, 29, 47–48, 306, 334
whisks, 51
white chocolate
    about, 36
    Blueberry and White Chocolate Shortbread, 106–7
    Cherry White Chocolate Filling in My Favourite Rugelach, 111
    Cherry White Chocolate Scones, 253
    Chocolate-Filled Nanaimo Bars, 169
    Chocolate Gâteau with White Chocolate Cream Cheese Swirl, 195–96

Double Trouble Chocolatey Chip Cookies, 78
Three Chocolate Fun Blondies, 143
Triple Chocolate Almond Biscotti, 216
White Cake with Lemon Curd and White Chocolate Whipped Cream, 308, 309, 311–12
White Chocolate Cherry Cookies, 77
White Chocolate Icing, 330
whole-wheat cake and pastry flour, 27
whole-wheat flour, 27
wire mesh sieves, 61
wire racks, 54, 66

yeast
    about, 19, 29, 31, 283, 371
    storage, 371
yeast breads
    about, 7, 272, 283–85
    Challah, 287–89
    Cheese Danish, 300–1
    Cinnamon Raisin Whole-Wheat Bread, 292–93
    flour in, 26, 27, 283, 284, 285
    Multi-Seed Bread, 290
    Special Occasion Chocolate Coffee Babka, 294–95
    Sticky Cinnamon Buns, 296, 299
Ye Olde Fashioned Sour Cream Coffee Cake, 367
yogurt, 42

zest, adding, 90
zesters, 61
Zucchini Cheese Muffins with Sun-Dried Tomatoes, 237–38